DATE DUE

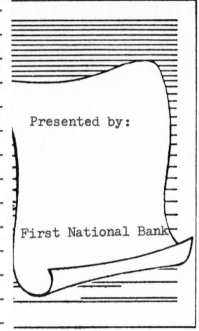

Presented by:

First National Bank

EDESSA

'THE BLESSED CITY'

THE POOL OF ABRAHAM (HALIL RAHMAN GÖLÜ), with Halil Rahman Camii at left

EDESSA

'THE BLESSED CITY'

BY J. B. SEGAL

'The city that . . . was ruled by Christians
and alone served the Lord when, long ago,
the whole world in the East was under
the sway of pagans.'

Pope Eugenius III to King Louis VII of France
1 December 1145

OXFORD
AT THE CLARENDON PRESS
1970

Oxford University Press, Ely House, London W. 1

GLASGOW NEW YORK TORONTO MELBOURNE WELLINGTON
CAPE TOWN SALISBURY IBADAN NAIROBI DAR ES SALAAM LUSAKA ADDIS ABABA
BOMBAY CALCUTTA MADRAS KARACHI LAHORE DACCA
KUALA LUMPUR SINGAPORE HONG KONG TOKYO

PRINTED IN GREAT BRITAIN

TO

LEAH

WHO WAS WITH ME

AT ALL TIMES

PREFACE

THIS book is the product of five visits to Urfa—in 1952, 1956, 1959, 1961, and 1966. It is with pleasure that I express here my gratitude to the persons and institutions whose help made those visits fruitful and enjoyable: the Turkish Department of Antiquities at Ankara and its courteous officials, the local representatives of the Ministry of Education, and the staff of the newly-erected museum at Urfa; the British Institute of Archaeology at Ankara under whose auspices my researches were conducted, its former Directors, Professor Seton Lloyd and Professor Michael Gough, and its staff, notably Mr. F. de la Grange; the Central Research Fund of the University of London, the Pilgrim Trust fund administered by the British Academy, and the School of Oriental and African Studies, all of which contributed generously towards the expenses of various expeditions; the companions whose friendship stood the test of the Anatolian summer, Professor Donald Strong and Dr. Michael Ballance, Mr. Arthur North, Dr. Géza Fehérvári, and above all, the late Professor Storm Rice whose brilliant talents and whose enthusiasm on my first three visits to Urfa converted the remains of the past into the living experience of the present. To my colleagues who have allowed me to exploit their great knowledge, Professor C. J. Dowsett, Dr. D. N. MacKenzie, Dr. V. L. Ménage, Professor H. W. F. Saggs and Professor E. Ullendorff, I am deeply indebted. No less a tribute should be paid to my predecessors in the study of the history of Edessa, both at the desk and in the field, without whose scholarly labours and integrity this work could not have been written, particularly Pognon, Sachau, and Cyril Moss—but especially Rubens Duval whose *Histoire d'Édesse* remains a model of erudition; if the present volume in some measure supersedes it, this derives from the security in which the student can pursue his enquiries in modern Turkey.

The plans of Urfa were prepared by Mr. Arthur North during a survey of the city in 1959; they have been revised in the light of information I obtained on later visits and were then redrawn by Mr. A. F. de Souza. The coloured reproductions of the mosaics—based upon my own rubbings and photographs on the site—are the work of Mrs. Seton Lloyd, and appear here by kind permission of Messrs. Thames & Hudson. My debt to the patience and the remarkable skill of the staff of the Clarendon Press can be measured only by those authors who have had the good fortune to entrust a typescript to their capable hands and who are the envy of their confrères in the academic world.

My last word of thanks is directed to the successive Valis and Mayors and, most of all, to the townspeople of Urfa. Wherever my inquiries took me—in the courtyards of the whitewashed mosques, in the markets, at the coffee-house by the shady fish-pools, in the orchards, or on the rough slopes of the Citadel—I met with hospitality that asked for no reward. These are worthy inhabitants of a great city.

CONTENTS

LIST OF PLATES

PRINCIPAL ABBREVIATIONS

Abh. K. Morg.	*Abhandlungen für die Kunde des Morgenlandes*
Acta Or.	*Acta Orientalia*
AJSL	*American Journal of Semitic Languages and Literature*
Anal. Boll.	*Analecta Bollandiana*
Arch. or.	*Archiv orientální*
AS	*Anatolian Studies*
BGA	*Bibliotheca Geographorum Arabicorum*
BO	*Bibliotheca Orientalis Clementino-Vaticanus*
BSOAS	*Bulletin of the School of Oriental and African Studies*
Bull. corr. hell.	*Bulletin de correspondance hellénique*
BZ	*Byzantinische Zeitschrift*
Bar Heb.	Bar Hebraeus
Cah. arch.	*Cahiers archéologiques*
Chr. min.	*Chronica minora*
Chr. ad 1234	*Anonymi auctoris chronicon ad annum Christi 1234 pertinens*
'Chr. Zuqnin'	'Chronicle of Zuqnin'
CRAI	Académie des Inscriptions et Belles-Lettres. *Comptes rendus*
CSCO	*Corpus scriptorum christianorum orientalium*
CSEL	*Corpus scriptorum ecclesiasticorum latinorum*
CSHB	*Corpus scriptorum Historiae Byzantinae*
DACL	*Dictionnaire d'archéologie chrétienne et de liturgie*
Dion. T–M.	Dionysius of Tell–Maḥre
Doc. Add.	*Doctrine of Addai*
EI	*Encyclopaedia of Islam*
FHG	*Fragmenta Historicorum Graecorum*
HTR	*Harvard Theological Review*
HUCA	*Hebrew Union College Annual*
JA	*Journal asiatique*
JBL	*Journal of Biblical Literature*
JNES	*Journal of Near Eastern Studies*
John Ephes., History	John of Ephesus, *Ecclesiastical History*
John Ephes., Lives	John of Ephesus, *Lives of the Eastern Saints*
'Josh. St.'	*Chronicle of 'Joshua the Stylite'*
JRAS	*Journal of the Royal Asiatic Society*
JRS	*Journal of Roman Studies*
JTS	*Journal of Theological Studies*
Mél. S-J	*Mélanges de la Faculté Orientale (Mélanges de l'Université Saint-Joseph)*

Mich. Syr.	Michael the Syrian
OC	Oriens Christianus
Pat. Syr.	Patrologia Syriaca
PG	Patrologia Cursus Completus . . . Series Graeca
PO	Patrologia Orientalis
RA	Revue d'Assyriologie et d'Archéologie orientale
RB	Revue biblique
RAC	Reallexikon für Antike und Christentum
Recueil, hist. occ.	Recueil des Historiens des Croisades: Historiens occidentaux
Recueil, hist. or.	Recueil des Historiens des Croisades: Historiens orientaux
REI	Revue des Études islamiques
REJ	Revue des études juives
Rendic. Lincei	Rendiconti della Reale Accademia (Atti della Accademia Nazionale) dei Lincei
Rev. arch.	Revue archéologique
RHR	Revue de l'histoire des religions
ROC	Revue de l'Orient chrétien
ROL	Revue de l'Orient latin
RQH	Revue des Questions Historiques
RSE	Revue des sciences ecclésiastiques
RSO	Rivista degli studi orientali
ThLz	Theologische Literaturzeitung
TU	Texte und Untersuchungen
YCS	Yale Classical Studies
ZA	Zeitschrift für Assyriologie und verwandte Gebiete
'Zach. Rh.'	Chronicle of 'Zacharias Rhetor'
ZDMG	Zeitschrift der Deutschen morgenländischen Gesellschaft
ZDPV	Zeitschrift des Deutschen Palästina-Vereins
ZNW	Zeitschrift für die neutestamentliche Wissenschaft und die Kunde der älteren Kirche
ZS	Zeitschrift für Semitistik und verwandte Gebiete
ZWT	Zeitschrift für wissenschaftliche Theologie

SCHEME OF TRANSLITERATION

	SYRIAC	ARABIC
b	ܒ with *qushshaya* or *rukkakha*	
d	ܕ with *qushshaya* or *rukkakha*	
ḍ		ض
dh		ذ
g	ܓ with *qushshaya* or *rukkakha*	
gh		غ
h	ܗ	
ḥ	ܚ	
k	ܟ with *qushshaya*	
kh	ܟ with *rukkakha*	خ
l	ܠ	
m	ܡ	
n	ܢ	
p	ܦ with *qushshaya*	
ph	ܦ with *rukkakha*	
q	ܩ	
r	ܪ	
s	ܣ	
ṣ		
š, sh	ܨ ܫ	
t	ܬ with *qushshaya*	
ṭ	ܛ	
th	ܬ with *rukkakha*	ث
w	ܘ	
y	ܝ	
z	ܙ	
ʿ	ܥ	
ʾ	ܐ; frequently omitted at the beginning and the end of a word	

A short vowel is usually followed by the reduplication of the next consonant.

Shewa mobile in Syriac or Hebrew is normally shown by *e*; compound *shewa* is treated as a full vowel. Long vowels are marked wherever desirable.

Foreign proper names and nouns in common use are spelt in the conventional manner.

INTRODUCTION

THE TRAVELLER APPROACHING URFA FROM THE WEST—along the route taken by caravans in quest of the spices, the gems, and the muslin and silk of India and China, by the cohorts of Roman Byzantium, by pilgrims and students—has little inkling of the prospect that awaits him until he is a few miles from the city. Then the winding road falls sharply; the barren brown hills give way to trees and orchards, and beyond to the south, as far as the eye can see, stretch the corn-fields of the plain of Harran. Suddenly the white cubes of the new housing estates of Urfa come into sight. A later turn of the road reveals the domes and minarets of the mosques. And finally, far away, two slender columns crowned by Corinthian capitals appear on the crest of the Citadel mount, towering over the countryside, a lonely relic of the Roman period.

The order in which the landmarks of Urfa emerge is strangely significant. They represent three successive stages in the history of the city. Today Urfa is a thriving city of some eighty thousand inhabitants, the seat of a Vali and the chief town of an extensive province. Modern suburbs have sprung up to the east and north-east of the city—evidence of the vitality of the new Turkey. But in medieval times, too, Islam left its mark upon the habits and appearance of the city; those who frequented its mosques won a considerable reputation for piety. The historian may, however, be pardoned for looking back yet further to a more distant age when this city, under the name of Edessa, had more than local fame. For over a millennium it held a unique position in Christendom, whether its rulers were Roman, Byzantine, Arab, Turkish, Armenian, or Latin. Tradition associated it with Jesus himself and the early missionary activities of Christianity. To it came pilgrims from Mesopotamia and Persia and even from the Far East; its legends were known and venerated in western Europe centuries before the Norman conquest. Its monasteries and caves were the dwelling place of saints, scholars, and poets. It was celebrated in the civilized world as the birthplace of Syriac literature and philosophy.

It is of this early stage in its history that the present work will seek to treat, citing wherever possible the words of contemporary writers. Thereafter —with the cruel disaster of 1146—its Christian community dwindled. The city, now under the name of Urfa, declined in the course of time into relative obscurity, as the chief town of a remote province of Turkey. Edessa had disappeared from the pages of history. A few of its ancient monuments have emerged in recent years (though much has fallen victim to the encroachments of modernization)—inscriptions, cave-tombs, mosaics, and pieces of sculpture; its mosques and minarets, themselves old, stand probably on the site of older churches and synagogues; the Citadel, now in ruins, still dominates the town, while below the fish-pools are a quiet memorial to the beliefs of two millennia ago.

I

THE BEGINNINGS

IN THE FOURTH CENTURY St. Ephraim the Syrian wrote, in his
commentary on Genesis, that Nimrod 'ruled in Erekh which is Orhay
(Edessa)'. He was recounting a legend that was widely credited in
western Asia. Later writers went further. St. Isidore, for example,
maintained that Nimrod 'built Edessa, a city of Mesopotamia, after he had
migrated from Babylon, and ruled in it, which aforetime had been named
Erekh'. We need not take these learned theologians too literally. It was
customary in the Near East (and, indeed, in Europe also) for the proud
inhabitants of an ancient city to ascribe its foundation to a powerful figure of
mythology. The Biblical Nimrod was famed as a builder. His name is attached
to several pre-Islamic sites in present-day Turkey; only a giant, it is felt,
could have assembled the huge monuments of a remote pagan age.[1]

At Orhay, the choice of Nimrod as founder had much to commend itself
in later centuries. In Jewish and thereafter in Moslem tradition, Nimrod was
the foe of Abraham. The association of Nimrod with their city encouraged
the people of Orhay in the belief that the patriarch himself had dwelt there.
Forty kilometres to the south stood the pagan centre of Harran which claimed
Abraham as a resident and displayed to Christian pilgrims the places where
he had lived; and Harran's claim finds support in the Bible text. Other sites
in this region seem to be mentioned in the Bible—Paddan and, as personal
names, Serug, Terah and Naḥor.[2] Had not the celebrated Christian city of
Orhay a stronger title to one of the great fathers of monotheism?

The names of Nimrod and Abraham cling to this city and its environs to
the present time. The mount on which stands the Citadel is commonly called
the 'throne of Nimrod'; the barren hills with the ruins of Deyr Yakup, once
a famous monastery, which lie to the south of the city walls are the 'hills of
Nimrod'. Two mosques beside the fish-pools, the modern *balıklar*, below the
Citadel are named after Abraham. The pools figure in local folk tales of
Nimrod. Nimrod, we are told, bound Abraham between the two great

---

[1] By Jacob of Edessa and other Syriac
writers, Nimrod is identified as Ninus son of
Belus, the eponymous founder of Nineveh.

[2] Gen. 11:20 ff., cf. 24:10 ff., 28:2 ff. Serug
is the name of (probably) the district in which
stood Batnae—the classical Anthemusia—to
the south of Harran; Terah and Naḥor are
mentioned, in cognate forms, in cuneiform
records, the latter especially in texts from
Mari; Paddan continued to be used of a
locality near Harran during both Christian and
Moslem times.

columns that still stand on the Citadel mount and slung the patriarch into the valley. Where he fell, miraculously unharmed, appeared the pool known to this day as Birket Ibrahim, the 'pool of Abraham', whose fish are the 'fish of Abraham'. By the pool was erected the Halil Camii, the mosque of the 'Beloved [of God]', a Moslem epithet for Abraham. In a cavern beside another mosque, Makam Ibrahim, or 'the place [of prayer] of Abraham', the infant Abraham was hidden, so another tale relates, from the enmity of Nimrod. A third account tells how King Nimrod sought to destroy Abraham with fire. Abraham knelt in supplication to Heaven; two springs of water emerged at the places where his knees touched the ground and extinguished the flames.[1] These are the springs that feed the *balıklar*. One of the two pools is called, as we have seen, the 'pool of Abraham'; the other is the 'pool of Zulha' after, it is generally held, the wife of Potiphar, Zulaikha. But it is difficult to see what Potiphar's wife is doing in this setting. Perhaps at one time it was the pool of Sulkha, as Moslems name the mother of Nimrod.[2]

The identification of Orhay with Erekh stems, of course, from the Biblical passage, 'and the beginning of [Nimrod's] kingdom was . . . Erekh' (Gen. 10:10). To the commentators the similarity of the names was irresistible.[3] The theory is untenable, since we know now that Erekh (Uruk) lay in southeast Mesopotamia, and over five hundred miles from Orhay. Modern theories on the origin of the name Orhay are no less improbable.[4] It can hardly be a secondary form of the name Osrhoene, the province in which it stood. Scholars have regarded Orhay as a mutilated form of καλλιρρόη '[the city of] beautiful flowing [water]'—or as derived from a Semitic root *wrh*, water, Arabic, *wariha*, well-watered.[5] These theories should be regarded with caution since they assume that the city acquired its name only in the Seleucid period.

---

[1] Similar stories about Abraham and Nimrod are related by Ṭabari and other Moslem writers; they are found earlier in Jewish legend.

[2] For another, and more probable, hypothesis, see p. 8 below. There may be an echo of the name Nimrod in the 'Marud' mentioned by Jacob of Edessa in the late seventh or early eighth century. He states that the 'Chaldaeans' —here the pagans of Harran—maintained that 'first everything was darkness and waters before there were gods and men, and the spirit hovered over the waters and created these seven [planets]. . . . And it made Bel first and after him Marud as lords of the gods'. Nimrod may be referred to obliquely by Jacob of Serug, 'On the Fall of the Idols', where among the gods of Harran are Bar Nemre and 'Mar[i] of his dogs'; but cf. p. 57 below on Marilaha. In one passage Bar Hebraeus attributes the

foundation of Orhay to Enoch 'whom the Greeks call Hermes Trismegistos'; it was, he claims, the least of the cities which he founded. Elsewhere Bar Hebraeus regards Nimrod as the founder of Orhay.

[3] Strangely enough, this equation is offered by the author of a *Life* of the Edessan martyrs, Shmona and Gurya, in the early fourth century. He writes, 'in the days of Qona, Bishop of the city of Erekh'.

[4] It is a counsel of despair to accept the view of one Syriac chronicler that Orhay was founded by Orhay son of Ḥewya (i.e. Serpent; see p. 106 below). It is unlikely, too, that Orhay is a by-form of the name Aryu, founder of the Edessan dynasty, p. 16 below.

[5] This etymology would then be parallel with the derivation of the name Edessa from the Macedonian *voda*, water (cognate with Greek ὕδωρ); see p. 6 below.

Orhay has been identified with the Biblical Ur of the Chaldees, not only by scholars but also by modern worthies of Urfa.[1] There is no satisfactory evidence for this hypothesis. It was not held by the bishop of the city who acted as cicerone to Egeria, the pilgrim abbess from Aquitania, in probably the fifth century—although he knew that she wished to be shown the sites with Biblical associations, and was about to visit the shrines of Abraham at nearby Harran. In fact, at Harran, Egeria was informed that Nisibis was five stages distant and Ur of the Chaldees a further five stages—and in the hands of the Persians. Nor is it mentioned by the writers of Christian martyr- ologies and the poets of Orhay in the fourth, fifth, or sixth centuries, who lost no opportunity to vaunt the pre-eminence of their city. The earliest Syriac chronicler to identify Orhay with Ur of the Chaldees appears to be the Jacobite Metropolitan, Basil bar Shumana, the friend of Zangi, who conquered Edessa in the twelfth century. And we may note that if Ur of the Chaldees were Orhay, the first stage of migration of Teraḥ and Abra- ham, one of the most significant migrations of antiquity, would then be reduced to a journey of fifty kilometres, almost to the status of a Sabbath- day walk.

There were other towns in ancient Mesopotamia called Uru, or Ur-a. One appears in records of Ugarit as subject to the Hittites, another was clearly in north-eastern Mesopotamia. We read of a 'great Ur' and a 'little Ur'. They are scarcely to be identified with our Orhay; as the Metropolitan Basil perceived, the element 'Ur' may mean no more than 'city'.[2] Indeed, the readiness of St. Ephraim and others to equate Orhay with Erekh would rather suggest that the early form of the name may have been URH or URḤ or URK.[3]

However this may be, it can be assumed that the persistent tradition of an early, certainly pre-Seleucid, foundation of the city is probable, if not certain. It could hardly be otherwise if one considers the geographical situation of Orhay. No power, seeking to maintain control of the region, could afford to neglect this site. It lay at the junction of ancient highways. One, the road from Armenia, descended from the great centre of Amid (Diyarbakr), and

---

[1] The Imam of the Halil Camii expressed this opinion to the present writer in 1959. In 1956 another respected citizen of Urfa declared that the name Urfa was derived from Orpheus of Greek mythology. The present writer scoffed at the theory. A few days later he discovered the Orpheus mosaic in a cave cut out of the rock at Urfa (see p. 52 below)! He has learnt to be less ready to scoff—but the theory of the derivation from Orpheus must nevertheless be rejected because Urfa as the city's name is not clearly attested before the Turkish period; see p. 255.

[2] Basil, cited by Michael the Syrian, dec- lares: 'After the flood, in the time of Noah, King Nimrod . . . built Orhay. He called it "Ur", that is, "town", and as the Chaldaeans lived there he added "hay", that is "that town [of the Chaldaeans]", just as Urshalem (Jerusalem) signifies "town of Shalem".'

[3] We may note that in the inscription of Shahpuhr I the name Orhay in Mid. Persian is [']WLḤ'Y and in Parthian 'WRḤ'Y. So Har- ran is [ḤR]'NY in Mid. Persian and Ḥ'RN in Parthian, in Greek it is Καρραι; Aleppo is ḤRPY in Parthian

debouched from the mountains into the plain at this spot. Thence it continued southwards to Harran and along the river Balikh, across the Euphrates, and beyond to the great cities of Syria in the west and south. At Orhay the north–south road meets an east–west road which linked Nisibis, and beyond Nisibis, the Iranian countries and India and China in the east with the fords of the Euphrates in the west. Along this road caravans carried, in Seleucid and also, we may presume, in pre-Seleucid times, spices and gems and muslin from India, and silk from China to the populous towns of Asia Minor and the Mediterranean seaboard.

The region, then, within this great curve of the Euphrates, played a significant part in the movement of trade and conquest from the riparian lands of the Tigris to the Euphrates and Syria. We expect to find allusions in cuneiform records. In the third millennium, Bilak (probably a city on the river Balikh) provided wine, according to texts of Lagash; and the town Ballihu was among the cities captured by Nabopolassar at the end of the Babylonian kingdom. Duru, on the river Gullab, about twenty kilometres east of Orhay, was subject to the Assyrians in the ninth to eighth centuries B.C. Campaigns in which Ashurnaṣirpal (884–859 B.C.) subjugated the Aramaean tribes of this area, and hunted lions by the Balikh and wild boars by the Euphrates, are recorded on the gates newly discovered at Balawat near Mosul.[1] They mention tribute paid by the city of Serug. The successor of Ashurnaṣirpal, Shalmaneser III, captured the cities on the Balikh called Kitlala and Til-sha-mar-ahi (or Til-mar-ahi).

Our early texts refer most frequently, however, to Harran, the city to which, according to the Bible, Abram and Sarai came, and whence Isaac and his son Jacob took their wives. The moon god of Harran, Sin, was called upon to ratify treaties as early as the nineteenth century B.C. and the fourteenth century B.C., and as far away as north Syria in the eighth century. The temple of Sin was restored by Shalmaneser III in the ninth century, two centuries later by Ashurbanipal (whom Sin and Ningal 'in the fidelity of their heart crowned with the lordly tiara'), and finally by Nabonidus in the twilight of the Babylonian empire. The letters from Mari show the area around the Balikh to be occupied in the nineteenth century B.C. by a confederation of semi-nomad tribes, who were especially active in the region of Harran. Raids were frequent, safety was to be found only in the towns. Fortresses were garrisoned largely by local troops under loyal sheikhs. Shamshi-Addu, ruler of Assyria, mounted a carefully organized expedition to conquer the region of Harran—possibly to keep open the trade route. Five centuries later, the Assyrian Adadnirari I annexed the province under a *turtanu*. With Ashur, Harran in the tenth century enjoyed exemption from taxation, and the privilege was restored by Sargon in the late eighth century. It was a fief in

---

[1] See the reference on p. 18 n. 7 below.

special relationship to the Assyrian king. In the ninth to eighth century B.C., its *turtanu* was the highest military commander of the Assyrian empire, who held the politico-religious office of *limmu* after the king himself. Esarhaddon visited the temple of Harran on his way to the conquest of Egypt; not long afterwards Ashurbanipal installed his brother there as High Priest. It was at Harran that the Assyrian forces under Ashuruballiṭ made their last stand before retreating westward in about 610 B.C., and, by historical justice, Harran was the residence of Nabonidus, the last king of Babylon.

It is certainly surprising that no obvious reference to Orhay has been found so far in the early historical texts dealing with the region, and that, unlike Harran, its name does not occur in cuneiform itineraries. This may be accidental, or Orhay may be alluded to under a different name which has not been identified.[1] Perhaps it was not fortified, and therefore at this time a place of no great military or political significance. With the Seleucid period, however, we are on firm historical ground. Seleucus I founded—or rather re-founded—a number of cities in this region. Among them, probably in 303 or 302 B.C., was Orhay.

The genius of Alexander had introduced a radical change in the technique of warfare. The meteoric speed with which he moved across the scene of events was unparalleled. It was based upon a novel disposition and use of fighting material. An army was now a carefully co-ordinated machine— various types of infantry to take the shock of battle, cavalry to gather swiftly the fruits of victory, artillery both for siege and in the field, engineers with a wide range of equipment, an intelligence service, and even the rudiments of a medical service, and survey and geographical units to maintain the force with the skill and assurance of science. Campaigns were mounted in any season of the year; rapid movement ensured the advantage of surprise. In the military sphere this new conception of time and movement was as far-reaching as the invention of the aeroplane in the twentieth century.

The cities of the plain, among them Harran, now became vulnerable.[2] But Orhay was admirably fitted to meet the new military situation, for with its great strategic importance it combines great natural strength. Within the broad curve of the Euphrates it commands a fertile hinterland, and it stands at sufficient distance from the river—eighty-five kilometres east of Zeugma and Birtha (Birecik), forty-five kilometres south-east of Samosata—to be forewarned against attack from the west.[3] The city lies wedged against the

---

[1] The city Urshu, well known from cuneiform inscriptions, almost certainly lay west, not east, of the Euphrates.

[2] There were, however, Macedonian settlers at Harran already in 312 B.C., presumably for political reasons; we hear of a Macedonian

element in that city as late as the time of Pompey, p. 10 below.

[3] On his campaign against the Persians, however, Alexander advanced eastwards to Nisibis, not through Zeugma but through Thapsacus, by the valleys of the Balikh and the Gullab.

foothills of the Anatolian massif. On two sides the hills form a natural rampart, and they were easily reinforced by a double row of walls. To the south-east the city is exposed to easy access from the plain of Harran; but this side is commanded by a high mount of limestone rock, crowned with a citadel which towers over both city and countryside. Water is supplied by a river flowing from the north-west along a deep wadi to enter the city in the south-west; emerging in the east it joins the Gullab, itself a tributary of the Balikh. It was called in Syriac Daiṣan, in Greek Scirtos—both names mean the 'leaping [river]'. The title was appropriate.[1] It was a troublesome little stream whose waters, swollen by the onrush of the winter rains and the melting snows of the mountains to the north, brought sudden disaster upon the city and its inhabitants at least once in every century. Dependence on the river whose twenty-five sources lie at some distance in the high lands would, however, have put the city at the mercy of a determined besieger. Fortunately there are copious springs of water within the circuit of the city walls, feeding the famous fish-pools.

Like other cities established by the Seleucids, Orhay received new names. On coins of Antiochus Epiphanes (died 163 B.C.) it is called 'Antioch by the Callirhoe', or 'Antioch by the beautiful flowing [water],[2]—a reference, no doubt, to the fish-pools as well as the river of Orhay. The same charming epithet is found also of Hierapolis (Mabbog, Bambyce), where also was a celebrated pool of fish, sacred to Atargatis, the 'Syrian goddess', whose cult is described by Lucian; and the two cities were confused by Strabo.[3] The conferment on Orhay of the name Antioch may have implied that a military colony there had been raised to the status of a city; it then had partial autonomy in issuing coinage, with the effigy, but not the royal superscription, of Antiochus Epiphanes. We may note that Nisibis, with which Edessa had direct links, was refounded at the same time under the name of Antioch Mygdonia.

More enduring was another name given to Orhay, probably at a somewhat earlier date. The city received—under, according to tradition, Seleucus Nicator—the name of Edessa. Why its Seleucid conquerors bestowed upon it the name of their own capital in Macedonia we do not know. Perhaps the luxuriance of its waters—the name of the Macedonian Edessa, now Vodena, is derived from *voda*, water—or its situation among the hills recalled to some nostalgic general the characteristics of his native town.[4] This was the name

---

[1] The name may have been used elsewhere in the neighbourhood of Edessa and with somewhat different application; see p. 54 below.

[2] So also in Pliny, but there this may be the result of confusion; Pliny incorrectly maintains that the city bore the name Antioch before it was called Edessa ('Edessa, that was formerly called Antioch, named Callirrhoe from its fountain . . .').

[3] See p. 46 below.

[4] We should not regard seriously the statement of a Syriac chronicler that Edessa was named after the 'oldest and first' daughter of its founder Seleucus, and was allotted to her as her dowry. Nor should we accept the suggestion

by which Orhay was to achieve renown—and this is the name by which it will be called henceforward in the present work.[1]

We may conjecture the appearance of the Mesopotamian Edessa in the Seleucid period. Roman coins carry a portrait of the city goddess seated on a mound with the figure of a river deity swimming at her feet. The theme is a hackneyed one and it was shared by Edessa with neighbouring cities. She was none the less well entitled to it as her emblem, and doubtless from an early time. We have observed that the Citadel mount and the river and springs and pools were prominent features of the city.

On these natural features was superimposed a scheme of town planning whose shape seems to be preserved to the present day. With the contours of the ground narrowly confined between the foothills and the river-bed, this could scarcely have been otherwise.[2] The engineers of the Byzantine Emperor Justinian, it is true, carried out important alterations to the course of the river to the north and west of the city, but with one exception this still followed the lines of the hills and valley bed.[3] The walls to the north and west could not but run alongside the wadi; to the south they included the springs and pools necessary for the supply of water. Sluices and river gates in the west admitted the river, which flowed out of the city into the plain through sluices and river gates in the east. There were four road gates, sited, with fair precision, at the four cardinal points of the compass. These continued in use, though under different names at different epochs, until the twelfth century—three of them until the present time.[4] The defences probably consisted of both an outer and an inner wall; in Byzantine times, we are told that in the intervening space was built a covered colonnade, and the inner wall must therefore have already been constructed. As in other cities in the East designed under the Seleucids, the main streets ran in straight transverse lines—north–south and east–west, and they have largely survived until modern times.

Only part of the Citadel mount was included within the walls in Seleucid times. This was rightly regarded as a defect in the city's defences by the Byzantines, and they enlarged the circuit of the walls to include the whole hill.[5] The Citadel was presumably the residence of the Seleucid governor, as later it was of the kings of Edessa. Its present complex covers an area of

---

of a modern scholar that the name Edessa is a distortion of Syriac Ḥadatta, or the new (city); this is nowhere attested in records, and presents serious philological difficulty.

[1] In Syriac, however, the city continued to be called Orhay; the name Edessa occurs only rarely in Syriac chronicles, and usually under the influence of Greek.

[2] An idealized description of the building of Edessa by Seleucus in a Syriac chronicle is of interest. The town was given, we are told, a strong and high wall, with four towers—the author adds that a little of one of them still remained in his time—and 'four splendid and fortified citadels at the four corners of the city'. In addition, palaces, temples, and markets were provided, and a carefully planned water supply ensured adequate irrigation.

[3] See p. 187 below.   [4] Pls. 5 a, b, 6.
[5] See p. 188 below and Pl. 4a.

approximately 400 by 80–120 metres, but it has been subject to reconstruction so often that we cannot hazard a guess as to its appearance under the Seleucids. The two fish-pools lay below and due north of the Citadel mount.[1] One is called today Birket Ibrahim, the pool of Abraham, the other Birket Zulha, the pool of Zulha, named after Zulaikha the wife of Potiphar. It has already been suggested that at one time the second pool was named Birket Sulkha after the mother of Nimrod. But it is equally possible—and, indeed, there is some evidence for this outside Edessa[2]—that the pool was originally called Seloq, after Seleucus; the name of the reputed founder of the city was in widespread use at Edessa.[3]

Beside the pools there stood in Seleucid times, according to tradition, a great pagan altar. And nearby—possibly at the end of the second century A.D.—was to be erected the church that came to be venerated far and wide as the oldest Christian shrine of Edessa.

[1] Frontispiece and Pl. 9a.   [2] See p. 55 below.   [3] Cf. pp. 16 f., 28 n. 4, 42 n. 3.

II

EDESSA UNDER THE KINGS

THE EARLY SELEUCIDS founded military colonies and cities on a scale never before seen in Mesopotamia—no fewer than ten were established in the area of Edessa. But with the death of Antiochus Epiphanes in 163 B.C., this policy had become ineffective as an instrument of direct government. Continuous warfare and internal dissension had weakened the central administration in Syria, and the vast distances over which the comparatively small numbers of Greek colonists were extended made difficult the day-to-day control of even individual strongholds. The structure of Hellenistic law and civic organization remained, and in some areas the Seleucid era continued in use until it was superseded by the Moslem system of dating;[1] but active political power in Mesopotamia passed out of the hands of the Seleucids and their representatives. The final turning-point came in the winter of 130–129 B.C., when a large part of the army of Antiochus Sidetes—after gaining some initial success in Babylonia and Media—was destroyed by the Parthians. Thereafter Syrian kings did not attempt to assert their rule beyond the Euphrates.

The vacuum left by the Seleucids was occupied by the Parthians—apart from some twelve years of domination by Tigranes of Armenia from 89 B.C. Parthian suzerainty did not involve rigid or centralized control; and several regions of Mesopotamia acquired some degree of autonomy. Some were ruled by families of Arab or Nabataean stock, notably the regions of Hatra and Singara to the east, Mesene to the south, and Anthemusia and Edessa in the west. Edessa became the seat of an independent kingdom, according to a tradition which seems trustworthy, only shortly before the defeat of Antiochus Sidetes. The reason is evident. Edessa was the most prominent city in the region which was now called the province of Osrhoene—a name that may be derived from Orhay, the native name of Edessa.[2] The province was

---

[1] In a document from Edessa dated A.D. 243, the Seleucid era is referred to as 'the former reckoning', presumably in contrast to the Roman system of chronology. At Edessa, the Seleucid era began from October 312 B.C., as among the Macedonians; the names of the months are, however, Semitic. Jacob of Edessa, in the first century of the Moslem period, refers to 'this era of the Greeks, that is, the era

of the Edessans'. Eastern Christians continue to employ the Seleucid era in certain contexts at the present time.

[2] If we accept as original the form Orrhoene. Pliny calls the people of the region Orroei or Orrhoei; a Latin inscription at Rome (to be dated after 242; see p. 30 n. 3 below) has the form Orrheni, and Dio Cassius has 'Ορροηνοί. (The name Μαννουορρα Αὐυρηθ in Isidore of Charax is

bounded to the west, the north-west, and the south-west by the Euphrates. As long as Seleucid Syria clung to its political pretensions in Mesopotamia, it could not relinquish interest in the crossing points of the Euphrates from Samosata to Callinicos. Through Zeugma—but from the second century A.D., through Caeciliana near Hierapolis—passed the road that linked Antioch, the western capital of the Seleucids, with their eastern capital, Seleucia on the lower Tigris. Another road went northwards to Nisibis, the great mart of the eastern frontiers—called appropriately in Syriac Ṣoba, the meeting-place—and crossing the northern Tigris led to Arbela, with a diversion to the south. Batnae (Serug), Harran, Resaina (Resh'aina), as well as Edessa, were important staging points on these routes.

We have virtually no contemporary allusions to Edessa's role on the international scene during the early Seleucid period. For the later period we must rely largely upon Roman historians (in both Latin and Greek), and these, it should be remembered, have little immediate concern for a theatre of operations so remote from the imperial capital. Nevertheless, it is clear that whenever Rome intervened in this region of Mesopotamia she came into contact with Edessa.

Sextilius led a Roman expedition against Tigranes of Armenia. Allied with Tigranes and defeated with him in 69 B.C. was the phylarch of Edessa.[1] A few years later, in the winter of 65–64 B.C., the soldiers of the Roman general Afranius,

returning through Mesopotamia to Syria . . . wandered from the way and encountered many hardships by reason of the winter and the lack of supplies. His troops would have perished had not the people of Harran, Macedonian colonists, who dwelt somewhere in that vicinity, received him and helped him forward.[2]

Evidently Edessa too showed friendship to the Romans, for in Pompey's settlement of the East, after the defeat of Tigranes, Abgar of Edessa was confirmed as ruler of his city.[3]

It was the same Abgar of Edessa who, twelve years later, in 53 B.C. was an actor in one of the most crushing disasters that ever befell a Roman army. Crassus, determined to win a reputation by victory over Parthia—and, it is alleged, fired by the example of Lucullus who had captured great booty at Nisibis and Tigranocerta—led his forces across the Euphrates. The events that ensued are vividly portrayed by Plutarch:[4]

obscure.) The suffix *ene* is used to denote a Seleucid eparchy, the subdivision of a satrapy. Another form of the name is Osdroene. Procopius derives the province's name from an eponymous king, Osroes; this name, like Orroes, Osdroes and Cosdroes, is a variant of the Persian Khusraw.

[1] Probably Abgar I, Piqa (the stammerer), 94–68 B.C.

[2] Dio Cassius.

[3] Abgar II, 68–53 B.C.

[4] Dio Cassius, writing a century after Plutarch, adds nothing of substance to his account, except to maintain that the Osrhoenians actually joined the Parthians in their onslaught on the legions. This allegation is to be treated with caution if the arguments advanced here about Abgar are valid.

While Crassus was still . . . considering [his course of action] . . . there came an Arab phylarch, Ariamnes by name,[1] a crafty and treacherous man, and one who proved to be, of all the mischiefs which fortune combined for the destruction of the Romans, the greatest and the most consummate. Some of the soldiers who had served under Pompey in these parts knew the fellow had profited by the kindness of that commander and was thought to be a friend of Rome; but now, with the knowledge of the [Parthian] king's generals, he tried to work his way into the confidence of Crassus, to see if he could turn him aside as far as possible from the river and the foothills, and bring him down into a boundless plain where he could be surrounded. . . . Accordingly, coming to Crassus, the barbarian (and he was a plausible talker too) lauded Pompey as his benefactor and congratulated Crassus on his forces. But then he criticized him for wasting time in delays and preparations . . .

At this time, therefore, after the barbarian had persuaded Crassus, he drew him away from the river and led him through the midst of the plain, by a way that was suitable and easy at first but soon became difficult when deep sand succeeded, and plains which had no trees, no water and no limit anywhere which the eye could reach, so that not only did thirst and the difficulties of the march exhaust the men but also whatever met their gaze filled them with obstinate dejection. For they saw no plant, no stream, no projection of sloping hill, and no growing grass—but only sea-like billows of innumerable desert sand-heaps enveloping the army. This of itself was enough to induce suspicion of treachery. . . .

Cassius . . . privately abused the barbarian. 'Basest of men', he said, 'what evil spirit brought you to us? With what drugs and jugglery did you persuade Crassus to pour out his army into a yawning abyss of desert and follow a route more fit for a nomad robber chief than for a Roman *Imperator*?'

But the barbarian, who was a subtle fellow, tried to encourage them with all servility, and exhorted them to endure a little longer; and as he ran along by the side of the soldiers and gave them his help, he would laughingly banter them and say, 'Is it through Campania that you think you are marching, longing for its fountains and streams and shade and baths (to be sure!) and taverns? But remember that you are traversing land on the borders of Assyria and Arabia!' Thus the barbarian played the tutor with the Romans, and rode away before his deceit had become manifest, not, however, without the knowledge of Crassus—he even persuaded him that he was going to work in his interest and to confound the counsels of his enemies.

The terrible fate of Crassus and most of his army need not be retold here.

Was Abgar a traitor to Rome, or was his advice to Crassus well-intentioned but unwise, or even misunderstood? Modern historians judge Abgar less harshly than does Plutarch. His situation was, by any standards, unenviable. Edessa lay in the political and cultural sphere of Parthia. Abgar must have respected the power of the Romans, and he may have felt gratitude to Pompey; but his sympathies doubtless inclined towards the Parthians. It may have been shame at the defeat of Crassus that led Roman historians to ascribe it to causes other than the incompetence of their general—the

---

[1] The name is probably derived from the epithet 'Aramaean'—less likely is a derivation from 'Armenian'. Abgar in other narratives is also called by his patronymic Maz'ur.

severity of local conditions and the treachery of allies. Their arguments are not convincing. The countryside of Harran in May does not present the alarming appearance described by Plutarch, nor are villages and watering points far apart. As for the behaviour of Abgar, Roman historians are free with accusations of perfidy against Arab chieftains;[1] today we would judge them guilty of no greater crime than unwillingness to commit their fortunes to a cause in which they had little interest. Indeed, there is evidence that may wholly acquit this Abgar of treachery. From a Syriac chronicle, it appears that there was a break in the continuity of the rule of Edessan kings between 53 B.C., the year of Crassus's defeat, and 52 B.C. It is not impossible that Abgar, far from being perfidious, as Plutarch would have us believe, remained loyal to his Roman ally and paid for his steadfastness by the loss of his throne.[2]

The defeat of Crassus restored Parthian hegemony over all the lands to the east of the Euphrates. A century passed before Edessa re-appeared in Roman history. In A.D. 49 the king of Edessa, another Abgar,[3] was a member of a delegation which went to Zeugma to receive Mihrdad (Meherdates), prince of Parthia and Roman nominee for the throne of his country. The 'dishonest' Abgar detained Mihrdad 'day after day in the town of Edessa'. We may suppose that he provided him with lavish entertainment, since the Parthian, notes our annalist, was an 'inexperienced youth who identified the acme of fortune with dissipation'.[4] Abgar finally accompanied Mihrdad on his expedition to the East, and Romans attached to the Edessan the blame not only for the delay—winter had already set in—but also for the circuitous route which was taken. Mihrdad, with his escort, passed through the mountains of Armenia and through Adiabene. But before he could put his claim to the test of battle, he was deserted, first by the king of Adiabene, then by the king of Edessa; defeated and captured, he was mutilated by the Parthian king Godarz (Gotarzes). It may well be that it was the treachery of this Abgar that led Plutarch, sixty years later, to ascribe similar behaviour to the earlier Abgar of the time of Crassus.

Viewed through the eyes of the Romans, the name Abgar of Edessa could, it must be admitted, be equated too easily with temporizing and duplicity. In A.D. 114 Trajan arrived at Antioch to open the campaign that was to

---

[1] So for example, Tacitus writes, 'The contingents . . . of the Arabs took their departure, in accordance with the levity of their race and with the fact, proved by experience, that barbarians are more inclined to seek their kings from Rome, than to keep them'.

[2] A different reason, it is true, is offered by a Syriac chronicle: 'The Edessans were without a master for one year by reason of strife through desire for the chieftainship'. It should also be observed that Crassus was guided from Harran to his death at Sinnaca, by a certain Andromachus. The latter was ill-disposed towards the Romans; he was leader of the pro-Parthian party at Harran, and he later became ruler of the city under the Parthians. Roman historians may have transferred the perfidy of Andromachus to Abgar.

[3] Abgar V, Ukkama (the Black), 4 B.C.–A.D. 7 and A.D. 13–50. Tacitus calls him 'Acbar, king of the Arabs.'

[4] Tacitus, *Annals*.

provide a final settlement of the eastern provinces of the Roman Empire. The envoys of the king of Edessa[1] came to him with gifts and a message of friendship, excusing the king's tardy submission by his fear of the Parthians—though it was only five years previously that, according to one source, he had purchased his kingdom from Parthia for a large sum of money. Trajan visited Edessa, and was entertained by the king, who, we are told, brought in his son to perform a 'barbaric dance.' Abgar's protestations of loyalty, his costly gifts—250 horses and mailed horsemen, suits of armour, and a large store of arrows—and the intervention of his handsome son, who had become a favourite with the Emperor, combined to induce Trajan to restore the Edessan to his throne. The neighbouring phylarch of Anthemusia, who, like Abgar, had failed to pay his respects to Trajan, was less fortunate. He fled, and it was at Abgar's suggestion that the Roman troops captured his capital town Batnae and annexed his territory. But Abgar was not to be trusted. In 116 when Trajan was resting after his conquest of Adiabene and Ctesiphon, Edessa joined a general insurrection in Mesopotamia; Roman garrisons were massacred or expelled. The Romans exacted swift vengeance. Lucius Quietus was sent to restore order. He besieged and captured Nisibis. Edessa was recovered and laid waste by fire and the sword, and its king seems to have perished in the disorder.[2]

On Trajan's death in 117, his conquests east of the Euphrates were renounced by his successor Hadrian. To the throne of Edessa, which appears to have been left vacant for two years, was appointed a Parthian prince, Parthamaspat, who had been elevated by the Romans to the throne of Parthia but rejected by his own countrymen. In 123, however, the native dynasty seems to have been restored at Edessa with the accession of a king Ma'nu.[3] A generation later, early in the reign of Emperor Marcus Aurelius, the Parthians resumed the offensive against Rome. The king of Edessa, another Ma'nu,[4] was replaced by a Wa'el bar Sahru (who struck coins with the effigy of the king of Parthia and with the legend in Syriac),[5] and the Parthians crossed the Euphrates into Syria. Ma'nu took refuge in the Roman camp, but his return was not long delayed. In 165 Avidius Cassius laid siege to Edessa; its citizens slaughtered the Parthian garrison and admitted the Romans. By a peace treaty in the following year, the ruler of Osrhoene became a client of Rome; Ma'nu was restored with the title of Philorhomaios.

Thirty years later a ruler of Edessa again broke his pledge of loyalty to

[1] Abgar VII, A.D. 109–116.

[2] According to the biography of Emperor Antoninus Pius, a king Abgar was persuaded by that Emperor to return to Edessa from eastern Parthia. It has been suggested that this is the Abgar in whose reign Edessa was sacked by Lucius Quietus, and that he had in fact escaped to the east. More probably, however, the reference is to a later king, perhaps Ma'nu VIII; Abgar may well have been regarded as a generic name for the kings of the dynasty of Edessa. [3] Ma'nu VII, A.D. 123–39.

[4] Ma'nu VIII, A.D. 139–63 and 165–77.

[5] Pl. 28b (i).

Rome. In 194, in the unrest which followed the murder of Emperor Pertinax, there was a general pro-Parthian rising in Mesopotamia. Abgar of Osrhoene[1] joined the ruler of Adiabene in laying siege to Nisibis. They later claimed, in an embassy to Septimius Severus, that they had attacked Nisibis because it had supported his rival Pescennius Niger; it is more likely that they hoped that the Roman hold had weakened, and that they could regain their independence. Their hopes were not realized. They could not take the city though they destroyed some supporters of Niger. Subsequently they offered to return their Roman prisoners to Severus, but they showed no inclination to yield forts which they had taken or to admit Roman troops. Severus swiftly defeated 'Abgar, King of the Persians' and his allies, and awarded Nisibis the status of *colonia*. For a while he appointed a procurator in charge of Osrhoene, feeling perhaps that the pro-Parthian party at Edessa was still strong. Soon, however, he gave the throne back to Abgar. This time Roman confidence in the king of Edessa was justified. When Severus returned to Rome the Parthians crossed the Tigris and besieged Nisibis. But Abgar, who had adopted the Roman names of Lucius Aelius Aurelius Septimus, identified himself with the Roman cause, and gave his sons as hostages to Rome and also offered the services of his skilled archers. Severus, after routing the Parthians in an easy campaign in 197–8, again declared Osrhoene a client state, and recognized Abgar's authority as 'king of kings'. He invited Abgar to visit Rome. The reception there of the king of Edessa was, declares a Roman historian, the most lavish accorded to a foreign potentate since Nero welcomed Tiridates of Armenia in A.D. 66. Abgar's journey must have taken place after 204 when the Emperor returned home.

Abgar the Great died in, probably, 212. He was succeeded by his son Abgar Severus,[2] but the independence of Edessa was drawing to its close. Caracalla, preparing his expedition against Parthia sent a friendly invitation to the king of Edessa to visit him, possibly at Rome; when the king arrived, he was seized and deposed, on the pretext that he had ill-treated his subjects while claiming that he was introducing them to Roman practices. In 213–14, probably in January 214, Edessa was proclaimed a *colonia*.[3]

The events of the following years are obscure. Edessa's coins show that she used the titles Aurelia Antonina; under Macrinus, these were replaced by Opellia Macriniana. Subsequently, the colony carried the names Marcia, Aurelia, Antoniana, and later Alexandria or Alexandriana, combined in various ways. According, however, to a Syriac chronicle, a king Ma'nu son of

[1] Abgar VIII, commonly called the Great, A.D. 177–212. It has been maintained that this king should be regarded as Abgar IX—incorrectly, as has been shown by A. R. Bellinger and C. B. Welles, *Y.C.S.* v, 1935, 150.

[2] Abgar IX, Severus, A.D. 212–14; he had no doubt taken the name Severus as a compliment to the Emperor, after the victorious Roman campaign against Parthia in 197–8.

[3] Caracalla spent the winter of 216–17 at Edessa. He was assassinated in spring 217 while on a visit to Harran.

Abgar reigned for twenty-six years until 240;[1] he can have been king only in name and without effective powers.

Coins of Edessa demonstrate that between 214 and 235, under Caracalla, Macrinus, Elagabalus, and Alexander Severus the city was a *colonia*; from the time of Alexander Severus and until 242 it was, like Batnae, a *metropolis*. Ma'nu seems to have been succeeded by an Abgar[2] who, according to numismatic evidence, must have accepted, at any rate nominally, the suzerainty of Emperor Gordian III. But the capture of Nisibis and Harran by the Persian Shahpuhr I, and his advance deep into Syria brought Gordian to Mesopotamia. The Romans recovered Harran and Nisibis; a victory at Resaina led to the restoration of the *colonia* of Edessa. In May 243 the city was administered by a Roman Resident and two *strategoi*, and that may have been already the second year of this form of government. King Abgar seems to have withdrawn to Rome with his wife. The monarchy had come to an end after about 375 years.[3]

The kingdom of Edessa had been established when the Seleucids withdrew to the west of the Euphrates, abandoning Mesopotamia to the Parthians; it came to an end when Rome imposed her direct rule on the eastern provinces. It could maintain itself under the disinterested suzerainty of Parthia or when Rome was content with exercising only an indirect hegemony. It could not survive open conflict with a major power. Nevertheless, that the dynasty of Edessa should have lasted 375 years is a remarkable record in a region so exposed to discord and violence at so restless a period of history. The kings who performed this feat of supple statecraft merit our attention. With the discovery, in the last eighty years and notably in the last two decades, of inscriptions and other monuments at Urfa, we are now in a position to assess the pattern of life at Edessa under the monarchy.

---

[1] Ma'nu IX A.D. 214–40.

[2] Abgar X, Frahad, A.D. 240–2.

[3] See p. 30 n. 3 below on the Latin inscription at Rome, erected probably by Abgar X. It may be significant that under Abgar X, from, that is, 240–2, Edessa seems to have had a monopoly of minting bronze coins in northern Mesopotamia. After 242, this duty and privilege was divided between Edessa, Harran, Nisibis, and Singara. The list of the kings of the dynasty of Edessa may be reconstructed as follows (the early names and dates should, however, be regarded with caution): Aryu, 132–127 B.C.; 'Abdu bar Maz'ur, 127–120; Fradhasht bar Gebar'u, 120–115; Bakru I, bar Fradhasht, 115–112; Bakru II, bar Bakru, alone, 112–94; Bakru II and Ma'nu I, 94; Bakru II and Abgar I, Piqa, 94–92; Abgar I, alone. 92–68; Abgar II, bar Abgar, 68–53; interregnum, 53–52; Ma'nu II, 52–34; Paqor, 34–29; Abgar III, 29–26; Abgar IV, Sumaqa, 26–23; Ma'nu III, Saphlul, 23–4; Abgar V, Ukkama bar Ma'nu, 4 B.C.–A.D. 7; Ma'nu IV, bar Ma'nu, 7–13; Abgar V (second time), 13–50; Ma'nu V, bar Abgar, 50–7; Ma'nu VI, bar Abgar, 57–71; Abgar VI, bar Ma'nu, 71–91; interregnum, 91–109; Abgar VII, bar Ezad (Izates), 109–16; interregnum, 116–18; Yalur (or Yalud) and Parthamaspat, 118–22; Parthamaspat, alone, 122–3; Ma'nu VII, bar Ezad, 123–39; Ma'nu VIII, bar Ma'nu, 139–63; Wa'el bar Sahru, 163–5; Ma'nu VIII (second time), 165–77; Abgar VIII, the Great bar Ma'nu, 177–212; Abgar IX, Severus bar Abgar, 212–14; Ma'nu IX, bar Abgar, 214–40; Abgar X, Frahad bar Ma'nu, 240–2.

The foundation of the kingdom of Edessa is ascribed by Syriac chroniclers to the year 180 of the Seleucid era—that is to 132–131 B.C.[1] The first king is said to have been a certain Aryu. This name is the Canaanite-Aramaic term for lion; in the ancient Semitic, and particularly the Arab world the names of animals are frequently found as the appellation of tribal groups and of individual members of tribes, but whether we should look here for totemistic affiliations is open to question.[2] Armenian writers[3] claim the rulers of Edessa as Armenian, successors of Abgar[4] son of Arsham, who moved his capital there from Metsbin (Nisibis). The names of the kings of Edessa and their fathers' names do not lend support to the theory. Some of these names are Iranian (like Fradhasht, Ezad, Frahad); we shall see that Edessa lay largely within the cultural milieu of Parthia. Others (Maz'ur, Abgar, Wa'el) are in use in Arabic. But most striking, because they are least easy to explain, are those names which terminate in the suffix 'u' (Ma'nu, 'Abdu, Bakru, Gebar'u, Sahru). They are undoubtedly Nabataean. In ethnic origin the Nabataeans were Arab;[5] their activity and area of settlement extended from southern Palestine to Syria, Arabia, and the Persian Gulf. Their language, however, was a branch of Aramaic particularly close to Arabic, written in a peculiar script. Significantly, the language of most of the inscriptions of Edessa at the time of the monarchy is Syriac, and this was the language of its townspeople and its scholars during the following centuries. Syriac as a principal member of the Aramaic group of languages is related closely to Nabataean in structure and vocabulary.

While, however, the rulers of Edessa were largely of Nabataean stock, the general population was more mixed in origin. There must have been considerable intermarriage between the colonists from Macedonia or Asia Minor or Syria, and the native population. In the sixth century John of Malalas alleges that Seleucus Nicator had described Edessa as 'half-barbarian (μιξοβάρβαρος) Antioch'. Inscriptions show that the name Seleucus was popular at Edessa in the period of the monarchy; the name Antiochus is also found, though less frequently. Under the influence of Rome, Edessans

---

[1] Five years earlier, according to a late Syriac chronicler; he regards the date of the conquest of Mesopotamia by the Parthians as the date of the beginning of the kingdom at Edessa.

[2] Another hypothesis on the origin of this name is given on p. 72 n. 2 below.

[3] Possibly also Jacob of Edessa, if our text of his chronicle is reliable. Armenian 'histories' on this period consist of a medley of legends.

[4] This name, which is characteristic of the dynasty of Edessa, is said to mean 'lame' in Syriac; cf. p. 73 below. The name is still found, of a Christian bishop, in the tenth century. In Arabic the word denotes a person with an umbilical hernia, a paunchy person; it is found also in Arabic as a personal name. The association of Abgar with Iranian has been doubted; the etymology from Armenian awag-ayr, 'great man', suggested by Moses of Khoren is certainly to be rejected. Tacitus uses the form Acbar, while Plutarch gives Agbar as well as Abgar. The proper name Abgar is found in Palmyrene inscriptions. The form Agbar occurs already in the Aramaic inscription of Nerab which was inscribed probably in the seventh century B.C.

[5] By Pliny, Tacitus, and Plutarch, the Edessans are termed 'Arabs'.

also adopted Latin names—Marcus, Marcia, Aurelius, Aurelia, Severus, Antoninus, Augustina, to mention only a few. Some Jews of the city had Hebrew names, Joseph and Samuel, others were called Seleucus, Gordian, Ezad. But the texts of the time of the monarchy, and the period immediately following, provide an overwhelming number of Syriac names; few names are Nabataean.

It is probable that before the Aryu dynasty seized power, the city of Edessa, like others in the Seleucid empire, was administered by two *strategoi* or civic magistrates, who gave their names to the years. They are mentioned in a document written shortly after the end of the kingdom and they appear not infrequently in later texts, notably in the Edessan martyrologies. But we do not find any reference to them in the sparse texts of the period of the Aryu dynasty; we may infer that their office had been suppressed by those autocratic monarchs.

The kings of Edessa did not, it should be observed, arrogate to themselves absolute power. Like Arab tribal chieftains, they ruled through a council of elders, possibly sheikhs, and including, no doubt, members of the royal family. In one account the king's principal courtiers are styled the 'chiefs of those who sat with bended knees'.[1] Roman historians term the rulers of Edessa phylarchs, and rightly so. Edessa at the end of the monarchy was still divided, at least formally, into districts allocated to φυλαί or clans; each was administered by an *archon*.[2]

Yet, although he was, in theory, no more than the first among his peers, the king of Edessa retained the outward tokens of power, as well as its substance, firmly in his hands. His regnal year provided the official system of dating, side by side with that of the Emperors. He resided in a 'great and beautiful palace'—here the term for palace is Iranian—at the 'source of the springs' which fed the famous fish-pools. The palace was destroyed in the floods of A.D. 201, and rebuilt on the same spot some years later. After the kingdom had come to an end, pilgrims to Edessa were shown the marble statues of the kings and the fish-pools inside the palace buildings.[3] Fearful of a recurrence of the floods, Abgar the Great constructed a 'winter house as a royal dwelling' (in one text called a 'castle') on the Citadel mount in, apparently, 205–6.[4] His nobles lived in mansions, that is in lesser state, in the proximity of the king's residence. In death also the kings were shown deference. They were buried

---

[1] Iranian nobles seem to have adopted a similar squatting posture. But this description of the Edessan nobles (in the *Doctrine of Addai*) is doubtful, since by a minor change in the text (*waʿda* for *qaʿda*) we may read 'chiefs of those who sat in the [king's] council'.

[2] The view has been advanced that Abgar's court was organized on Hellenistic, rather than on Oriental lines; Abgar's envoys to the Roman governor are described in the *Doctrine of Addai* as the 'chiefs and honoured men of [Abgar's] kingdom', and this corresponds exactly with the πρῶτοι καὶ προτιμώμενοι of Hellenistic kingdoms. We should not, however, ignore the Parthian and Arab influence, and the tribal structure of Edessa at this period.

[3] See p. 33 below and Pl. 10*a*.

[4] Pl. 9*a*, 36.

in a tomb tower[1] erected by Abgar VI in A.D. 88–9; one writer describes it as a 'great sepulchre of ornamental sculpture'.[2]

A significant symbol of royalty was the special head-dress that was the prerogative of the king.[3] Tiaras of silk were conferred by the king on all the chiefs and commanders and other high dignitaries of the kingdom, and these appear in sculptures of Edessa and the neighbourhood.[4] Among Parthians the wearing of the tiara was an honour 'shared by those who sat at the royal table and allowing men of merit . . . to speak counsel and vote in the assemblies'. At Edessa, if we may trust the account of a late martyrology, the principal pagan priests carried tiaras embossed with gold. Only the king, however, was entitled to wear a diadem with his tiara. The distinction is shown clearly on some coins of Edessa. On the obverse side Abgar the king wears his full regalia of tiara and diadem, while on the reverse appears a certain Ma'nu with only a tiara and the Greek legend 'Pais'. This term may be an abbreviation of *paṣ(griba)*, the chief officer of the kingdom.[5] The importance of the prerogative of the royal head-dress is vividly recalled in the biography of Aggai, the legendary bishop of Edessa, the first after the Apostle Addai. When the reprobate son of Abgar the Great ascended the throne, he instructed Aggai, who evidently had a monopoly of this craft, 'Make for me a tiara of gold as thou didst make for my fathers'. Aggai refused, and by order of the king was put to death for his act of *lèse-majesté*.

Taxation was in the hands of the king, as we shall observe later. He alone had the power to remit taxes. We read of a 'master of imposts' a few years after the end of the monarchy, who ensured that fees were paid on the sale of a slave girl by a woman of Edessa.[6] The king also controlled the military forces of the state. During the campaign in which Crassus was defeated in 53 B.C., King Abgar II was present with his troops. Abgar VII, it will be remembered, presented Trajan with horses and mailed horsemen, suits of armour, and arrows in A.D. 114. Some eighty years later, Abgar the Great offered Emperor Severus the services of his skilled archers. Archery was a favourite pastime at Edessa and the archers of the region were famous already in the ninth century B.C.[7] Osrhoenian archers formed a crack unit in

---

[1] Syriac *naphsha*.

[2] The Syriac is obscure. The rendering given here is based, following Duval, upon the amendment of one letter in the text; it receives support from the instruction of the *Testament* of St. Ephraim, 'In your sepulchres do not place me, for your ornaments do not help me'. Less probable is the rendering, also with a slight emendation of the text, 'great sepulchre of coloured sculpture'.

[3] On some coins of Edessa a sceptre is shown before the face of the king.

[4] Notably in the reliefs of high-ranking

officers of the kingdom at Sumatar Harabesi, p. 58 below.

[5] Perhaps this Ma'nu, the *paṣgriba*, is the father of Queen Shalmath, whose statue stood on a column on the Citadel mount at Edessa; p. 19.

[6] This interpretation of the text may be accepted, although it has been doubted by some scholars.

[7] Archers of the Balikh region are shown on panels recording the achievements of Ashurnaṣirpal II engraved on gates erected at Balawat near Mosul and now being deciphered.

the Imperial army which Maximinus led to Germany. They revolted against him on the death of Alexander Severus in 235, and raised a Senator named Quartinus to the purple, with fatal consequences for their nominee. But the subservience of the military at Edessa to the royal household is eloquently shown by the Syriac inscription on the column on the Citadel mount that was erected by the military governor of the town:

I Aphtuḥa the *nu[hadra]* son of Bars[h. . . .][1] m]ade this column and the statue which is on it to Shalmath the Queen daughter of Ma'nu the *pa[s]griba* wife of [. . . the kin]g my lady [. . . . .].[2]

The administration of Edessa was evidently efficiently organized, as befitted a Hellenistic foundation, with a corps of officials with clearly defined precedence and functions. In the narrative of the conversion of king Abgar to Christianity we read of a 'second in the kingdom', whom the Apostle Addai healed of his gout. This personage, it may be noted, was called, 'Abdu bar 'Abdu—his name, then, is probably Nabataean like those of many of the kings of Edessa. The 'second in the kingdom' no doubt carried the Iranian title of *pasgriba*;[3] perhaps he may have been not Viceroy, but heir-apparent to the throne. Certainly he was the highest-ranking officer in the kingdom. The *pasgriba* Ma'nu, mentioned on the column inscription in the Citadel, was father of the queen of Edessa, and he may be that Ma'nu whose head appears on the reverse side of a coin of Edessa. Another principal office of state was that of the 'ruler of the Arabs', or *Arabarchos*, who probably governed the marches to the east of Edessa.[4] The dignitary called *nuhadra* was probably of lower rank than the *Arabarchos*, for the son of an *Arabarchos* seems, according to a Syriac inscription of probably the second century, to have held the rank of *nuhadra*. Like *pasgriba*, the title *nuhadra* is Iranian.[5] In Parthia in the third century A.D., it was held by the governor of a town and its environs, and at Edessa in the same period the *nuhadra* may have been in charge of local administration. He is also likely to have had military functions, for the Persian general who invaded Osrhoene in 354 carried the title of *nuhadra*.

(I owe this information to the kindness of Dr. R. D. Barnett and Dr. E. Sollberger of the British Museum.) But Mesopotamia was probably renowned for its archers much earlier. In the region of Amid (Diyarbakr), was found the commemorative stele of Naramsin, grandson of Sargon, erected in about 2300 B.C. The use of bowmen by that victorious general may have contributed largely to his success. On the stele his troops are depicted in loose formation, not in the compact phalanxes of the Sumerians, lightly clad, and armed with bows and arrows. Palmyra too furnished bowmen for the Roman army at the time of the Civil War, who were under the command of Antony. They are said to have taken part in the fighting against the Jews at Jerusalem in A.D. 70 and in campaigns in Europe and Africa under the Severi. Archers appear in tableaux at Dura Europos.

[1] Probably Barshuma, or Barshelama, or Barsamya.　　　　　　[2] Pl. 29a.

[3] This is evident from the early 'Hymn of the Soul', p. 31. In inscriptions at Hatra are found the forms *PŠGRB'*, or *PZGRYB'*; the Parthian form is *pasagriw*.

[4] See p. 22 below.

[5] Parthian *nakhwadhar, nokhadhar*.

Public order in the city was maintained by the city watchman, the *geziraye*, a term possibly also of Iranian origin. After the disaster of 201, the king gave instructions that some *geziraye* should sleep on the walls from October to April in order to give notice of the approach of river floods. There were also city surveyors and other experts, 'wise men' or 'knowledgeable men', in municipal administration, as well as workmen employed on the upkeep of the royal buildings. Characteristic of the personal rule of the kings of Edessa seem to have been the *sharrire*, or commissioners, probably persons whom the king chose as his confidants. An important official with the status of *sharrira*, was the king's *tabulara*, or secretary;[1] we shall refer in a later chapter to the role of Ḥannan, secretary to King Abgar, in the dissemination of Christianity at Edessa. Two *sharrire* of the city were in charge of the archives in which official documents were deposited. They may have been in some degree the equivalent, under the kings, of the *strategoi* of pre-monarchy days. At Dura in the third century, contracts were often witnessed by the '*strategos* and Steward of the city'; at Edessa in 243, a document is certified by a *strategos* who carries the title of *bahora*, the Inspector, that is, who confirmed its bona fides. Later, in the Byzantine period, the office of the *sharrire* was greatly reduced in popular prestige. Already in martyrologies of the fourth century they had become minor officials who set down in writing and then reported to the authorities the actions of the citizens.[2]

The archives of Edessa had a reputation for reliability. Eusebius gives an account of the beginnings of Christianity there, which, he states, had been translated into Greek from the Aramaic 'archives of Edessa which was at that time ruled by its own kings'.[3] A Syriac chronicle of Edessa has survived, and provides us with extracts from the city's archives. For the most part they are brief, and belong, in their present form, to the sixth century. But the description of the flood at Edessa in A.D. 201[4] shows that records must have been compiled at greater length; and the vividness and detail of this narrative mark it as authentic and contemporary—written, that is, during the monarchy, and at the specific command of the king. A wide range of documents was admitted to the archives. They are described, at the end of the monarchical regime, as the 'sacred and profane archives of Edessa'. Centuries

[1] This is the equivalent of the Latin *tabularius*, not *tabellarius*, courier, as Eusebius and Rufinus. The latter is *rahṭa* in Syriac; it occurs in the memorial inscription of a cave outside Urfa, probably of the second or third century, which reads: 'I, Rabbai son of 'Abshelama the courier, made for myself this tomb, for myself and for my children and for my heirs, and for GNY' my son'.

[2] The Syriac term was evidently not understood by the translators of the martyrologies into Greek, and they omit it. In the Syriac version of the history ascribed to Zacharias Rhetor, the epithet *sharrire* is used of Senators at Rome.

[3] The establishment of archives at Edessa is ascribed by the Armenian Moses of Khoren to the Romans. A Syriac chronicle declares that Jesus was on the earth for thirty-two years, 'according to the testimony which we have found in the truthful book of the archives of Edessa, which errs in naught but makes known everything truthfully'.

[4] See p. 24 below.

later, the records of Edessa were still arranged in the two categories of episcopal and lay; and, indeed, this is the pattern followed by most Syriac histories. The writer of the spurious martyrology of Sharbil claims that it was written down for deposit in the 'archives of the city where the royal charters are placed'. Not only, however, were events of public significance recorded there, but even the deeds of a private commercial contract, like the sale of a slave girl, were kept in the official archives.[1] Transcripts were made by the 'scribes of Edessa'—under the monarchy by the 'king's scribe'—or by clerks (*exceptores*).[2] It was then signed by witnesses and by the inspector of contracts, and certified by the *strategos baḥora* (as we have already remarked) in the presence of the parties to the transaction.

The nobles of Edessa, who were in attendance on the king and were entitled to wear a tiara, are called in Syriac documents variously 'grandees', or 'chiefs', or 'commanders'. We do not know what was the exact significance of these titles; but all nobles could be described as 'free men'. Many must have acquired Roman citizenship. Probably this status became general only in the last decades of the monarchy, through Caracalla's grant to Edessa of the status of *colonia*. In the Edessan contract of 243, the parties to the contract and most of the city officials bear Roman names, an indication of citizenship; the names of their fathers, on the other hand, are Semitic. The Resident and one of the two *strategoi* are Roman knights, a rare distinction, since we do not hear of any citizen of Dura with this rank, and few are mentioned even in the inscriptions of Palmyra.

The 'free men' built mansions in the 'High Street'[3] in the vicinity of the king's palace. No doubt they derived their wealth from landed property, owning villages outside the city. But some may well have been merchants, dealing in the products that were brought by caravans to Edessa from the East, especially along the ancient road from Nisibis. Merchants were evidently known at court. It was Tobias son of Tobias from Palestine with whom Addai lodged according to legend, and Tobias was requested to introduce the Apostle to the king. The 'strangers of the lands of Nisibis[4] and Harran' who attended the preaching of Addai the Apostle were, no doubt, merchants from the two great commercial centres to the east and south of Edessa.

An important element in Edessan society were the artisans. Some were employed by the king and housed near his own residence, presumably at his expense. The 'husbandmen[5] and artisans who (worked with their) hands' are

---

[1] A duplicate of the document was given to the purchaser of the slave, presumably in case of resale or in defence of his title to the girl. Cf. *Doctrine of Addai*: 'The records of the kings, where the ordinances and laws are laid up and [the contracts] of the buyers and sellers are kept with care, without any negligence whatever.'

[2] The clerks, we are told, recorded the details of the trial and sentence of the martyred Ḥabbib, see p. 85 below.

[3] On this name see p. 181 n. 3.

[4] Syriac, Ṣoba.

[5] Or 'workmen'; Syriac, *pallaḥe*.

categories mentioned by name after the 'chiefs and freemen of the king and commanders' in the account of the assembly summoned by Abgar to hear Addai the Apostle. After the flood of 201, the artisans were instructed to remove their booths from beside the river and they were allowed to erect them only at the distance from the river that was prescribed by the surveyors and the other experts of the municipality. Workmen, including, we may assume, artisans, who sat in the colonnades and carried out their occupation beside the river, were also forbidden to spend the night in this area during the autumn and winter months when there was fear of unexpected flooding—eloquent evidence of the paternalism of the king.

That there were slaves at Edessa under the monarchy, as afterwards, is shown by a Syriac document, dated 243, found at Dura Europos. This is the contract of sale of a slave girl, Amath-Sin, aged about 28 and purchased from an Edessan woman by a man of Harran for the price of 700 *denarii*. The Harranian may have bought her for resale. The seller disclaims responsibility if the slave were to run away from her new owner, and possibly also if she were to develop some defect, after a probationary period of six months—a usual clause in contracts of this nature from early times.

Abgar decreed, after the flood of 201, that the taxes should be remitted both 'of those who were inside the city and those who dwelt in the villages and on farms'. These villages and farms lay in the agricultural country around the city; and their inhabitants were bound to the population of the city by ties of consanguinity and economic dependence—as in other regions of the early Near East. Beyond the zone in which the villages stood, lived the people of the uncultivated lands. They were at an intermediate stage in the transition from nomadism to settled life. Close to the villages were the semi-nomads, the 'Arab, who spent part of the year tending the fields, part tending their flocks. Further afield were the pure nomads, the Beduins, who were always on the move, living in tents, refusing to accept the authority of the city and deriving their livelihood not only from cattle rearing but also from highway robbery and pillage. It is these whom Greek and Roman writers call Saracens; Syriac writers call them Ṭayyaye, from the Beduin tribe Ṭayy, with whom they were most familiar.

The Beduins were no respecters of persons; they harried the half-settled 'Arab, as well as the caravans of merchants and city dwellers. It was probably, then, as much to defend the 'Arab as to protect the roads against the Ṭayyaye that the office of *Arabarchos*, in Syriac *shalliṭa de'Arab*, was established at Edessa. A text of Dura Europos, dated A.D. 121–2 mentions 'a *strategos* of Mesopotamia and Parapotamia, and *Arabarchos*', who was also collector of taxes and held Parthian rank. Cicero ridiculed Pompey by describing him as an *Arabarchos* who acted both like a Parthian official and a rough Arab chieftain. But the jurisdiction of the *Arabarchos* of Edessa probably did not extend far from the environs of the city. The title *shalliṭa de'Arab* appears in Syriac inscriptions at Sumatar Harabesi, in the rugged Tektek plateau. Here, at an intersection of wadis some sixty kilometres south-east of Edessa and thirty kilometres east-north-east of Harran, is an important oasis, on which, to the present day, nomad shepherds converge with their flocks and herds. In one inscription dated A.D. 165 found at Sumatar, a *shalliṭa de'Arab* prays for the life of his 'lord the king' and his sons, referring, no doubt, to Wa'el, son of Sahru, the pro-Parthian king of Edessa. Another *shalliṭa de'Arab* has inscribed a memorial in honour of a certain Aurelius Ḥaphsai, his 'lord and benefactor'.[1] The *shalliṭa de'Arab*, we may conclude, controlled the marches to the east of Edessa on behalf of the ruler of that city.

How far did the authority of the kings of Edessa extend? In late Roman times Edessa was the principal city of Osrhoene, which may derive its name from the city.[2] But we do not know where the boundaries of that province stood. They are not defined in the accounts of the settlement of this region by Pompey, Trajan, Hadrian, and their successors as Emperors of Rome, and no doubt they varied in the course of time. The natural frontier to the west is, of course, the river Euphrates. A Syriac inscription of Birtha (Birecik) records the construction of a burial place by its ruler (*shalliṭa*) in A.D. 6; he was, we are told, tutor to the son of a certain Ma'nu bar Ma'nu.[3] Ma'nu, however, has no title, and therefore cannot reasonably be identified as king of Edessa. Another Syriac inscription, on a tomb tower at Serrin on the Osrhoenian bank of the Euphrates opposite Mabbog, was dedicated in A.D. 73 by, probably, a religious notable,[4] but again it has no obvious association with Edessa. Nevertheless, we know that the king of Edessa went in A.D. 49 to escort Mihrdad, the pretender to the throne of Parthia, from Zeugma to Edessa, and we may assume that the territory as far as the Euphrates was subject to Edessa at this time. Less certain is the situation to the east of the city. Mihrdad was accompanied by the army of Edessa as far as Adiabene;

---

[1] It is tempting to identify (with Pognon, *Inscriptions sémitiques* 37 f.) this Aurelius with the Aurelianus son of Ḥaphsai, who was Roman governor of Osrhoene after the abolition of the monarchy in the third century. But the considerable interval in dates makes the theory untenable.   [2] p. 9 above.

[3] This, the oldest Syriac inscription, reads: 'In the month of Adar of the year 317, I, ZRBYN bar Ab[gar] ruler of Birtha, tutor of 'WYDNT bar Ma'nu bar Ma'nu, made [this bu]rial place [for my]self and for ḤLWY', mistress of my house and for [my] children [. . .]. Whoever will enter this b[urial place] and shall show respect [lit., see] and shall give praise— all the [gods shall bless him].'

[4] 'In the month of the former Teshri of the year 385, I, Ma'nu the *qashshisha*, *budar* of Naḥai, son of Ma'nu, grandson of ŠDRW NḤ', built this *naphsha* (tomb tower) for myself and for my sons, at the age of ninety. Whoever shall give praise, all the gods shall bless him, dwelling and life shall he have. [But] he who shall come and ruin this work and these bones . . . atonement for sin [? or 'burial'; this word would then be Nabataean or dialectal] he shall not have, and sons who shall cast dust upon his eyes shall not be found for him.' The interpretation of this text is due to the perception of A. Maricq (Maricq–J. Pirenne, *Classica et Orientalia*, 135, 141 ff.) The term *qashshisha* probably has religious significance (see the present writer's article in *Iraq* xxix, 1967, 6); on *budar* see pp. 57 ff below.

and there is evidence that the ruling houses of Edessa and of Adiabene were connected by alliance, if not by ties of blood.[1] In A.D. 194 the armies of Edessa and Adiabene were associated in the siege of Nisibis—evidence of unsettled conditions, and perhaps also of the need to assert control of the trade route. Certainly the oasis of Sumatar Harabesi recognized the authority of Edessa in A.D. 165.[2] To the south of Edessa there must have been rivalry between that city and Batnae, capital of Anthemusia. Both were the seat of an Arab or Nabataean monarchy, and Batnae, like Edessa, was a considerable centre of commerce.[3] The king of Edessa evidently encouraged the Romans to annex Anthemusia in, probably, A.D. 115, and may have profited as a result. But even Harran, no more than forty kilometres south of Edessa, maintained the status of *colonia*; it retained its traditional system of government and remained virtually independent of Edessa until a very late date.[4]

We receive a graphic picture of the topography of Edessa itself from the account, in the *Chronicle of Edessa*, of the flooding of the city in A.D. 201. It is written in crisp Syriac, and must have been composed not long after that memorable November night. It merits quotation in full:

In the year 513 in the reign of [Septimius] Severus and the reign of king Abgar, son of king Ma'nu, in the month of the latter Teshrin, the spring of water that comes forth from the great palace of king Abgar the Great became abundant; and it rose abundantly as had been its wont previously, and it became full and overflowed on all sides. The royal courtyards and porticoes and rooms[5] began to be filled with water. When our lord king Abgar saw this he went up to a safe place on the hill, above his palace where the workmen of the royal works reside and dwell. While then the experts[6] were considering what to do about the excess of waters which had been added, there took place a great and abundant downpour of rain during the night. The [river] Daiṣan came before the usual time and month and foreign waters came, and they found the sluices closed with large plated iron [bars] and with reinforced iron bolts. Since no ingress was found for the waters, a great lake formed outside the city walls and the waters began to descend between the battlements of the walls into the city. King Abgar standing on the great tower called '[the tower] of the Persians', saw the waters by [the light of] burning torches and ordered that the gates and the eight sluices[7] of the eastern[8] wall of the city should be removed from [the place] where the river came out. But at that very moment the waters broke down the western wall of the city and entered into the city. They destroyed the great and beautiful palace of our lord king and removed everything that was found in their path—the charming and beautiful buildings of the city, everything that was near the river to the south and north. They caused damage, moreover, to the nave[9] of the church of the Christians. In this

---

[1] Pliny, it is true, assumes that the Orroei extended from the Euphrates in the west, to the Tigris in the east and to Armenia in the north, but he is writing with obvious imprecision.

[2] See p. 23.   [3] Cf. p. 137.

[4] On the traditional enmity between Edessa and Harran see the present writer's *Edessa and Harran* (Inaugural lecture delivered on 9 May 1962).

[5] Or 'courtyards and porticoes and royal houses'.

[6] Lit., wise men.

[7] One editor reads, 'gates of the eight sluices'.

[8] The text has 'western'; see, however, pp. 7, 156.

[9] Or 'shrine'; Syriac, *haikla*.

incident there died more than two thousand persons; while many of them were asleep at night, the waters entered upon them suddenly and they were drowned.

In face of this disaster King Abgar acted energetically.

When the city was full of the sound of wailing and when king Abgar had seen this damage that had taken place, he ordered that all the craftsmen of the city should take away their booths from beside the river, and that no one should build a booth for himself beside the river; through the expert [skill] of the surveyors and knowledgeable men, the booths were placed as far as the breadth of the river [allowed] and they added to its former measurements. For even though the waters were great and abundant, the actual breadth of the river was small; it received the waters of twenty-five streams in their confluence from all sides. King Abgar ordered that all those who resided in the portico and carried out their occupation opposite the river should not pass the night in their booths from the former Teshrin to Nisan, but that all the winter time five of the *geziraye* who guard the city should pass the night on the wall above the place where the waters enter the city. When at night they observed and heard the sound of foreign waters beginning to enter the city and . . .[1] Whoever heard [this] sound and was negligent and did not go out [and shout], 'Behold the waters' would be punished for contempt because he had despised the order of the king. This order was instituted from the time when the event happened in this wise until eternity.

But our lord king Abgar ordered a building to be built as his royal dwelling, a winter house [in] Beth Tabara—and there he used to dwell all the winter time; in the summer he would go down to the new palace that had been built for him by the source of the spring [of water]. His nobles also built for themselves buildings as dwelling places in the neighbourhood in which the king was, in the High Street[2] called Beth Saḥraye.[3] In order that the former tranquillity of the city should be established, king Abgar ordered that unpaid taxes from those who were inside the city and from those who dwelt in the villages and on farms should be remitted, and that taxes should be suspended from them for five years until the city had grown rich in its population and adorned with its buildings.[4]

This narrative confirms the course of the river through the city from west to east and the location of the king's palace by the pools. The 'safe place on the hill' which the king climbed to examine the flood for the first time cannot be the high ground in the north-west of the city since he would then have been obliged to cross the path of the waters. It must have been the

---

[1] A few words are missing here.

[2] Or, less probably, 'Corn market'.

[3] That is, palace-enclosure area, or area of pedlars.

[4] The Chronicle adds: 'Maryahb son of Shemesh and Qayoma son of Magraṭaṭ (the vocalization of the last name is uncertain)— these scribes of Edessa wrote down this event at the order of king Abgar, and Bardin and Bulid who were in charge of the archives of Edessa received it and placed it inside them [in their capacity] as *sharrire* of the city'. An account of this flood in the anonymous '*Chr. Zuqnin*', of probably the eighth century, provides addition-al details. The exits of the river in the eastern wall of the city were blocked by the accumulation of scum carried from the hills and from the city streets. Those houses of Edessa that were made of bricks and clay collapsed under the pressure of the flood waters. Bodies and wood and domestic articles were carried away in the stream; beds, some with their dead owners still upon them, were swept through the east wall into the plain. These details may, however, be a description of a flood of Edessa nearer to the time of the writer than that of A.D. 201; see pp. 203 f. below.

Citadel mount which would have commanded a fine bird's-eye view of the river. It was there that the king built his winter house, and it was there that, according to legend, the Apostle Addai addressed the people of Edessa assembled at the invitation of the king.[1] Beth Saḥraye, where the nobles constructed their mansions, was probably the eastern portion of the present Citadel mount[2] and the high land further to the east and north. In the vicinity is the cave in which was found the Family Portrait mosaic; the dignified mien of the personages in this mosaic marks them as noblemen living in easy circumstances.[3]

The 'tower of the Persians', from which Abgar examined the floods for the second time, must have been near the palace or even inside the palace. Possibly it was on the site of the tower that still stands, south of Birket Ibrahim.[4] The Christian Church of Abgar's time—later it was called the Old Church—was evidently well known to the narrator, since he mentions it without introduction or explanation. It must have been situated east of the palace and on low ground. If we assume that the mosques of present-day Urfa stand on the site of Christian churches, the most probable location of the church would be Makam Ibrahim.[5]

Nothing is left today of the 'charming and beautiful buildings' of the city of Edessa at the time of Abgar the Great. Of Abgar's palace and the mansions of the nobles all that survives are the fish-pools, and the two graceful columns standing high on the Citadel mount among ruined towers and arches and fallen debris. The two columns are on bases that were subsequently reinforced, and their twenty-seven courses are each two half-drums of stone, with bosses to aid the builders to hoist them into position.[6] The style of their Corinthian capitals assigns them to the late Roman period, and this date is confirmed by the script of the Syriac dedication to Queen Shalmath on the eastern column. Shalmath may well have been the wife of king Abgar the Great at the end of the second and beginning of the third century. Her statue, like the inscription, must have faced the city. We may assume, then, that the columns stood at the northern entrance to the complex of buildings,

---

[1] See p. 78 below and Pl. 36.

[2] Cf. p. 188 below, on the constructions at Edessa in the time of Justinian.

[3] Plan II and Pl. 1.

[4] Modern writers have maintained that this tower stands on the place where once was the famous School of the Persians; the hypothesis is possible since here was erected a Jacobite Church of the Mother of God, p. 185 below.

[5] Plan I and Pl. 32b.

[6] In the second century A.D., bosses for lifting heavy stones were probably no longer used in the West, but they were employed by builders in Hellenistic times and may well

have survived in the eastern provinces. The space between the columns at Urfa is 1,040 cm. From the present surface of the ground the height of the base of the eastern column is 255 cm., of the western column about 275 cm.—the surface of the ground was evidently uneven also at the time of the erection of the columns; the other dimensions of the bases are 415 × 507 cms., and 375 × 390 cm., respectively. The height of the courses is irregular, ranging between 41 cm. and 48 cm., with an average of about 45 cm. The total height of the columns, including the bases, capitals and copings, is therefore about 15 metres. Pl. 9b.

and there are superficial indications, among the ruins, that a row of buildings on the mount lay to the south, in line with the columns. The columns are identical in form and structure, but only approximately similar in size. They appear to be free-standing. Their function, and that of the buildings around them, in the second and third centuries is far from certain.[1] It is strange that only one carries an inscription referring to a statue; we would have expected the statue of the queen to be accompanied, and no doubt preceded, by a statue of the king. Perhaps they were part of a colonnade; there are grounds, albeit somewhat slender, for maintaining that the building in which they stood was a pagan temple.[2]

In recent years the cemeteries of Edessa have yielded useful information. To the north-west, west, and south-west of the city, the foothills of the great Anatolian plateau fall sharply to the plain. Here are cave-tombs— 'houses of eternity' they are called in Syriac, as also in Palmyrene—cut in the rock to the number of perhaps a hundred. Three main cemetery areas were in use at Edessa during the time of the monarchy, and the decades immediately following. In the low hills west of the Citadel, beside the modern village with the suggestive name of Kırk Mağara, 'Forty caves', is a cluster of burial places on either side of the wadis. Jews also were buried here, if one may judge from the brief inscriptions in Hebrew and Greek; on one side of the entrance to a tomb is carved also a five-branched candelabrum, or *menorah*. Other tombs at Kırk Mağara are pagan. One is decorated with the relief of a funerary banquet and a Syriac inscription with the date A.D. 201–2, the year of the flood at Edessa in the reign of Abgar the Great.[3] This western cemetery seems to have extended also northwards, towards the modern Vadi Manci. In it was probably the resting-place in the fourth century of St. Ephraim, laid at his own request among the poor and criminals, but soon afterwards transferred to the tomb of the bishops of Edessa. Due south of the Citadel, the cave of the Family Portrait mosaic, probably depicting a noble family, lies in a southern cemetery which spreads westwards and, more important, eastwards to the present Eyüp Mahallesi. The dates of mosaics in this area range between A.D. 228 and 278, but one inscription has the date 208–9. A third cemetery is to be found beyond Justinian's dam to the north-west of the walls. That this was less favoured than the other cemeteries in pagan times, we may deduce from a comparison of the dress of the personages of the Tripod mosaic with the more ornate costume of the Family Portrait mosaic and the Funerary Couch mosaic in the southern area. Later, however, with the triumph of Christianity at Edessa, the northern cemetery appears to have become more popular. Here was built the shrine of the Confessors at

---

[1] We must reject the elaborate theory that these columns represent Dioscoroi or twin deities, as propounded by J. R. Harris, *Cult of the Heavenly Twins*, 1906, and elsewhere.

[2] Cf. p. 53 below; for the text of the inscription see p. 19 above.

[3] See p. 28 n. 4 below.

the place where the martyrs of Edessa were interred; the memory of the shrine is probably perpetuated in the modern name of this quarter of Urfa, Şehitlik Mahallesi, the quarter of the martyrs' tomb.[1]

With few exceptions, these cave-tombs are of modest dimensions, ranging from 285 cms. square to 300 × 317 cm., while the cave of the rich Family Portrait mosaic is only 250 cm. square. Where a cave leads to an inner cave the outer one is larger—one outer cave is 470 × 400 cm., the inner cave about 290 cm. square. The entrance to many of the cave-tombs is scarcely visible until one approaches close to the opening. A few have frame mouldings over the arched doorway, or one or two pilasters on either side, some also have figures in the pediment, possibly putti and tritons; one had four fluted columns.[2] Inside the cave-tombs the walls are ornamented with carvings in the cornice, sometimes with vine leaves. Ranged around the walls are conventional arcosolia, some of them so hollowed out, whether artificially or from natural causes, that they have almost become sarcophagi; the arcosolia vary in dimensions from 170 × 95 cm., to 220 × 100 or even 125 cm. The niche in which they are set has either an arched or a triangular head. The architectural décor of the arcosolia varies in its degree of elaborateness. Often the wall below the shelf on which the body rested was shaped to represent the legs of a couch, sometimes the niche of the arcosolium is framed in a carved cornice with a pilaster on either side, crowned with a capital, with rosettes or eagles with swags or vine leaves or putti. A few have the familiar winged Victories with wreaths in their outstretched hands. Three are decorated with a relief on the rear wall of the arcosolium, depicting the deceased man reclining at a funerary banquet.[3] One cave has a bust over the entrance on the inside, and in the soffit of the niche two busts look down on the arcosolium. Other caves have no carvings, but elaborate mosaics on the floor which we describe later. A small number have inscriptions in Syriac, either in the mosaic or carved on the walls; of these some carry dates, but all are in a script which enables us to assign them to the period of the monarchy or shortly afterwards.[4]

[1] Today, however, the citizens of Urfa ascribe the name of the district to the burial there of Turks killed in the defence of the city against the French after the First World War. For the location of the cemeteries, see the cave-tombs on Plan II.

[2] Now in the Urfa museum.

[3] We may also ascribe to the period of the Edessan monarchy two other bas-reliefs of a funerary banquet in a cave tomb at Kara Köprü, north of Urfa; see Pognon, op. cit. p. 179 and Pl. XI, and p. 55 below.

[4] See Pls. 1–3, 16–27, 43–4. The tomb at Kırk Mağara, with a bas-relief of a funerary banquet, has the inscription: 'In 513 I, Seleucus

bar Moqimu made for myself this burial place, for myself and for my children and for my heirs'; the tomb was therefore set up in A.D. 201–2. Other tomb inscriptions in the same area are briefer. One has simply: 'Moqimu bar Seleucus', another: 'Raḥbu, daughter of Seleucus', a third: 'Magdal, daughter of ʿAbedallat, dust! alas!', a fourth: 'This is the image of Barʿatha so[n of . . .]', a fifth, ' . . . daughter of . . ., sister of Barshemesh . . .'. In the cemetery area of Eyüp Mahallesi is an inconspicuous cave with the inscription over the central niche: 'In the month Adar in the year [5]20, I, ʿAbsha bar Barʿatha made for myself this tomb, for myself and for my children'; the tomb was

Two methods were used for closing the entrance to the cave-tombs. One, in Şehitlik Mahallesi, has a rectangular stone slab swinging on an upper and a lower hinge. It was closed from the outside by means of a chain which drew a bar across into a socket in the jamb of the door; it was evidently opened by inserting through the 'letter box' of the door the bar which had grooves corresponding to those of a socket in the jamb. More frequently, however, a flat circular stone 'door' was man-handled across the opening, and housed in a recess outside the entrance when the tomb was open.[1]

While these cave-tombs were the usual place of burial, some wealthy Edessans buried their dead in a tomb tower, Syriac *naphsha*; a sepulchre of this type was erected, we have already observed, for the members of the Aryu dynasty in A.D. 88–9. Several tomb towers are found at Kasr al-Banat and elsewhere in the Tektek mountains, some eighty kilometres from Urfa, and reference has been made to the tomb tower with an inscription at Serrin on the bank of the Euphrates.[2] None, however, has survived at Urfa itself. The nearest tomb tower to the city, which still stands, is that at Deyr Yakup in the bare hills about seven or eight kilometres to the south. Here, high in a wall, is a reclining figure; probably—for the stone is too weather-beaten to allow us to distinguish the details clearly—the figure has the high head-dress of a priest or noble,[3] and his head rests on a cushion. Nearby, over the entrance to the upper storey of the tomb tower, is found a bilingual inscription in Greek and a script resembling Palmyrene, and another inscription wholly in the near-Palmyrene script;[4] these texts have been assigned, on the basis of the writing, to the second century. At one time, there must have been more towers at this place, since a monastery which had the Syriac name *naphshatha*, 'the tomb towers', was established here in the sixth century. Its pagan associations are indicated by a chronicle of, probably, the Islamic period, stating that the monastery stood 'in the midst of the hills where there is a great pagan altar standing to this day'.[5]

The inscriptions in a near-Palmyrene script at Deyr Yakup underline the close relations that must have existed, in the time of the monarchy, between

constructed, then, in A.D. 208–9. In this cemetery was found the only example so far discovered at Urfa of a tomb to which access is gained through a vertical shaft. It has arcosolia on each side below ground, and was roofed over by a large stone slab or slabs. Two Syriac inscriptions beside the tomb are too fragmentary to be read; on one may be the word, '[s]isters'. On a third inscription we read: 'This is the grave of John the Gov[ernor], son of Theophylactos, sh[ared by] his spouse, daughter of John, captain of the troops of the Greeks, and [this is the grave] of Theophylactos their

son and of all of them'. This text may, on grounds of script, be assigned to the third century. On inscriptions at Urfa see the articles in *BSOAS* by the present writer and the bibliographies there.

[1] Pls. 21*a*, 22*a*.

[2] See p. 23 above.

[3] See the photograph (here published for the first time) at Pl. 39*b*.

[4] Both inscriptions at Deyr Yakup state simply: 'Amashshemesh wife of Shardu bar Ma'nu'; Pl. 30*b*.

[5] Cf. p. 105 below and Pl. 39*a*.

the leaders of Edessan society and the West. At this early period, trade brought the merchants of Edessa into touch with cities far beyond Palmyra. We have several allusions, confirmed by independent sources, to the important role of merchants in the dissemination of cultural and religious ideas.[1] There was constant traffic between Edessa and Adiabene, through Nisibis. In the first century A.D. the ruling house of Adiabene was Jewish, and its members made frequent and prolonged visits to Jerusalem. The Jewish community at Edessa had considerable influence on the thought and practices of their city, as we shall see; and the host of the Apostle Addai, who converted Edessa to Christianity, was, the Syriac tradition tells us, a certain Tobias, from Palestine and presumably a Jew.[2] Towards the end of the monarchy, Edessa was under the political control of Rome. Abgar's emissaries in the story of Addai submit their reports to the Roman Governor of Syria. But it was, no doubt, the fashions of Rome itself that were followed at Edessa. The visit to the Imperial capital by Abgar the Great at the invitation of Septimius Severus was, we have observed, an occasion of some magnitude, clearly intended to make an impression on a potentially useful ally. The reception accorded to Abgar suggests that nothing short of extreme magnificence would have had the effect that the Emperor desired; Edessans must have been familiar already with the ordinary luxuries of the capital. The Edessans, concerning whom two inscriptions have been found at Rome, may have arrived there as exiles or hostages, but it may be assumed that they assimilated themselves to Roman society.[3]

It was, however, Greek culture, transmitted to the East by Alexander and his successors, that left an impress on Edessa. The coins of Edessa carried legends in Greek.[4] This was more than a formal convention. We have noted that one part of the bilingual text at Deyr Yakup near Edessa was in Greek, and that Greek is found side by side with Hebrew on the early Jewish funerary inscriptions at Kırk Mağara.[5] On the Edessan document of 243 the

[1] For Mesopotamia see p. 68. The importance of Edessa in the commercial world of the time is shown by the fact that nearly half the coins minted between A.D. 220 and 251 that were discovered at Dura Europos had originated there (41 per cent—48 per cent); Nisibis and Antioch are far behind with respectively 17 per cent—30 per cent and 16 per cent—18 per cent.

[2] This, however, is not mentioned in the Greek tradition presented by Eusebius.

[3] It was probably Abgar X, Frahad who set up a tomb at Rome to his wife Hodda. His brief Latin inscription contains conventional formulae: *D M Abgar Phrahates filius rex principis Orrhenorü Hodda conjugi bene merenti fec.* At Rome too, a Greek inscription records in elegiac verse the death, at the age of twenty-

six, of a certain Abgar, son of 'the former King Abgar'. The tomb was erected by the deceased man's brother, Antoninus; they were perhaps the sons of Abgar IX, Severus.

[4] The earliest known coins of Edessa after the Seleucid period have legends in Syriac. They were minted under the pro-Parthian king Wa'el, his successor Ma'nu Philorhomaios who was restored to the throne by the Romans, and the next king, Abgar the Great, probably in the early part of his reign. Thereafter the legends are in Greek.

[5] See pp. 27, 42. A Greek inscription appears beside two busts on a relief now in the Urfa museum, and may be dated Sel. 488 (A.D. 176–7), if our decipherment is correct. The text appears to read: 'The year HTTY, the month Gorpiaios, Zabdibōlos'. The use, however, of

Inspector signs in Greek. Wealthy Edessan families under the monarchy had already acquired the habit of sending their sons to be educated in the Greek-speaking lands to the west of the Euphrates, to Antioch or Beirut or Alexandria, or to Greece itself. The practice is perhaps reflected in the 'Hymn of the Soul' of the *Acts of Thomas*, which probably derives from a Syriac source and was composed not later than the first century A.D.; there the prince is dispatched to seek his 'precious pearl' in Egypt. The Edessan philosopher Bardaiṣan is said to have sent his son to attend the academies of Athens, and it is held that he acquired there his competence in poetry and music. This tradition is late, but it contains an element of probability. The Edessan *Book of the Laws of Countries* demonstrates, in both its structure and its argument, how deeply the school of Bardaiṣan was influenced by Greek systems of philosophical exposition. Edessa was to win renown in Syriac-speaking Mesopotamia as a centre of Greek learning.

Nevertheless, at the time of the monarchy, as also, indeed, later, Greek civilization must have affected only a small section of the population of Edessa. Bardaiṣan himself, like St. Ephraim a century and a half later, is reputed to have had little or no first-hand knowledge of Greek. Hellenistic conventions of law and civic organization and the Seleucid era were maintained at Edessa after the withdrawal of Seleucid power, but in this Edessa was at one with the rest of Mesopotamia. In the struggle between Rome and Parthia for authority over Mesopotamia, Edessa was usually on the side of the latter. Seen from Rome, Abgar of Edessa was a Parthian, and this notion continued well into Byzantine times when even Syriac poets describe Edessa as 'Parthian' or 'daughter of the Parthians'. The titles of high officials of the kingdom, *paṣgriba* and *nuhadra*, were Iranian. As we shall observe later, the dress of the menfolk of Edessa was also Iranian (though women, as elsewhere in Mesopotamia, wore Roman costume). In the Edessan mosaics, human figures are represented in the frontal mode that has been regarded as characteristic of Iranian art. Adiabene, Edessa's ally, lay wholly within the Parthian sphere; and Theodoret writes of Adiabene as 'belonging to the Parthians, but now called Osrhoene'. We have noted that even in the vicinity of Abgar's palace at Edessa was a 'tower of the Persians'. The river Gullab was still called 'the river of the Medes' 250 years after the end of the monarchy. Edessa's position on the 'silk road' to Nisibis, thence to India and the Far East, must have brought traders from the East.[1] Bardaiṣan is credited with an account of the history and practices of the Indians, derived, it is held, from an Indian embassy that passed through Osrhoene on a visit to Emperor Elagabalus in about 218.

the Macedonian month name and the following proper name seem to point to a Palmyrene origin. Pl. 14*b*.

[1] See p. 137 below, for Ammian's description of the fair at Batnae in the fourth century.

The cross currents of western and eastern civilizations produced an invigorating atmosphere at Edessa. Its royal court, at the end of the second century, was evidently a scene of gaiety and movement and also of some sophistication. It has been already suggested that Edessans of this period were familiar with the luxuries of the West. In the first century the Parthian pretender Mihrdad, who was accustomed to the frivolities of Antioch, was not unwilling to dally at Edessa. Trajan, too, was obviously impressed by his entertainment there (including the 'barbaric dance' performed by the son of his royal host). The winter baths, not far north of the fish-pools,[1] may well have been built under the monarchy of Edessa; in the north-west of the city, by the walls, was a hippodrome which, tradition averred, had been presented to the king by Augustus himself.

The men of Edessa maintained, as a pastime, the skill as bowmen for which the Osrhoenians were famous in war, and they were keen followers of the chase. We have vivid representations of animals in the tableaux that have survived—the birds, lion, and gazelle of the Phoenix and Orpheus mosaics (dated A.D. 235-6 and 228 respectively), and the fierce boar of the border of the now fragmentary Animal mosaic.[2] Julius Africanus, a visitor to Edessa at the end of the second century, recounts that, on a hunting expedition, a terrible forest bear leapt out of a thicket, to the consternation of the bystanders; it was slain by Prince Ma'nu who coolly shot an arrow into each eye of the beast. Bardaiṣan himself was no mean archer, as Julius relates in a vivid passage. On one occasion he asked a handsome young man to stand opposite him, and then outlined the youth's form upon his shield with arrows, like a painter with a brush,—his head, 'the gleam of the eyes, the junction of the lips, the symmetry of the chin', and finally the whole figure of the youth. The spectators were amazed 'to see that the bow could be not a warlike implement but a [source of] delight and a pleasant sport': the young man gazed with astonishment at his picture.

Under the monarchy, Edessans cultivated the liberal arts with vigour. Their architects must have attained a high degree of skill. At Sumatar Harabesi in the Tektek mountains, the monuments, of which two towers are round and of exactly the same circumference, another is an exact square, and another is round and set upon a square base, are aligned with perfect precision; they are, no doubt, the work of Edessans or foreign craftsmen working under the direction of Edessans.[3] In the city itself porticoes were erected in public places, and we have, in the two Corinthian columns on the Citadel mount, a relic of the magnificent buildings of royal Edessa. We have alluded to representations of the funerary banquet and the other somewhat florid

---

[1] The remains of a hypocaust on this spot were seen briefly by the present writer in the summer of 1959, before the site was incorporated into the municipal water installations.

[2] Pls. 43, 44 and 17b–20.

[3] See the photograph on Pl. 40a.

sculpture in the cave-tombs outside the walls of Edessa. Stone figures in relief at Sumatar, both in a cave cut in the rock and on the sacred mount, are no doubt by Edessan sculptors of the second century.[1] At Sumatar, too, is a free-standing statue of a man in Iranian costume, a great sword at his side, which may have been erected in the same period.[2] Statues were evidently a familiar feature of Edessa itself. One of the columns on the Citadel mount was crowned, as we have seen, by a statue of Queen Shalmath. The Aquitanian abbess Egeria who visited the city in, probably, the fifth century, was impressed by the statues in the summer palace by the pools, which were probably set up under the monarchy. She writes;

> [The bishop] led me to the palace of king Abgar, and showed me there the statue which, as they said, was a very close likeness, made of marble of such lustre that it might have been of pearl. From the features of king Abgar it was truly seen that this man was greatly wise and dignified. . . . Nearby was a statue also made of the same marble, which he said was [the representation] of [Abgar's] son Magnus, also with something of grace in his features.[3]

There were other representations of Abgar at Edessa that survived to the time of Egeria, apparently by the west gate through which, according to tradition, the letter of Jesus had been brought to Abgar. Egeria adds, 'The holy bishop also showed us a memorial[4] of Abgar and of all his family which was very beautiful but made in the ancient fashion.'

A few small miscellaneous reliefs of uncertain provenance, but probably from the region of Edessa, are preserved at Urfa and may be ascribed to the period of the monarchy.[5] They include three reliefs of a nude male and a half-nude female exchanging embraces, the busts of two male personages holding a scroll, a Victory and some tritons. Two pieces of free-standing sculpture of particular interest have survived at Urfa. Both have undated Syriac inscriptions and both are likely to belong to this early period. One, a full-length relief, shows a seated woman, and at her side the figure of her daughter in miniature; it was erected by her husband. The other is a bust of a handsome lady called Shalmath, also set up by her husband, and also with a miniature full-length figure of her daughter by her side.[6]

We now have records of eight mosaics from Edessa,[7] most of them found within recent years, and all to be attributed to the last years of the monarchy or the decades immediately following. We can speak of a school of Edessan

---

[1] See Pl. 40b, 41, and Pognon, op. cit.

[2] See the photograph on Pl. 13a. The similar statue found at Harran may belong to the same period; photograph on Pl. 13b.

[3] Egeria's 'Magnus' is presumably Ma'nu IX, who reigned from 214–40; if, however, the legend of Abgar Ukkama were accepted, he would be Ma'nu V (A.D. 50–7).

[4] Latin, memoria.

[5] On a bas-relief of two busts accompanied by a Greek inscription, which may belong to the second century, see p. 30 n. 5 above.

[6] See the photographs on Pls. 12 a, b, 15 a, b.

[7] Nine, if we regard the mosaic published by Clermont-Ganneau and analysed by E. Renan as having been found at Urfa; see the present writer's article, BSOAS xxx, 1967, 297.

mosaicists. They attained a considerable degree of accuracy in their work, carefully distinguishing between brown and grey eyes, and black and grey hair. Their artistry is evident from the grouping of their subjects. The mosaics reflect, too, the taste of the Edessans for bright and varied hues and the distinction of their costume; and by the sophisticated and comfortable mien of the personages which they depict we are reminded forcibly of the portraits of merchants of medieval Europe.[1]

Edessans had a lively partiality for music in early, as in later, times. Bardaiṣan's poems were set to music; and they still retained their attraction for the young aristocrats of Edessa two centuries after the poet's death. St. Ephraim sought to counter the insidious charm of these pagan hymns by forming choirs to sing his own canticles and responses. His labours had little success, for forty years later Bishop Rabbula was dismayed to find that Bardaiṣan's songs had lost none of their popularity at Edessa. Music and musicians played a significant role in the pagan religion of this area, as we shall see later. Orpheus with his magic lyre is the theme of a beautiful Edessan mosaic of the last decades of the Aryu dynasty.[2]

Letters, too, were evidently popular under the monarchy; the city's reputation in Christian times as the seat of a famous academy was based on a tradition of long standing. The Syriac inscriptions on the statues, on the walls of tombs, and in the mosaics are neatly written. We have evidence, however sparse, of nicety of style. The Tripod mosaic has a short epigram:

> Whoever despises
> the expectations of [his] last [days],
> and mourns [his] first [days]—
> he shall have a goodly latter end.

The sentiment, that only the man who scorns long life and repents of his youthful errors may deem himself worthy of life after death, is expressed skilfully. The second and third lines rhyme; and the poem seems to be constructed by stress, not, like later Syriac verse, by a syllable count. There is an adroit antithesis between 'last [days]' and 'first [days]', and a punning play on two Syriac words.[3] The text is a pleasant reminder of the mannerisms of good Semitic poetry. Of equal distinction is another Syriac epitaph, also in the southern cemetery of Edessa, whose archaic script assigns it, too, to the early period.[4]

Pleasant is the resting-place of Shalman, son of Kawkab.[5] Greetings to thee[6] . . . and they answered thee, and they called thee and thou didst answer them—those whom thou

---

[1] See Pls. 1–3.
[2] Cf. p. 52 below.
[3] 'ḥritha, line 2; ḥartha, line 4.
[4] See Pl. 30a.

[5] Or 'Star'.
[6] Here may be read, among lacunae, '. . . thy essence . . .'.

didst touch. Thou hast seen the height and the depth, the distant and the near, the hidden and the manifest.[1] And they supervise the uses of thy reckonings, . . . giving rest[2] . . .

We need not hesitate, then, to attribute strenuous literary activity to the Edessa of the later years of the monarchy. Unhappily little is extant whose authorship can definitely be regarded as Edessan. The touching epistle of Mara bar Serapion was written by a pagan of nearby Samosata to his son as the author was taken captive to Seleucia, possibly at the end of the second century. The Oration to Antoninus Caesar, a discourse on free will and sin, is ascribed incorrectly to the philosopher Melito of Sardis; it was composed probably by a Christian, and perhaps in Osrhoene in the third century. Edessa, or the neighbourhood, may have been the place of composition of the Syriac text of the *Acts of Thomas*, written probably in an Iranian milieu and in the first decades of the third century.[3] To this epoch belong, too, the translations into Syriac of the Old and New Testaments. Whether the translators performed their work in Osrhoene or Adiabene cannot be decided,[4] but the question need not detain us. The lucid and flowing style of much of these translations must have been the common heritage of a wide area of Syriac-speaking Mesopotamia. That it was shared by Edessa, is shown by the extract from the city archives describing the flood of 201 which has already been given; this must have been written close to the event and displays qualities of freshness and clarity.

The giant of Edessan literature in the period of the monarchy was Bardaiṣan. The names of the members of his family seem curiously allegorical. His father is said to have been called Nuḥama (revival, resurrection) and his mother Naḥshiram (hunting); his son, famous for his musical accomplishments, was Harmonius, and his own name means nothing more than 'son of Daiṣan', the river of Edessa. Bardaiṣan himself, however, was real enough. He was born at Edessa in 154, the son, it is maintained, of pagan parents who had fled from Parthia.[5] One tradition relates that he was instructed in the lore of the heathens at Hierapolis, the famous cult centre of the Syrian goddess, Atargatis. According to another tradition, Bardaiṣan was educated at Edessa with the future Abgar the Great; certainly he frequented the court

[1] Or 'rising [of the sun or stars]'.
[2] The Gnostic overtones of this remarkable, but obscure, inscription recall the remark of St. Ephraim on Bardaiṣan: ' . . . he counted six essences; four essences he placed in the four directions (of the compass), one he placed in the depth, another in the height'. See also p. 38.
[3] See p. 44 below. It has been claimed that the Odes of Solomon (which, like the *Acts of Thomas*, contain Gnostic expressions) were composed at Edessa; the evidence is, however, circumstantial and slender.
[4] Tatian probably composed the Syriac of the Diatessaron in the West before his return to 'Assyria' (no doubt, this is Adiabene; see pp. 68–70) in A.D. 172. But the style of his version is presumably that of his own homeland.
[5] Porphyry, *de Abstinentia*, iv, 417, describes Bardaiṣan as a 'Babylonian'—probably because of his fame as astrologer; p. 50.

of Edessa. Julius Africanus admired Bardaiṣan's prowess as archer. He was converted to Christianity by, we are told, a certain 'Bishop' Hystasp, and composed polemics against the heresy of Marcion. But Bardaiṣan's independence of mind made it difficult for him to conform to prescribed dogma; and he was expelled from the Church by ʿAqi, the successor of Hystasp. He is credited with having subsequently founded his own sect. The Bardaisanites are said by no less an authority than Jacob of Edessa to have continued at Edessa until the late seventh or eighth century; Moslem writers allege that his followers were to be found between Wasiṭ and Baṣra in southern Iraq in the tenth century, and even in Khorasan and Chinese Turkestan.

These assertions may be based on misunderstanding, for there was a tendency, particularly among Moslem theologians, to group miscellaneous heresies under a single ill-defined heading. They show, however, how deep and lasting was the impact of Bardaiṣan, not only on his contemporaries, but also on succeeding generations. During his lifetime—he died in 222—he composed some religious and philosophical treatises, a treatise on the conjunction of the planets, a history of Armenia, written when he fled to that country in the reign of Caracalla, and a history of India. Even his enemies acknowledged his charm and his keenness of perception. Eusebius, a century later, calls him 'a most able man' and 'a powerful disputant'. St. Ephraim writes of 'the dirt of the wiles of Bardaiṣan', but he was forced to admit that 'Bardaiṣan is found to speak with subtlety': and showing unwonted mercy towards a heretic, Ephraim declares, 'Ye sons of the good [God], pray for Bardaiṣan, for in his heathenism there went a Legion in his heart but our Lord in his mouth'.

A prose work attributed to the school of Bardaiṣan was probably composed by his disciple, Philip; it is entitled the *Book of the Laws of Countries*.[1] Brief extracts may convey something of the shrewdness and humanity of Bardaiṣan; these qualities are evident even though the text may have been revised by a Christian apologist.

If you want to learn it is helpful to learn from older people . . . , but if [you want] to teach it is not necessary for you to ask them anything but to persuade them to ask what you wish. . . . It is a good thing to know how to ask questions. . . .

There is nothing that men have been commanded to do which they cannot do. . . . We are not commanded to carry heavy burdens of stone or timber or other things—which only those who are strong in body can do, or to build fortresses or found cities—which only kings can do, or to steer ships—which only sailors know how to steer, or to measure and divide the earth—which only surveyors know. . . . But we have been given commandments ungrudgingly according to the bounty of God, which any man who has a soul can perform with joy. . . .

---

[1] It receives this name because it offers examples of the laws of peoples ranging from the 'Seres' and Indians in the East to the Greeks and Britons in the West. See on its contents p. 44 below.

It is easier to do good than to abstain from evil. For good is part of man, and therefore he rejoices when he does it, but evil is the activity of the enemy and man does these odious things when he is disturbed and unhealthy in his nature. . . . By its nature the lion eats flesh; and for this reason all lions are eaters of flesh. . . . And the bee makes honey by which it sustains itself; and for this reason all bees are honeymakers. And the ant lays up for itself a store in summer, that it may sustain itself from it in the winter; and for this reason all ants do likewise. . . . But men are not governed in this manner; but in the things belonging to their bodies they maintain their nature like animals, and in the things which belong to their minds they do that which they wish, as being free and with power and as the likeness of God. . . .

When God wishes, all things can be without confusion; there is nothing that can restrain his great and holy will. . . .

In the constitution of a new world all evil movements will cease and all rebellion will come to an end; and the foolish will receive persuasion, and short-comings will be made full, and there will be peace and well-being by the gift of the Lord of all creatures.

The genre of literature, however, which Bardaiṣan made peculiarly his own, was poetry. He composed a hundred and fifty hymns, the number of the Psalms of the Bible, around the themes of his religion and philosophical doctrines. The rhythm of his poetry was marked by stress, as was the epitaph of Shalman bar Kawkab. The hymns were then set to music and achieved immediate and lasting popularity. St. Ephraim declares sadly:

[Bardaiṣan] created hymns and united them with musical accompaniment, and he composed psalms and introduced metres: with measure and weights he divided words, And the simple he corrupted with bitterness in sweetness, the sick who did not choose healing nourishment.

Fragments of Bardaiṣan's verse have survived in the work of St. Ephraim, unfortunately too scanty for us to judge their poetic merit.[1] We have, however, a longer extract quoted by an eighth century theologian, Theodore bar Koni, in which Bardaiṣan expounds his cosmological theories.[2]

. . . Five essences from old were they in essence; but they relaxed and strayed.

At last they were convulsed,[3] as though by some mischance; the wind blew in its might; one crawled[4] and met its fellow.

The fire kindled the forest, the black cloud which no fire begot, grew thick; the limpid air grew foul.

They were mingled all together, their elect origin was assailed. They began to bite each other like ravening beasts.

Then sent their Lord to them a word of thought. He bade the wind to cease; it turned its course to itself.

---

[1] They have now been edited by H. J. W. Drijvers, *Bardaiṣan of Edessa*, 130 ff.
[2] See p. 44 below.

[3] Or 'were set in motion'.
[4] The text is obscure.

The wind blew on high, . . . was quelled by force. The foulness was reduced to its depths.[1]

The air was radiant in its midst; quiet and repose were there, and the Lord was praised for his wisdom, thanksgiving went up for his grace.

From that mingling and blending that was left, from the . . . essences he wrought the whole creation of the upper and the lower things.[2]

And lo, the natures, all of them—with created things they hastened, to purify themselves and remove what was mingled with the nature of evil.

In the cultured society of Edessa we find, as we should expect, a liberal attitude towards womenfolk. Women are shown in dignified poses in the family groups of the mosaics and stone reliefs in the cave-tombs. Several memorial texts are inscribed to women. Statues to women were evidently not uncommon; not only was the statue of Queen Shalmath erected on the Citadel mount, as we have seen, but the two free-standing statues that have survived at Urfa are of women. The tomb tower at Birtha, on the Osrhoenian bank of the Euphrates, was for the 'mistress of the house' as well as for the owner and his children. In two cases, moreover, a tomb near Edessa was prepared in honour of a woman. One was apparently dedicated by the dead woman's nephew; the other carries a long text to the memory of the deceased woman, while at the side is a curt sentence, in memory of a man who, if we judge from his name, may be the woman's father![3]

Women, then, enjoyed respect at Edessa, and held an honoured position in the family. So highly was their chastity regarded that not only was an Edessan woman who had committed adultery put to death, but one against whom a charge of adultery had been preferred received summary punishment. Nevertheless, it should not be thought that they were the equals of men in the eyes of the law. Women were entitled to their own property, but the Greek legal practice was followed which required them to be represented at a formal transaction by a guardian; if a woman were married the guardian was her husband. In the document of 243, therefore, the signature of the Edessan woman who sells a slave is countersigned by her husband. That the women in the family groups of the mosaics and of the reliefs in cave-tombs are unveiled, may not mean that the veil was not used at this time, but that in these portraits it is necessary to identify their features. We observe too that in these tableaux the wife of the occupant of the tomb (but in one mosaic the mother-in-law of the deceased) is shown on his left. It was, no doubt, the right side that was considered the more honourable, and here stand the children of the dead man. So, too, in the Family Portrait mosaic a daughter stands with her brothers to the right of her father, but she stands after her brothers. Significantly, it is only in the Tripod mosaic, set up by a family of relatively

---

[1] Drijvers, op. cit., 101, translates, 'and the confusion was suppressed by force and flung into its abysses'.

[2] Ibid. translates, 'of the elements he made all creation, that which is above and that which is below'.   [3] See p. 59 below.

modest means, that the female figures, a wife and a daughter, carry a spindle as a reminder of their domestic duties. Perhaps we may conclude that the higher a family's place in the social scale the more generous its attitude to women.

From the mosaics and, to a lesser extent, from sculpture,[1] we obtain a remarkably clear picture of women's dress at Edessa at this period of history. The undated Family Portrait mosaic displays a family of well-to-do burghers. In it, the adult women wear tunics heavily embroidered along the whole length of the sleeves, and also at the front in the case of the mother of the family; over their tunic is a long robe of a different colour secured with a brooch on the left shoulder. Their hair is in plaits, and they have pointed slippers on their feet. In the somewhat modest family of the Funerary Couch mosaic (dated A.D. 278), the wife of the deceased is seated on an armchair with her feet resting on a stool, beside her husband's couch, and has a similar, but less ornate, costume; while her daughter's dress is still simpler. So, too, the Tripod mosaic, found in the northern cemetery area outside the city—the other two mosaics are from the southern cemetery area—shows an adult woman in plain costume, her hair falling in long curls. Young girls, in both the Family Portrait mosaic and the Tripod mosaic, wear no robe; their tunics are fastened with a broad belt. All the costumes are gaily coloured. The women wear jewellery, golden bracelets and a golden clasp to fasten the outer garment; the statues show women wearing a necklace either of tooth-shaped beads or pieces of gold.

Most striking is the head-dress of the women of Edessa, as illustrated by the mosaics and statues. In the Family Portrait mosaic the wealthy adult women wear high hats, slightly tapered at the peak. The hats are of four different coloured tiers, or, more probably, two bands of material of other colours are wound around the middle of the hat; over this is draped the outer robe falling on either side like a veil.[2] The same head-gear appears in other mosaics, in the full-length statue at Urfa, and in the funerary banquets on the reliefs in stone at Urfa and Kara Köprü. In the less prosperous family of the Tripod mosaic, however, the mother's hat is broader and less high and has only one band. Here we may have a link with another type of head-dress. In the stone bust found at Urfa the miniature figure of the daughter has the high hat of the mosaics. But her mother, Shalmath, perhaps more in the current fashion, has the lower hat, with one band around it, and draped with a cloth; it has a brooch in front. This form of head-dress survived until modern times. In 1844 the missionary, Mr. Badger, drew at Urfa a sketch of a woman with a hat resembling that of Shalmath, but made

[1] Pls. 1–3, 16b, 17a, 12 a, b, 25b.
[2] This hat is reminiscent of the steeple head-dress or 'hennin' that was the mode in Europe in the fifteenth century.

of silver plate—and, incidentally, also wearing the necklace of tooth-shaped beads of the mosaics and statues of third century Edessa.[1]

Girls wore less elaborate head-gear than their elders. In the Funerary Couch mosaic a girl wears no hat, but has her robe simply draped around her head. In the Tripod mosaic another girl has a Phrygian cap like her brother. In the fashionable Family Portrait mosaic, a grand-daughter, standing in the background, has three rounded combs in her hair, a style which appears also in another Edessan mosaic, now destroyed.[2]

Male society at Edessa was no less fastidious in its dress. From the mosaics we observe that they wore shirts reaching to the knees, of a simple form in the case of boys. The belts of the Tripod mosaic are ornate, that of the father in particular, which has a double clasp. Trousers are of the familiar Iranian type reaching to the ankle or mid-calf; some are baggy, others less full. In the Tripod mosaic, the trousers of the deceased man seem to be gathered at the bottom with a cord held by two tassels. Boots reach to mid-calf, but in the elegant Family Portrait mosaic the menfolk wear slippers, cut away at the back (as in the Near East today), and with triangular flaps on top.

Over his shoulder, the central personage in the Tripod mosaic carries what may be a cloak; and he has a triangular ornament on the front of his shirt. Young men in the Funerary Couch mosaic have loops on their left shoulder, presumably to hold a cloak. But the menfolk of the Family Portrait mosaic wear over their shirts a narrow-sleeved *quftan*-like coat. The sons have elbow-length sleeves, whereas the father's sleeves reach to his wrists, as in the dress of King Abgar on coins of the reign of Gordian III. This resembles the garment known in Arabic as the *qaba'*, a garment whose use had become restricted in the ninth century, but was even then still worn generally by the pagans of Harran.[3] All the men of the Family Portrait mosaic have what appear to be epaulettes on each shoulder, perhaps a sign of rank but apparently without parallel elsewhere.

The father in this mosaic wears a necklace with a pendant (an unknown hand has removed the tesserae), while his son Ma'nu, who is probably the father of the young girl in the background, is adorned by a golden necklace, although he was evidently the youngest son. But the most distinctive feature of dress among the men, as among the women, of Edessa was evidently their head-dress. The central personage to whom a tomb is dedicated is always distinguished from the rest of the family by his hat. In the Funerary Couch mosaic he wears an elaborate form of Phrygian cap; the other male members of his family have their head uncovered. In the Tripod mosaic the children wear Phrygian caps;[4] the head-dress of the deceased man is missing

[1] Most clearly on Pl. 12*b*.

[2] See Pls. 1–3, 16*b*.

[3] According to Ibn al-Nadim the *qaba'* was the dress of the 'companions of the rulers' (or 'those in charge of the administration'). It was in use in Egypt at a later period. See the author's article, *AS* iii, 1953, 117.

[4] So also in the mosaic from Urfa now at

—the mosaic has been damaged—but one figure extends to him what must be a cap of state of elegant shape. In the Family Portrait mosaic, two of the three sons wear their hair elegantly waved; in much the same fashion, a figure on a second century relief at Sumatar wears his hair uncovered, but secured by a band, a bow and a loop at either side. The son next to the central figure of the Family Portrait mosaic wears a Phrygian cap, a sign perhaps that he is the eldest son. But the portly figure of the father is distinguished by a magnificent turban. It is the only turban of this sort in the Edessan mosaics; the nearest we come to this fine head-gear is a hat of ostrich or peacock feathers, on the relief of a funerary banquet at Kara Köprü near Urfa. There is one allusion in literature to turbans at Edessa, and significantly it occurs in a description of a pagan festival, two or three centuries after this Family Portrait mosaic. We read there that the crowd celebrated the occasion by going up 'to the theatre toward evening, clad in linen garments, wearing turbans and with their loins ungirt'. That attention was paid to head-gear by males also at Edessa will not surprise us. We have already observed that the king wore a diadem with his tiara as token of his elevation to the throne and that tiaras without a diadem were conferred on nobles as a sign of rank.[1]

The people depicted in the mosaics and statues of Edessa were evidently pagan. This is clear on negative grounds alone; in the inscriptions and décor appears none of the formulae or the symbols which are obligatory in Christian and Jewish memorials.

The Jews of Edessa looked eastward to more powerful Jewish communities in north-eastern Mesopotamia. In Adiabene, the ruling family adopted Judaism in the first century A.D. The story of Queen Helena of Adiabene and her two sons was so widely current that nearly three centuries later the biographies of another Queen Helena, mother of Emperor Constantine the Great, were largely modelled on it. In the second century the Jews of Adiabene were still numerous. But the greatest Jewish community of this region was at Nisibis. This was a stronghold in which Jews of northern Mesopotamia took refuge in times of persecution, because, writes Josephus, 'the inhabitants, who were many, were all warlike men'. Here were stored the contributions of the Jews of this region to the Temple at Jerusalem. Here, too, was the seat of a Jewish academy, whose fame spread not only to south Mesopotamia, but also to Palestine; it is no accident that it was in the time of the celebrated Rabbi Judah ben Bathyra of Nisibis, the first of that name in the Talmud, that the kings of Adiabene became Jewish.

We have observed how close were the relations between Edessa, Nisibis,

Istanbul, and in the relief of a marble block from Urfa which is at Istanbul too; see Pls. 17a, 14a. The latter carries a Syriac inscription of which the only words that are certain are, 'Of our lord . . . revered . . . of Shemeshgram'.

[1] See p. 18 above.

and Adiabene.[1] They were linked by the 'silk road'.[2] Merchants had abandoned the southerly route, across the plain of Harran, where their caravans were exposed to the pillage and the blackmail of the Beduins; they preferred the comparative safety of the route that skirted the mountains by way of Edessa. We are not surprised, then, to discover that the Jews of Edessa included merchants in cloth, and that they were men of substance. A synagogue stood in a prominent position in the centre of the city; another seems to have been situated in front of the old Cathedral church of Edessa. The Jews of Edessa lived on easy terms with their neighbours. They shared with pagans the cemetery of Kırk Mağara. There, three inscriptions in Hebrew and one in Greek commemorate Jews, and their mixture of Hebrew, Macedonian, Roman, and Parthian names indicates a degree of assimilation to the general population. But the Jews maintained their separate identity for we find also a *menorah* engraved on the wall outside a cave.[3] The sympathies of the Jews seem to have been with the Parthians rather than with the Romans. When Trajan's forces advanced to the East in 114–15, they were opposed by the Jews of Edessa, Nisibis, and Adiabene, who paid, we are told, a heavy price in lives for their contumacy.

All the names of courtiers at Edessa that are mentioned in the annals are pagan. But Jews in the city may have been known to the king. At any rate, we are told that Abgar requested Tobias son of Tobias from Palestine, at whose house at Edessa Addai stayed, to bring the Apostle to him, and although much of the traditional account of the introduction of Christianity to Edessa is evidently unhistorical, this statement bears the stamp of truth. Indeed, the swift progress of Christianity at Edessa is sufficient testimony to the influence of the Jews. It is a truism that the advance of the new religion was most rapid in those places where Jews lived firmly established and in security. In north Mesopotamia, Christian evangelists found in the Jewish communities tools ready to hand for the diffusion of their faith; for they were close-knit congregations, respected by their neighbours, willing to accept the Christians as allies against the dominant paganism, well acquainted with the methods of analysis and argument best suited to the theological climate of the country, and well acquainted too with the doctrines of the Old Testament. The last factor is by no means the least in importance. We have alluded to

---

[1] See pp. 12 ff.

[2] On the involvement of Jews of Nisibis in trade in silk see Neusner, *A History of the Jews in Babylonia*, i, 'The Parthian Period'.

[3] Pognon, op. cit., 78 ff. All three Hebrew texts have peculiarities of language, which may be explained on dialectal grounds. One appears to read: 'This is the tomb which . . . its middle which is [to be] rented', but both the writing and the interpretation are difficult. If, however, this inscription follows the usual formula it is to be translated, 'This is the tomb of Rasha of M . . . agir'. The second text reads: 'The Lord give rest (or 'The Lord has given rest') to the soul of Joseph'. The third is bilingual, being in Greek and Hebrew; the Greek is more legible and reads: 'This is the tomb of Seleucus bar Ezad and Iamia bar [. . . an]d Samuel bar Gord[. . .], the Jews'. Pls. 16a, 31a.'.

the possibility that it was at Edessa that the Bible was translated into Syriac. Some passages certainly reflect orthodox Jewish interpretation. Through the medium of these admirable renderings into the local speech, monotheism and the stories of Israel were spread among the people.

The traditional account of the evangelization of Edessa[1] makes brief acknowledgement of the part played by Jews. 'The Jews also', it declares, 'conversant with the Law and the Prophets, who sold soft [stuffs], were also persuaded and became disciples and made the Christian confession.' Further evidence of the influence of the Jews at Edessa may be provided by a strange passage in a Syriac treatise of the third century. It states that, 'the people of Mesopotamia also worshipped the Hebrew [woman][2] Kuthbi, who saved Bakru[3] the patrician of Edessa from his enemies.'[4]

We have no record elsewhere of this incident, and it can scarcely be regarded as historical. It has been suggested that the name Kuthbi is derived from the common Semitic root *ktb*—to write, and that the word does not refer to a 'Hebrew woman' but should instead be interpreted as 'Hebrew writing'. We now know that the Nabataeans worshipped a deity Kuthba or Kuthbai presumably 'writing'; and writing is regarded by Arabs as a special skill of the Nabataeans. The rulers of Edessa were, we have deduced, Nabataeans. But here writing is associated with Jews. We may assume that the Edessans knew of the Jewish practice of affixing a Biblical text to the doors of a house or the gates of a city (*mezuzah*); this practice was certainly observed by the Jews of Palmyra.[5] And, indeed, the Talmud informs us that the Jews of Adiabene were so devoted to the practice that they placed the *mezuzah* outside their lodgings wherever they travelled. It may, then, have been from the Jews that Edessans derived their deep regard for the sacred letter which they affixed to the gate of their city, as we shall observe in a later chapter.[6]

The last hundred years of the monarchy at Edessa was a time of religious ferment throughout the Near East. Orthodox Christianity contended with the theories of the followers of Marcion; the Gnostic schools, notably that of

---

[1] *Doctrine of Addai.*

[2] The late variant, 'Arab (woman)', should be rejected.

[3] It has been suggested that Bakru is to be identified with Paqor who reigned at Edessa in 34–29 B.C. In 40 B.C., shortly before he came to the throne, another Paqor, king of Parthia, invaded Syria and intervened in the domestic quarrels of the Maccabean rulers of Palestine. The Parthians opposed Herod of Judea; and this is reflected in the tradition of Edessa that it was their king Paqor who carried out a campaign against Herod. The passage in 'Pseudo-Melito', however, is too obscure to admit of historical explanation.

[4] The passage here, from the text incorrectly ascribed to Melito (p. 35 above), is difficult. The term for 'saved' is unusual, although it is found elsewhere; the word 'patrician' (Syriac *abaya*) occurs nowhere else, but cf. p. 69 below. The words 'Bakru the patrician' could be a misreading of the Syriac letters of 'Abgar Ukkama'—but one would expect the reverse process, for the name of Abgar Ukkama was too well known to invite 'correction'.

[5] Bible texts, notably Deut. 6 : 4–9, have been found affixed to the lintels of doorposts at Palmyra.

[6] pp. 75 f.

Valentinus, devised complex schemes of cosmogony and philosophy, and the ground was being prepared for the Manichaean doctrines based upon dualistic conceptions of the forces of creation. The syncretistic temper of the times is well illustrated by the strange sect of the Elkesaites. The doctrines of the Elkesaites were an intermixture of Judaism, Christianity, and paganism: the acknowledgement of a single god, the rejection of earlier prophets, the veneration of water as the source of life, belief in the male and female principle of Christ and the Holy Spirit, and belief in reincarnation—for Jesus was reincarnated, the sect held, in their prophet-founder Elkesai. The latter was alleged to have come from a city, 'Serai', in Parthia. Parthia, it should be recalled, comprises also the area of Harran and Edessa, and the name Serai (from the Chinese term for silk) may allude to the silk trade which brought prosperity to the inhabitants of those cities.

At Harran, the so-called 'Sabians' (according to texts written at a late date but describing the practices of an earlier period) directed their prayers to spiritual beings which acted as intermediaries between men and a Supreme Deity; these beings inhabit and guide the planets, that stand to them in the relation of the body to the spirit. The activity of these spiritual beings produces movement in space, and this creates material things, plants and animals and men. But matter is bad by nature, and human beings have prejudices and passions: only through the influence of the spiritual beings are they endowed with love and amity, knowledge and feeling. The Sabians therefore rejected the teaching that a human prophet can mediate between man and the Supreme Deity. They did not believe in resurrection in the conventional sense, but every 36,425 years, they maintained, a new order of men, animals, and plants is created afresh.

That Gnosticism, born of Oriental theism and Hellenistic philosophy, was familiar to Edessans is evident from a memorial inscription which has already been cited.[1] There are undoubtedly Gnostic elements, too, in the *Acts of Thomas*, composed probably at this period, in part possibly at Edessa itself. In the writings of Bardaiṣan also, scholars have discovered Gnostic philosophy and there is some basis for their assertion. A hymn attributed to Bardaiṣan maintains that first there existed five basic elements: wind, fire, light, water, and darkness or matter. From these warring elements the *Logos* arranged the universe; Bardaiṣan here follows the theories of Hermogenes.[2] In the *Book of the Laws of Countries*, members of the school of Bardaiṣan are seen to wrestle with the problems of good and evil, free will and fate. The workings of human nature and man's outer circumstances, it is affirmed, depend on fate, but his moral decisions are free, and faith is all important:

. . . Those who have not faith . . . are not competent to speak and to instruct, and they do not easily incline themselves to hear. For they . . . have no confidence upon which

[1] See p. 34 above.   [2] Cf. p. 37 above.

they may hope. . . . But [God] exalted [man] by Freewill above many things and made him equal with the angels. . . . The nature of man is . . . that he should be born and grow up and beget children and grow old . . . and that he should die. But that everything is not in our will is apparent. . . . Rubies and honour and health and sickness and children and various objects of desire are subject to Fortune and are not in our own power. But . . . just as we see that Fortune crushes Nature, so we can also see the Freewill of men repelling and crushing Fortune itself; but not in everything. For it is proper that the three things, Nature, Fortune, and Freewill should be maintained in their lives until . . . the measure and the number be fulfilled, as it seemed good before Him who ordained how should be the life and perfection of all creatures and the state of all Beings and Natures.

Bardaiṣan denied the resurrection of the body. Like the followers of Elkesai, he held that the body has some admixture of impurity; it would not be recreated by a holy God. St. Ephraim considered this doctrine heretical. Bardaiṣan, however, believed in the resurrection of the soul. He was philosopher and astrologer rather than theologian; and he sought to reconcile Christian beliefs with the Hellenized astrology of the 'Chaldeans' and his own philosophical speculations.[1] His individualistic outlook could not but clash with orthodox dogma. Nevertheless, the heretical views ascribed to him by Christian theologians at a later date may be little more than the projection of their own arguments in defence of orthodox doctrine; the fact that these arguments were bitter may indicate that the followers of Bardaiṣan at his native Edessa at one time outnumbered those who professed 'orthodox' Christianity.

The philosophy of the Gnostics could, however, appeal only to an elect few. It did not provide the framework of ritual observance that would retain the loyalty of the populace. Before we assemble the evidence for the religious beliefs and practices of pagan Edessa we must consider, however summarily, those of cult centres with which Edessa had direct contact.

Mention has been made of the association between Edessa and Palmyra. At Palmyra a prominent role in the pantheon was occupied by astral deities—principally Bel, the ancestral solar god, and Malakbel, Yarḥibol and 'Aglibol, who were, respectively, solar and lunar deities, Beltis, the consort of Bel, Shemesh, the sun god, Nabu (Mercury), Be'elshamin, god of the heavens, and also 'Athar'atha (Atargatis), perhaps 'Athar with the attributes of 'Atha, who was regarded as the deity of the sea or lake or as the Tyche, the 'palladium' of the city. Palmyra had its triads of gods: Bel, Yarḥibol, and 'Aglibol; or Be'elshamin, 'Aglibol, and Malakbel. At Harran, too, which lay at no great distance from Edessa, it was a planet deity, Sin the moon god, that ruled the pantheon; he is mentioned in records as far back as the nineteenth century B.C. and his emblem is found over a wide area. But Sin was also the

---

[1] Contact between the *Book of the Laws of Countries*, and later Christian writings has been established by T. H. Nissen, *ZNW*, ix, 1908, 190, 315.

dominant member of a triad, to which belonged the sun, and Ishtar or Venus;[1] and the other planetary deities, Saturn, Jupiter, Mars, and Mercury, were worshipped at Harran by the so-called Sabians until the eleventh century A.D.

Mabbog, Greek Bambyce,[2] better known as Hierapolis, the holy City, was linked to Edessa by an important highroad. Both cities were regular staging points along the route which crossed the Euphrates at Zeugma (but from the second century A.D. at Caeciliana near Mabbog) and led to Nisibis in the east and Singara in the south-east. Ptolemy and Chinese sources of the third century show the route to have been used by caravans travelling between Antioch and the Far East. Already in the first century A.D. the neo-Pythagorean philosopher, Apollonius of Tyana, passed through Hierapolis on his celebrated journey to India, and the same way was probably taken by the Indian embassy which visited the Roman Emperor in about A.D. 218 in the time of Bardaiṣan. The close link between Hierapolis and Edessa in both trade and war continued long after the fall of the Aryu dynasty. But the fame of the temple of Hierapolis was widespread. It derived its wealth, according to Lucian of Samosata, from worshippers in Babylonia and Assyria, as well as from Cilicia, Phoenicia, and Arabia, and even from Egypt and Ethiopia. With Edessa it had specially close connection; Strabo even confuses the two cities, 'Bambyce lies four parasangs[3] distant from the river [Euphrates], and they call it both Edessa and Hierapolis, and in it they worship the Syrian goddess Atargatis.' Bardaiṣan, the philosopher of Edessa, is said by a late but persistent tradition to have passed his early years at Hierapolis and to have been instructed there by a pagan priest. The link between the cities survived in Christian times; the envoy of Abgar to Jerusalem is held to have passed through Hierapolis, and this city remained on the route of pilgrims, as well as of armies, from Antioch to the East.[4]

The chief deity at Hierapolis was the Mother Goddess, Atargatis, or 'Athar'atha, Syriac Tar'atha, known to the people of Western Asia under many names, but identified in Greek as Hera. Her Hierapolitan cult was carried to Europe; it was widely observed in the cities of Syria and Mesopotamia. Her consort was Hadad or Zeus, and a triad was completed by a young god, called in Greek Apollo. Side by side with this triad, other planetary deities were worshipped at Hierapolis, for example the sun, Atlas (perhaps Kronos, Saturn), Hermes (Nabu, Mercury), Eileithyia, Aphrodite

---

[1] Arabic 'Uzzā, cf. 'Aziz, p. 106 n. 1 below.

[2] *Bombyx* is the silkworm of the Near East, while Chinese silk is termed *sericum*.

[3] About twenty-three kilometres.

[4] Constantius took the road through Hierapolis on his return to the west from Edessa in 361, and the same route was followed in the other direction by Julian when he invaded Parthian Mesopotamia. The martyrs, Dom-nina and her two daughters, were conducted to Hierapolis by their military escort, after fleeing to Edessa in 305 or 306; they drowned themselves in the river nearby. (This martyrology may, however, be legend rather than history.) In, probably, the middle of the fifth century Egeria travelled through Hierapolis on her pilgrimage to the shrine of St. Thomas at Edessa. See further pp. 78, 216 n. 3.

(Venus). Within this pattern Atargatis was regarded as the moon, Hadad as Jupiter, Apollo, in warlike costume, as Mars.

The great temple of Bel at Palmyra stood in the middle of an esplanade of Corinthian columns nearly fourteen metres high; around it was a wall, and the entrance was from the west. At Harran the arrangement and order of temples built to the planets, and the heights of the idols seem to have conformed to the distance from the earth of each planet as calculated by astronomers. Each temple had its peculiar shape and colour, the idol was of a particular substance and to each deity was allotted his day of the week.[1] At Hierapolis the temple to Atargatis was surrounded by a wall; it was orientated to the east, the entrance was from the north. It was ablaze with gold and sweet with incense. In an inner shrine, open to the air, which only certain priests might enter, stood three golden statues: Atargatis, borne on lions, carried in one hand a sceptre, in the other a distaff, on her head were rays and a tower, and she had the attributes of several goddesses including Athene, Aphrodite, and Selene; Hadad, borne on bulls, had the attributes of Zeus; and between the two was an emblem, called 'Sēmēion' by the people of the country[2], resembling the standard of the Roman legions, and surmounted by a dove. Elsewhere in the temple were idols of the other deities, and only the sun was represented by a throne without a statue. Apollo, according to one source, was shown in armour, with a spear in his right hand, a flower in his left. Outside the temple stood statues of demigods with animal attributes, and of kings and queens, heroes and priests, and a bronze altar.

The temple personnel at Palmyra were dressed in long-sleeved white robes falling to the calves, on their heads they wore a high conical bonnet, and their feet were bare.[3] The same costume was worn by the numerous priests at Hierapolis. But there the High Priest, who was elected to his office for one year, alone wore purple robes and a golden tiara. Also at Hierapolis there were a lower order of temple attendants who were musicians with pipes and flutes, a number of women possessed by frenzy, and men who, under the emotional sway of the music of flutes and tambourines, of singing, gesticulation, and dancing, castrated themselves outside the temple of the Mother Goddess. Special dress was worn by crowds of pilgrims who performed ritual sacrifice; the pilgrims for each city were instructed by a host, 'whom the Assyrians called "teacher" '.

Temple ceremonial at Palmyra, as elsewhere, included sacrifice, the offering of libations and incense, and the recital of prayers. Worshippers held up their right hand in a gesture of adoration, in their left hand they grasped a flower or a bunch of twigs as an aspergillum; sometimes they held cups,

---

[1] Details are given in the present writer's 'The Sabian Mysteries', in E. Bacon, ed., *Vanished Civilizations*, 1963, 201.

[2] Lucian, *de Dea syra*, refers to them as 'Assyrians'.

[3] This is admirably illustrated in tableaux of the latter half of the first century A.D. at Dura Europos.

perhaps of wine. At Dura Europos by the Euphrates, not far from its junction with the Khabur, are painted representations of the rites of Palmyra probably of the first century A.D. A figure in priestly dress dips, with his right hand, a branch or plant into a high vase, with three bulbous protuberances near the top and a fluted base, resting upon a tripod; the vase is filled with a transparent liquid, possibly holy water. In the priest's left hand are a ewer, a bowl and two knives. Another priest, a bowl and two knives in his right hand, appears to throw incense, with his left hand, into a burning censer. The act of plunging a branch, presumably for lustration, into a vase is repeated in other tableaux at Dura, but the officiant may, evidently, be a layman for in one painting he is depicted not in priestly garments. At Harran worshippers prayed towards the north (less probably, according to some writers, to the south) at sunrise, noon, and sunset; they performed ablution before prayer. There, too, they wore a special costume appropriate to the planet to whom their supplications were addressed, and made offerings appropriate to the deity. A late account, from the ninth century A.D., describes the procession of a sacrificial black bull festooned with garlands and bells and escorted by singers and musicians. At Hierapolis sacrifice was made twice daily, to Hadad in silence, but to Atargatis with violent musical accompaniment. Sometimes the animal victims were thrown to their death; the same fate befell children sacrificed by their parents.

A significant role is played at all these shrines, as at others in the ancient Near East, by running water. At Palmyra the great temple of Bel stood beside a brook flowing from the sacred spring of Ephca;[1] each year gifts were thrown into the sulphurous waters of the spring as an offering to its *numen*, and perhaps oracles were sought and given. A temple of the moon near Harran was at the 'Sabian' shrine of the 'idol of the water' who had returned to the well outside the city after a flight to India,[2] and there ceremonies were carried out on the twentieth day of each month, and especially on the twentieth of Nisan.[3] At Hierapolis, too, were hydrophoric rites; water was brought there twice yearly from the 'sea', and poured into a chasm outside the temple with complex and obscure ritual.[4] In the temple were statues of mermaids. The water flowed into a lake in close proximity to the temple in which were

[1] An early Syriac text recounts the myth, widespread in different forms throughout the Near East, of Balthi (cf. Beltis at Palmyra), the queen of Cyprus who loved Tammuz, prince of Phoenicia; when her lover was killed in the Lebanon by her jealous husband, Hephaestus, she remained at Gebal and died in the city Aphaca (cf. Ephca at Palmyra) where Tammuz was buried.

[2] The text reads at this point, 'in the days of Asta' followed by a variant 'Troinicos', perhaps reflecting a form of the name Stratonice, a

reputed founder of the temple of Hierapolis; D. Chwolson, *Ssabier und der Ssabismus*, 1856, ii, 40, 300.

[3] The calendar of the 'Sabians' is said to have included also solemn rites of bathing at Serug.

[4] Cf. the *Oration* of 'Melito': '. . . The Magi charged Simi, the daughter of Hadad, that she should draw water from the sea and cast it into the well [in a wood at Mabbog], in order that the [unclean] spirit should not come up [and] commit injury'.

fish of immense size, sacred to Atargatis. The fish were never eaten; some were so tame, relates Lucian, that they came when summoned by name, and one carried a design in gold on its fin. In the middle of the lake was an altar to which devotees of the goddess swam and performed religious ceremonies. The lake was visited on solemn occasions by the deities, led by Hera. There was a lake of sacred fish at the temple of Atargatis at Delos, and similar lakes were to be found at other temples in Palestine, Syria, Asia Minor, and elsewhere; Xenophon in the *Anabasis* remarks on the lake of fish that he visited by the Chalys near Aleppo.[1] Aelian, who was a contemporary of Bardaiṣan, alludes to a legend that Hera bathed at a source of the Khabur after her union with Zeus; there, we are told, the air is always fragrant, and tame fish leap (σκιρτῶσιν) in shoals. Not far away in modern times is a small lake of sacred fish at the main source of the Balikh, 'Ain al-'Arus, also called after Abraham 'Ain Khalil al-Raḥman, fifty kilometres south-south-east of Urfa; nearby are two springs, to which are attributed healing qualities. Twenty kilometres east of 'Ain al-'Arus is another source of the Balikh called 'Ain Seloq.

In the temple courtyard at Hierapolis roamed tame lions, bears, eagles, horses, and great oxen. The beginning of spring was marked by the most important festival of the year, of which examples may be found elsewhere in the Near East, a circumambulation of images of deities, and then the solemn conflagration of trees to which offerings of animals and garments and precious metal had been attached. Curious and apparently without parallel was the Hierapolitan rite of two wooden columns, some sixty metres high (according to Lucian) at the entrance of the Temple to the north. Lucian ascribes to them phallic significance. One carried inscriptions dedicated, Lucian tells us, by Dionysos to Hera. Twice a year a man, with a rope around his waist, would climb one of the columns, mounting as one climbs a date-palm in Arabia or Egypt, with the help of projections up the height of the column. Having arrived at the top, he would lower another rope and hoist up wood, clothing, and other objects in which he sat 'as it were in a nest'. He remained on the summit for seven days, and made supplication—for what is uncertain; either that no flood should come again upon the earth or for the welfare of the people, especially for the devout who brought gifts to the foot of the column. If this *phallobates* fell asleep he would be roused to his duties by a scorpion.

At Palmyra and at Dura we have evidence of the reverence paid to the dead. Outside the city walls were grottoes in which the dead were buried; the wealthy erected for themselves funerary towers, some several storeys high. The dead, mummified and often with death masks, were laid on *loculi*. These tombs, or houses of eternity, sometimes had inscriptions cursing the

---

[1] See especially F. J. Dölger, *Der heilige Fisch*, 1922.

impious who might disturb the dead. They were decorated with sculpture or paintings. Here are depicted the conventional eagle and winged Victory; in some tombs the deceased is portrayed standing or reclining as at a banquet, often with members of his family, the mistress of the house holding a distaff or spindle. The figures are dressed in formal, ornate costume. Sometimes the dead person has a crown, or a palm, or a tablet or a roll of parchment. A man, but not a woman or child, may hold a cup of wine, evidence that only men participated in the banquets which were so frequent a feature of daily life. These banquets probably had religious significance, since wine was sacred to the god Bel. At Harran there was a complex scheme of mysteries, of which we have garbled accounts from a late Arabic source, and mysteries may well have figured in the Atargatis cult at Hierapolis.

When, now, we turn to Edessa under the monarchy, we find that its inhabitants worshipped the planets like their neighbours of Palmyra, Harran, and Hierapolis. Observation of the stars was the link, indeed, between popular religion and the complex cosmological schemes of the philosophers. Bardaiṣan, as we have mentioned, was a skilled astrologer and wrote a treatise on the conjunction of the planets, and the *Book of the Laws of Countries* which was the work of his school shows familiarity with astrological concepts. One of the gates of Edessa was called Beth Shemesh, after the temple of the sun that must have stood there.[1] The crescent moon is depicted on coins of Edessa at this period; on the tiara of King Abgar it is accompanied by one, two, or three stars.[2] The planets appear in the personal names of Edessans, in Syriac texts, both at Urfa itself and in its immediate neighbourhood, on the walls of tombs, on mosaic floors, and in literature. Among them, to cite only a few, are 'maidservant of Sin (the moon)', 'servant of Bel (Jupiter)', 'greeting of 'Atha (Venus)', 'Shemesh (the sun) has determined', 'servant of Nabu (Mercury)'.

Mention of other astral deities is found at Edessa. ZYDallat and other theophorous names combined with Allat show that some Edessans worshipped that goddess, in common with the pagans of Arabia. The name Bar Kalba at Edessa and at Sumatar Harabesi[3] suggests the worship of the Dog star. The sixth-century poet Jacob of Serug, who lived most of his life at Edessa and Batnae, maintains that at Harran was a deity with the strange title of 'Mar(i) (lord) of his dogs'; perhaps this means the hunter Orion, at whose heels are the constellations Canis major and Canis minor. A striking passage in the *Doctrine of Addai* describes the scene at Edessa at the time of the introduction of Christianity:

I saw this city that it abounded greatly in paganism which is against God. Who is this Nabu, a fashioned idol to which ye bow down, and Bel which ye honour? Behold, there

---

[1] Cf. pp. 184 f.
[2] Other coins of Edessa have one or two or four stars without a crescent.
[3] On this site, see p. 56 below.

are among you those who worship Bath Nikal like the men of Harran your neighbours, and Tarʿatha like the men of Mabbog, and the Eagle like the Arabs,[1] and the sun and moon as others who are like you. Do not be led astray by the rays of the luminaries or the gleaming star.

We have discussed the worship of Nabu, Bel, and Tarʿatha (Atargatis) of Mabbog, and the sun and moon. Bath Nikal is no doubt daughter of Ningal, consort of Sin the moon deity, and herself perhaps to be identified with Tarʿatha. The Eagle may be the term given, as it was by later Arabs, to the constellation of the Lyre, which includes one of the brightest stars in the northern hemisphere. It may, on the other hand, be the symbol of Jupiter. In the fragmentary Animal mosaic in Şehitlik Mahallesi at Urfa,[2] all that remains of the centre are outstretched wings and a hand grasping a staff. Perhaps this is a representation of Zeus and his eagle; perhaps it told the myth of Ganymede.

We meet with legends, in the Syriac literature of Edessa of this period, that have much in common with those of contemporary cities, particularly of Hierapolis. In the *Doctrine of Addai*, on the introduction of Christianity to Edessa, the Apostle relates the discovery of the Cross at Jerusalem by Queen Protonice, wife of Emperor Claudius. The queen's name may be a variant of Stratonice, wife of the king of Assyria, and one of the reputed founders of the temple of Hierapolis. Protonice in this story obviously reflects Helena, mother of Constantine the Great, whom history credits with the finding of the Cross. But local legend confused this Helena with an earlier queen Helena, who was renowned for her adoption of Judaism and her largess to the temple at Jerusalem, and the latter was queen of Adiabene, which was popularly called 'Assyria'.[3] In the Syriac *Oration*, too, incorrectly ascribed to Melito of Sardis we read that:

the Syrians worshipped ʿAthi of Adiabene who sent the daughter of Belaṭ, the woman-physician and she healed Simi, daughter of Hadad king of Syria; after a time, when leprosy came upon Hadad himself, ʿAthi entreated Elisha the Hebrew and he came and healed him of his leprosy.

These names remind us of the cult of Hierapolis—Hadad and ʿAthi (ʿAtha, ʿAtharʿatha) are its chief deities, and Simi is the Sēmēion, the golden emblem that stood between them in the inner shrine of the temple. ʿAtha, however, was worshipped also at Edessa.[4] The cure of leprosy by Elisha the Hebrew echoes the healing of Abgar of Edessa of a sickness, by some identified with leprosy, by another Hebrew, the Apostle Addai.[5]

Finally, another passage of this *Oration* declares, 'Concerning Nabu that is in Mabbog what shall I write? That it is the image of Orpheus the Thracian magus all the priests in Mabbog know.' It has been suggested that the

---

[1] Syriac, ʿArbaye.
[2] See p. 32.
[3] See pp. 68–70 below.

[4] Cf. p. 50.
[5] Leprosy and lepers were carefully avoided by the pagans of Harran.

confusion between Nabu and Orpheus derives from a misinterpretation of the symbols of this image; the tablet and stylus of the planet-god have been mistaken for the musical instruments of the legendary bard. Music played, we have noted, a prominent part in the temple at Hierapolis. It was equally prominent at Edessa.[1] But there is a more striking analogy: in the Eyüp Mahallesi at Urfa the beautiful Orpheus mosaic has been found.[2] The musician is seated, a lyre in his hand; around him are a lion, a gazelle, and birds in attitudes of becoming docility. The Orpheus theme had acquired a considerable following in Rome's eastern provinces, and a variation on the motif is probably to be identified in the representation of David in the synagogue at Dura Europos. More significantly, the Orpheus mosaic of Edessa was set up in A.D. 228, in the reign of Alexander Severus, who was Syrian by origin. He had been proclaimed Emperor in 222; in 231, three years after the mosaic had been completed, he passed through Edessa on his way to the East. A biography of the Emperor informs us that busts of Abraham, Jesus, Apollonius of Tyana, and Orpheus stood together in his private chapel. The cult of Orpheus was evidently acceptable at Edessa, as at Hierapolis, in the syncretistic atmosphere of that time. Its diffusion stemmed from the attraction of its mysteries, their teaching of recompense in an after-world and particularly the feeling of reassurance and security which they imparted in an age of emotional and social unrest.

The priests of Edessa, as of the neighbouring shrines, wore a high headdress or tiara like the nobles. The High Priest, however, wore special garments, much the same as those of his counterpart at Hierapolis. A martyrology of Edessa tells us that the 'chief and ruler of all the priests was greatly honoured above all his comrades. And he was clad in splendid and magnificent vestments, and a silken (tiara) embossed with figures of gold was set upon his head.' We shall see later that the High Priest at Edessa, as elsewhere in Osrhoene, and as at Hierapolis, seems to have been nominated for one year only.

Outside the temple at Hierapolis stood statues of demigods, heroes, kings, and priests; below the Citadel mount at Edessa were statues of the kings of the Aryu dynasty. So too, at Edessa a great pagan altar which later writers vaguely ascribed to the Seleucids stood below the Citadel mount. There were evidently other altars at Edessa. Of one we read in the *Doctrine of Addai* 'What is the great altar which ye have built in the midst of this town, to which ye come and go and on which ye pour libations to demons and sacrifices to devils?' At a festival in Nisan:[3]

the whole city assembled near the great altar which was in the midst of the town opposite the office of Records,[4] all the gods having been assembled and having been adorned and

---

[1] See p. 34. [2] Pl. 44. [3] April.
[4] A slight emendation of the text is required to give this meaning.

seated in honour, both Nabu and Bel with their companions. All the priests were offering sweet incense and libations, and the odour of the holocausts was diffused and sheep and oxen were slaughtered, and the sound of music and the drum was heard in all the town.

This altar was permitted, even according to the tendentious *Doctrine of Addai*, to survive into the Christian period. The chief priests of Edessa, fired by zeal for the new religion, are said to have 'run and thrown down the altars on which they sacrificed before Nabu and Bel—except the great altar in the midst of the town.'

It is possible that at Edessa were observed also some less conventional features of the cults of her neighbours. Elsewhere in Osrhoene, temples seem to have faced eastwards like that of Hierapolis.[1] But exactly as at Hierapolis there were two great columns at the north entrance to the temple (according to Lucian of Samosata), one bearing a dedication by Dionysos to Hera, so it may be no coincidence that the great columns with Corinthian capitals on the Citadel mount at Edessa stand also on the edge of the cliff to the north of a complex of buildings. One of the Edessan columns, too, bears a dedication, not to a goddess but to a queen.[2] The statue of Queen Shalmath looked towards the city below. Twice a year, it will be recalled, one of the columns at Hierapolis was climbed by a representative of the cult to pray either that no deluge should again afflict the earth or that the pious should prosper.[3] By some scholars the practice has been associated with the activities of stylites,[4] for Edessa was also celebrated for its stylites.[5] Nor should we ignore the fact that the winter palace of Abgar was erected on the Citadel mount (beside a temple?) to avoid a repetition of the disaster of 201, when his palace by the fish-pools was destroyed by flood waters,[6] since the *phallobates* of Hierapolis may have implored the deities never again to send flood waters on the earth.

Much of this is surmise. In some practices, however, the analogy between Edessa and the neighbouring cult centres is certain. The flower in the hand of the statue of Apollo at Hierapolis finds a parallel in the Tripod mosaic.[7] There a male personage proffers what may be a cap of state;[8] to his right a female figure holds in her right hand a small golden or yellow object, perhaps a jewel, but more probably a flower. More striking is the gesture with two

---

[1] Cf. 56 f. below on Sumatar Harabesi.

[2] For a possible explanation see p. 56 below on the role of Abgar in the development of religion at Edessa.

[3] He ascended by means of wooden bosses. The stone bosses at Edessa have a different function, p. 26 above. Has Lucian misunderstood the function of the bosses on the Hierapolitan columns?

[4] This interpretation has been rejected by other scholars, notably H. Delehaye, *Les Saints*

stylites, 1923.

[5] p. 109 below. The father of Simeon Stylites the Younger, it should be added, was a native of Edessa.

[6] Lucian's statement that the *phallobates* of Hierapolis made himself a 'nest' on the top of the columns recalls the use of minarets and other high buildings throughout this region by storks; no one disturbs their nests, Pl. 33*b*.

[7] Pl. 3.

[8] See p. 41 above.

leaves in the hand of the figure of the deceased in the Family Portrait mosaic. This is to be related to the scene of the Tripod mosaic where the deceased extends a leaf towards a vase standing on a tripod and containing probably holy water. We have here an exact parallel to a ritual of Palmyra in which the deceased grasps a flower or a bunch of twigs. The action is illustrated in yet greater detail in the tableaux of Dura Europos where the officiant, not necessarily a priest, holds out a branch towards a vase of liquid standing on a tripod, as in the Tripod mosaic. The deity, to whom the rite is directed, is suggested by a relief and a statue of Atargatis at Hatra;[1] in the former the goddess holds a leaf in her right hand, in the latter in her left hand.

Edessa, like Hierapolis and other cult-centres of the area, was celebrated for a well of healing waters that was, as we shall see, a holy place in the Christian period and later. Rites of incubation are performed there, indeed, to the present day.[2] Like Hierapolis, Edessa had its sacred fish. The statuettes of tritons, now in the Urfa museum, recall the reliefs of figures, half women, half fish, found at Membig (Mabbog) by travellers in the seventeenth and eighteenth centuries. A more certain analogy is to be seen in the two pools of Edessa, which are, like the famous pools of Hierapolis, full of carp of remarkable size and in astonishing numbers. Egeria, who examined them in, probably, the fifth century, observed that she had 'never seen fish of such size, so gleaming and succulent'. In the nineteenth century, the English missionary Badger was told that the fish were never eaten by the Moslems of Urfa—although, he adds, Christians often partook of 'the forbidden dainty, the fish being easily secured in the streams which flow from the pond through the gardens. They generally cook them with wine sauce, and declare them excellent.'[3] Still today the fish are treated as sacred, and are never caught. They are fed with bread, and so tame are they that they will leap inches out of the water to snatch at morsels of food.[4]

Remarkably enough, the same features are reflected in Aelian's description of the pools at the source of the Khabur, and there too, we are provided with an association with the cults of Hera at Hierapolis and Edessa. The pools of the Khabur were, we are informed, sacred to Hera, and, like an echo of the 'leaping' river of Edessa, the Scirtos or Daiṣan, its shoals of fish are said to leap (σκιρτῶσιν). Has Aelian confused the source of the Khabur with the source of the Balikh, that today has sacred fish and nearby springs with healing properties? A source of the Balikh is named after the patriarch

---

[1] On Hatra see also p. 60 below.

[2] Cf. p. 72 below.

[3] Niebuhr, who visited Urfa in 1766, also states that the fish were sometimes eaten in spite of the veneration with which they were regarded; so, too, Buckingham in 1823.

[4] See photograph on Pl. 7b. The pools were examined by Tavernier in 1644. He remarked that they 'were so full of fish that if you throw them in a little bread they will follow you from place to place as you walk by the side of the pond'.

Abraham, like the northern pool of Edessa, the Birket Ibrahim, whose fish are 'Abraham's fish'.[1] The Balikh has another source, not far away, and this is called 'Ain Seloq, the fountain of Seleucus; and it may be conjectured that the name of the southern pool at Urfa, Zulha, is a corrupt form of the same name, Seloq.

Reverence for the dead was a feature of the cult-centres of this region. We have, however, no more than one written allusion to funeral ceremonial in Osrhoene, that is in the inscription of the tomb-tower of Serrin, dated A.D. 73. It invokes a curse on the person who may disturb the dead man's remains and, it continues, 'sons who shall cast dust upon his eyes shall not be found for him'.[2] As we have observed, the cave-tombs and funerary towers of Palmyra had their counterpart at Edessa. The bodies of the deceased were laid upon the platforms of the *loculi*. The relief at Deyr Yakup provides an excellent illustration of the method employed. The figure there lies face upward, his head resting upon a cushion and wearing a formal high head-dress to signify his status as priest or noble.[3] A common decoration of the cave-tombs was the ritual banquet, for it appears in the reliefs of no fewer than two tombs outside Urfa and two tombs at Kara Köprü near Urfa, and also in one mosaic at Urfa itself—evidence that it may have been as important an element in Edessan life as it was at Palmyra and elsewhere. One of the reliefs near Edessa is accompanied by an inscription which informs us that the tomb was made for a certain Seleucus in A.D. 201–2. Beside him stand his wife, and son and daughter. A more striking picture of a funerary banquet is shown in the mosaic, which is dated A.D. 278. The deceased man reclines, his left elbow resting on a cushion (as in the reliefs of Palmyra) and in his hand a stoup of wine. The couch is inlaid and has ornate carved legs. To the left of the dead man, his wife in elegant robes and a high head-dress is seated in an armchair, her feet on a footstool. Around him are his six children, one holding a napkin, the other what may be a spice-box.[4]

We have observed that Bardaiṣan rejected the theory of corporeal resurrection but believed in the survival of the soul. Nevertheless some pagans in Osrhoene must have maintained belief in the actual resurrection of the body also. One tomb inscription at Edessa warns that 'he who shall move my bones—may he have no latter end';[5] and the Serrin inscription declares that the devout will be blessed by all the gods and 'dwelling and life shall he have', presumably in the world to come. The two points of view are well elaborated by two mosaics at Edessa found in recent years. The Orpheus mosaic points to the existence at Edessa of the cult whose followers observed forms of ceremonial and moral self-abnegation; they avoided contact with birth and death, and abstained from animal foods and other possible causes of

---

[1] Cf. pp. 2, 49 above. [2] See p. 23 n. 4 above. [3] Cf. pp. 18, 52; Pl. 39*b*.
[4] Pl. 25*b*, 2. [5] See p. 59 below.

pollution. They did so in order, as they felt, to safeguard the purity of the soul so that ultimately it would arise free from uncleanness. They maintained, like Bardaiṣan, the immortality of the soul. The theme of the Phoenix mosaic, on the other hand, dated A.D. 235–6, reflects a different view. It depicts a tomb in the shape of a conventional arcosolium; above it stands a wreathed pillar, and surmounting the whole is the phoenix, symbol of the renewal of life.[1] Only when the funeral rites are properly conducted, we may conclude, will resurrection follow, that is, resurrection of the body.

It is evident that paganism at Edessa incorporated much of the beliefs and practices of neighbouring cult-centres, notably those of Hierapolis. But a significant change in direction seems to have occurred under a certain King Abgar. The *Book of the Laws of Countries*, written possibly at the beginning of the third century, provides almost contemporary evidence. It states explicitly that, 'when Abgar the king believed (in Christ) he decreed that anyone who castrated himself should have his hand cut off. And from that day to this time, no man castrates himself in the country of Edessa.' This Abgar is credited, then, with abandoning a rite that was a central feature of the worship of the Mother Goddess at Hierapolis. It was the same Abgar whom Christendom was later to associate with the evangelization of Edessa, though we need not assume that he was himself a convert to the new religion.[2] It was also Abgar the statue of whose wife possibly appeared on a column at Edessa, in the place where Hera's figure appeared at Hierapolis. What were the influences that would have led Abgar to take this momentous step? The age in which he lived was witnessing a change in religious environment that was to have far-reaching effects not only on Edessa itself, but on the more general development of religion in Mesopotamia.

Light has been thrown on this development by monuments recently discovered at Sumatar Harabesi in the Tektek mountains. At this deserted oasis, sixty kilometres south-east of Urfa, a group of seven or eight ruined buildings, of different shapes, perhaps tombs,[3] form an uneven arc, at varying distances, around a central mount—a bare narrow rock, fifty metres high and of about the same length. The mount has an uninterrupted view to the east; and clearly it was a sacred place. On its northern flank are two reliefs. One is the bust of a male personage, without a hat but with his hair secured by a headband, a bow and a half-loop on either side of his head;[4] the other is a full-length statue of a man wearing the same long coat as that shown in the Family Portrait mosaic of Edessa.[5] Both reliefs have Syriac texts at their side. One states that the full-length relief was put up at the command of

---

[1] Pl. 43.
[2] Cf. p. 70 below.
[3] See p. 32 above.
[4] Cf. p. 41. The pagans of Harran wore

their hair in long locks to the surprise of the Caliph al-Maʾmun, when he visited the city in circa 830. See the text in Chwolson, op. cit.
[5] On this costume see p. 40; Pl. 40*b*, 41.

'the god'; another, beside the bust, requests that certain persons, who are named, be 'remembered before the god'. But a third inscription explicitly identifies the god. It declares that the bust was made, 'to Sin the god for the life of Tirdat[1] bar Adona and for the life of his brethren.' Another inscription, unfortunately difficult to decipher, seems to refer to the deposit of a treasure and ends, '. . . I behold him, and lo! I am Sin the god.[2]'

On the bare summit of this sacred mount, among several brief dedicatory inscriptions, is one which declares, 'Remembered be 'Absamya son of Adona the *nuhadra*; [may he be] remembered before Marilaha.' Two other texts are given pride of place on the mount. One, on the western side, states:

In the month of Shebaṭ in the year 476,[3] I, Tirdat bar Adona, ruler of the 'Arab, built this altar and set a pillar to Marilaha for the life of my lord the king and his sons and for the life of Adona my father. . . .

In an inscription on the eastern side of the mount is written:

In the month of Shebaṭ in the year 476[4] . . . we set this pillar on this blessed mount and erected the stool for him whom my ruler feeds.[5] He shall be *budar* after Tirdat the ruler and he shall give the stool to him whom he feeds. His recompense shall be from Marilaha. And if he withholds the stool,[6] then the pillar will be ruined. He, the god, lives.[7]

The text was evidently inscribed by a group of 'Arab over whom Tirdat had authority as ruler, or *Arabarchos*. The year in which these texts were written— another Sumatar text has the date Adar 476 (approximately March 165)—was a turning-point in the history of Osrhoene. The Roman armies occupied Edessa and expelled its pro-Parthian monarch Wa'el in the following November. The 'king' of the Sumatar text is probably the king of Edessa, the principal city of the province. There was a direct political connection between Sumatar and Edessa at this time.

There was also a religious bond between the two places. The chief deity of Sumatar is evidently referred to as Marilaha, 'the lord god'.[8] The 'Arab of the place set a stool and a pillar on the eastern side (ritually the more

[1] Parthian, Tirdad (Tiridates).

[2] This reading is probable, but not certain.

[3] Approximately February A.D. 165.

[4] A list of five names follows.

[5] Lit., 'nourishes'. The phrase could also be rendered, 'whose shepherd is my ruler'.

[6] The reading on which this translation is based (Syriac *nkl'*) is to be preferred, on grounds of script, to Syriac *npl'*, i.e. 'if the stool falls'.

[7] After a fresh examination and recording of this inscription in 1966, I now read Syriac *ḥy* instead of my previous *yd'n*. S. Shaked in A. D. H. Bivar and Shaked, *BSOAS* xxvii, 1964, 28 ff., interprets the text differently: '. . . and we erected the stool to whoever feeds Him (i.e. the god). My ruler shall be *Bwdr* after Tirdat the ruler, and

he shall give the stool to whoever feeds Him. His recompense shall be from Marilaha. If the stool falls and the pillar is ruined, [yet] He, the God, knows us' (following my earlier reading of the last word). Shaked suggests that it is the deity who is fed, and that the *Bwdr* is called 'ruler' as a priestly title, but with rank inferior to that of Tirdat, ruler (of 'Arab).

[8] The importance of the shrine at Sumatar Harabesi seems to be attested by remains at another site in the Tektek mountains now called Sanimağara. There, an altar is situated on the summit of a mount. It faces eastwards like the mount at Sumatar. But a large stone stands orientated towards Sumatar Harabesi— and perhaps towards Harran. Pl. 42.

important)[1] of the sacred mount for the *budar*, who succeeded Tirdat and was fed by him in a ceremonial meal. For this action Tirdat would be rewarded by Marilaha. If, on the other hand, he did not give his successor access to the stool, the sacred pillar would fall and, we conclude, Marilaha would be angry. Tirdat, in token of his consent, set up on the same day an altar and a pillar on the western side of the mount.

The motif of a pillar surmounted by horns or a crescent is a not uncommon lunar symbol in this region. We find it, beside the shape of a serpent, carved on the wall of a cave outside Urfa.[2] It occurs also on reliefs in a cave cut from the rock at Sumatar Harabesi, together with male figures and dedicatory inscriptions in Syriac; these include one to an *Arabarchos* and his son the *nuhadra*, and to two other *Arabarchoi*. The same motif is found on coins of Harran of the reign of Septimius Severus, and on stelae from Harran of the time of the Babylonian king Nabonidus centuries earlier. The moon god Sin, the peculiar deity of Harran, was, we observe, worshipped also at Sumatar.

Of different significance are the stool and pillar as the cult emblems of Marilaha. They appear in miniature on an Edessan coin of the reign of Elagabalus (218–22).[3] They are also inscribed on coins of that Wa'el of Edessa in whose reign the Sumatar inscriptions were dedicated. On these coins is shown a temple with a pediment and steps leading up to it; inside is a 'cubic cult object, on a base supported by two curved legs'.[4] This is evidently religious furniture. A star may be seen in the pediment of the shrine, no doubt an indication of planet worship.[5]

The objects in the temple on the Wa'el coins are a pillar and stool; the pillar does not have horns or a crescent. The stool is evidently the symbol of office of the *budar*. The term *budar* is found already in the Syriac inscription, dated A.D. 73, on the tomb-tower of Serrin on the Osrhoenian side of the Euphrates. This tower was erected for a *budar* of the deity Naḥai; the *budar* had also the religious title of *qashshisha*, elder.[6] A form of the title *budar* seems to have been in use among the pagans of Harran (who also used Syriac in their liturgy). In the course of induction into their mysteries—the account is unfortunately transmitted only in garbled form in the Moslem period and by someone who knew Syriac but little Arabic—the novice was called 'son of the *bughdariyyun*'.[7] In the incantation at these mysteries were also allusions to

---

[1] Cf. p. 47.   [2] See below p. 106.

[3] The coin may, however, be assigned to the reign of Caracalla.

[4] G. F. Hill, *Catalogue of Greek Coins of Arabia. . . .*; cf. the catalogues of G. Macdonald and J. Babelon.

[5] The legend on the coins may be read as 'LH 'NḤY, 'the go d Nahai'; Pl. 28a.

[6] The text is given on p. 23 n. 4. In Christian

Syriac *qashshisha* denotes 'priest'; see my article in *Iraq* xxix, 1967, 6. Under the form *gšyš'* it appears as the title of a personage, possibly a religious dignitary, on an Elymaean inscription of Khuzistan of the first or second century A.D., Bivar and Shaked, op. cit. 272.

[7] BDR is possibly to be read in an inscription found at Saʿadiya near Hatra and dated April 125, Fuad Safar, *Sumer* xvii, 1961, 9 ff., and

the 'house', perhaps temple, of the *bughdariyyun*. It is reasonable to suppose that at pagan Edessa also in the reign of Wa'el there was a priestly dignitary called *budar*. As at Sumatar, a sacred stool was handed down from *budar* to *budar*; if the chain of transmission were broken, the pillar which stood on it would fall. A stool of office seems to be alluded to in contemporary Elymaean inscriptions;[1] and we know that in the seventh century the chief of the pagans of Harran occupied a stool of office, and was elected annually.

Among the ceremonies on the appointment of a *budar* at Sumatar was evidently a ritual meal. Here too, confirmation may be found in the description of the mysteries at pagan Harran. There novices partook of special food of which some, at least, was consecrated. Ritual feeding seems to be mentioned also in the Elymaean inscriptions which refer to a ceremonial stool.[2] It is not unreasonable to infer that at pagan Edessa also ceremonial meals were part of the induction ceremony of a *budar*.

Let us return to Marilaha, the deity recorded at Sumatar Harabesi. At Kirk Mağara outside Edessa a Syriac inscription, undated but probably of the second or third century, reads:

I G'W, daughter of Barshuma, made for myself this burial place. I ask of you who come after [and] who may enter here, move not my bones from the sarcophagus. He that shall move my bones—may he have no latter-end, and may he be accursed to Marilaha.[3]

Who was this Marilaha? In Nabataean, and we have noted that the rulers of Edessa were largely Nabataean, *mara* is one of the epithets used of the divinity Be'elshamin, 'lord of the heavens'. This deity is attested over a great area of the Near East, notably among Aramaeans, and from a very early period. At Palmyra Be'elshamin holds an important place in the pantheon in the first centuries of the Christian era, but he is not, like Bel, a national god; he seems to have had wider associations. He is called variously 'great god', 'lord (*mara*) of all', 'lord of the universe (*mara de'alma*)'. There are strong grounds for supposing that it was Be'elshamin who is worshipped as the 'anonymous god', that is the object of numerous dedications at Palmyra between A.D. 111 and 268 and is styled impersonally 'he whose name is blessed for evermore (*le'alma*)'. Both deities are called 'good and merciful', both form a triad with Malakbel and 'Aglibol, and both are identified as

---

my article in *Iraq*, loc. cit. The passage records the dedication of 'a garden and altar of Marilaha of Qarqabesh' and adds, 'made by ZN' the BDR (or, 'this BDR') who attends (*ḥny*) to those who see [visions] in dreams'. There may, on the other hand, be confusion in the Sa'adiya text between BDR ḤNY and the BDR NḤY (that is, of the deity Naḥai) of the Serrin inscription, p. 23 n. 4, cf. n. 5 above. For Marilaha at Hatra, see p. 60 below.

[1] At Tang-i Sarvak; see Shaked, op. cit. 287 ff. Two texts read: '. . . Bel-dosha, who is *rabbani*, with Aserya(?) and Antiochus, who are at the Gate. Bar Basi, taking the stool'; another: '. . . Orodes, taking the stool . . ., feeds, bowing upon him, worships'.

[2] Above n. 1.

[3] At the side is a brief text, also in Syriac, perhaps in memory of G'W's father; it reads: 'Remembered be Barshuma bar Wa'el'. Pl. 29b.

Zeus. At Hatra, a small kingdom about eighty kilometres south of Mosul, inscriptions, in a derivative of Aramaic script and contemporary with the kingdom of Edessa, indicate that, there too, the divinity that was invoked most frequently was Be'elshamin. He was the 'great god' and 'king'. But near Hatra, we find also an inscription to a local deity Marilaha; and coins from Hatra carry the legend 'Sin Marilaha'. Was Sin here elevated to a supreme role, or was he identified with a central deity Be'elshamin?

The pagans of Edessa knew the deity Be'elshamin, for his name is found among the proper names of the mosaics. Sin, the moon god, also played an important role in the planet worship of the city. But it is not profitable to speculate upon the precise identity of a godhead Marilaha. Cults appeared, merged, and disappeared in this region of the East and at this period. We cannot seek to resolve the disorder into a tidy pantheon in which each deity is allotted his particular sphere, with peculiar attributes and functions. It is sufficient to observe that the general atmosphere over a large area of northern Mesopotamia and Syria during the first centuries of the Christian era favoured the conception of a single godhead, whether he stood alone above all other deities, or whether he was attended by lesser deities and merely *primus inter pares*. At Harran, Be'elshamin was worshipped as 'chief of the gods' certainly as late as the fifth century, but probably for considerably longer. The pagans there, the so-called Sabians, worshipped the seven planets, like the pagans of Edessa. But, as we have already observed, they believed that the planets, the habitation of deities or themselves deities, were no more than the agents of a Supreme Being who had delegated to them the administration of the universe. The qualities of this single divinity were beyond human powers to describe; he was too great and too remote to require the worship of man.[1] Indeed, we find a trend towards the system in which one deity stood at the peak of the pantheon much earlier at Harran. Already in the sixth century B.C. in the inscriptions of Nabonidus, king of Babylon, at Harran, the chief god is raised to the status of a universal deity above all the other gods. He is addressed as 'king of the gods', and 'greatest of the gods and goddesses'.

It has been suggested that it was the influence of the Jews at Edessa that paved the way for the triumph of Christianity there, and there is weighty evidence for this view. But friendship and sympathy alone do not win converts to a new religion; indeed, it was the belief, in this area and at this time, in a single divinity of cosmic proportions that must already have provided

---

[1] We may recall in this context that the Koran uses the term *hanif* of a person who professed monotheism before the appearance of Judaism and Christianity—before, that is, Moses and Jesus; in the opinion of Muḥammad the true *hanif* was Abraham. Harran at the time of Muḥammad had long been the centre of the Syriac *hanpe* (*hanpe* is cognate with *hanif*, although, it should be observed, some modern scholars doubt a direct semantic connection between the two words)—and Harran was the home of Abraham. *Ḥanif* is, in some measure, a synonym of 'Sabian'. The sacred book of the 'Sabians' was the 'volume of the Hanifites'; they offered to the sun and moon the 'greater and lesser incense of the Hanifites'.

the monotheism of the Jews with a ready hearing. The motif of a divine trinity was familiar in this region of the ancient East, and the hope in life after death was, as we have seen, widespread at Edessa. The idea of a human-divine mediator won an immediate response. In this environment Christianity could not fail to appeal.

III

THE BLESSING OF JESUS AND THE TRIUMPH OF CHRISTIANITY

A T THE BEGINNING OF THE THIRD CENTURY there was a Christian church in a prominent quarter of Edessa,[1] but probably the majority of the population was still pagan. A century later, not only was Christianity the dominant faith in the city, but the story of its evangelization had become famous throughout Christendom. Edessa was acclaimed as the first kingdom to adopt Christianity as its official religion.

Eusebius relates in his *Ecclesiastical History*, completed in 324 or 325, that Abgar, king of Edessa, 'the most celebrated ruler of the nations beyond the Euphrates', was afflicted with a disease 'beyond human power to heal'. Abgar wrote to Jesus begging him to cure his ailment.[2] Eusebius gives the text of the correspondence between Abgar and Jesus, extracted, he claims, 'from the archives of Edessa which was at that time ruled by its own kings',[3] and translated from Syriac into Greek:

A copy of a letter written by Abgar the toparch[4] to Jesus and sent to him at Jerusalem by the courier[5] Ananias:[6]

'Abgar Ukkama, the toparch, to Jesus the good Saviour[7] who has appeared in the district of Jerusalem, greeting. I have heard concerning you and your cures, how they are accomplished by you without drugs and herbs.[8] For, as the story goes,[9] you make the blind recover their sight,[10] the lame walk, and you cleanse lepers,[11] and cast out[12] unclean

---

[1] See foot of p. 24 above.

[2] Perhaps cf. Matt. 4 : 24, 'And [Jesus's] fame went throughout all Syria: and they brought unto him all sick people that were taken with divers diseases and torments, and those which were possessed with devils, and those which were lunatic, and those that had the palsy; and he healed them.'

[3] The Syriac *Acts of Thaddaeus*, which was perhaps the source of the account of Abgar in Eusebius, and was composed probably towards the end of the third century has, 'You have in written documents the evidence of these things, which is taken from the Book of Records which is at Edessa; for at that time the kingdom was still standing. In the public documents, therefore, that are there, in which is contained whatever had been done by those

of old up to the time of Abgar, these things also are found preserved there up to the present hour. But there is nothing to hinder our hearing the very letters themselves which are taken by us from the Archives, and have the following form of words translated out of Syriac into Greek.'

[4] *Doctrine of Addai* omits 'toparch' throughout.

[5] Better read 'secretary', p. 20 above.

[6] Syriac, Ḥannan.

[7] *Doc. Add.*, 'physician'.

[8] *Doc. Add.*, 'roots'.

[9] *Doc. Add.*, 'by your word'.

[10] *Doc. Add.*, 'open the [eyes of the] blind'.

[11] *Doc. Add.*, adds 'and the deaf you make to hear'.

[12] *Doc. Add.* omits.

spirits and demons, and you cure those who are tortured by long disease[1] and[2] you raise dead men. And when I heard of all these[3] things concerning you[4] I decided that it is one of two things,[5] either that you are God and came down from Heaven to do these things, or are the Son of God for doing[6] these things. For this reason I write to beg you to hasten[7] to me[8] and to heal the suffering which I have.[9] Moreover, I heard that the Jews are mocking you,[10] and wish to[11] ill-treat you. Now I have a city very[12] small and venerable[13] which is enough for both of us.'[14]

The reply from Jesus to the toparch by the courier Ananias:[15]

'Blessed are you who believed in me, not having seen me, for it is written concerning me that those who have seen me will not believe in me, and that those who have not seen me will believe[16] and live.[17] Now concerning what you wrote to me, to come to you, I must first complete here all for which I was sent, and after thus completing it be taken up to Him who sent me;[18] and when I have been taken[19] up, I will send to you one of my disciples to heal your suffering[20] and give life to[21] you and those with you.'[22]

Eusebius then narrates the outcome of the exchange of letters between Abgar and Jesus; this account too, he asserts, has been translated from Syriac, but here he does not claim that the text is derived from the city archives:

Now after the ascension of Jesus, Judas who was also Thomas, sent Thaddaeus to him as an Apostle, being one of the Seventy, and he came and stayed with Tobias the son of Tobias. Now when news of him was heard, it was reported to Abgar, 'An Apostle of Jesus has come here, as he wrote to you'. So Thaddaeus began in the power of God to heal every disease and weakness so that all marvelled.

And when Abgar heard the great and wonderful deeds that he was doing, and how he was working cures, he began to suspect that this was he of whom Jesus had written saying, 'When I have been taken up, I will send to you one of my disciples who will heal your suffering'. So he summoned Tobias, with whom Thaddaeus was staying, and said, 'I hear that a certain man of power has come and is staying at your house. Bring him to me'. Tobias came to Thaddaeus and said to him, 'The toparch Abgar summoned me and bade me bring you to him in order to heal him'. And Thaddaeus said, 'I will go up since I have been miraculously sent to him'.

---

[1] *Doc. Add.*, 'your word'.

[2] *Doc. Add.* adds 'moreover'.

[3] *Doc. Add.* adds 'wondrous great'.

[4] *Doc. Add.*, 'which you do'.

[5] *Doc. Add.* omits.

[6] *Doc. Add.*, 'that you do all'.

[7] *Doc. Add.*, 'come'.

[8] *Doc. Add.* adds 'as I worship you'.

[9] *Doc. Add.* adds 'for I believe in you'.

[10] *Doc. Add.*, 'murmuring against you and persecuting you'.

[11] *Doc. Add.* adds 'crucify and seek to'.

[12] *Doc. Add.* omits.

[13] *Doc. Add.*, 'beautiful'.

[14] *Doc. Add.*, 'two to live in it in tranquillity'.

[15] *Doc. Add.* inserts, 'Go and say to your Lord who has sent you to my presence'.

[16] Cf. John 20: 29, 'Jesus saith unto him, Thomas, because thou hast seen me, thou hast believed: blessed are they that have not seen, and yet have believed.'

[17] *Doc. Add.* omits, and inserts 'in me'.

[18] *Doc. Add.* has, 'that for which I was sent here is now finished and I am going up to my Father who sent me'.

[19] *Doc. Add.*, 'gone'.

[20] *Doc. Add.*, 'and to heal and make sound the suffering that you have'.

[21] *Doc. Add.*, 'turn to everlasting life'.

[22] *Doc. Add.*, 'all those who are with you'. It adds, 'And your city shall be blessed and no enemy shall ever be master of it again'; see p. 73 below.

So Tobias rose up early the next day and taking Thaddaeus came to Abgar. Now as he went up while the king's grandees were standing present, as soon as he entered a great vision appeared to Abgar on the face of the Apostle Thaddaeus. And when Abgar saw this, he did reverence to Thaddaeus, and wonder held all who were standing by, for they had not seen the vision which appeared only to Abgar. And he asked Thaddaeus, 'Are you of a truth a disciple of Jesus, the son of God, who said to me, "I will send you one of my disciples who will heal you and give you life"?' And Thaddaeus said, 'Since you have had great faith in him who sent me, I was sent to you for this reason. And again, if you believe in him, the request of your heart shall be to you as you believe'. And Abgar said to him, 'I have had such belief in him as to have wished to take force and destroy the Jews who crucified him, had I not been prevented from this by the Roman Empire', And Thaddaeus said, 'Our Lord has fulfilled the will of his Father, and after fulfilling it has been taken up to the Father'. And Abgar said to him, 'I too have believed on him and on his Father'. And Thaddaeus said, 'For this cause I put my hand on you in his name'. And when he did this immediately he was healed from the disease and the suffering he had. And Abgar wondered that just as he had heard concerning Jesus so he had in fact received through his disciple Thaddaeus, who cured him without drugs and herbs, and not only him but also Abdus the son of Abdus who had the gout; for he too came and fell at his feet and received his prayer at his hand, and was healed. And the same Thaddaeus healed many of their fellow-citizens, performing many wonderful deeds and preaching the word of God.

And after this Abgar said, 'O Thaddaeus, it is by the power of God that you do these things, and we ourselves have wondered. But in addition to this I beg you, explain to me the coming of Jesus, how it happened, and concerning his power, and by what power he did these things of which I have heard'. And Thaddaeus said, 'I will now be silent, but since I was sent to preach the word, summon for me tomorrow an assembly of all your citizens, and I will preach before them'. . . . So Abgar commanded his citizens to assemble in the morning and to hear the preaching of Thaddaeus, and after this he ordered him to be given gold and plate. But he did not receive it, saying, 'If we have left our own things, how shall we take those of others?' These things were done in the 340th year.

The extract from Eusebius has been given at length, because it received wide dissemination in the then civilized world. Upon the story of the evangelization of Edessa rests largely the claim of the city to pre-eminence in Christendom. Yet the authenticity of the story is doubtful; it may be regarded, indeed, as one of the most successful pious frauds of antiquity.

The central feature of the story is, of course, the correspondence with Jesus—and particularly the letter of Jesus himself, for the letter of Abgar may have been composed subsequently in order to provide the background for the letter of Jesus. The appearance very shortly after their death of 'authoritative' documents ascribed to holy personages is a well-known phenomenon in the Near East and elsewhere; in this way writings were ascribed posthumously to, for example, Muḥammad. This letter of Jesus cannot, however, have been written by him, nor is it to be assigned to the years immediately following his death. First, the earliest mention of the incident is in the time of Eusebius, but the conversion to Christianity of an important monarch at this early period would not have been ignored by Christian writers for close on 300 years. Secondly, Edessa was, from, at any rate, the third century, under the ecclesiastical jurisdiction of Antioch, but her Christian community is unlikely to have accepted this subordinate role had her ruler and the majority of her citizens adopted Christianity shortly after the crucifixion.[1]

The account of the correspondence between Abgar and Jesus and the rest of the Abgar episode arose, it is clear from Eusebius, in the Syriac-speaking region east of the Euphrates. How far does it represent the probable course of events? In particular, did Edessa receive Christianity from Palestine in the south-west, or from the East?

At the beginning of the Christian era Edessa lay in the Parthian, not the Roman, sphere of interest, and its people spoke Syriac not Greek. St. Thomas, it may be assumed, is introduced into the Abgar narratives because it was to him that Jesus declared, '. . . Blessed are they that have not seen, and yet have believed',[2] and this feature is central to the story of Abgar. But it is Parthia and the region to the east of Parthia of which Thomas was the evangelist; and nowhere in the earlier versions of the proselytization of Edessa is it claimed that St. Thomas himself came to the city.

Now it seems likely that there were three stages in the evolution of the identity of the evangelist to whom is ascribed the conversion of Edessa to Christianity. The Addai whom Syriac-speaking Edessans regarded as their Apostle may well have been an historical personage. A missionary of this name is held—and there is no reason to gainsay the view that this account has a basis of fact—to have brought Christianity to Adiabene at the end of the first, or early in the second, century.[3] He may have introduced it to Edessa. Relations between Edessa and Adiabene were of the closest. Nor should we overlook the important bond of language, for Syriac was the speech of both Adiabene and Edessa.

Addai, however, was unknown to the Greek church. His identification with Thaddaeus, one of the Twelve Apostles—though Eusebius, perhaps by way of compromise, calls him one of the Seventy—was easy enough. The

---

[1] In the translation from Greek into Syriac of the *Apocryphal Acts of the Apostles*, St. John is said to have declared, 'Let the nations of the earth hear that the city of Ephesus was the first to receive thy Gospel before all cities and became a second sister to Edessa of the Parthians' (cf. p. 31). This claim for the priority of Edessa cannot, however, be older than the fourth century.   [2] John 20 : 29.

[3] The legend is widely held in the Eastern Church. It is repeated in the chronicle attributed to Meshiḥazekha, written perhaps in 550–69 (but the authenticity of this work is doubtful; see Peeters, *Anal. Boll.* xliii, 1925, 261 ff. and most recently J.-M. Fiey, *L'Orient syrien* xii, 1967, 265 ff.). Sozomen attributes to Edessans and Armenians the introduction of Christianity to Persia. Late narratives purporting to relate the conversion to Christianity of Nisibis and the territories of the East by Mari and other disciples of Addai (for example, the *Acts of Saint Mari*) are a farrago of legend. East Syrian writers generally regard Addai as the founder of the Church of eastern Mesopotamia; he is said to have been the disciple of a certain Mari.

Thaddaeus of Matt. 10 : 3[1] and Mark 3 : 18 is called Judas brother of James in Luke 6 : 16 and Acts 1 : 13 (cf. John 14 : 22); he is probably the brother of James, author of the Epistle of Judas and brother of Jesus. The name Judas was readily associated with Addai, of which, indeed, it may be a cognate form.

The use of the name Judas also assisted the introduction into this complex of legends of the more famous personality of St. Thomas. The Semitic name Thomas denotes 'twin', and has special significance for the brother relationship already connected with Thaddaeus–Judas. It was, as we have noted, Thomas who preached to the Parthians, Medes, and other peoples of the East—as Addai preached to the people of Adiabene. The *Acts of Thomas* describe the mission and martyrdom of the Apostle; they were composed probably in Syriac, possibly at Edessa itself, at the end of the third century. Here the Apostle is regularly called Judas Thomas, just as Eusebius writes of 'Judas who was also Thomas' as having dispatched the mission of Thaddaeus. The association of Thomas with Thaddaeus-Addai integrated the evangelization of Edessa within the direct apostolic tradition.

We may seek to assign approximate dates to this course of development. At the time of the visit of Egeria to Edessa, Saint Thomas was himself regarded as the evangelist of the city; the abbess makes no mention of Addai or Thaddaeus. This was probably in the middle of the fifth century. A copy of the letter of Jesus found at Kırk Mağara near Urfa belongs to an earlier stage, for it refers to 'Thaddaeus that is Thomas'. On epigraphic grounds this inscription is to be ascribed to the fifth century, but it may be older.[2] The Addai–Thaddaeus–Thomas nexus may be taken back yet further, to the first half of the fourth century at the latest. It can scarcely be coincidence that in the account of the spread of Manichaeism at that time, two of Mani's assistants are named Addai and Thomas. Addai the Manichaean proselytized in the region east of the Tigris, where the Christian Addai laboured for his faith;[3] Thomas was possibly the companion of his master Mani when he carried out an evangelizing mission in India, as the Apostle Thomas had done for the Church. This is no doubt the reflection of the activities of Christian evangelists.

The role of King Abgar is equally central in the story of the introduction of Christianity to Edessa. The tradition of the recognition of Jesus by eastern potentates was early; and though Abgar was not one of the three magi who paid homage to the new-born Messiah,[4] he at least confessed, it is claimed, the divinity of Jesus before the crucifixion and paid homage to him.

---

[1] 'Lebbaeus whose surname was Thaddaeus'.
[2] See p. 75 below.
[3] It is interesting to observe that Theodore bar Koni states that the sect of the Mandaeans was founded by a beggar called Ado who was born in Adiabene but settled in Mesene. The founder of Manichaeism is also said to have been brought up in Mesene; see on Spasinou Charax, p. 67 below.

[4] A late Syriac legend relates, however, that the three Wise men from the East came to Edessa.

But when we examine the identity of the Abgar of the narrative of Eusebius, we find that here too there has been confusion of names. Eusebius accepts the traditional view that the royal protagonist of Christianity at Edessa was Abgar Ukkama, the Black, who reigned in the lifetime of Jesus. The facts suggest otherwise. Again we must look to the East for the solution of the problem.

The romantic story of the royal house of Adiabene was celebrated at Jerusalem and left a deep impression on the contemporaries of Jesus. Josephus relates that the king of Adiabene, who had married his sister Helena, sent his favourite son Ezad to stay with Abennerigos, king of Spasinou Charax at the head of the Persian Gulf.[1] The young prince won the affection of his host, who gave him in marriage his daughter Samachos[2] and also appointed him governor of one of his provinces. On the death of his father, Ezad returned home to ascend the throne of Adiabene; we are told that he then conveyed some of his relatives as hostages to Emperor Claudius.[3]

While Ezad was at Spasinou Charax, Josephus continues, a Jewish merchant named Ananias converted to Judaism some women in the king's harem and then also Ezad himself. He accompanied Ezad when the latter returned to take over the government of Adiabene; they found that the queen mother, Helena, had also, apparently independently, adopted Judaism. Ezad, despite some dissuasion on the part of Helena and Ananias, allowed himself to be circumcised. He prospered, and the king of Parthia accorded him rule over Nisibis, and certain privileges usually reserved for Parthian rulers. The nobles of Adiabene were hostile to the Judaism of Ezad, but in vain. An Arab king Abias, whom they encouraged to oppose Ezad was defeated; the king of Parthia, Walagash (Vologases I), proposed to attack Ezad, but was diverted by an invasion from the East. Shortly afterwards, Ezad died. Both he and his mother Helena, who survived only a little longer, were buried at Jerusalem. There their piety and generosity had won great renown.

Of the historicity of the events related by Josephus there need be no doubt. Ezad ascended the throne of Adiabene in A.D. 36. He was therefore a contemporary of Abgar Ukkama of Edessa.

There are remarkable parallels between the history of Spasinou Charax and that of Edessa. Spasinou Charax was built by Alexander, but, like Edessa, refounded by Antiochus IV under the name of Antioch. Shortly before 129 B.C., it became the seat of an Arab dynasty, of which the first ruler was Hyspaosines or Spasines, exactly at the time of the emergence to power of the Aryu dynasty at Edessa. At Spasinou Charax, as at Edessa,

---

[1] This king is probably to be identified with the Abinergaos of a coin of Spasinou Charax, dated A.D. 10, and Adin[e]rglos of a coin of A.D. 22. His Semitic name was evidently 'Abe[d]nergal.

[2] The name appears in various forms: Σαμάχως, σαμαχός, σαμμαχώ, Συμαχώ, etc.

[3] This should be Tiberius; see p. 69 below.

Aramaic was freely employed; indeed, both kingdoms had Aramaic legends on their coinage after the destruction of Seleucia in A.D. 164.[1] The names of some of the kings of Spasinou Charax indicate that they worshipped planets (Nergal and Bel), as did the kings of Edessa.[2] The name, too, of the daughter of the king of Spasinou Charax was probably not Greek but Aramaic; *sumaqa* means red, and may have been derived from the natural colouring of the region.[3] In fact, an Abgar of Edessa, who reigned apparently from 26–23 B.C., bore the nickname of *sumaqa*. Perhaps we should note that the Abgar of the Syriac Addai–Abgar legend also received as his nickname a colour, *ukkama*, black, which has some resemblance to *sumaqa*.

Spasinou Charax, in Semitic, Karkha deMaishan, was capital of the kingdom of Mesene. At the period with which we are dealing, it was one of the main ports to which ships brought the products of India and the Far East. From Mesene the goods were transported up the Euphrates to Babylon, the route taken by Apollonius of Tyana on his return from India in about A.D. 47; alternatively they were carried up the Tigris and thence to Adiabene in the East, and to Nisibis and Edessa in the West. In the 'Hymn of the Soul' of the *Acts of Thomas*, the prince declares, 'I quitted the East and went down. . . . I passed through the borders of Maishan (Mesene), the meeting place of the merchants of the East, and I reached the land of Babylonia.' The prince's route on his return to the East was the same; he passed Babylon on the left and came 'to the great Maishan, to the haven of merchants which sits on the shore of the sea'.[4] The 'Hymn of the Soul', probably composed originally in Syriac, certainly antedates the main text of the *Acts of Thomas* and may go back to the first century A.D.

The story of religious development in Adiabene and that of Edessa seems to be almost inextricably interwoven. The Jewish merchant of Spasinou Charax, Ananias, who converted Ezad, has the same name as Abgar's emissary to Jesus, Ananias—in Syriac, Ḥannan. Merchants played a part also in the proselytization of Edessa; Addai stayed at the house of the, presumably Jewish, merchant, Tobias.[5] And sympathizers to Christianity came, we are told, to Edessa in the guise of merchants to witness the acts of Addai and then to return home to spread the faith in 'their own country of the Assyrians', that is, Adiabene.[6] The piety of Queen Helena of Adiabene is also reflected in the Edessan story. She came to be confused with Helena, the mother of Constantine the Great, who found the Cross at Jerusalem. This event is

---

[1] Aramaic lettering appears on coins of Spasinou Charax for the first time after 78–77 B.C.; but during the interval between that date and the fall of Seleucia most of the coinage has Greek legends.

[2] Abinergaos (p. 67 above) and Attambelos.

[3] 60–70 kilometres from the site of Spasinou

Charax is Muḥammera, the red [place].

[4] There was also direct communication between Mesene and Palmyra, as we know from Palmyrene inscriptions dated between A.D. 8 and about 163, and another of 193.

[5] See p. 63 above.

[6] See p. 79 below.

related by Addai, in the Syriac account of the proselytization of Edessa, although there the queen has the name of Protonice, wife (it is supposed) of Emperor Claudius.[1] Josephus relates that Ezad of Adiabene left some of his family as hostages with Claudius. But the emperor should rather be Tiberius, who was alive at this time; in the histories of both Adiabene and Edessa the intrusion of the name of Claudius seems to require a common explanation.[2] The name of the Arab Abias, who opposed Ezad, may be echoed in the odd title, 'patrician (Syriac, *abaya*) of Edessa' which was given to the Arab 'rescued by the Hebrew [woman], Kuthbi'.[3] And, finally, the reluctance of Helena to countenance the circumcision of Ezad may be reflected in the Edessan legend that Abgar prohibited cultic castration.[4]

The account, then, of Jewish activity at Spasinou Charax and Adiabene has been converted into the story of Christian activity at Edessa. In Adiabene Christianity spread rapidly and at an early date, if we may credit our sources. Tatian, who had already composed the Syriac harmonized version of the Diatessaron in the West, returned to 'Assyria' (that is, no doubt, Adiabene) as a professing Christian in A.D. 172. The evangelist of both Edessa and Adiabene is called Addai. In Adiabene, as at Edessa, Christian missionaries appear to have relied on the friendship of the Jews. We have seen that at Edessa there was an important Jewish community,[5] while at least one text indicates a tradition that the early Christian bishops of Adiabene carried Jewish names.

It seems likely that Christianity, like both the most celebrated theologians of Edessa in the first centuries, Bardaiṣan and St. Ephraim, originated in the East. We would expect it to have been conveyed along the high road through Nisibis.

Early evidence of Christianity at Nisibis is provided by the Greek grave inscription of Abercius. He is almost certainly to be regarded as a Christian of Hieropolis in Asia Minor who visited, in the latter half of the second century, the communities of his co-religionists. In the inscription we read: 'I saw the Syrian plain, and all the cities—[even] Nisibis, having crossed the Euphrates. Everywhere I found people with whom to speak'. Eusebius refers to a synod in Osrhoene (in another document this is expanded to, 'Edessa and the region of Adiabene') and 'the cities there', which was convened as early as about 197 to express its view on the date of Easter. The account may be dismissed as spurious; but it need not be beyond credibility. Bardaiṣan was an acknowledged Christian at Edessa in the second century; and there was a church there in 201.

Nor, indeed, should we reject as wholly apocryphal the account of the

---

[1] See pp. 77 f. below.
[2] See p. 73 below.
[3] See p. 43 above.
[4] See p. 56 above.
[5] See p. 42 above.

conversion of King Abgar to Christianity; the legend may well have a sub-stratum of fact. It no doubt arose while the monarchy was still popular at Edessa. Scholars have maintained, with good reason, that the king in whose reign Christianity made a notable advance in Edessa was not Abgar Ukkama, but his namesake Abgar the Great, whose long reign spanned the latter half of the second, and the beginning of the third centuries. Both were sons of Ma'nu. Abgar Ukkama's wife is said to be Shalmath daughter of Mihrdad (Meherdates);[1] the wife of Abgar the Great may also have been a Shalmath, the daughter of Ma'nu whose statue stood on the column of the Citadel mount.[2] In the legend the king of 'the Assyrians' (that is, of Adiabene) at the time of Abgar Ukkama is called not Ezad (as in Josephus) but Narsai. And in fact the king of Adiabene at the time of Abgar the Great was called Narseh; he was drowned in the Great Zab by the Parthians for his pro-Roman sympathies.[3]

Abgar the Great may have been well disposed towards the Christians; he need not have actually adopted the new religion. His contemporary Julius Africanus calls him a 'holy man'; elsewhere he is called 'most pious and learned', but he is not termed a Christian. The coins of Edessa carry the portrait of this Abgar—a bearded head, wearing with assurance and dignity the great tiara and diadem of his office.[4] He was, we are told, friendly with Bardaiṣan, the philosopher-poet of Edessa, and he must have been a man of culture. He was a wise administrator, concerned with the welfare of his subjects. It was he who outlawed the practice of castration at Edessa—but this need not have been, as our source suggests, under the influence of Christianity. For Abgar was also a man of the world. He had, no doubt, like Bardaiṣan, met ambassadors from India, and he visited Rome towards the end of his life.[5] We should not forget that even the idealized Abgar of the Addai legend did not submit altogether to the principles of Christianity, for tradition has it that the great altar in his palace remained; there, like some kings of Israel, he continued to worship the planets in the privacy of his own courtyards. Abgar the Great is likely to have favoured Christianity for reasons of state. He was too shrewd a statesman not to have foreseen the growing threat to the independence of Edessa. Rome could no longer control this region from afar through puppet princes. The Parthians menaced her com-munications with the East, and she could keep the roads open only by maintaining garrisons to the east of the Euphrates herself. In these circum-stances Abgar's friendship for the Christians was sound policy. It secured

---

[1] See pp. 78 f. This may be a reminiscence of the Parthian prince who visited Edessa at that time; p. 12 above.

[2] See p. 19 above.

[3] Procopius relates that a 'toparch' Abgar visited Rome in the reign of Augustus; he is confusing Abgar Ukkama with Abgar the Great, p. 14 above.

[4] Pl. 28b (i).

[5] There is no foundation for the hypothesis of Harnack that Abgar was in direct touch with Eleutherius, Bishop of Rome from 174 to 189.

for him the sympathy of an important group of his subjects; at the same time it strengthened his position through the respect for authority and order, which was an inherent quality of the Christian community.

When this has been said, however, an explanation is still required for the choice of Edessa as the scene of the Christian acts of healing which are a central feature of the Abgar–Addai story.[1] Disease was the source of constant anxiety in the ancient Near East, the ability to cure disease was a divine gift. From the very inception of the Church, Christians were taught to regard the care of the sick as work of prime importance, and the Syrian Christians devoted much of their energies to medicine. Already in 410, if not earlier, the churches and monasteries of eastern Mesopotamia had infirmaries attached to them, and the same was true of western Mesopotamia. At the hospital at Nisibis were facilities for the training of students as at the famous Christian medical college of Beth Lapaṭ.[2] Physicians at the Persian court were Christian, and Christians continued to hold this position at the court of the Caliphs. In large degree, no doubt, the eminence of Mesopotamian Christians in medicine derived from their role as the transmitters of Greek civilization, and particularly of Greek science, to the East. Not only Christian speakers of Syriac, but also the pagans of Harran and the vicinity were celebrated for their knowledge of the natural sciences. At Edessa in the second century Bardaiṣan took special interest in scientific matters. So too did St. Ephraim; and medicine in particular is a favourite theme in his poetry.[3] It is related that, towards the end of his life, he administered the works set up by Edessans for the relief of the poor and sick.[4] A leper hospital was established by Bishop Nona near the Gate of Beth Shemesh in the middle of the fifth century. Indeed, the attention lavished by the people of Edessa on their less fortunate fellow-citizens attracted villagers to the city; during a plague even the Byzantine soldiery maintained an infirmary for the sick and dying. So highly were physicians accounted that one of their number was entrusted by Byzantium with the mission of persuading Khusraw to spare Edessa in 544.[5]

There was good reason for the preoccupation of Edessans with healing. We have observed the significant role of running water at the pagan shrines

---

[1] The Syriac *Doc. Add.* lays stress on the powers of Jesus as healer. There he is the 'good physician', while in the Greek version of the story of Addai, in Eusebius, he is the 'good Saviour', p. 62 above.

[2] Weh-Andyok Shahpuhr, later Gunde-Shahpuhr.

[3] Notably in his 'Carmina Nisibena'.

[4] It may be significant that legend recounts a visit by St. Ephraim to St. Basil of Caesarea.

The latter set up hospices for the poor. One is described by Gregory of Nazianzus as a vast edifice with rooms for the sick, a hospital, and a sanatorium; it was intended, like those of Edessa, principally for lepers and for travellers who sought asylum. Other places, notably Ephesus, Daphnae near Antioch, and cities in Egypt, had similar institutions, mostly with resident physicians and cooks.

[5] See pp. 138, 148 below.

with which ancient Edessa had association: the well near Harran, the spring of Ephca at Palmyra, the fountains, the fish-pools, and also a celebrated well at Hierapolis.[1] So too at Edessa there were the two fish-pools each fed by a fountain. More important was the well outside the south wall of the city, now the Bir Eyüp,[2] the well of Job, whose healing qualities are well attested. It was near by that were built the shrines of Saints Cosmas and Damian, the physician-martyrs, and an infirmary and hospice. Not far away was the leper hospital of Bishop Nona to which reference has been made. It may be significant too that it was in the south of the city that the church of Michael the Archangel stood, and possibly also another dedicated to St. Dometius, both popularly associated with healing. Zangi, conqueror of Edessa in 1164, bathed in the waters of Bir Eyüp to cure his gout. In the twelfth century, the well was called the 'well of those who suffer from elephantiasis'.[3] So popular were its supernatural qualities that it was in the open country behind the well that, in the thirteenth century, Christians of all denominations assembled, when the city was affected by drought, and for four days made supplication for rain. To the present day the sick pass the night at the well, particularly those suffering from skin ailments,[4] and this quarter of Urfa is called the Eyüp Mahallesi, the quarter of Job.

It is not fortuitous, then, that 'Abdu bar 'Abdu, the deputy of Abgar in the Acts of Addai, is said to have been cured of gout by the Apostle. What was Abgar's 'incurable disease' is not related in the early versions of the legend. Procopius in the sixth century maintains that the king, like his deputy, suffered from gout. At a later date, certainly in the ninth century, it was held that he was afflicted with leprosy, and that he was called the Black by way of euphemism. Perhaps, on the other hand, he had been smitten by blindness, and received his epithet for that reason.[5] It will be recalled that Abgar saw a vision on the face of Addai, to the surprise of his courtiers to whom the miracle was not vouchsafed.[6] A story is told of a deacon who was healed

---

[1] See p. 48 above.

[2] Did this originally carry the name of Jacob? Compare Julius Africanus, *Chronography*, 'the shepherd tent of Jacob at Edessa, which had survived to the times of the Roman Emperor Antoninus, was destroyed by fire.' Job was associated with healing by the waters of a spring, cf. the well at the mosque of Eyüp at Constantinople, and particularly Koran, xxi, 83 f.; xxxviii, 41 ff. Pl. 38.

[3] The form of leprosy called elephantiasis Graecorum is termed in Syriac, *aryana*, leonine. The latter term is scarcely to be connected with the name of Aryu, the founder of the dynasty of Edessa.

[4] See Badger, *Nestorians*, 326. This was confirmed by me recently at Urfa. Pococke,

who visited Urfa in the eighteenth century, reported that its waters would heal 'all foul and scrophulous disorders'. In the middle of the seventeenth century, Thévenot, an acute observer, noted that men and women bathed at the well and that its waters healed leprosy.

[5] Syriac, *ukkama*, black, may be related to *kmh* which is used of both blindness and blackness, opposed to *hwr* which is employed of both sight and whiteness. A visitor at Urfa in 1838 and 1839 records the popular belief there that anyone who eats fish from the pool of Abraham will be smitten by blindness.

[6] This is curiously echoed in the tenth century. When the portrait of Jesus arrived at Constantinople from Edessa in 944, the sons of the usurper Romanus Lecapenus were unable

of eye-ache by the use of water at the shrine of St. John at Edessa.[1] Probably, however, Abgar's ailment was lameness, a concomitant of gout. 'Lame' may be the meaning of the name Abgar, and here too may be the explanation, by popular etymology, of the frequent appearance of the Emperor Claudius in the Abgar tradition.[2] There is a curious anecdote about the healing of a lame person, by contact with the sacred kerchief on which were imprinted the features of Jesus, one mile from Edessa—the distance at which stands Bir Eyüp outside the walls.[3] Elsewhere we read that Abgar bathed in a well called Kerassa in the Greek text; this may be a corrupted form of the Syriac *karoza*, preacher, used possibly of Addai. Certainly the emphasis on baptism in Christian practice may have made bathing in the waters a popular activity.

The 'letter of Jesus' was, we have suggested, not authentic; and it was declared apocryphal in a decree of Pope Gelasius in 494. Ephraim of Edessa seems to allude to it only in the most obscure terms, and only in his *Testament*:

Blessed is the town in which thou dwellest, Edessa, mother of the wise; by the living mouth of the Son hath it been blest by the hand of his disciple. That blessing will dwell in it until the holy one revealeth himself.

Nevertheless, the legend of the correspondence between Abgar and Jesus became famous throughout Christendom. In the course of time it received various accretions. Probably the earliest was a sentence attached to the 'letter of Jesus'; 'Your city shall be blessed and no enemy shall ever be master of it'.[4] The sentence does not appear in the text of Eusebius which, it will be remembered, is said to be derived from the Edessan archives of the time of the monarchy. Nor is it directly mentioned by St. Ephraim. It is, on the other hand, referred to in a letter to St. Augustine, dated 429. It was known also to Jacob, Bishop of Serug near Edessa (451–521), and in the chronicle of his contemporary, 'Joshua the Stylite'; the latter considers its effectiveness proved by the ignominious withdrawal of the Persian king Kawad from the siege of Edessa in 503.

For some time the additional sentence was not known in the West. We learn this from the Latin journal of the Aquitanian abbess Egeria; the date of her visit to Edessa is unfortunately uncertain, but it may be assigned to

to distinguish the features of Jesus on the kerchief; but, we are told, the legitimate claimant to the throne, Constantine Porphyrogenitus, saw them clearly.

[1] Nau, *PO* viii, 1912, 157; unfortunately the text cannot be dated. It may be observed that Bishop Nona built a shrine to St. John the Baptist as well as the infirmaries of Saints Cosmas and Damian; p. 184 below.

[2] Cf. Latin, *claudus*, Syriac *bgr* denotes 'close', like Latin *claudo*.

[3] Legend relates also that the Persian king Khusraw sent to Edessa for the portrait of Jesus in order to heal his daughter of a demon. The Edessans conveyed a copy of the portrait to Persia; the demon fled before it, and the king returned it to Edessa with gifts.

[4] *Doc. Add.* adds, 'again'.

the middle of the fifth century. The bishop of Edessa, she tells us, related to her that the city was besieged by the Persians a short time after Abgar (she means the Abgar Ukkama of the legend) had received the 'letter of Jesus'. The king took the letter, and

with all his army prayed in public. Then he said, 'Lord Jesus, you promised us that no enemy will enter yonder city; but behold the Persians are attacking us'. When he said this, holding that letter in his raised hand, suddenly such thick darkness appeared outside the city

that the Persians could not approach the walls. They sought to divert the water supply—which, at that time, the bishop implausibly maintained, was derived from the Citadel mount; straightway springs of water appeared inside the city. The Persians withdrew in shame. Whenever, continued the bishop, Persian forces appeared before Edessa, the letter of Jesus was produced and read, and the enemy was repelled.

The bishop took Egeria to the gate through which, it was held, the letter of Jesus was brought to Edessa. There he prayed, recited the letter and prayed again. He told her that from the day that the letter was brought to Edessa 'until the present day no unclean person and no one in sadness passes through that gate, and no dead body is taken out through that gate.' Finally Egeria took from the bishop a copy of the 'Abgar–Jesus correspondence', for, she remarks, 'it seemed more fitting to take it there from him because it appears that less has reached us at home, for indeed what I have received here is at greater length.' In western Europe at that time, then, the 'letter of Jesus' probably did not contain the sentence with the promise to Edessa of immunity from capture.

The sentence was evidently missing also from the letter with which the readers of Procopius, in the mid-sixth century, were familiar. In his account of the Abgar–Jesus correspondence he writes:

[Jesus] added also that never would the city be liable to capture by the barbarians. The final portion of the letter was entirely unknown to those who wrote the history of that time, for they did not even make mention of it anywhere; but the men of Edessa say that they found it with the letter, so that they have even caused the letter to be inscribed in this form on the gates of the city instead of any other defence.

Procopius doubts the efficacy of the promise; he adds, with characteristic cynicism, 'The thought has occurred to me that if Christ did not write this thing as it has been told, nevertheless, since men have come to believe in it, he wishes to keep the city uncaptured for this reason, that he might never give them cause for error.'

Belief in the impregnability of Edessa arose, as we have remarked, after the time of St. Ephraim, but probably not long afterwards. With the disastrous defeat of Julian in 363, Mesopotamia was open to the Persians. The cession of Nisibis to the enemy left Edessa in the front line as one of the principal bulwarks of the eastern provinces of Byzantium, and it must have appeared a miracle to the Edessans that their city remained free from attack. The thought of Nisibis was probably present in their minds, if we may judge from the bishop's account to Egeria of the miraculous deliverance of Edessa from the Persians. His story is wholly inappropriate to Edessa; its water supply could never have been derived from the Citadel mount, and the springs of water inside the city and the fish-pools were scarcely the outcome of miraculous intervention. But the diversion of waters played an important part in the attack by Shahpuhr II on Nisibis in 350, described vividly by St. Ephraim who was an eye witness of these events, and by Emperor Julian in his panegyric in honour of Constantius.

We may safely ascribe to the end of the fourth century the insertion of the final sentence of the letter. By the fifth century the legend of the correspondence between Abgar and Jesus was popular and widely credited, in spite of its official rejection by Pope Gelasius in 494. The date of the inclusion in the letter of the promise of Jesus to Abgar is confirmed on archaeological grounds. Copies of the letter inscribed in Greek have been found on two stones at Euchaita in northern Anatolia, on a stone at Philippi in Macedonia, and finally on a stone at Kırk Mağara near Edessa itself; none appears to have been discovered in Syriac. The function of the Euchaita inscriptions is uncertain, but the Kırk Mağara inscription was standing by a grave, while that at Philippi was on the city gate. All, significantly enough, contain the sentence about the impregnability of Edessa; all belong to the fifth century, if not earlier.[1] A copy of the correspondence was discovered also at Ephesus on a stone over the door of a house, but this is of later date. The Greek text of the letter of Jesus has been found also written on papyrus, perhaps as an amulet. Here the last sentence takes another form, reminiscent of Jesus as the Light of the World. Texts of the Abgar–Jesus correspondence are frequent in Coptic, and in many forms—on stone, on parchment, on ostraca, and as amulets on papyrus. One text, written by a monk in Upper Egypt, should even be dated, it has been suggested, to the middle of the fourth century. All these copies give both letters of the correspondence, and usually they contain the last sentence of the Greek 'letter of Jesus'. Various forms of the legend, much expanded, are extant in Ethiopic and Arabic. In pre-Norman England the story of Abgar was translated from Latin into Anglo-Saxon at about A.D. 1000 and appears in the local liturgy of the time.[2]

---

[1] One of the inscriptions at Euchaita is badly mutilated; the letter of Abgar is missing, and part only of the letter of Jesus remains. The latter, however, contains the sentence about the impregnability of Edessa. See further von Dobschütz, *Christusbilder*, and Kirsten. The inscription from Kırk Mağara is shown on Pl. 31b.

[2] The story of Abgar reappears elsewhere in the West far from Edessa in, for example, the Passion of St. Eutropus of Saintes; Eutropus, like Ḥannan, visits Jesus at Jerusalem before the crucifixion.

How long before the time of Procopius was the letter of Jesus inscribed on the gate of Edessa? It was not there (as we have seen) in the time of St. Ephraim. Nor can it have been inscribed before 378. The author of the so-called *Romance of Julian* was familiar with the topography of Edessa,[1] and he has a curious account of a blessing sent to the city by Constantine the Great, but removed by the Arian Emperor Valens who died in that year. He does not mention the letter on the gate. The inscription was not on the wall during the visit of Egeria, probably in the middle of the fifth century. We may therefore assign its appearance in writing on the city gate to the second half of the fifth century.

The 'letter of Jesus' had acquired the function of a palladium to protect the city of Edessa from her enemies. In time a rival claimant appeared, the portrait of Jesus. In the Syriac *Doctrine of Addai* which cannot have been composed, at least in its present form, before about 400, (though its contents may, in fact, be earlier) we are told that two 'chiefs and honoured men' of the court, together with Ḥannan, Abgar's secretary, visited the Roman governor in Syria. Thence they went to Jerusalem. Ḥannan saw Jesus and wrote down his Acts; on returning to Edessa he related to Abgar all that he had witnessed. Abgar sent him back to Jerusalem with a letter to Jesus couched in language closely resembling that of the letter in Eusebius. The account of this second journey of Ḥannan to Jerusalem has an artificial ring. He left Edessa on 14 Adar (the day of the Jewish festival of Purim, one month before the Passover), and found Jesus at Jerusalem on Wednesday 12 Nisan (three days before the Passover) at the house of Gamaliel the High Priest.[2] Jesus made a reply to the letter of Abgar—orally, not in writing. Ḥannan, however, was also the royal painter, and

he took and painted a portrait of Jesus in choice paints, and brought it with him to his lord king Abgar. And when king Abgar saw that portrait he received it with great joy and placed it with great honour in one of the rooms of his palace. And Ḥannan the secretary[3] related to him all that he had heard from Jesus, his words being set down in writing.

The text goes on to relate the subsequent arrival at Edessa of Addai, his works of healing, and the evangelization of the city with the approval of Abgar.[4]

In the *Doctrine of Addai*, that is, in the early fifth century, the portrait has a comparatively minor role. But an analysis of later allusions to the portrait

[1] The Jews of Edessa, alleges the author of the *Romance*, offered to open to Julian the South gate of the city—the appropriate gate, as he was on his way to Harran; and Jovian, on his return from Persia, entered Edessa, it is claimed, through the East gate.

[2] The improbability of Ḥannan's arrival at Jerusalem just before the Crucifixion requires no comment. For the interval of three days see p. 79 below on the death of Addai; on the significance of this period of time see the present writer's *The Hebrew Passover*, 1963, 144. The implicit reference to Purim may suggest Jewish influence in this narrative.

[3] Syriac, *tabulara*, see p. 20 above.

[4] See pp. 78 f. below.

shows that gradually it increased in sanctity. In the earliest version, it was the work of the painter Ḥannan, in later accounts it could be painted only with the assistance of Jesus, finally it was wholly the work of Jesus himself. It had become now the impression of the features of Jesus which he had himself left on a kerchief, and it was divine—'not the work of [mortal] hands', as it was termed, a phrase that may occur for the first time in 569. The abortive siege of Edessa by Khusraw I Anosharwan in 544 is described factually by Procopius, writing some two years later; he ascribes the success of the defenders to their courage and resourcefulness. But the chronicler Evagrius, writing fifty years after Procopius, holds that the discomfiture of the Persians was the work of the sacred portrait of Jesus. When all seemed lost, the bishop was instructed in a vision, to discover the portrait hidden between some tiles in the city wall. The Edessans sprinkled water on the portrait and cast the water towards the enemy; his siege-works were consumed by fire. In certain circles the portrait had apparently replaced the letter as the palladium of Edessa.

Both letter and portrait existed side by side. We shall see that from the reign of Justinian there was a Melkite (Chalcedonian) community at Edessa, maintained with Byzantine support, as well as the Jacobite (Monophysite) community; each had its own bishop. The portrait may well have been the special property of the Melkite community, while the letter of Jesus was prized by the Jacobite community, who objected to images of Jesus, at any rate in the fifth and sixth centuries. We have observed that sacred writing was a Semitic concept;[1] writing was highly esteemed by the Edessans, of whom the majority belonged to the Jacobite congregation. But for western Syria and Byzantium, portraiture by painting or sculpture was a more familiar medium. The portrait of Jesus at Camuliana existed already at the end of the fourth century, and was brought to Constantinople in 574.[2] Western influences may underlie the devotion paid to the Edessan portrait of Jesus. Significantly, there is confusion between the sacred kerchief of Edessa in the East and the veil of Veronica or Berenice of Paneas in Palestine in the West. The legends of Paneas and Edessa are curiously interwoven. The evangelist Addai is said to have been born at Paneas—or at Edessa. The *Doctrine of Addai* recounts the finding of the Cross at Jerusalem by the wife of the Emperor Claudius, called Protonice; this is possibly a variant of the name Berenice.[3] Berenice of Paneas dedicated a statue of Jesus as a thanksgiving offering on being healed from sickness, and a Greek author of the early fifth century alleges that she was princess of Edessa. And, finally, when both

[1] See p. 43 above.

[2] This portrait, together with a copy from Melitene were both regarded as 'not the work of [mortal] hands'; see further von Dobschütz, *Christusbilder*, and A. Grabar, *Martyrium*, ii, 343 ff. See on the cult of images, E. Kitzinger, *Dumbarton Oaks Papers* viii, 1954, 83.

[3] For a different explanation of the name, see p. 51 above.

the portrait and the letter of Jesus, or at least copies of the portrait and the letter, were transported from Edessa to Constantinople in 944, the Greek community there received the former, we are told, with jubilation and adoration; the latter was largely neglected.[1]

In time 'true' copies of the portrait and the letter multiplied at Edessa with the proliferation of sects. The Jacobites, as well as the Melkites, claimed to have the genuine portrait; a later report holds that there were three portraits in the city, the third presumably belonging to the Nestorians. Even a portrait of Jesus found, significantly enough, at Hierapolis (Mabbog) was given divine sanction. A legend was recounted which declared that the original portrait was deposited there by the messengers conveying it from Jerusalem to Edessa; it then left its imprint on the tiles, as on the tiles in the city wall at Edessa in the account of Evagrius. So too with the letter. It was taken, as we have remarked, to Constantinople in 944. But in 1032 another 'genuine' letter of Jesus was dispatched to the capital by the general George Maniaces. And even then the people of Edessa still maintained that the original letter remained safely in their hands.

The Syriac *Doctrine of Addai*, it has been shown, relates how Ḥannan, the king's secretary, brought the portrait of Jesus to Edessa. This document then gives an account, perhaps highly redacted, but nevertheless not without a basis of fact, of the evangelization of Edessa. It is a somewhat lengthier version than that of Eusebius; since it reflects local colouring it merits brief summary here.

Addai, introduced to the court by his host Tobias,[2] preached before the king and his mother Augustina, his wife Shalmath, daughter of Mihrdad (Meherdates), and his nobles. He recounted the works of Jesus and expounded the tenets of Christianity. He related, too, the finding of the Cross at Jerusalem by Protonice, wife of the Emperor Claudius, and how with it Protonice's daughter was restored to life. Abgar and all his court 'glorified God and made their confession in Christ'.

Abgar instructed 'Abdu to proclaim by herald to the whole city that they should attend at the 'place which is called Beth Tabara, the wide space of the house of 'Awida son of 'Abednaḥad', to hear the doctrine of Addai the Apostle. All the city

assembled, men and women, as the king had commanded . . . chiefs and freemen of the king and commanders and husbandmen,[3] all of them, and artisans who [worked with their] hands, and Jews and pagans who were in this town, and strangers from the region

---

[1] Is it significant that the Melkite historian Agapius (Maḥbub) of Mabbog (Hierapolis), who wrote in the tenth century—probably before 944—mentions the portrait as being kept at Edessa but omits mention of the letter?

[2] That Tobias, or his father, came from Palestine is mentioned in the Syriac text, but not by Eusebius.

[3] The Syriac term *pallaḥe*, could also denote 'workmen', possibly 'soldiers', see p. 118 below.

of Ṣoba[1] and from Harran, and the rest of the inhabitants of all this region of Mesopotamia.

Addai preached again, declaring that he was not 'a physician of medicines
and roots . . . but a disciple of Jesus Christ'. He refuted the worship of the
planets and of idols, he glorified Jesus and urged his hearers to acknowledge
him also. The city, led by Abgar, his son Maʿnu, and his mother and wife,
accepted the new faith. The king encouraged Addai to build a church, and
gave him generous gifts so that Addai's word 'should be of authority and
prevail in all this town'. In a scene of enthusiasm

the chief priests of this town, . . . ran and threw down the altars on which they sacrificed
before Nabu and Bel their gods, except the great altar in the midst of the town. . . . And
Addai . . . baptized them . . ., and those who used to worship stones and stocks sat at his
feet, . . . even Jews conversant with the Law and the Prophets . . . who sold soft [stuffs]—
they too were persuaded and made the Christian confession.

Aggai 'who made the silken [garments] and tiaras of the king', and Paluṭ,
and Barshelama (who is also called ʿAbshelama) and Barsamya

ministered with [Addai] in the church which he had built. . . . A large multitude of
people assembled day by day and came to the prayers of the service and to [the reading
of] the Old Testament and the New [Testament] of the Diatessaron.[2] They also believed in the resurrection of the dead. . . . They kept also the festivals of the Church at
their proper season. . . . Moreover, in the places round about the city, churches were
built and many received from [Addai] the hand of priesthood. So the people of the East
also, in the guise of merchants, passed over into the territory of the Romans in order to see
the signs which Addai did. And those who became disciples received from him the hand
of priesthood, and in their own country of the Assyrians they found disciples, and made
houses of prayer there in secret from fear of those who worshipped fire and adored water.

Narseh, 'king of the Assyrians', enquired of Abgar about the deeds of Addai,
and 'was astonished and marvelled'.[3]

Finally Addai

was seized with that disease of which he departed from the world. And he called for
Aggai . . . and made him administrator and ruler in his own place. And Paluṭ who was a
deacon he made presbyter, and ʿAbshelama[4] who was a scribe he made deacon.

He admonished them concerning their conduct. Three days later, on 14 Iyar,
Addai died.

And the whole city was in great mourning and bitter distress on account of him. Nor
was it only the Christians who grieved over him, but the Jews also and the pagans who

[1] Nisibis.

[2] This rendering is based on an emendation
of the Syriac text, involving a very small
change (s for wn). The passage may, however,
be an interpolation; see p. 80 below.

[3] At this point is inserted the account of a
correspondence between Abgar and Emperor
Tiberius; the former requests the Emperor to
avenge on the Jews the death of Jesus, and the
request is carried out to Abgar's satisfaction.
The passage is obviously apocryphal. We have
here the echo of a legend that is included in the
cycle of the Veronica portrait. In it Emperor
Tiberius, falling sick, desired to see the portrait of Jesus, worshipped it and was healed.

[4] That is, Barshelama (above, this page).

were in this same town. But king Abgar grieved over him more than all—he and the grandees of his kingdom. . . . And with great and exceeding honour he conveyed and buried him like one of the grandees when he dies, and he placed him in a great sepulchre of ornamental sculpture[1] in which those of the house of Aryu, the ancestors of king Abgar, were laid. . . . And all the people of the church . . . celebrated the commemoration of his death from year to year.

Our narrator describes the conduct of Aggai and his colleagues as so meritorious that 'even the priests of Nabu and Bel divided the honour with them at all times'. Some years, however,

after the death of king Abgar there arose one of his rebellious sons who was not satisfied with tranquillity, and he sent word to Aggai, as he was sitting in the church, 'Make me a tiara of gold[2] as you made for my fathers of old.' Aggai sent word to him, 'I will not leave the ministry of Christ . . . and make the tiara of evil.' And when he saw that he did not obey him he sent and broke his legs as he was sitting in the church and expounding. And as he was dying he adjured Paluṭ and 'Abshelama, 'Lay me and bury me in this house for whose truth's sake, behold, I am dying. . . .' And there was a great and bitter mourning in all the Church and in all the city, beyond the grief and mourning which was in its community, like the mourning which there had been when the Apostle Addai died.

This narrative was certainly composed long after the events it purports to describe, even if we identify Abgar with King Abgar the Great. The statement that it was necessary for the Christians of 'the country of the Assyrians', presumably Adiabene, to practise their religion in secret seems to imply a date after 226. With the emergence of the Sasanid dynasty at about that time, and the growth and influence of the Zoroastrian priesthood it became impossible for Christian evangelists to work in the Persian empire. That Persians coming from the East to Roman territory should disguise themselves as merchants suggests a still later date. Only with the treaty of Jovian in 363 were the frontiers between Persia and Byzantine Mesopotamia clearly defined; previously they could be crossed with impunity. But the text in its present form cannot be much later than the end of the fourth century or the beginning of the fifth century. The Diatessaron, a harmonized, composite version of the four Gospels, was, our writer maintains, in use at Edessa at this time.[3] The reference may be an interpolation. Nevertheless, the fact that it appears without any words of condemnation is significant; this version of the New Testament was superseded in official use at Edessa by the Separate Gospels before, or at the very latest during, the lifetime of Bishop Rabbula (died 435 or 436).[4]

---

[1] See p. 18 above. The royal tomb may have been in the neighbourhood of Abgar's castle, p. 17 above. Harnack has suggested that Syriac *birtha*, castle, has been corrupted into 'Britannia', in a text of *c.* 500.

[2] See p. 18 above.

[3] Syriac, *Evangelion daMehalleṭe*.

[4] See p. 93 below.

The account of the evangelization of Edessa in the *Doctrine of Addai* compresses into the space of one or two generations events that extended, we may assume, over several. The writer himself, indeed, does not claim that heathenism was uprooted at Edessa. The great pagan altar in the centre of the town was permitted to stand; pagan priests were honoured, though they had to share their privileges with Christians. But most important is the summary in the *Doctrine* of the internal development within the Church of Edessa. In a brief sequel to the death of Aggai, we read that

because he died suddenly and quickly at the breaking of his legs, he was not able to lay his hands upon Palut. And Palut himself went to Antioch, and received the hand of priesthood from Serapion, bishop of Antioch, the same Serapion who also received the hand from Zephyrinus, bishop of the city of Rome,[1] (who was himself) of the succession of (those who had received) the hand of priesthood of Simon Peter, who had received it from our Lord. . . .

It is probable that here we have the echo of a change of direction in the government of the Church of Edessa. The legendary Addai and his successor Aggai may represent the early period in which it was largely autonomous but still looked eastward for its strength. Bardaiṣan, like St. Ephraim 150 years later, came to Edessa from Parthia. But Palut (the name is probably Greek) evidently represents a strain more acceptable to the dominant Greek-speaking church. He admitted the ecclesiastical authority of Antioch. Zephyrinus was Pope from about 198, and the submission of Edessa to Antioch may therefore belong to the early third century. There was a tendency to omit Aggai from the list of the leaders of the Edessan church, and to consider Palut the direct successor of the Apostle Addai.[2] Christians of Edessa even came to be called 'Palutians', perhaps to emphasize their opposition to other groups like the Arians. Ephraim condemns the practice with characteristic scorn:

Their hands have let go [*plṭ*] of everything. There are no handles to grasp. They even called us Palutians, but we have spewed [*plṭ*] them out and cast away [the name]. May there be a curse on those who are called by the name of Palut, and not by the name of Christ. . . . Palut too did not want men to be called by his name. If he were alive he would curse with all curses, for he was the disciple of the Apostle [Paul] who suffered pain and bitterness over the Corinthians when they abandoned the name of the Messiah and were called by the names of men.

There was no question, by the time of Ephraim, of the independence of the church of Edessa from the general body of Christendom.[3]

---

[1] An incorrect version reads here, 'Antioch'.
[2] So in the late martyrology of Sharbil.
[3] It must not, however, be assumed that the Palutians were heretics; this is pointed out by Jacob of Edessa in his twelfth letter to John the Stylite, citing the passage from S. Ephraim. On the contrary, declares Jacob, Palut was an orthodox and righteous man.

In the popular mind, a rapid advance in the diffusion of Christianity was to be attributed to the sufferings of Christian martyrs and their emulation by their co-religionists. Among the martyrologies ascribed to Edessa are those of Sharbil, Babai, and Barsamya.

Sharbil was, we are told, 'chief and commander of the pagan priests' of Edessa, and was converted to Christianity at a great pagan festival on 8 Nisan in 416 Sel. (A.D. 104). In that year, a decree reached the city from the Emperor Trajan, insisting that sacrifices and libations to the gods be increased throughout the empire and that those who refused to participate should be tortured and put to death. Sharbil met his death at the hands of the Governor after fearful threats and an exchange of somewhat wearisome harangues. As Sharbil died his sister Babai caught his blood; and for this she too was killed. Barsamya, bishop of the Christians, who had converted Sharbil, was arrested on the following day, in spite of demonstrations by the public in his favour, and imprisoned and tortured. But dispatches arrived unexpectedly with an Imperial Edict of toleration for the Christians. Barsamya was released amidst the plaudits of his flock.

The date attributed to these events is at fault; they should be assigned to the persecution of 250–1 in the reign of Emperor Decius, rather than to that of Trajan. Nevertheless, the account of the martyrdom of Sharbil and Babai, and the threatened execution of Barsamya cannot be regarded as having historical validity. It is true that the writer appears to display some knowledge of the locality of Edessa, but in fact his narrative has drawn heavily on the *Doctrine of Addai*.[1] Moreover, the miraculous intervention of the decree of toleration which, like a *deus ex machina*, saved Barsamya at the last moment, underlines the improbability of the story. Barsamya himself is not known to us as a bishop of Edessa; he is one of the followers of Aggai, successor of Addai, whose story is given in the *Doctrine of Addai*. The *Acts of Sharbil, Babai, and Barsamya* were probably composed after the time of Ephraim of Edessa (died 373), and after a Syriac Calendar of 411, in which Sharbil and Barsamya are not mentioned, but possibly before Rabbula's time (died 435 or 436), and certainly before Jacob of Serug (died 521).[2]

[1] The names of leading citizens of Edessa, the names of the heathen deities, and the description of the robes of the High Priest echo passages in the *Doc. Add.*, while *sharrire* and the archives of Edessa were matters of common knowledge. There are only two references to the topography of Edessa in the Sharbil story, and both are found elsewhere. 'The great altar in the middle of the town' is in the *Doc. Add.*, and the 'cemetery of the father of 'Abshelama the bishop' is a clumsy allusion to the 'cemetery built by 'Abshelama son of Abgar' in the martyrology of Ḥabbib. That the original text of the Sharbil 'martyrology' may have been in Greek is indicated by the frequent transliterations of Greek terms into Syriac. Notable is the use of the name 'Edessa' in the Syriac version instead of the usual 'Orhay', even in the phrase 'Edessa of the Parthians'!

[2] Another martyrology that has been associated with Edessa is that of Isaac, Bishop of Karkha, Shahpuhr, Bishop of Beth Nicator and three laymen. This, too, is apocryphal and of little value; it may have been composed at Edessa by the beginning of the sixth century.

The spurious martyrologies of Sharbil, Babay, and Barsamya may be intended to show that the nobles of Edessa, and its bishop, were prepared to make the supreme sacrifice for Christianity. For in the reign of Diocletian there were indeed martyrs at Edessa, but these were ordinary villagers, not sophisticated city dwellers.[1] The accounts of the martyrdom of Shmona, Gurya, and Ḥabbib (unlike those of Sharbil, Babai, and Barsamya) deserve to be accepted as historical documents. They may not have acquired their present shape before about A.D. 360, but they have 'a naturalness and tone of real feeling' that suggest they were based on the narrative of a contemporary. They may indeed be preserved largely in the form in which they were set down by that Theophilus, who claims (according to our present text) to have witnessed the execution in, probably, 309 and 310.[2] Whoever he was, the writer of the *Acts* of these three martyrs knew the topography of Edessa well, and he reflects in a sincere, direct style the atmosphere of the city at this time.

In 303, it was decreed that copies of the Scriptures throughout the Empire were to be surrendered and destroyed, churches were to be demolished, and Christian worship forbidden. Christians were deprived of their honours. Christian priests, later laymen also, were instructed to worship Zeus and the Emperor (not, as so improbably in the *Acts* of Sharbil and Barsamya, the local deities Bel and Nabu). These regulations were interpreted with varying degrees of severity in the East. At Edessa the Governor summoned to his presence two villagers, Gurya and Shmona, who were encouraging other Christians in the villages to remain firm in their faith. They were thrown into prison. At first the Governor was hesitant about his course of action. After consultation with the authorities at Antioch, however, he threatened Shmona and Gurya with fearsome punishment; they suffered the tortures of stretching and dragging and scourging, but refused to yield. They were confined in the prison known as the 'Dark pit', from August to mid-November 309, Shmona undergoing more tortures, but not Gurya because he was weak and old. The day of reckoning was not far off:

On the 15th November in the night that dawns into the third day of the week, when the cock had crowed twice, the Governor had risen and gone down to his Court of Justice, and with him was all his corps of officials, and there were torches and flambeaux[3] lighted before him. And when he had sat down on his tribunal in the Basilica by the winter baths, at the same time he had sent eight soldiers with the gaoler for Gurya and Shmona;

---

[1] So also in Adiabene, as Kirsten points out, Christianity seems to have spread first in the villages rather than in the cities.

[2] One chronicle states that Ḥabbib was martyred in the persecution by Licinius 'after that of the days of Diocletian'. Another chronicler seems to maintain that the martyrdom of Shmona and Gurya was in A.D. 306–7. It adds that '[Licinius] also seized Qona, Bishop of Edessa, and Shaʻduth the presbyter, and Aitallaha the deacon, and while he was tormenting them Licinius was killed. The victorious Constantine ordered that the persecution should cease, and then they were released.' This is no doubt echoed in the apocryphal martyrdom of bishop Barsamya.

[3] The rendering is doubtful.

and he brought them up from that pit. And they carried Shmona, because he was not able to walk on his right foot, on which that iron buckle had been fastened, and had sprained his knee joint; but Gurya, though he was walking on his feet, was held by two soldiers, one on his right and one on his left, first on account of the affliction of his imprisonment and secondly because of his age.

The Governor offered to allow them to return home and rejoin their families and relations and recover their property, if they would do obeisance to the sun. Shmona replied that they worshipped the Creator of the sun. The Governor said that he did not wish them to die at his hand; Shmona retorted that they were dying for the name of Jesus, in order to be delivered from the second death which lasts for ever. Again the Governor pleaded with them to save themselves, but they rejoiced at the prospect of death.

[The Governor] had commanded the executioner to take with him ten soldiers and go forth and take them outside the city far away, because of the city folk, that no one in the city should be grieved on their account. And when the executioner had received the command of the Governor . . ., he went forth by night hurriedly by the West gate of the city; and behold, a cart happened to be going forth and he made them both sit in the cart, before the city folk were awake. And he carried them off to a hill to the north of Edessa to a certain height called Beth Alah Qiqla,[1] which is to the south-west[2] of the fountain of water that goes into the city.

They were glad that the moment of 'crowning' had arrived, and asked the executioner to let them pray, and both he and the Roman soldiers begged them to pray for them also. The martyrs asked that their spirits should be received in peace and their bodies gathered at the Resurrection. Both Shmona and Gurya looked towards the East, knelt and asked the executioner to do his duty; he slew each of them with one blow of the sword. The soldiers left their bodies there side by side and went into the city.

And as they were coming in, large crowds met the soldiers because day had dawned and they had gone forth to inquire where they had carried off the holy ones, and they were asking the soldiers, 'Where have ye carried off the Confessors?' They said to them, 'Beth Alah Qiqla.' And many were the folk that had gone forth to search for the holy martyrs. Now there was with the first crowd that had gone forth the daughter of Shmona the Confessor; and folk from all the city had gone forth, men and women, and they had laid out their bodies and gathered the dust on which their blood was sprinkled. And many of them had brought fine garments and many cloths and perfumes and spices and much balm . . ., and they wrapped them in clean cloths and in those garments and with the balm and with the spices and with grave bands; and they laid them in one coffin and one grave which was there, saying over them psalms and anthems and hymns and litanies.

The sad scene was repeated less than a year later, and again the narrator is said to be the same Theophilus, who witnessed the death of Shmona and

---

[1] See p. 182 below.   [2] This is probably an error for 'north-west'; see p. 182 below.

Gurya. Licinius had commanded that there should be sacrifices and libations offered to Zeus; but the persecuted

cried out of their own free will, 'We are Christians', and they were not afraid of persecution, because those who were persecuted were more numerous than those who were persecuting. Now Ḥabbib, who was of the village of Tell-Ṣhe and had been made a deacon, was both going about to the churches in the villages secretly, and ministering and reading the Scriptures, and was encouraging and strengthening many by his word, and admonishing them to stand fast in the truth of their belief, and not to be afraid of the persecutors. . . . When the city informers[1] had heard . . . they went in and made known to . . . the Governor that was in the Citadel of Edessa. . . . The Governor made a report to the Emperor, asking for instructions because they had heard that Constantine . . . in Gaul and in Spain was a Christian and did not sacrifice.

Licinius replied that the Christians were to be killed by fire or by sword. At this time Ḥabbib was at Zeugma. The Governor ordered his family and fellow-villagers to be arrested and put in gaol. Hearing this, Ḥabbib went to Edessa and handed himself over to the chief officer of the guard; and although the officer told him that if no one had seen him he should go away and no harm would befall his family, Ḥabbib insisted on being taken to the Governor.

The Governor interrogated him. He refused to worship the statue of Zeus, declaring that he was not afraid of torture, and was scourged. On the following day he was brought from prison and again threatened with torture if he refused to worship the statue; he repeated that he was not afraid, since God forbade the worship of created things. He was hung and combed, but still refused to sacrifice to idols. After much argument the Governor declared:

I know that all you say is in order that my rage and the anger of my mind may be excited, and that I should give sentence of death against you speedily. I will not therefore be hurried on to that which you desire, but I will have patience . . . in order that the affliction of your tortures may be increased.

Once more Ḥabbib refused to obey the Emperor. Finally,

the Governor began to give the sentence of death against him; and he called aloud before his corps of officials, and said, the freemen of the city also hearing him . . ., 'I command that the strap be cast into his mouth as into the mouth of a murderer, and that he be burnt by a slow lingering fire so that the torture of his death may be increased.

And [Ḥabbib] went from the presence of the Governor, with the strap thrust into his mouth, and a multitude of the people of the city was running after him. Now the Christians were rejoicing that he had not turned aside nor abandoned his state of life,[2] and the pagans were threatening him because he would not sacrifice. And they took him out by the West gate, (the gate) of Arches,[3] over against the cemetery which was built by ʽAbshelama, son of Abgar. Now his mother was clad in white, and she was going out with him.

[1] Syriac, *sharrire*; see p. 20 above.
[2] Syriac, *qeyama*, which has an ecclesiastical connotation; see p. 136 below.
[3] Or 'Vaults', see p. 185 below.

And when he arrived at the place where they were going to burn him, he stood up and prayed, and all those that were going out with him. . . . And while Ḥabbib was standing they dug a place, and took him and set him up in the midst of it, and they fixed up by him a stake. . . . And when the fire burned and its flames ascended fiercely they called out to him, 'Open your mouth'. And the moment he opened his mouth his soul mounted up; and they exclaimed, both men and women, with the voice of weeping. And they drew him up out of the fire, and they threw over him fine linen and choice unguents and spices, and they seized upon some of the faggots for burning him and they carried him, both brethren and laymen, and wrapped him up and buried him by Gurya and Shmona, the martyrs, in the same grave in which they were placed, on the height which is called Beth Alah Qiqla, saying over him psalms and hymns, and carrying his burnt body in procession affectionately and honourably. And even some Jews and pagans took part in shrouding and burying his body with the Christian brethren. . . . There was one spectacle of grief spread over all those within [the community] and those without, and tears were running down from all eyes, while everyone was giving glory to God. . . .

Now the impression we receive from these vivid accounts is clear: this was not so much a struggle between Christians and pagans as between Edessans and alien rulers. The Abgar and Addai stories tell of king and Apostle, the Sharbil, Babai, and Barsamya 'martyrologies' are of High Priest and bishops. But the Gurya and Shmona and Ḥabbib narratives are of simple village folk, well versed in the text of the Syriac Bible, but men of little influence except that of their own merit and their own actions. The execution of Gurya and Shmona was carried out stealthily so that it should not arouse the anger of the city folk. Executioner and the Roman soldiery alike sympathized with the martyrs, 'called them happy . . . and secretly cherished and honoured them, while afraid of the Imperial authority'. Even the Governor was reluctant to enforce the decrees of the Emperor. The Edessans evidently had no fear in showing respect to the martyrs' remains. So, too, Ḥabbib was escorted to his death by a crowd of Christians, and after his death he was buried with honour and even with the participation of Jews and pagans. The Christians showed no hesitation in declaring their faith, 'because those who were persecuted were more numerous than those who were persecuting'. Edessa was now a Christian city.

The shadowy figures of the *Doctrine of Addai* and of the *Acts of Sharbil, Babai, and Barsamya* belong to legend—like the early figures of the Aryu dynasty at Edessa and the 'bishops', Hystasp and 'Aqi, of the Bardaiṣan biographies. But with Shmona, Gurya, and Ḥabbib the Church of Edessa had reached historical times. Bishop Qona, who began to build the Cathedral of Edessa in, probably, A.D. 313, started a line of bishops of Edessa that was sometimes disturbed, but was not broken for a thousand years.[1] Edessa was represented at the Council of Nicaea in 325, and at all important ecclesiastical

---

[1] Qona has been credited by one scholar with the promotion of the Separate Gospels as the standard text; there is, however, no concrete evidence for the hypothesis.

assemblies thereafter. The churches and religious institutions of the city increased in number, and the Church authorities disposed of considerable revenue. Their activities largely governed the social life of Edessa, as we shall see in a later chapter.

The outstanding personality of the fourth century at Edessa, and the most celebrated Father of the Syrian church, was St. Ephraim. His career should be seen outlined against the troubled events of the period. The hostility in Mesopotamia between the West and East had grown sharper. It was now a conflict of faith as well as of politics, since after 313 Christianity had become the official religion of the Roman Empire, of which the capital was now Byzantium. Ephraim was aware of the conflict from his earliest years. He was born in about 306 at Nisibis or its neighbourhood, that is, on the borders of the Empire. His parents may have been pagan, but he was reared in a Christian atmosphere. In his youth he came under the influence of three well-known bishops of Nisibis, Jacob, Babu, and Walagash (Vologases), and especially under that of Jacob; he calls Nisibis the 'daughter of Jacob'. Tradition attributes to him an active part in the desperate but successful defence of Nisibis against the attack by the Persian army in 350,[1] and his early 'Carmina Nisibena' gives us a graphic account of the event. Ephraim probably composed his hymns 'Concerning Paradise' and 'Against Heresies' at this period of his life. When Nisibis was ceded to the Persians by Jovian in 363, Ephraim was already a distinguished writer.

Under the terms of the treaty between Byzantium and the Persians, the Christian population of Nisibis was authorized to withdraw freely to the West. Ephraim lived for a short time at Amid, and then settled at Edessa where he spent the last ten years of his life. He refused advancement to high ecclesiastical office; according to legend he worked as a bath-attendant on first coming to the city. But he was an active preacher, as well as an adviser to the leaders of the Church of Edessa. There is no direct evidence that he founded, or taught at, the School of the Persians, a theological academy at Edessa which was celebrated in the Eastern Church for the remarkable attainments of its teachers and students; but it would be strange if he were not associated with it. A biographer relates that, so great was the trust of his fellow-Edessans in Ephraim, he was requested to administer relief work among the poor during a famine towards the end of his life. Before he died, in 373, Ephraim asked to be buried among the graves of the destitute and criminals; but shortly afterwards his remains were moved, we are told, to the place of burial of the bishops of Edessa. Under the name of Khudr

---

[1] The *Life* of St. Ephraim must be regarded with caution, in particular those sections that describe his career at Nisibis, since it contains details that are also in the *Life* of Jacob of Nisibis. Pl. 6b.

Elias,[1] the holy man was revered at Urfa until recent times by Moslems also, and a spring festival was held near his tomb in the Armenian Church of St. Sargis (Sergius) to the west of the city.[2]

Ephraim's biographer relates that he

ate no food but barley and dry pulse and occasionally vegetables; his drink was water. His body was dried on his bones like a potter's vessel. His clothes were of the many-coloured rags of the dust heap. He was short in stature. He was sad at all times, and he did not indulge in laughter at all. He was bald and beardless.

Ephraim shunned the social life of the city. He is said to have lived in one of the innumerable caves in the hillside outside Edessa, and it is this that may have given him the reputation of a hermit. Certainly he had sympathy with monasticism. In his letter to the hermits who dwelt in the hill-country, he encourages them to live in solitude, in faith and prayer, like Jesus in the wilderness, without fear of wild beasts or hunger. They would not 'be soiled by the sinful mire of the town', for they had 'cast off . . . the yoke of the world and the tyranny of possessions'. They did not 'fear the voice of those in authority . . . like the owner of property and riches'.

But Ephraim is unlikely, on the other hand, to have tolerated the excesses of asceticism and of self-mortification which too often were practised by the Christian solitaries of Mesopotamia. He accepted loyally his vows of poverty and chastity, but he was a man of action also. He was a scientist as well as a theologian,[3] and he had a high regard for the learning of others, even of his enemies. He recognized the importance of pastoral duties. He rebuked the Edessans who opposed their Bishop Barsai:

Thou [God] didst console Samuel when the fools rejected him, and didst say that it is thee whom the people rejected. Thy church . . . hath rejected thy priest; through him thy children have shown their hatred of me. . . . [Barsai] is poor, they are rich, he is tolerant, they are quarrelsome, he is gentle, they are rough, he is humble, they are oppressive. . . .

The new shepherd came forth—from the beginning he was met with violent rain and clouds, and they have confused his assistants. They took pleasure in the wolves; they thought the shepherd to be a wolf. When the eyes of the assistants have been dulled by darkness, their sight and their knowledge will be restored by thy light, and they will turn to the shepherd and tend his sheep.

---

[1] The appearance of Khudr at Urfa must be later than the mid-seventeenth century since it is not mentioned by Evliya Çelebi. Badger describes the chapel of Sargis 'commonly called Khudr Elias. In the courtyard a descent of four steps led to a grotto with four recesses and a cave with eight tombs including the remains of St. Ephraim and St. Theodorus.' St. Theodore was a favourite saint of the Edessans, see pp. 190, 239 f. below. Hasluck, *Christianity and Islam under the Sultans*, i,

47–9, associates St. Theodore Stratelates of Euchaita, the dragon-killer, with the nephew of Khudr buried in a nearby tomb (I owe this reference to my colleague Dr. V. L. Ménage). It may not be accidental that Euchaita was acquainted with the letter of Abgar, p. 75 above.

[2] On, it appears, 28 Nisan; it should be remarked that this date was a day of pilgrimage among the pagans of Harran.

[3] See p. 167 below.

As a writer Ephraim was exceptionally prolific. He poured out a stream of metrical homilies and hymns, commentaries on the Scriptures, expository sermons, and polemical tracts. They were quickly translated into Greek, Armenian, Coptic, Arabic, Ethiopic, and Latin; their influence extended, not only throughout Mesopotamia and Syria, but through the whole of Christendom. Ephraim was acquainted with the work of Greek philosophers, but possibly little with that of Greek theologians. It is doubtful, in spite of legends to the contrary, whether he was greatly proficient in the Greek language: he certainly did not understand Persian. Of Syriac style, however, he was a master, and he earned eulogies that were bestowed on him in his own day and shortly afterwards—Prophet of the Syrians, Lion of Syria, Harp of the Holy Spirit, Pillar of the Church. His work, it must be confessed, shows little profundity or originality of thought, and his metaphors are laboured. His poems are turgid, humourless, and repetitive. In his hymn to maidens in praise of Virginity are the banal verses:

Do not trust in wine, for it is an impostor and an agitator that surrenders thy fortress, that the captive-taker may come and take captive thy freedom into handmaidenship, that thy love may follow his will.

And when moreover thou hast lost thy true Bridegroom and got in his stead a false one, when thou hast the consolation that even if thou hast lost but yet thou hast found, [what will it profit thee]? For his love is lying and deceitful; it alights on everything, it does not cleave to thee—and then the regret will be great.

Youthfulness is like a branch of first-fruits that is fair in the summer, and when its fruits and its leaves have been stripped off it becomes hateful, and everyone turns his face from it, and what was desired of all becomes despised of all. O inexperience, do not show thy beauty to those outside; when it becomes hateful and aged, those that see despise it.

There is little, too, that is novel in his praise of Edessa:

O Edessa, full of chastity, of wisdom and intelligence, clothed with prudence and judgement, adorned with the girdle of faith, armed with the helmet of unchangeable truth and the breastplate of charity, the universal ornament.

But Ephraim's writings reflect his courage, his sincerity, his unswerving zeal for the faith and his sympathy for the poor. He knew well the lives and thoughts of the ordinary man:

Let us rejoice . . . in the needs of all of us, for in this way unity is produced for us all. For inasmuch as men are dependent on one another, the high bend themselves down to the humble and are not ashamed, while the lowly reach out towards the great and are not afraid. And also in the case of animals we exercise great care over them. Obviously our need of everything binds us in love towards everything. . . .

If other thoughts occurred [to the husbandman] so that he pondered and reasoned as to whether the seed was sprouting or not, or whether the earth would fail to produce it or would restore it again, then the husbandman could not sow. . . . The husbandman who cannot plough with one ox cannot plough with two thoughts. Just as it is useful to plough with two oxen, so it is right to employ one healthy thought. . . .

This is the greatest knowledge [of the sages] that when they do not know a thing, they confess that they do not know it. For if a man confesses about something that he knows it, and then something else that he does not know it . . . in both these cases he has spoken the truth, and because he does not lie in either of them his truth is victorious. . . .

Like children playing on a wide staircase, when one sits on the lowest step his companion in order to anger him sits on the middle step, and in order to resist both another sits on the upper step—even such are the heralds of Error. . . .

It is in his prose *Refutations* that we observe most clearly Ephraim's attitude towards the principal enemies of the Church in his day, who were the followers of Marcion, Bardaiṣan, and Mani. Ephraim, it has been well stated, 'may be described as a Monist and a Materialist—that is to say, he recognises only one self-existing original entity or being, that is, God'.[1] He was outraged by the elaborate structure of the universe devised by the heresiarchs, which appeared to him to deny the unity of God. His arguments are marshalled with the vehemence of debating points. Too often his words are virulent, 'We have not come to stir up now the mire of Bardaiṣan, for the foulness of Mani is quite sufficient. For behold our tongue is very eager to conclude at once and flee from him.' At times he resorts to scorn, 'They did well who skinned the lying Mani, who said that Darkness was skinned, though it has neither hide nor sheath-skin.' But sometimes his sarcasm is not unjustified:

Oh, what [is to be said] of a teaching whose failures are more than its artifices [can remedy]? For as often as they need an argument they bring forward such proofs as these, and as often as an allegory suits them they concoct such tales as these.

The Church of Edessa was fortunate to have in Ephraim a doughty champion at a time when its fundamental tenets were challenged.[2]

The Arian community seems to have flourished at Edessa in the reign of Constantius, of whom Ammian writes that, 'the plain and simple religion of the Christians he obscured by a dotard's superstition; by subtle and involved discussion about dogma, rather than by seriously trying to make them agree, he aroused many controversies'. Somewhat later, the Arians of Edessa aroused the wrath of Emperor Julian. 'In the insolence bred by their wealth', he asserts, they attacked the followers of Valentinus, the Gnostic leader, and committed 'such rash acts as could never occur in a well-ordered city'. Julian ordered their money to be given to the soldiers as *largitiones* and their lands to be confiscated to the Imperial exchequer.[3] He could not refrain

---

[1] F. C. Burkitt in *St. Ephraim's Prose Refutations* (ed. C. W. Mitchell) II, 1921, cxv.

[2] For Ephraim on the Jews and pagans, see pp. 101 f., 105 below.

[3] *Res privata.*

from adding, sarcastically, that they would appreciate his command, 'since by their own admirable law they are bidden to sell all they have and give to the poor, so that they may attain more easily to the kingdom of Heaven.' Julian, who hated Christian Edessa, continues:

I publicly command you citizens of Edessa to abstain from all feuds and rivalries, else will you provoke even my benevolence against yourselves, and, being sentenced to the sword and to exile and to fire, you shall pay the penalty for disturbing the good order of the Empire.[1]

Subsequently, with the encouragement of Emperor Valens, the Arians of Edessa grew more confident. Valens himself visited Edessa in about 372. It is reported that he threatened the orthodox Christians there with a choice between death and apostasy to Arianism. Only when the people went out in multitudes to await martyrdom at the 'famous and splendid shrine' of St. Thomas outside the city, was he persuaded to revoke his ultimatum.[2] Nevertheless, Bishop Barsai and some leading clerics were expelled from Edessa in September 373, three months after the death of Ephraim; they were followed into exile by crowds of devout followers. But with the death of Valens in 378, the triumph of the Arians was over. The orthodox clergy returned and resumed possession of their churches.

Ephraim had done his work well. As he claimed, the heresies of Marcion and Mani seem to have found little popular support at Edessa. The Bardaisanites, however, still provided an opposition to be reckoned with, in the time of the next Church leader of Edessa of whom we have much information, the famous Bishop Rabbula. Born at Qenneshrin, near Aleppo, the wealthy son of a pagan father and a Christian mother, Rabbula gave away his possessions and renounced his family to become a recluse. He passed through a period of severe asceticism, and then was appointed Bishop of Edessa in, probably, 411 or 412. Conscious of his own ability, he did not offer the usual show of reluctance to accept high office in the Church. His was an austere personality; he was constant in prayer and fasting, and simple in his dress and food, and his tableware. His clergy were forced to refrain from all luxuries. Rabbula did not build new churches like his predecessors; instead, he built infirmaries for the sick and needy, both men and women. We have still the canons ascribed to Rabbula and drawn up for the guidance of monks and clergy; they have the impress of his severity.[3]

Against heretics and dissenters Rabbula acted with characteristic vigour. The nobles of Edessa who still hankered after the songs of Bardaiṣan, and the remnants of Arians and Marcionites were persuaded to accept baptism and re-enter the orthodox fold. Jews, we are assured, though with evident

---

[1] 'Epistle to Hecebolios'.   [2] See p. 175 below.   [3] See p. 135 below.

exaggeration, were accepted into the Church in their thousands, and pagans in their tens of thousands. A synagogue in the centre of Edessa was converted into the Church of St. Stephen[1] and four pagan temples were destroyed.

Dissident Christian sects had multiplied, if we may credit our sources, for instance the Borborians, who were suspected of shameful practices, and the Sadduceans, who claimed to have visions. Some, we are told, originated at Edessa.[2] These were the 'Udaye, whose founder was an archdeacon in the region of Edessa at the time of the Council of Nicaea. He adopted some of the teachings of Bardaiṣan, and founded his own church which received adherents in Mesopotamia, Palestine, and Arabia, and even among the Scythians and Goths. There were the Mesallians (in Greek, Euchites), who appeared at the same time, followers of a certain Adelphus of Edessa. He practised asceticism in Sinai and in Egypt and returned while still a young man to Edessa to live in constant prayer, privation, and solitude. Adelphus, relates Philoxenus of Mabbog, 'relied on rules of life . . . but he had no humility. [He received] hallucinations of devils instead of divine contemplation . . . as if he had no need of labours and physical mortification.' He taught that the mystic power of prayer could overcome sin and bring man to perfection. These doctrines represented a threat to the established Church, for Adelphus and his disciples preyed upon the gullible and ignorant; he and his sect were beaten, harried into exile, and condemned again and again by ecclesiastical councils. Less dangerous was the simple poet-monk of Edessa, Aswana, who, in the first half of the fourth century, composed hymns that were still sung over two centuries later. Of him Philoxenus writes that:

Satan deceived him too and brought him out of his cell and set him on the hill called 'Stadium'[3] and showed him the shape of a chariot and of horses and said to him, 'God has sent for you to cause you to depart in a chariot like Elijah.' And in his childishness he was deceived and went up to stand upon the chariot. The whole phantasm disappeared under him and he was precipitated down from a great height and died a ridiculous death.

At the hands of Rabbula all these aberrations received short shrift. Errant monks were obliged to make their choice between confinement within monastery walls or exile from the province of Osrhoene, unless they submitted to the discipline of the Church.

But within the Church the situation had changed since the days of Ephraim. It was no longer possible for the orthodox to present a uniform front. The whole body of Christendom was divided by the arguments over the Natures of Jesus. The Dyophysite party, led by Diodorus of Tarsus,

---

[1] See p. 182 below; plan II.
[2] There is no convincing evidence to indicate that the heresy of Quq was evolved at Edessa, as has been asserted. [3] See p. 164 below.

Theodoret, and their partisans, had achieved approval in high places with the preferment of Nestorius to the patriarchate of Constantinople in 428. Nestorius acted with assurance. 'Give me', he exclaimed to Emperor Theodosius II, 'the earth freed of heretics and I shall give you Heaven in return; help me to fight the heretics, and I shall help you to fight the Persians.' At first Rabbula appeared to hesitate. Then he revealed himself as a bitter opponent of Nestorius and threw his authority on the side of the Monophysite leader, Cyril of Alexandria. He summoned a Council at Edessa in 431, burnt the writings of Theodore of Mopsuestia, and travelled tirelessly to councils outside his diocese to press the Monophysite cause.

Rabbula died in 435 or 436. His authority in his province was undisputed, but his spirit of partisanship was to leave an unhappy legacy of bitterness. The Dyophysites spoke of him as 'the tyrant of our city who persecuted even the dead under the guise of religion', referring to his attack on Theodore of Mopsuestia and his works. The Monophysites declared that not only all the Christians of Edessa but even pagans and Jews participated in the mourning at Rabbula's funeral. Like Ephraim, Rabbula had been active not only as pastor but also as writer; he translated into Syriac at least one of the works of Cyril of Alexandria, at Cyril's own request. Of his literary work little has survived, but it is evident that he was a skilled theologian and controversialist. Whether Rabbula himself is to be credited with the ban at Edessa on Tatian's composite version of the Gospels, the Diatessaron, and with the insistence upon the use of the Separate Gospels in the liturgy, is open to question. The Diatessaron may have been largely replaced in official use before his time, probably by the Old Syriac version rather than by the Peshitta.

Rabbula's successor in the see of Edessa, Hiba (Ibas), was not unfavourable to the Nestorian party, an indication of how evenly balanced were the opposing factions of Monophysites and Dyophysites at this time. Before his appointment to the bishopric, Hiba had been on the staff of the School of the Persians. He was dubbed 'the Translator', because he was member of a group of scholars who had translated into Syriac the works of Diodorus and Theodore of Mopsuestia. To Theodore he was greatly attached, and it was for this reason in particular that Hiba incurred the hostility of extreme Monophysites: he is said to have been expelled from Edessa by Rabbula in 431. His celebrated letter to Mari of Beth Ardashir, in which he described the doctrinal strife at Edessa, had helped Nestorian doctrines to take root among the Eastern Christians. Popular passion over religious dogma ran high at Edessa. It was fanned by personal antagonisms. Hiba was no less high-handed than his predecessor; but, unlike Rabbula, he was also fond of worldly pleasures. 'The jockey bishop', his enemies called him, and accused him also of the vices of simony and nepotism and the misappropriation of Church property.[1] His opponents in Osrhoene, under the leadership of Uranius, Bishop of Himeria, appealed to the Patriarch of Antioch, and Hiba promptly excommunicated those priests among them who were members of his own diocese. Both parties were summoned to Antioch, and the Patriarch ruled, in 448, that Hiba had not exceeded his rights. The Monophysites then used their influence at Court to impress their views on the Emperor. A commission was set up at Tyre and Beirut, and again found Hiba innocent of the charges of heresy and misconduct preferred against him. The commission, however, imposed restraint on the bishop's autocratic treatment of his subordinates and his handling of Church funds, and required him to pronounce his disapproval of Nestorius in public.

Nevertheless, when Hiba returned to Edessa before Easter 449, he found that, in spite of his vindication by the commission, popular agitation had been whipped up against him. The hostility between Monophysites and Dyophysites had, Hiba later complained, divided Christendom; Christians 'could not go [freely] from country to country and from town to town, but were becoming a source of ridicule to pagans and heretics'. Hiba left the city to seek help, as he was entitled to do, from the military commander. Meanwhile, at Edessa, Monophysites demonstrated before the Governor, who had newly arrived from Constantinople, shouting:

... No one wants an enemy of Christ! No one wants a corrupter of orthodoxy! To exile with the confidant of Nestorius! ... To exile with the despoiler of the temples! To exile with the companion of Nestorius! ... No one wants the enemy of the faithful! No one wants Judas Iscariot! Iscariot to the gallows! Holy Rabbula, pray for us! Hiba has violated your faith! ... Go and join your companion Nestorius! An orthodox bishop for the church! No one wants the accuser of upright faith! No one wants the friend of the Jews! No one wants the enemy of God! Rid us of Hiba and deliver the world! To the circus with the hater of Christ! To the stadium with the brood of the impure! ... No one wants Hiba! Remove his name from the Diptychs! Holy Rabbula, throw Hiba into exile! To the mines with Hiba! We entreat, we are making no command. We do all this for Christ.

The Governor reponded to these appeals and to petitions from notables of the city. Hiba was thrown into prison; it may be suspected, indeed, that the Governor had been given instructions to take this step before he left the Court. A Synod was convened at Ephesus in August 449, the so-called Robbers' Synod, which condemned Hiba in his absence[2] and ordered his deposition. But two years later, the Council of Chalcedon effected a compromise between the moderate elements of both Monophysites and

---

[1] See pp. 130 f. below.
[2] Condemned with Hiba were Flavius of Constantinople, Domnus of Antioch, Theo- doret of Cyrrhus, Irenaeus of Tyre, Eusebius of Dorylaeum, Daniel of Harran, and Sophronius of Tella.

Dyophysites. Hiba then pleaded for the reconsideration of his case, and was reinstated at Edessa. He remained there until his death in 457.

Hiba was succeeded by Nona, who had occupied the see during the two years of Hiba's exile from Edessa. Under Nona, who accepted the rulings of the Council of Chalcedon but was not actively opposed to the Dyophysites, there seems to have been a recrudescence of activity among the supporters of Nestorius. Bishop Cyrus followed Nona in 471, and resolved to take decisive action. He persuaded Emperor Zeno to close the School of the Persians at Edessa and to expel the staff. On the site of the School was erected a church. Thus came to an end, in 489, a centre of theological learning and disputation which, for over a century, had contributed greatly to the reputation of Edessa in eastern Christendom. It was, it is true, the last outpost of Nestorianism in the Byzantine empire; it is only with the conquest of Edessa by Persia in 609 that Nestorians were to return to western Mesopotamia. But the School was also an important source from which Persian Christians derived their knowledge of Greek culture, and where they studied the profane and ecclesiastical masterpieces of the West; it has been appositely called 'a communicating door between East and West'. Antipathy between Persians and Syrians had, however, never ceased to hamper the School. Nestorians ascribed its closure by 'the crafty worker, the mad dog, and the teacher of deceit' to envy of the Nestorian scholar, Narseh. Western theologians at Edessa, they alleged, resented the superiority of the Persian, who had not received the conventional training in Greek logic. There were also, it was hinted, allegations of treason against Narseh, which caused him to leave Byzantine territory precipitately. Monophysites, on the other hand, while admitting that 'Persians are in general keen enquirers', maintained that 'the holy Cyrus . . . tore up the bitter plant [of heterodoxy] by its roots'. The exiled scholars had already before 489 begun to make their way across the frontiers to Nisibis; some attained high office in the hierarchy of the Persian Church, others (notably Narseh himself) taught in the Academy of Nisibis, and conferred upon it a renown that spread far beyond the boundaries of Persia.

At Edessa the wearisome struggle was now between Monophysites and Chalcedonians. The less extreme among the former were largely placated by the document of union (*Henoticon*) of Emperor Zeno, which reaffirmed the decisions of all synods except those of Chalcedon. Notable exponents of Monophysitism, in the region of Edessa, were John, Bishop of Tella and Philoxenus (Aksenaya), Bishop of Mabbog. The latter had studied theology at Edessa, and instigated a new translation of the whole Bible from Greek into Syriac which was completed in about 508. He was an active advocate of his views; but the writer of the so-called 'Chronicle of Joshua the Stylite', describing the celebration at Edessa of the pagan spring festival in 498, rebukes Philoxenus. The bishop of Mabbog, he states, 'was at that time in Edessa—of whom beyond all others it was thought he had taken upon himself to labour in teaching—yet he did not speak on this subject more than one day'. Paul, who had obtained the see of Edessa in 501, also professed support for Monophysite doctrines. But in 519 occurred another of the sudden reversals of fortune that make the ecclesiastical history of this time so bewildering. The successor of Zeno, Anastasius, had been inclined to favour the Monophysites. The following emperor, Justin I, however, eager to reconcile the western and eastern Churches, insisted on recognition of the decisions of the Council of Chalcedon, and there arose the Melkite, or Imperial group, to maintain these decisions.

There opened now a long period of fierce persecution of Monophysites. The oppression is well documented, though allowance must be made for the bias of our Monophysite sources. Among the most implacable leaders of this campaign, in north Mesopotamia, were the Patriarch of Antioch, Euphrasius, his successor, Ephraim of Amid, Count of the Orient (of whom even his enemies wrote that he was 'just in his deeds, not greedy of bribes, able and successful'), Asclepius, Bishop of Edessa, and Abraham bar Kilai, Bishop of Amid. We are given a list of fifty-four Monophysite bishops, including the great Severus of Antioch, who were removed from their sees. Not only monks and nuns, but also laymen were driven from their homes. They were beaten with swords and sticks, they suffered hunger and thirst and exposure; soldiers harried them, giving them no time to eat or to rest. Even persons with whom Monophysites found shelter were punished. Many priests perished miserably in exile. Philoxenus of Mabbog died at Gangra, suffocated by smoke from the kitchen of the hospice, over which he was incarcerated. John of Tella travelled widely in secret, ordaining priests and deacons and encouraging his fellow Monophysites to hold fast to their beliefs.[1] In February 537, he was apprehended in the mountains of Persian Mesopotamia and extradited; he died, after torture, a year later at Antioch.

In these events Edessa was closely involved. Its inhabitants had largely declared for Monophysitism. In 519 Bishop Paul was taken by force out of the Baptistry, where he had sought refuge, and was deported to Syria. Permitted to return after forty days, he still refused to accept the Synod of Chalcedon and was sent into exile at Euchaita in 522. His successor Asclepius became hated for his violent onslaughts on Monophysites, in which he used also local army detachments. Edessan monks, notably those of the Monastery of the Orientals, a few miles south of the city, were expelled. In April 525, Asclepius seized ten monks and threatened them with torture on the following day, unless they would accept Melkite tenets. During that night, however, the river Daiṣan overflowed into the city, and there was great destruction of

[1] See p. 151 below.

lives and of property.[1] The Monophysite party, feeling that Heaven had shown its approval of their cause, ran to stone the bishop; but Asclepius, like the Administrator of the city, had prudently withdrawn and made his way to Antioch. He received little sympathy there. Patriarch Euphrasius took him up to the pulpit and, pointing at the wretched bishop, invited his congregation to 'come and see this second Noah in his Ark, saved from the second Flood'. Shortly afterwards Asclepius died.[2] In 526 Paul wrote to the Emperor, accepting the Synod of Chalcedon, and was permitted to return to his diocese.[3]

The Monophysites showed remarkable fortitude in adjusting their affairs to the changed situation. There is extant a document setting out the ecclesiastical canons of 'the holy Fathers in time of persecution', regulating the relationship between Monophysites and the Chalcedonian 'heretics'. Monophysite priests were permitted to take refuge in the martyries of their enemies. They were forbidden to give them communion; they were forbidden to partake of food with non-Monophysites, and their lay followers were permitted to do so only under duress. Though Monophysitism had been reduced by persecution to its lowest ebb, it was, nevertheless, able to survive with the help of Empress Theodora at Constantinople, although her husband, Justinian, favoured the Melkites. She caused two Monophysites, Theodore and Jacob, to be consecrated as bishops, the latter to the see of Edessa in 542. Jacob, nicknamed Burd'aya[4] because he wore a horse-cloth as his cloak, is described as

fulfilling the work of the ministry to all the orthodox believers, not only by organizing the clergy and by ordaining into priesthood, but also by consoling and comforting and edifying and strengthening and teaching all the party of believers everywhere. . . . Whenever he went to any district, he would complete all the works of his ministry in one night perhaps and one day, and would pass the next night thirty or forty miles or more farther on; and whenever news of him was heard in one district, and his pursuers went out after him, the brave man would be found heroically fulfilling his work in another district, while those who were running after him beat the air in exasperation and bit their fingers . . . He resolutely refused to allow even a travelling companion to carry any gold or silver or bronze with him or any food upon the journey . . . He would also not consent to avail himself of the use of an animal for riding or for driving, but he used to carry out his travelling on foot, since besides being fortified by divine grace he possessed also a body sound by nature.'[5]

---

[1] See p. 156 below.
[2] Euphrasius himself perished in November 527 when, during the earthquake of Antioch, he fell (or was pushed) into a cauldron of boiling wax; according to another account, however, he was buried below a ruined house and throughout the day his wailing was heard from under the debris.

[3] There has been much discussion on the motives of Paul. For the most recent analysis see T. Jansma, *L'Orient syrien* x, 1965, 194. According to one Syriac chronicler, Paul was removed as a result of intrigue at court by the brother of Asclepius, whom he had slighted.
[4] The cognate form Burd'ana is also frequently found.   [5] John Ephes., *Lives*.

Jacob founded new Monophysite churches in Syria, Mesopotamia, and Asia Minor, ordaining twenty-seven bishops, and priests in such numbers—the figure of 100,000 is given—that the patriarch of Constantinople was led to address to him a friendly remonstrance. So great was the impact of his personality (he died in 578) that the Monophysites are commonly called after him the 'Jacobites'. He spent little time in Edessa, but through him Edessa became famous as a centre of Monophysite doctrine.[1] The Melkite party also continued there; and from this time Melkites and Monophysites had each their own bishop, churches, and monasteries in the city. A Melkite contemporary of Jacob Burd'aya was Bishop Amazonius (or Amidonius), who built the Melkite cathedral; its beauty is celebrated in a well-known hymn.[2] Later Melkite bishops of Edessa were Epiphanius, Severus (killed by the General Narseh), and Theodosius (or Theodore).

During the later years of Emperor Justinian, the persecution of Monophysites was relaxed. We are told that at the beginning of the reign of Justin II (565–78) an attempt was made to reunite the two factions of the church; it failed, and the attack on the Monophysites recommenced. In the reign of Maurice (582–602) there was a fresh wave of persecution. The Emperor's nephew, the Bishop of Melitene, came to Edessa and ordered the monks of the Monastery of the Orientals to accept the Synod of Chalcedon. They refused, and about four hundred were slaughtered in the moat outside the South Gate of Edessa.[3] Later the scene of the martyrdom was commemorated by a shrine. Others of the Monophysites were killed, and many were driven out, as they participated in their services. Melkites took possession of Monophysite churches and monasteries. In time the persecution was brought to an end, but only, claimed the Monophysites, through supernatural intervention; an eclipse, an earthquake, plague, and drought, brought home to the oppressors the wickedness of their deeds.

In 609 the Persian king Khusraw II Abarwez captured Edessa. Against the wishes of its inhabitants, he imposed on them a Nestorian bishop. At first the Monophysites were ill-treated, and their bishop, Paul, fled to Cyprus. Later, however, they were preferred to the Melkite party, who were more directly identified by the Persian authorities with Imperial Byzantium. Melkite bishops were, it appears, expelled throughout Mesopotamia; the Monophysites, on the other hand, were permitted to practice their rites freely and to reoccupy their churches. A Bishop Yunan was sent from Persia to minister to the Jacobite community of Edessa. When, after a brief stay at Edessa, Yunan returned to his own country, he was replaced by a certain

---

[1] Jacob's monastery was that of Pesiltha near Tella. He died on his way to Egypt to settle a dispute at Alexandria and was buried on the Egyptian frontier. In 622, it is related, his body was removed by a ruse and reburied in his own monastery. [2] See p. 189 below.
[3] At that time still called the Gate of Beth Shemesh.

Isaiah. It should be noted that Isaiah belonged, like Yunan, to the eastern branch of the Jacobite Church; evidently the Persians regarded it as inexpedient to nominate a bishop who might accept the ecclesiastical authority of Antioch.

The Monophysites welcomed the accession of Emperor Phocas, who had dethroned their oppressor Maurice,[1] although Phocas was no less a devout Chalcedonian and disapproved of Monophysite doctrines. But Phocas, in his turn, was removed by Heraclius. The new Emperor visited Edessa during his campaign in the East in, probably, 628. He was impressed by his reception, and by the numbers of monks and scholars in the city. Learning that they were Monophysites, he determined to restore them to the official Church, declaring, 'How can we abandon so admirable a people [and allow them to remain] outside our [community]?' But his politic intentions were thwarted by what a Monophysite historian himself calls 'the fervour of zeal or, to tell the truth, the simplicity or lack of breeding' of the Jacobite bishop, Isaiah. The latter refused to permit Heraclius to receive the oblation in the Cathedral, as was the privilege of a reigning Emperor, unless he first anathematized the Council of Chalcedon and the Tome of Leo on which were based the rulings of the Council. Enraged, the Emperor expelled the bishop from his cathedral and handed Monophysite churches to the Melkites. Many Monophysite monks defected to their rivals. Isaiah was accompanied into exile by members of aristocratic families of Edessa who had endowed the local Monophysite church with 'treasure of gold and silver and [the revenue of] gardens and mills and shops and baths'. They hoped that when Heraclius returned to his capital they would recover their property. But they had not foreseen the cataclysm that was soon to engulf the whole of the Near East. Mesopotamia, impoverished and weakened by constant warfare, was an easy prey to the Arabs. In 639 Edessa fell to the Moslem general 'Iyaḍ.

The Moslems punctiliously ordered the Christians of Edessa to maintain the situation which obtained at the time of the capture of the city. Melkites therefore kept the property, including the churches, of their rivals. The Monophysite historian, however, comments philosophically:

The God of vengeance . . . seeing the cruelty of the Byzantines, who, wherever they ruled, plundered cruelly our churches and monasteries and condemned us without mercy, brought from the southern land the sons of Ishmael, to deliver us through them from the hands of the Byzantines. And indeed, we have suffered some hurt because the catholic churches, having been snatched from us and given to the Chalcedonians, have remained with them—for when the cities submitted to the Moslems, the latter gave to

[1] Curiously, however, there is evidence that the Monophysites, as well as the Melkites, were devoted to the memory of Maurice and that he was considered a saint by both sects; see, for example, Janssens, *Byzantion* xi, 1936, 499.

each confession whatever shrines were to be found in their possession; and at this time the Great Church of Edessa . . . had passed from us. Nevertheless, the advantage to us was not small, in that we were delivered from the cruelty of the Byzantines and from their evil and their wrath and their bitter zeal against us, and we had rest.[1]

Among Monophysite Edessans, hatred of the Melkites outweighed even their fear of the Moslems.

What was the position of the Jews during the four centuries after the end of the kingdom at Edessa? When the Christians of Edessa, like their co-religionists elsewhere in the Roman Empire, were persecuted by the Imperial authorities at the beginning of the fourth century, they had the open sympathy of the Jews. We are told that Jews mourned at the funeral of Ḥabbib, one of the three martyrs of Edessa. But the Christians of Mesopotamia owed more than this to the Jews. The Church of Edessa had a twofold strain in its development, Semitic (that is Aramaean), as well as Greek. Partly for this reason, it stood remote from the rest of Christendom, and partly, no doubt, because of its ignorance of the Greek language. Nevertheless, it throve. The vitality of the Edessan church, in spite of its isolation, may be ascribed in no small degree to the resources, both moral and theological, of the Jews of Edessa.

The influence of Jewish learning and tradition upon the early Christianity of north Mesopotamia is apparent from the writings of Aphraates, who lived near Mosul in the first half of the fourth century. His tractates are among the most ancient of any Syrian Church Fathers; they made a deep impression on his contemporaries. Aphraates was acquainted with the Targum and the Talmud, although his acquaintance with them was not necessarily first-hand. He employs a Jewish chronology, and even his metaphors in a few passages are Jewish. It is possible that he had knowledge of Hebrew. There seems little doubt that his fellow-Christians in this area, like early Christians elsewhere, maintained Jewish practices; they avoided, for example, eating meat before the blood had been removed, and at the Passover they ate unleavened bread. Several of the homilies of Aphraates are, it is true, directed against the Jews. His theological arguments follow familiar lines. He does not spare his attacks upon the Jews—but they are upon Judaism and the Jewish contemporaries of Jesus, not upon the contemporaries of Aphraates himself. He writes without rancour. Several times he addresses himself to a Jewish disputant, calling him 'doctor' or 'wise man'.

When we turn to Edessa we find that the position there was much the same. Allusions to Jews in the *Book of the Laws of Countries*, whose authorship is ascribed to the school of Bardaiṣan and which was written probably in the third century, are not unfriendly. They stress the observance of the

[1] Mich. Syr.

laws of circumcision, and of rest from work on the Sabbath by Jews wherever they are domiciled. But in the latter half of the fourth century the situation was very different. Antipathy between Christians and Jews had become deep-seated. The writings of Ephraim show bitter hostility towards the Jews, although he, like Aphraates, was greatly indebted to the example of Jewish teaching for the construction and logic of his arguments. We can only surmise the reasons for the change; they almost certainly are to be found in the course of events in which Ephraim had himself been an actor. In the struggle between the Christian population of Nisibis and the Persians, the Jews of Nisibis are likely to have supported the latter. They were aligned against Byzantium. It is true that Emperor Julian acted towards the Jews and wrote about the Jews with some kindness and sympathy, but his sympathy stemmed from hatred of Christianity; the Jews were pawns in the desperate struggle of paganism against the growing power of Christianity. Sozomen writes that, in favouring the Jews, Julian 'was not actuated . . . by any respect for their religion, . . . but he thought to grieve the Christians by favouring the Jews. . . . Perhaps he also calculated upon persuading the Jews to embrace paganism and sacrifices.'[1]

The turning point in Jewish-Christian relations at Edessa must have come with the treaty between Byzantium and Persia in 363. By this treaty the frontiers between the two empires were sharply defined. Edessa lay firmly in the orbit of Byzantium; Nisibis had become a Persian stronghold. To merchants of west Mesopotamia this spelt poverty and decay, for the frontiers cut the caravan route along which was carried the produce of India and the Far East. To the Christians of west Mesopotamia the treaty meant isolation from a great centre of their faith. But to the Jews of Edessa, for whom association with Nisibis was vital,[2] it was a disaster from which they never recovered. Without Nisibis, they were left leaderless as well as impoverished. They had nowhere to turn for help. The political power of the pagans, unreliable allies in time of need, had been broken with the defeat and death of Julian. The Christians no longer needed the Jews as allies in their struggle with heathendom. The Jews were despised and rejected. At Callinicos in 388 Christians burned the synagogue. Theodosius ordered them to rebuild it, but at the urging of Ambrose the Imperial order was rescinded and even financial compensation was refused to the Jews. It is significant that the tolerant emperor felt obliged to instruct the military authorities in the East

---

[1] Ammian, an independent witness, relates how Julian sought to restore the Temple at Jerusalem but was deterred by supernatural balls of fire. Later writers greatly expanded the story. The acts of Julian were quickly overlaid with legend, and the 'histories' must be largely discounted. Bar Hebraeus, for example, is scarcely to be followed when he maintains that the Christians of Edessa 'slew the Jews who were their neighbours', on hearing that Julian had gone to Harran and 'offered sacrifice to idols and paid honour to the Jews'.

[2] See p. 41 above.

to punish anyone who looted synagogues or interfered with Jews holding religious services. Edessa was different only in degree from other places in the Byzantine empire; throughout the whole empire, where in the course of the fifth century only orthodox Christians were permitted to hold appointment as functionaries of the state, the name Jew had become a word of opprobrium.

Ephraim attacks the Jewish practice of circumcision and the Jewish Sabbath and dietary laws. He asks Jewry contemptuously:

Where is the beauty of thy youth, the glory of thine espousals? . . . Where is thy praise and thine honour, and thine adornment and thy splendour? Where is the house which king Solomon erected for thy glory? Where the priest . . . who waited in thy ministry? Where the girdle which was bound on him, the chain also and the turban? Where the fine linen and scarlet, the golden bell and the pomegranate? . . . Where are thy solemn assemblies, thy new moons and thy stated observances? Joy hath ceased with thee, the voice of the dance and thy singing; behold thy chants are funeral wailings in thy mouth and the mouth of thy children.

He reviles the Jews as murderers of Jesus. Death, he writes, declares that

the dead of the Jews are very hateful to me, even their bones are foul to me in the midst of Sheol. Would that I could find the means to cast their bones out of Sheol, for they make it stink. I wonder that the Holy Spirit has dwelt among a people whose smell is fetid.

When Monophysitism became the dominant creed of north-west Mesopotamia the position of the Jews became pitiable. Nestorian doctrine was attacked with fanatical virulence; Nestorianism could in some measure be regarded as close to the doctrines of the Jews, and in time Nestorians were equated readily enough with the Persians. An outstanding Monophysite churchman of his day reviled the Melkite bishops as 'impious men, renegades and New Jews';[1] but we read equally of 'the darkness of the cult of that fellow Nestorius—or rather, the Jewish odiousness and ugliness—I mean the duality of the Natures [of Jesus]'.[2] The Monophysite Emperor Anastasius abused the Nestorian clergy of his capital as 'you accursed Jews', and his words were echoed by the mob of Constantinople who screamed after the Nestorian patriarch, 'No one wants [this] Jewish bishop.'[3] Even the Fathers of the Church from Constantinople who attended the Council of Chalcedon in 451 shouted in unison, 'To exile with Dioscurus of Alexandria! God has cursed Dioscurus! . . . He who has communion with Dioscurus is a Jew!' We cannot wonder, then, that the Monophysites of provincial Edessa in their

---

[1] Elijah of Dara, in John Ephes., *Lives*. So Severus of Antioch fulminated against the 'Jewish Tome of Leo', 'Letters', ed. Brooks, *PO* xii, 321.

[2] Severus of Antioch, *Homiliae Cathedrales*, ed. Duval, *PO* iv, 80.

[3] '*Zach. Rh.*', ed. Brooks (*CSCO*, Scriptores syri 17), 43 ff.

execrations against the 'Nestorian' bishop Hiba should have exclaimed, 'No one wants the enemy of Christ! The foe of the Orthodox is wanted by no one! No one wants a Jew as bishop! . . . No one wants the friend of the Jews! No one wants the enemy of God!' And a century later the Monophysites denounced their persecutor, the Bishop of Amid, as 'murderer and Jew'.[1]

At Edessa, it is true, some signs of friendliness between Jews and Christians are recorded by our chroniclers, but they are few. The Jews of Edessa, we are told, took part in the general mourning at the death of Bishop Rabbula in 435. We are told, too, that they shared the wonder of gullible Christians at the egg that was laid in the town of Zeugma, bearing magical writings which foretold the victory of Byzantium over the Persians in 503–4. But the material and cultural decline of the Jews could not be halted. It was by order of Emperor Theodosius II that Bishop Rabbula converted a synagogue at Edessa into the church of St. Stephen. He received, his biographer informs us, thousands of Jews into Christianity. In the general poverty of Byzantine Mesopotamia the Jews suffered perhaps more than their Christian neighbours; during the famine of 499–500 at Edessa, Jewish women were permitted to bake bread. The purchase of flour, however, was evidently beyond the means of the Jews of Edessa, and the Jewish women were granted flour from the public storehouse.

Physical violence against the Jews was never far away. John of Ephesus described the unsavoury exploits of a certain recluse in a village near Amid who took pleasure in tormenting the Jews by, in particular, burning their synagogue, and John relates his story with pious praise for his hero. But this was the work of an obscure fanatic. The Byzantine authorities in the province of Osrhoene were usually fair in their treatment of the Jews. At Tella, about 100 kilometres from Edessa, the son of the bishop, Sophronius, brought a Jew named Hesychius into the episcopal palace when his father was away in about 448. He even ate with him the 'food of Jews', perhaps unleavened bread, which was forbidden to Christians by the canons of the Church,[2] and let him sit with him at table at about 4 p.m. during the week of Pentecost when Christians fasted. Then he introduced the Jew into church when a service was in progress, but this was too much for the folk of Tella. They drove the men out, and the *dux* gave them shelter in his *praetorion*. In the same town in 502–3 the Jews were accused of conspiring to hand over the city to the Persian army that was then besieging the walls, and an appalling massacre ensued. Indeed, in the seventh century relations between the Byzantine government and their Jewish subjects had so deteriorated that the

---

[1] John of Ephesus in '*Chr. Zuqnin*'.

[2] The Council of Laodicea declared, in Canon 38, that no one shall accept the un-leavened bread of the Jews or 'take part in their profanity'.

sympathies of Jews were held to be with the Persians during the wars of that period. Theodore,[1] brother of Emperor Heraclius, expelled the Persians from Edessa. Our chronicler continues:

Then he ordered the Jews who were at Edessa to be killed, because they had helped the Persians to do harm to the Christians. And when he began to kill them, one of them arose and came to Heraclius [at Tella] and . . . asked him to spare them and treat them kindly. And Heraclius wrote to [his brother] . . . and when the letter arrived he desisted from them.[2]

Nevertheless, although their lives had been spared, the Jews of Edessa were obliged to choose between baptism and exile to Persia.

The Jews appear only at intervals, and in a minor role in the histories of this period; the pagans lurk in the shadows, vague and indeterminate. With the death of Julian, the star of heathendom had set in the Byzantine empire. Pagan cults survived sullenly at Rome and Athens. They had a following at Beirut and Alexandria, largely with the connivance of local officials; and even at Constantinople itself a few individuals contrived to perform their devotions to the gods surreptitiously. In Mesopotamia the Beduins carried out sacrifices —sometimes, the story went, human sacrifices—to the planet Balthi or 'Uzzai, and their womenfolk poured out libations to the goddess on the roof-tops.[3]

The great centre of paganism in north-west Mesopotamia was Harran. While Edessa vaunted its fame as the champion of the universalist creed of Christianity, Harran clung the more obstinately to its local cults of Sin, the moon, and the other planets. In 363 Julian came to pay his respects at its shrines. The episode of the young philosopher-emperor, who cast himself in the role of a latter-day Alexander, but met his death in battle against the Persians, made a vivid impression on his contemporaries. It added fuel to the conflict between Harran and Edessa. 'He delayed [at Harran]', Ammian tells us, 'for necessary preparations and to offer sacrifices, according to the native rites, to the Moon . . . before the altar with no witness present.' The story of his visit was expanded with horrific but improbable detail by Theodoret, some seventy years later. Certainly the Christian community of Harran remained for long insignificant. We do not hear of a Bishop of Harran before 361, when Barsai was transferred from Harran to Edessa—but Barsai apparently had not ventured to reside at Harran. His successor as bishop of that town, the abstemious Vitus, made little headway there. Egeria found it wholly pagan, 'apart from a few clerics and holy monks'. In 449 this 'city of pagans'[4] required, we are told, a bishop of talent whose good works would attract and win over the heathens. Instead, Hiba of Edessa appointed to the see his nephew, Daniel, a young man of (it is alleged) loose morals. Daniel

---

[1] His name is given as Theodoricus by some writers.

[2] Agapius (Maḥbub) of Mabbog.
[3] See p. 145 below. [4] Lit., 'Hellenes'.

is said to have received at the altar the offerings of pagans who feared retribution for their sins, and this was contrary to Church canons; perhaps he sought in this way to convince them of the merit of Christianity. Nevertheless, centuries later, after the coming of Islam, Christian writers still felt an air of unclean mystery over the region of Harran where stonemasons found human skeletons fossilized in the rocks.[1] As far away as Persia it was known as a home of the black arts. The Persian king Khusraw I refused to accept money from the citizens of Harran who came to offer ransom for their city in 540; he said that their gift 'did not belong to him, because most of them are not Christians but are [followers] of the old faith'.[2]

For Harran and its pagans the writers of Edessa had a contempt born of conscious virtue. In the fourth century, St. Ephraim—in somewhat humourless vein, if one considers the relative age of Edessa and Harran—declared:

Thy waters are bitter and thy children harsh; O Harran, make thyself sweet with the Cross . . . My treasure, O Harran, is in thy vicinity, the famed and beauteous Edessa. O daughter, be like thy mother who is the salt of the universe, and with her doctrine season thy mind . . Thou, O Harran, art filthy. Behold, thy mirror is beautiful and pure; adorn thyself by her, the blessed one that is before thee.

Elsewhere he is more reassuring:

In Harran they have brought forth thorns in the desires [of men]. . . . [But] the thorns have changed to roses and lilies, a crown for the husbandmen who bore a crown of thorns . . . The way of reconciliation and the path of joy stretch from Edessa to the midst of Harran, and men go in concord from church to church.

But was Edessa herself, whom poets crowned with epithets like 'the first betrothed of Christ', free of blemish? Occasional allusions in histories and biographies, and scattered information from other sources enable us to build up a different picture. Even the *Doctrine of Addai* admits that the great altar in the midst of the town survived when the pagan priests were converted to Christianity; and a pagan altar was still to be found at a late period at the Monastery of the *Naphshatha*, or tomb towers, in the hills south of Edessa.[3] Names with pagan associations remained in the sixth century, like Kephar Ṣelem (village of the idol), outside the walls of Edessa, and Kephar Nabu (village of Nabu). Some are to be found to the present day, like Sarimaǧara or Sanimaǧara (cave of the idol).[4] There was a community of Manichaeans at Edessa in the fourth century and later, and we may recall the *bon mot* of Ephraim: 'because Mani was unable to find another way out, he entered, though unwillingly, by the doors which Bardaiṣan had opened'. The songs of Bardaiṣan were popular in the time of Ephraim, and his efforts to replace them by his own hymns and choirs were in vain, for they survived to the days of Rabbula.

[1] See p. 211 below.   [2] See p. 113 below.   [3] Cf. p. 29 above.   [4] Cf. p. 57 n. 8 above.

Emperor Theodosius in 382 commanded that a pagan temple of Osrhoene, probably at Edessa, should be permitted to remain open to the public—proof that a demand for its closure had been made—but that sacrifices which involved divination must be not performed there.[1] Later emperors re-enacted the laws against pagan rites; yet throughout the Empire they do not appear to have been enforced with severity. In the fifth century there were evidently still four idol sanctuaries at Edessa, which were destroyed by order of Bishop Rabbula. Finally, there are traces of a serpent cult at Edessa. Ephraim calls heretics 'sons of the serpent', and maintains that they 'enchant the serpent and charm the scorpion'. This is still echoed in Bar Hebraeus, who writes of 'the heresy of Gnostics, that is, those who worship the serpent'. We may recall that the founder of the royal dynasty at Edessa is said by one chronicler to have been Orhay, son of Ḥewya, that is, Serpent.[2] In a large cave just below the wall to the west of Urfa, the shape of a serpent flanked by a bull's head and disc is carved on either side of the central niche.[3]

At the end of the fifth century the men of Edessa celebrated a pagan spring festival with warm devotion and gaiety. In May 496:

they were present . . . on the Friday night [at the place] where the dancer . . . was dancing. They kindled lamps without number in honour of this festival, a custom which was previously unknown in this city. These were arranged by them on the ground along the river, from the door of the theatre as far as the Gate of Arches.[4] They placed on its bank lighted lamps, and hung them in the porticoes, in the Town Hall, in the High Street,[5] and in many other places.

Two years later, in 498, the scene is described again:

There came round again the time of that festival at which the heathen tales were sung; and the citizens took even more pains about it than usual. For seven days previously they were going up in crowds to the theatre at eventide, clad in linen garments, and wearing turbans with their loins ungirt. Lamps were lighted before them, and they were burning incense, and holding vigil the whole night, walking about the city and praising the dancer until morning, with singing and shouting and lewd behaviour. For these reasons they neglected also to go to prayer . . . and they kept saying that the inhabitants of the city in olden times were simpletons and fools. . . . And there was none to warn or rebuke or admonish.[6]

The chronicler seems to maintain not that the festival was an innovation at Edessa, but that the kindling of lamps at this celebration had not been

---

[1] Cod. Theod. xvi. x. 7, 8; but see Libanius, *Or.* 30. 7, 8. The statement by Julian, *Or.* iv, that the people of Edessa worshipped the sun and Monimos and Azizos (probably Mun'im and 'Aziz, representing the evening and morning aspects of the planet Venus) should be regarded with caution. We should no doubt read 'Emesa', which was celebrated for its cult in honour of the sun, for 'Edessa'; it may be observed that Ephraim, the contemporary of Julian, makes no mention of sun worship at Edessa.

[2] See p. 2 n. 4 above.

[3] Pl. 24*b*; above the bull's head is a disc.

[4] Or 'Vaults'; see p. 185.

[5] The Syriac text can also be rendered 'Corn market' but improbably; see p. 181 n. 3.

[6] '*Josh. St.*'.

known there before. Certainly the festival was, as he admits, pagan and popular. In the following year a plague of locusts seems to have caused the cancellation of the festival; and in 502 Emperor Anastasius issued a decree forbidding the public performance of dancing.

Jacob of Serug wrote in a letter in 521:

It is fitting that [Edessa] should be the first-born full of virtue at all times. For it is a blessed land that has received goodly seed and produced a crop of first-fruits in true faith. Even if there have come forth a few weeds, yet are they small in number and it is not to be despised on their account or to be called a field of weeds.

Jacob of Serug was a kindly man who thought well of his fellows. But, somewhat earlier, he had been obliged to write in gentle reproof to a certain monk, Stephen bar Ṣudaile, known as Stephen the scribe. He urges him to remember the penalty of sinfulness. It behoves us, he declares, not to lose, 'for the sake of an excellent life of but few days, the kingdom of heaven which has no end; [we should] flee from pleasures of short duration, lest through them we bring upon ourselves eternal torment.' Stephen had expressed disbelief in the eternity of the torments of hell. We learn more about Stephen from another letter, written by Philoxenus of Mabbog to two presbyters of Edessa, some ten or fifteen years previously. Stephen had once resided at Edessa, and at that time was living near Jerusalem. He had, Philoxenus maintains, expressed blasphemous opinions in books and letters, some of which he had sent to the presbyters. In them he taught 'impious and foolish' doctrines. He held that all creatures can become like God, that there is no Judgement, the same retribution being meted out to everyone, and that even demons will be consubstantial with the divine Essence; he preached, in fact, that all creatures will arrive at one Fulfilment, and that this will be made known in the mystery of the First Day of the Week, when God will be All in All, One Nature, One Essence, One Godhead. Philoxenus warned the presbyters not to allow these books to fall into the hands of others, particularly 'nuns dwelling within church precincts, lest they be led astray through the simplicity and weakness natural to women'.[1]

Evidently, then, heretical views were known, and even originated, at Edessa at this period. More serious was the actual performance of pagan practices by the leaders of local society. At Constantinople a number of well-known men and women, including physicians, sophists, and scholastics, were arraigned before Emperor Justinian who had ordered all pagans to accept Christianity under penalty of exile and the confiscation of their property; these people were charged with practising 'Manichaean'—a

---

[1] A. L. Frothingham, *Stephen bar Ṣudaili*. Whether Stephen is to be regarded as author of the *Book of the Holy Hierotheos*, as claimed by John of Dara and others, is possible but far from certain. In a study of bar Ṣudaile, F. S. Marsh comes to the conclusion that, from the little that we know of his tenets, Stephen could be the author of the third section of the book.

nondescript term for heathen—rites. They were executed and their property confiscated. At about the same time, another group of pagans was arrested in the capital; their leader, a patrician, committed suicide by taking poison. Some twenty years later there was another purge of distinguished persons accused of heathen practices. Five priests from Athens, Antioch, and Baalbek were burnt with their idolatrous writings. In 578 or 589 it was learnt that the pagans of Baalbek were persecuting the Christians, perhaps in revenge for the 'miraculous' destruction of their great and beautiful temple twenty years previously. By order of the Emperor the people of Baalbek were brutally punished by the army. The inquiry then led to Antioch. It was discovered that the vice-prefect of the city (who later committed suicide) had gone to Edessa to celebrate there the festival of Zeus with its Governor Anatolus. Anatolus vainly attempted to arrange an alibi with the bishop; but a statue of Apollo was found in his house, and he and his secretary were tortured and killed. Accusations were freely made against leading personalities, including the Patriarch of Antioch. One of the trials, which became a *cause célèbre*, lasted many years at Constantinople. The mob rioted both at the capital, where blame was laid at the door of the Jews, and at Antioch. But we hear nothing of rioting at Edessa, although the evidence of paganism there seemed to be beyond dispute: evidently at that city the revelations caused no public concern.

The pagans of Harran, among them the Governor himself, had been cruelly persecuted by Emperor Maurice. In 639 the approaching Moslem army gave them the opportunity to free themselves of their Byzantine oppressors. But before surrendering their city to the Moslems they consulted the people of Edessa for guidance. Evidently there was still an organized pagan community at Edessa. Jacob of Edessa at the end of the seventh century describes an argument between a Harranian devotee of the planets and an Edessan follower of Bardaiṣan. This is the last mention of overt paganism at Edessa. Where Christian divines had failed, Moslems succeeded with more subtle methods.

The Jews and the pagans of Edessa were, however, no more than minority groups, probably few in number and with little authority. By the fifth century, Edessa was a Christian city, 'very great and populous, most famous far and wide for its observance of religion'.[1] Its monasteries and academies were celebrated for the piety and the theological acumen of their scholars. Inside the city were 'many shrines and also holy monks, some living among the shrines, others further from the city in convents in more remote places.'[2] Outside the walls the hills, honeycombed with caves, were populated with devout, and sometimes also learned, anchorites 'in great numbers and

[1] Theodoret.   [2] Egeria of Aquitania.

[leading] so extraordinary a life that it can scarcely be described'. They ate neither bread nor meat, and drank no wine; their food was grass, as they 'dwelt in the hills, and continually celebrated God with prayers and hymns'.[1] Such was Abraham, the recluse of Qiduna and the supposed contemporary of St. Ephraim, who passed his days in fasting and vigil and squalor, but also in humility and charity. His redemption of his wayward niece is described by a Syriac writer with rare delicacy. A stylite, Theodoulos, is said to have spent forty-eight years on a pillar near Edessa, in the latter half of the fourth century; and many pillars seem to have been erected for this purpose in the vicinity of the city. The stories of Abgar's correspondence with Jesus, of the sacred portrait, and the evangelization of Edessa, whether by Addai or Thaddaeus or Thomas, were known wherever Christianity was propagated, from Britain to the remote regions of Iran. From all Christendom, pilgrims flocked to visit the shrines of Edessa with their holy relics of Addai and Abgar, of the martyrs Shmona, Gurya, and Ḥabbib, and the bodies of St. Thomas, St. Cosmas, and St. Damian.

[1] Sozomen.

IV

LIFE AT EDESSA, A.D. 240-639

THE MONARCHY IN EDESSA came to an end in about 242. Its dissolution was in no small degree the effect of the direct involvement of Romans and Persians in this area. Less than two decades earlier, in 226, the political situation in Mesopotamia had been radically altered by the emergence of the Sasanid dynasty. The new rulers of Persia followed a policy of national aggrandizement; eager to restore the empire of the Achaemenids, they conducted the war against Rome with determination. Ardashir captured Nisibis and Harran in 233 and threatened Edessa. In the confused fighting of the next ten years Nisibis and Harran changed hands twice; and in 243 the victory of Gordian III at Resaina seemed to have rolled back the Persian offensive. But Gordian was murdered shortly afterwards; and his successor, Philip the Arab, withdrew Roman forces from Mesopotamia, leaving only garrisons in the principal towns.

When the Romans intervened next, they met with disaster. In 260 Shahpuhr I, making his third incursion into Roman territory, laid siege to Edessa; and Emperor Valerian advanced across the Euphrates to its relief. Shahpuhr's inscription near Persepolis records the defeat of the Romans and the capture of the Emperor himself in the 'great battle beyond Harran and Edessa'. Edessa is not in the list of cities that then fell to the Persians, but the Roman army had been destroyed, and it would be surprising if the Persians had not entered the city. They could not, however, have occupied it longer than a few months. Roman troops under Callistus and the prince of Palmyra, Odainath, harried the Persian forces as they withdrew to the East after their sack of Antioch. For the next twelve years Palmyra was mistress of Mesopotamia, although she continued to acknowledge Roman suzerainty. Septimius Odainath assumed the titles 'King of kings and Restorer of the East'. But the territorial ambitions of Palmyra soon aroused the anger of Rome. The Palmyrene forces were defeated in the field, and in 272 Palmyra was occupied by the legions and her power crushed for all time. Rome's leaders were nevertheless unable to mount a successful offensive against the Persians. Aurelian and Probus planned campaigns in the East, but their energies were diverted elsewhere. Carus died suddenly before he was able to consolidate his victories in Mesopotamia. Galerius was defeated near Harran in, probably, 296. It was not until 298 that the Roman forces under the personal direction of Diocletian won back Mesopotamia and dictated terms to the Persians which placed the Imperial boundaries beyond the Tigris. A series of fortresses secured the frontiers; forty years of peace followed.

The restless Shahpuhr II renewed the Persian attack, first in Armenia, later in Mesopotamia. Three times he besieged Nisibis, in 338, 346, and 350. A battle at Singara in 348 was indecisive. Amid fell to the Persians in 359. In the following year Emperor Constantius stayed at Edessa, preparing for a fresh campaign against Persia; but news of the revolt of Julian reached him before his offensive was under way, and he returned to the West, to die on the journey in November 361. In March 363, Julian left Antioch on his much heralded drive towards the East; his forces, drawn from the whole Empire, are said to have totalled 65,000 men, perhaps the greatest expeditionary force of the Byzantine empire. At Batnae, we are told by one source, Edessan envoys offered him a crown.[1] He refused, however, to visit Christian Edessa; instead, he stayed for a brief time at Harran. The campaign of the young pagan Emperor ended, as the Christian moralists of Edessa never wearied of reminding backsliders, in catastrophe. The main Roman army worsted the Persians outside Ctesiphon, but progress was difficult, and in a minor engagement the Emperor was killed. Jovian extricated the Roman forces by a hasty truce, ceding to the Persians regions both to the east and west of the Tigris, Singara, and Nisibis, for a period, it was asserted, of 120 years. The new frontier line between the two empires lay along the river Khabur to the junction of the Nymphius and the Tigris. A contemporary historian describes the anger and grief of the people of Nisibis, who had three times beaten off Persian arms, when they saw a Persian, 'with the permission of the Roman Emperor, enter the city and raise the flag of his nation on the top of the Citadel.'[2] Desultory fighting continued nevertheless, and after prolonged negotiations a formal treaty was concluded only in 384.

During the following century Mesopotamia was free from war, apart from isolated outbreaks of fighting like that around Nisibis in about 424, and a further clash in 441. Edessa was, however, involved briefly in the politics of the capital. During the reign of Emperor Zeno, two of his generals, Leontius and Illus, rebelled at Antioch, the former assuming the title of Emperor, the latter that of 'Administrator of affairs'. Zeno sent an army against them, and they fled. 'They sent one of their supporters . . . to establish their authority in Edessa as a seat of government. The Edessans, however, opposed him, and closed the gates of the city, and guarded the walls after the fashion of war and would not let him enter.'[3]

At the beginning of the sixth century the Persian king, Kawad, reopened hostilities. A treaty of 422 had stipulated that Byzantium and Persia would

[1] This may be the *aurum coronarium* which it was customary for cities to offer to emperors   on their accession and on other festal occasions.   [2] Ammian.   [3] '*Josh. St.*'.

give each other military aid in troops or money, in case of need; and the Persians, on the strength of this clause had received an annual subsidy towards the expenses of operations to contain the Huns. Kawad claimed this as tribute and as acknowledgement of Persian suzerainty over the area.[1] Byzantium, on the other hand, pointed out that Nisibis had not been restored to the West in 483, under the terms of Jovian's treaty of 363, and discontinued the payment. In 502 Kawad suddenly attacked, and captured Theodosioupolis in Armenia through the treachery of the Byzantine commander. Then, aided by mercenaries recruited from the Huns and from the Beduins of al-Ḥira, he invaded the territory of Tella, Harran, and Edessa. The magi dissuaded him from attacking Edessa itself; the omens were unfavourable. Amid fell to him early in 503, and paid a terrible price for its gallant resistance of ninety-seven days, in the slaughter of, we are informed, over 80,000 of its citizens. Emperor Anastasius sought to buy off Kawad, 'that blood might not be shed on both sides', but in vain; war was declared in the same year. The Byzantine forces are said to have numbered as many as 52,000 men. In the autumn a powerful Persian army laid siege to Edessa, the Byzantine base of operations in this area, in spite of the warnings of a Christian sheikh that the letter of Jesus had assured its impregnability against an enemy. The citizens and garrison repaired the defences, although there was a shortage of supplies. According to an eyewitness account, a handful of Edessans beat off the Persians, with heavy losses to the besiegers. A second, more determined Persian attack was again repulsed by 'some few of the villagers who were in the city . . . [armed] with slings', without the intervention of the Byzantine troops. Kawad withdrew, wreaking vengeance on the Edessans by destroying churches and convents outside the walls of the city and laying waste villages in the vicinity.[2] Amid was recovered by the Byzantines in 504–5. Hostilities came to an end shortly afterwards, and a treaty was signed in 506.

On the death of Anastasius, the new Emperor, Justin I, apparently refused to pay the annual subsidy to the Persians. Raids by pro-Persian Beduins and a Byzantine invasion of Armenia led to a resumption of full-scale warfare in 527, the year of Justin's death and the accession of his nephew Justinian. Again, the countryside near the river Balikh and the Khabur was ravaged by Byzantine and Persian armies, who met with varying fortunes: the Byzantines won a battle at Dara in 530, only to be defeated at Callinicos the next year. The death of Kawad in 531 was followed a year

---

[1] This was vigorously rebutted by the Byzantines. John of Ephesus relates that, in claims and counter-claims by the envoys of Persia and Byzantium at the court of the Turks in about 571, the latter alluded to a statue of Trajan which still stood in Persia. No Persian would dare, they declared, to pass the statue mounted on horseback; evidence, they alleged, that the Persians still admitted the overlordship of Rome, and its successor Byzantium.

[2] See p. 157 below.

later by the signing of a new treaty, by which the Byzantines undertook to make a large payment of money to the Persians. But once more the peace was short-lived. In 540 the Persian king Khusraw I Anosharwan carried out an invasion deep into Syria, returning home by way of Mesopotamia. Like his father Kawad thirty years before, he is said to have wished to disprove the legend of the inviolability of Edessa. He was affected, however, by an illness when he reached the city, and permitted it, like Tella and Dara, to buy its immunity for 200 pounds of gold. In 544 Khusraw returned to besiege Edessa. The citizens refused his terms for surrender; negotiations proved fruitless. The walls were then defended with such courage that the Persian king was content to retire with a payment of 500 pounds of gold, instead of the 50,000 pounds that he had demanded.[1] An armistice between the empires was arranged in 545 or 546, and the Byzantines handed a large sum of money to the Persians; peace for fifty years was concluded in 562.

Scarcely ten years had passed before war broke out again, when Justin II refused to honour the undertaking to pay the subsidy now due under the treaty. In 573 the Persians removed the Byzantine threat to Nisibis, besieged and stormed Dara, and penetrated into Syria, though not without loss. Negotiations for a truce opened early in 575, but soon proved abortive. In the summer of the same year Khusraw invaded Byzantine Armenia and advanced westwards; but his army was forced to withdraw in disorder across the Euphrates. Truce talks were reopened and prolonged through 576–7 and into 578; they had reached the point of success when Khusraw died early in 579. War was resumed. While Byzantine armies were in the field against Persia in the East, a Persian army invaded the region of Edessa, Tella and Resaina in 580 and burned and harried the fertile countryside. Edessa successfully withstood a siege of three days. Again buildings to the north of the city were destroyed, and prisoners were killed by the Persians.

Spasmodic fighting followed, but a victory by Byzantine forces, in 586, east of Tella released Edessa from the danger of attack. In the same year Emperor Maurice succeeded to the throne. The conduct of the Byzantine campaign in Persia was imperilled when Maurice, bent on economy, decided that the soldiers' pay should be reduced by one quarter. A new commander, Priscus, was sent to take over the operations in 588, and came from Antioch to Edessa to spend Easter in the camp. But his unpopularity and news of the reduction in pay led the men to mutiny. Priscus took refuge at Tella, and after a hostile demonstration, he fled to Edessa and thence to Constantinople. The Persians sought to take advantage of the situation and laid siege to Tella, but the Byzantine army maintained its loyalty and beat off the in Persians, and even invaded Persia, where they won a considerable victory 590. In the meantime the Persians were faced with revolt. Khusraw II Abarwez

---

[1] See p. 158 below.

was expelled from Persia shortly after his accession, and fled to the protection of Emperor Maurice. After a brief stay at Circesion, at Edessa, where he was generously entertained[1], and at Mabbog, he was restored to his throne with the help of Byzantine arms.

The murder of Maurice in 602 served as the pretext for fresh hostilities, for Khusraw set out in the spring of 603 to avenge the death of his benefactor at the hands of Phocas. The commander of the Byzantine troops in Mesopotamia, Narseh, was also an opponent of Phocas. He seized Edessa, and, we are told, caused the Melkite bishop of the city, Severus, to be stoned. Meanwhile the usurper's force had divided into two: one army set out to besiege Edessa, the other went in pursuit of a person claiming to be the son of Maurice. Khusraw drove off Phocas's army outside Edessa in 604, and seems to have briefly occupied the city, possibly to meet Narseh. He subsequently withdrew, and Narseh himself left Edessa for Mabbog, where later he was induced to surrender to Phocas,[2] to be burnt alive in the capital. When Khusraw decisively defeated the forces of Phocas, Mesopotamia lay at his mercy. But complete control of the area was assured to him only with the capture of Edessa, probably in 609; he was then able to extend his rule over Syria and Palestine, and even Asia Minor and Egypt. At Edessa the Persians imposed, we are told, a heavy burden of taxation on its citizens, and pillaged the marble, gold, and silver of the churches. A historian explains that Khusraw had appointed an Edessan, Cyrus, as governor of the city. Cyrus requested the king to reduce the taxes. But later, Cyrus, angered by the slanders of his envious fellow-townsmen, advised the king to strip the city of its treasures. Subsequently Khusraw ordered the wholesale evacuation to Persia of the population of Edessa, perhaps from fear of the impending attack of the Byzantines. The Persian governor, was, however, a merciful man, and he dispatched the Edessans in small batches. Only one quarter of the citizens had left the city when a Byzantine army approached, and these were later permitted to return on the instructions of the Emperor.

The tables were quickly turned on the Persians. Phocas had been overthrown in 610 by Heraclius, and the new Emperor displayed outstanding generalship and energy. In a series of rapid campaigns he recovered Mesopotamia; he entered Edessa in, probably, 628. But he had little time to enjoy his triumph. Scarcely had peace been signed by Byzantium and Persia in 630—the terms included an exchange of prisoners—when the countries of the Near East were overrun by the armies of Islam. They conquered Syria in 636, Persia in 637, and Mesopotamia in 639. Edessa capitulated to the Moslems in 639.

[1] The view that Khusraw did not visit Edessa can scarcely be maintained in view of the description of this occasion by Edessan chroniclers.

[2] According to one source, the citizens of Edessa handed over Narseh in return for an amnesty.

The four centuries from the abolition of the monarchy at Edessa to its capture by the Moslems were marked, as we have seen, by nagging warfare between East and West. The Persian empire under the Sasanids probably represented the most serious threat that the later Roman Empire had to face on any of its frontiers, and against it were mustered the largest forces recorded in its history. In these circumstances Edessa was a fortress of exceptional importance. Even when Roman frontiers lay far to the east of the Tigris, Edessa's natural strength and strategic situation assured its status as a provincial capital and a military base. In 359 a certain Antoninus, who had deserted to the Persians with secret information about Byzantine plans of campaign, advised them that they could extend their rule to the West only if they secured Edessa in their rear. A few years later, with the surrender of Nisibis to the Persians in 363, Edessa became the principal military stronghold of the Byzantines in this region. The war between the empires was a war of mobility. Persian forces harrassed the country-side, set fire to the crops, and destroyed the villages and homesteads. The Beduin mercenaries in Persian pay did not use the usual lines of communication by water or road; with ever increasing boldness, they carried out forays across the desert paths, and withdrew as quickly as they had come. But these attacks could have no lasting effect as long as the Byzantines retained Edessa.[1] Fortunately for the West, the Persians had little liking for prolonged sieges, particularly in inclement weather. Dressed in the *sharwal*, they were 'weak and sick in winter time, unable to endure the cold and not able to prosecute a war at that season—as the proverb says, "At that time the Mede does not even put his hand outside his cloak".'[2] When, however, Khusraw II took Edessa in 609, the judgement of Antoninus was vindicated. Holding Edessa in the rear, the Persians were able to sweep across the Euphrates and extend their power far to the West and South.

For Rome, and later for Byzantium, it was necessary to maintain the active goodwill of the population of Edessa and of the countryfolk. There were obstacles. The language of the region was Syriac and strange to the West, although, as we shall observe, this problem was eased when the use of Greek became gradually more widespread among the Edessan intelligentsia. There was, too, a greater community of interest during these four centuries, as in earlier times, between Osrhoene and Persian Mesopotamia than between Osrhoene and Asia Minor, or even Syria; ties of cultural and social tradition united the inhabitants of north Mesopotamia on both sides of the frontier. A more powerful bond, however, was religion. In the second and third centuries the growing Christian population of Edessa may have had as

[1] Among the complimentary epithets bestowed on Rabbula in his *Life* was that of 'frontier fortress' of the faithful.

[2] *Chr. ad* 1234. The same chronicler tells us that at the siege of Amid the Persian soldiers 'seemed weak as they were dressed in their *sharwal*'.

little liking for the pagan rulers at Rome as for those at Ctesiphon. Christianity, it is true, originated in western Asia. But it had a firm foothold in Adiabene, east of the Tigris, and in Persian Mesopotamia, and it may well have reached Edessa from the East.[1] A turning point came with the emergence of the Sasanid dynasty in 226, for the heightening of national consciousness in Persia was accompanied by growth in the influence and power of the Zoroastrian priesthood. Official policy in Persia was now antagonistic to Christianity, in spite of the liberal attitude of individual monarchs; Christianity was a proselytizing religion, and Persians would not tolerate missionary activity among a Zoroastrian population. In the West, too, Emperor Decius, and later Licinius, persecuted the Christians, and for a while the followers of the new religion at Edessa were left without sympathizers in either camp. But in 313 came Constantine's Edict of toleration at Milan. Shortly afterwards Christianity became the official religion of the eastern Roman Empire. Thenceforward, the duel between the empires of Byzantium and Persia became a contest between Christianity and Zoroastrianism; and Edessa was perforce committed to Byzantium.

Sectarian conflict, however, weakened and finally severed this bond of religion. At the time of the closure of the School of the Persians at Edessa in 489, the majority of its citizens probably applauded the opposition of Constantinople to the Dyophysite Nestorians. Five years later, the Nestorian leaders in the East broke with the ecclesiastical authority of Antioch to found the national church of Persia. Politics now went hand in hand with dogma, and the Edessans were loyal to Byzantium. But in the following century more subtle differences of opinion caused a rift in the anti-Nestorian camp in the West. The Edessans were mostly Monophysite, and in the sixth century Monophysites were regarded by Constantinople as dangerous heretics. The antipathy between Monophysites and the official Melkite church of Byzantium was no doubt a reflection of the antipathy between dour provincials and the easygoing citizens of the capital. It was heightened by the persecution of Monophysites by Emperors Justin and Maurice, which left, as we have related, a legacy of bitterness at Edessa. The refusal of the intolerant Bishop Isaiah to give the sacrament to Heraclius at the Cathedral of Edessa and the harsh reaction of the Emperor was not an isolated incident.[2] The Edessans had come to bear an intense hatred for the Imperial church. It did not lead them to collaborate with the Persians; but it certainly encouraged them to admit the Moslems into the gates of Edessa. The uncompromising tenets of Monophysitism had much in common with the strict monotheism of Islam.[3]

Diocletian's victories had given Rome undisputed control over the region beyond the Euphrates. The administrative structure of the region was then

---

[1] See pp. 65 ff. above.   [2] See p. 99 above.   [3] See further pp. 99 f. above.

overhauled. The name of Mesopotamia was attached to a province east of the Khabur, with its capital at Amid, the area between the Khabur and the great loop of the Euphrates was called Osrhoene, and its capital was Edessa; both provinces remained within the ecclesiastical jurisdiction of the Patriarch of Antioch. These two provinces, Mesopotamia and Osrhoene, continued in existence throughout the Byzantine period and until the coming of the Arabs. Diocletian's administrative reform was justified on strategic grounds. The eastern province, of which the headquarters moved with the changing course of military operations, maintained direct supervision over the forward garrison towns, like Dara, founded in 507, and the forts along the frontier with Persia. Osrhoene provided a secure supply base in the rear. Its boundaries on the west and the south were the Euphrates, from some 100 kilometres north-east of Samosata to Circesion, and on the east from the lower Khabur to some 30 kilometres west of its junction with the Mygdonius, and then due north to a point about 20 kilometres north-west of Dara; the northern boundary seems to have passed near Mardin and thence, in a north-westerly direction, north of Severak to the Euphrates. It contained cities of no little importance: Birtha, Dausara (later, Qal'at Ga'bar), Callinicos (Nicephorion), and Circesion, all crossing points on the Euphrates, then Resaina (Theodosioupolis), Tella (Contantia), and Severak to the east and north-east of Edessa, and Batnae (Serug) and Harran to its south-east and south. But none had the strategic advantages of Edessa. Here was the natural focus of provincial activity during the four centuries of Roman-Byzantine Osrhoene; here was normally the residence of a military commander (*dux*), of the civil Governor of the province, and of the ecclesiastical authorities.

Edessa was the headquarters of the Byzantine army when Constantius prepared his campaign against Persia in 360. At the turn of the fourth century a factory for the production of shields and arms was established in the city. The commissary-general who sent provisions to the Byzantine troops fighting at Amid in 503 was stationed at Edessa, and in the following two years Edessa was the main base of Byzantium in Mesopotamia while the forward command was at Amid. In 531 also, the military headquarters was at Edessa, and again during the operations at Nisibis in the reign of Justin II.

There was evidently a large garrison permanently quartered at Edessa and in the immediate neighbourhood. In addition to the field army, there were *comitatenses*, combined in the course of time with units of the *palatini*, and also *limitanei* (*riparienses*), or frontier troops. As Procopius explains, these were, 'stationed . . . in all parts of the Empire's frontiers in order to guard the boundaries of the Roman domain, particularly the eastern portion, thereby checking the inroads of the Persians and Beduins.'[1] Procopius goes

---

[1] Procopius, like other Byzantine writers, calls them 'Saracens'; they are the Syriac 'Ṭayyaye'.

on to accuse Justinian of allowing the pay of the *limitanei* on the eastern frontier to fall four or five years into arrears, and of forcing them to depend on charity for their livelihood. There were also stationed at Edessa and the neighbouring towns *foederati*, foreign mercenaries,[1] furnished under treaty by allied tribes and fighting under their own commanders; among them were Huns, Germans, Illyrians, and Goths, some of whom rose to high rank. In Mesopotamia were found, as we shall see, units of Beduins, under a phylarch or paramount sheikh, corresponding to a *dux*, who served in the neighbourhood of their native country. By the time of Justinian, these organized foreign mercenaries had come to be termed 'allies' (σύμμαχοι); the term *foederati* was now applied to soldiers, mostly barbarians, who had enlisted as individuals and were formed into units under Byzantine officers, somewhat like the modern Foreign Legion. All these men were Byzantine citizens, and so accustomed were the Edessans to their presence that the Syriac word *rhomaya* indicated either a Byzantine Roman, or simply a soldier.

On discharge from the army, veterans were enabled to receive allotments of land in the area in which they had served, on which they settled and which they cultivated. By a law of 443, the lands of the *limitanei* became inalienable, and the sons of these soldiers would both enlist in their father's unit and inherit his property. Here perhaps lies the explanation of the use of the Syriac word *pallaha* at Edessa to signify both agricultural labourer and serving soldier; the latter is represented more exactly as *pallaha demalkutha*, *pallaha* of the Empire, or *pallaha stratiya*, military *pallaha*. Serving soldiers, like other public servants, were exempted from the onerous duty of acting as guardians or custodians. Soldiers, too, like merchants, were also to be granted long notice before being summoned to court as witnesses or being required to carry out other legal obligations, since journeys by soldiers to attend distant courts would have affected military efficiency. Indeed, a regulation of the fifth century permitted *limitanei* to be prosecuted only in military courts. Trials in which *limitanei* were involved were, no doubt, conducted in the first instance under the authority of the *dux*.

Recruits were raised by levy from among the rural population, and upon enlistment they were branded. In disciplinary matters they were subject to the control of their general, in Osrhoene of the local *dux*. The general could award any punishment, including death. Of one general we are told that, on the intercession of the bishop, he reduced a sentence of death by burning to death by decapitation. At times the troops were not amenable to discipline. In 505–6, at the request of the grandees of Edessa, the general ordered the Gothic soldiers to have rations allocated to them by the month. In anger they

---

[1] Edessan writers use the Greek term βοήθεια, transliterated into Syriac.

attacked him in his house, and he escaped by fighting his way out; but nothing more was heard of his proposal.

From the time of Diocletian the military command in the provinces was largely separated from the civil government, and regulations enacted by Constantine extended this process. But local recruitment and the provision of armaments, supplies, and billets to the troops were the responsibility of the civil authorities; when there was friction between the military and civilian command it was usually the wishes of the former that prevailed. Soldiers' rations were normally bread, meat, wine, and oil—in wartime, biscuits (*bucellatum*) instead of bread, and sour wine instead of wine. The grinding of corn and the baking of bread or biscuits were an obligation on the local population. Officials of the *curia*, the local council, supervised the transport of rations. In time of war the maintenance of troops placed a heavy burden on the citizens, as we shall see. Soldiers even deserted their camps in the cold of winter for the warmth of the town. For the ordinary citizen it was impossible to contact the military authorities except through the civil administration, and he had little or no redress against ill-treatment by the soldiery. He was fearful of arousing their ill will. In 505–6 Edessans, angered at the bad behaviour of the Gothic mercenaries, adopted the ruse of writing down complaints anonymously on sheets of paper and putting them up on the walls where public notices were displayed. The effect on their commander was immediate, for the troops were quickly withdrawn. The mother of a girl who had been abducted and enslaved by a Goth soldier brought the matter to the notice of his general, but indirectly, through the good offices of the bishop of Edessa.

The civil authority of the kings of Edessa was first replaced by that of a Resident, presumably the ἐπιστάτης τῆς πόλεως. The first civilian Governor of Edessa was, Syriac historians state, a certain Aurelianus Ḥaphsai in possibly 248–9. From his name we may assume him to have been a local notable, who had acquired Roman citizenship. The appointment of a native as the first occupant of such a post, after conquest, was a common practice in the Roman Empire at this time; indeed the Persian king Khusraw II installed citizens as Governors at both Amid and Edessa at the beginning of the seventh century. We have no certain record of the names of Governors of Edessa except for the year 449 and for the period covered by 'Joshua the Stylite'.[1] Under the highly centralized system of the later Roman Empire, appointment to the post of provincial Governor was made at Constantinople, and a Governor of Edessa might be the native of a region far removed from Mesopotamia. It was a matter worthy of comment for the chronicler that, when Amid was recovered from Persia in 504–5, 'the Emperor gave [its

---

[1] See pp. 123 f. below.

citizens] the Governor whom they requested'. The term of office of Governors seems to have been no more than a few years; a certain Alexander who was, as we shall note later, an administrator of exceptional talent, remained at Edessa only one year.[1]

In the fourth century and later, perhaps when the capital of the Empire moved to Constantinople, the provincial Governor of Osrhoene was called by local people by the Greek term *hegemon*, transliterated into Syriac; in his legal capacity and also in fiscal matters he is usually called *dayyana dathra*, judge of the region.[2] His residence was the *praetorion*, situated probably in the Citadel, which previously had been the residence of the kings, and his staff of officials were the *officion* or *praetoriani* with a *princeps* at their head; he gave official interviews to petitioners in his σέκρετον, or office. In, at any rate, the fifth century, his staff included both *palatini*, provincial representatives of the Imperial Government, and officers of the provincial administration, whom local documents call ταξεῶται.

The Governor's badge of office was evidently no longer a special head-dress like that of the kings. It was another symbol of authority that appears under the monarchy, the belt and sword of state, which is found already in the pre-Byzantine period on a statue at Sumatar Harabesi, and on a statue from Harran which may be equally early.[3] When the Governor went to visit the Emperor at Constantinople in 499–500, he set out 'girt with his sword' to show that he retained his office and had not been deposed. This may be related to the Byzantine practice of 'cutting the belt' as a sign of dismissal. Procopius accuses Justinian of cutting the belt of persons who had become unfit or old; Emperor Tiberius threatened leaders of Byzantine society with this punishment if they failed to attend an Imperial court of inquiry. The ceremony of cutting the belt was performed in public when the commander of the Byzantine army in Mesopotamia was removed from duty by Justin II.

Under Diocletian, the periodic requisitions in kind to maintain not only the army, but also the civil service, public transport, the court, and the food supply of the capital were converted into the 'indiction', an annual levy based on a register of land, stock, and heads of the rural population. The

---

[1] See p. 123.

[2] In the law codes of this region and period, the father who wishes to release a son from the *patria potestas* or to give him gifts must do so before the *dayyana*; a woman who wishes to take care of orphaned children must inform the *dayyana dathra*. The guardian of an orphan must not pay taxes on his behalf without the authorization of the *dayyana dathra*. The *hegemon* must be present when a man gives his son to be adopted by another person, and this may be done only if the documents are attested by the Emperor or the *dayyana* (here clearly a higher official than the local *dayyana dathra*). It is the *dayyana dathra* who asks the city notables (*rishane dameditta*) to appoint a guardian to look after orphans. When the Governor collects the capitation tax and seeks financial aid from the Emperor for his city he is called *dayyana*. Shameless people, we are advised, cannot hold the position of *dayyana dathra*.

[3] Photographs on Pl. 13*a*, *b*.

countryfolk were in consequence tied to the locality in which they were registered. This system, shown in fiscal units, could be adjusted simply year by year to meet the budgetary requirements of the Empire, whether in coin or in kind, and to find recruits for the army and labourers for public works. In addition to the annual indiction, special levies were, from time to time, imposed by the central authority upon the province for specific needs. There were also *munera sordida*, the grinding of corn and baking of bread for the troops, as we have indicated, and the supply of material for public buildings, the provision of artisans and unskilled labour, hospitality for soldiers and couriers, and the upkeep of fortified places, roads, and bridges. Frontier provinces like Osrhoene carried a particularly heavy burden.

Responsibility for the payment of taxes in each province was vested in its Governor. He, for his part, usually delegated the task of collection to the members of the local council, the *curia* or *boule*, and they in turn to their own agents. The *curia* not only had the distasteful task of collecting the taxes, but also the obligation of covering any deficits that might appear as the rates of taxation rose. The more *curiales* sought to renounce their station, the more the State insisted on their retaining it. Evidence for this situation is found, at Edessa, in a law prescribing that one son of each successive *princeps* of the *officion*, that is, head of the provincial civil service, must be enrolled in the city *curia*; this evidently was a device for maintaining a link between the government and the municipal administration. The Governor was usually ready to deal vigorously with recalcitrant taxpayers. At Edessa at the end of the fifth century the provincial Governor did not hesitate to use violence against landed proprietors in order to extort the taxes. The machinery for collecting taxes may have been slow and cumbersome, and sometimes taxes were written off because there was no hope of recovering them; nevertheless, by and large, defaulters must have been few.

The assessment of taxes was made, of course, by the central administration, and the annual indictions had to be signed by the Emperor himself. Remission of tax also could be granted only by the Emperor. This was normally on the recommendation of the provincial Governor. In 499–500 when locusts had ruined the crops around Edessa, the Governor went in person to Constantinople to report the disaster and perhaps to ask, as was his duty, for the remission of taxes; he returned with a large sum of money to distribute to the needy. In the three years 503–6 the taxes of Osrhoene were remitted by Anastasius, no doubt because of the heavy financial onus of maintaining the army, which was held to have reached a total of 52,000 men, in the war against Persia. The Emperor reduced taxes on villagers by two *folles* on the personal intervention of the Bishop of Edessa in 499–500, but he evidently did so with reluctance. Indeed, when the bishop went to Constantinople, in 504–5, to make representations to Anastasius that taxation should be reduced, he was rebuked, with some irritation, by the Emperor for deserting his post and also, we may infer, for assuming the prerogative of the Governor. Only the military authorities were on occasion empowered by the Emperor to tender advice about the taxes. When peace was concluded with Persia in 506, Anastasius gave the Byzantine commander and the commissary-general authority to reduce the taxes. They decided to recommend the remission of all the taxes of Amid, and half the taxes of Edessa.

There were other forms of taxation levied on landowners and gentry, but these were of minor importance. All these taxes fell, directly or indirectly, upon the rural population. One tax alone, the *collatio lustralis* or *chrysargyron* was paid, from the time of Constantine, by city dwellers. As its name indicates, it was originally exacted in gold and silver, but, from the reign of Valens, only in gold. Originally, it fell due on the accession and subsequent quinquennial celebrations of the Emperor, but by the fifth century it was collected every fourth year. It was paid by all *negotiatores*, that is, anyone making his livelihood by buying or selling or by charging fees—merchants, shopkeepers, craftsmen, and even moneylenders and prostitutes. It was assessed on the individual's capital assets, including his tools, his animals and slaves, and the numbers of members of his family. Exceptions were few. Doctors and teachers and painters and, after 374, rural craftsmen were immune, while veterans and the lower ranks of the clergy were partially immune. The *collatio lustralis* weighed heavily upon those who paid it. Few taxpayers were provident enough to save during the four years the amount required for the tax, and arrangements to pay by instalments were rare. At Edessa, a city in which, as we shall see, trade in luxury goods had a major role, the tax yielded 140 pounds of gold every four years. Yet the *collatio lustralis* provided no more than probably one-twentieth of the revenue of the empire, a clear indication of the agricultural bias of the economy and the minimal importance of industry and commerce. In 498, the *collatio lustralis* was abolished throughout the Empire by Anastasius, a shrewd financier; he made up the revenue from the *res privata*, the funds at his personal disposal. Its removal caused widespread rejoicing among the artisans at Edessa.[1]

The provincial Governor acted, then, as custodian of the finances of his area. Another major function which he carried out, on behalf of the Emperor, was the administration of justice. The Governor of Osrhoene had, if we may judge from the cries of the Edessan mob, the power to sentence to death by hanging, by burning, or in the Stadium, or to forced labour in the mines. The provincial law courts at Edessa were situated in the 'basilica by the winter baths' in the fourth century, at the end of the fifth century in the nearby Church of St. John. Governors acted as judges of first instance.

[1] See p. 139 below.

They were discouraged from delegating important cases to subordinate courts. But inevitably the poor were at a disadvantage in litigation with more important citizens. Fees were high, there were long delays, and bribery was not uncommon; throughout the Empire the shortest road to riches for a provincial Governor during the short tenure of his office lay through his activities in the courts. There was little that the authorities at Constantinople could do to rectify this situation. Dissatisfied litigants, with a few exceptions, had, it is true, a right of appeal to a higher court, in the case of Osrhoene to the *comes Orientis* or even direct to the Emperor. But, too often, an appeal would involve the expense of travel over a long distance, and this would nullify the advantage given by Diocletian's creation of smaller provincial units, each with its own court. Two institutions protected in some degree the poorer citizens—the office of the *defensor civitatis* and the episcopal courts; and to these we shall return later.[1]

At Edessa, as elsewhere in the Empire, justice in the Governors' courts appears to have been frequently frustrated through the venality of judges and the undue influence of the wealthy. The more striking then, is the tribute paid to Alexander, Governor of Osrhoene in 496–7, of whom we are informed that he tried cases, where necessary, in secret and without fees:

[He] placed a box in front of the *praetorion* and made a hole in its lid and wrote thereon that if anyone wanted to make something known and it was not easy for him to do so openly, he should write it down and throw [the paper] into [the box] without fear. By this means he learned many things which people wrote down and threw into [the box]. He used to sit every Friday at the shrine of St. John the Baptist and St. Addai the Apostle, and settle legal cases without any charge. So the wronged took courage and brought their cases before him, and he judged them. Some cases which were more than fifty years old and had never been inquired into were brought before him and settled.[2]

The Governor's powers extended throughout the province. But he also controlled the life of the capital city, Edessa; and it is to the activities of the Governor in this capacity that we have most frequent reference in the local chronicles. All the multifarious functions of local administration were vested in his hands; we are reminded, indeed, of the paternalistic attitude of the kings of the Aryu dynasty. In Byzantine times the place of the *nuhadra* of the monarchy was taken by the Administrator (Syriac, *medabberana*). He deputized for the Governor in his absence from the city, and he discharged minor duties on his behalf. It was, however, the Governor himself who was charged with the responsibility for the security of the area under his control. In 504–5, for example, the Governor with a subsidy of 200 pounds of gold from the Emperor restored the whole outer wall of Edessa, and also repaired the wall of Batnae which had fallen into disrepair. He it was, no doubt, who

[1] See pp. 125, 129 below.
[2] '*Josh. St.*' The translation presumes small emendations to the Syriac text, following Wright.

kept the roads in proper condition, and supervised the efficient working of the postal service. He superintended the upkeep of the aqueducts, which brought water into Edessa from the hills to the north, and the maintenance of an adequate supply of corn in the public granary. The Governor disposed of a body of secret police, *sharrire*,[1] and also a force of police with general duties. The latter controlled movement through the city gates, which seem to have been closed each night. No doubt they continued the custom, established under the monarchy, of manning the walls during the autumn and winter months to give warning when the river threatened to submerge the city. To judge from the loss of life in the floods of 303, 413, and 525, this task was not performed with great efficiency.

The streets of the city were lit at night. We read that in 504-5 the oil which had been supplied to the shrines and convents, to the amount of 6,800 *qeste*, was devoted to lighting the porticoes; instead the Governor made, from his own property, an allocation of 200 *qeste* to each shrine. Eight years previously the artisans of Edessa were ordered by the Governor to hang crosses over their booths on each Saturday night with five lighted lamps in them. The Governor supervised the organization of the markets. 'Joshua the Stylite' gives such precise details for each year of the prices of staple foods that these were evidently under constant review. The upkeep of the public baths and the hygiene of the city were also the responsibility of the Governor. In 496-7 order was given to remove the raised platforms built by the artisans in the porticoes, presumably to maintain freedom of movement in the streets. Our chronicler informs us that in 497-8 the Governor ordered the porticoes to be whitewashed, to the annoyance of the superstitious who felt that this was unlucky and presaged disaster.

A good Governor displayed a sympathetic interest in the welfare of the citizens. In time of drought or plague he would take the lead in making provision for the needy and sick. In 499-500 the Governor went to Constantinople to report direct to the Emperor the terrible famine at Edessa, and 'the Emperor gave him no small sum of money to distribute among the poor'. The Governor's deputy released corn from the government granary for sale to the public. In the following year the Governor 'blocked up the gates of the colonnades attached to the winter bath, and laid in it straw and mats so that [the poor] could sleep there.'[2] He accompanied the bishop and nobles at funeral processions in time of famine. He was in charge also of the cemeteries. During the famine of 499-500 many people died and the cemeteries were full; the Governor gave order that old graves beside the Church of Mar Qona[3] should be reopened. Some Governors of Edessa were enthusiastic builders. One constructed a covered walk[4] near the West Gate and a public

---

[1] See p. 20 above.   [2] 'Josh. St.'   [3] See p. 180 below.
[4] The Syriac term may be translated, less probably, 'rampart' or 'warm baths'.

bath, another repaired the city wall, the aqueducts and baths and his palace, and built, we are told, much else.

The administration of municipal affairs was, then, the responsibility of the Governor sent from Constantinople and his deputy, the Administrator. There were also civic functionaries chosen from among local people. The two *strategoi* whose office was, it has been suggested, suppressed by the kings of Edessa,[1] seem to reappear. We have observed that already in 243, when Edessa had just been brought under the direct administration of Rome, the *strategoi* are named in an official document, side by side with the Resident. They are mentioned too in the *Acts* of the Edessan martyrs, which reflects the situation at Edessa in the early fourth century; in a legal code of the following century we are told that if a widowed mother does not wish to take care of her child, a guardian may be nominated 'by the city *strategoi* who are the chief men (*rishane*)'. When Amid was occupied by the Persians in the early sixth century they appointed two representatives of the citizen body to act as its spokesmen, who were, in fact, *strategoi*. But these are no more than passing references. Already by the time of Diocletian, the *strategoi* had lost much of their power, and at Edessa these shadowy functionaries certainly provided no restraint on the autocratic power of the Governor.

Minor judicial powers were vested in two other personages in the city. The first was the bishop, who presided, as we shall observe, at his own court which tried lay, as well as ecclesiastical cases. The second was the *ekdikos* or *defensor civitatis*, whose office had emerged in the East, probably before Constantine the Great; by later emperors it was extended to the whole Empire. It was intended to protect humble citizens against exploitation by their more powerful fellows. Allusions to the *defensor civitatis* in the Syriac codes indicate that his jurisdiction at Edessa was limited. He could, for example, instruct the keeper of archives to release the text of a will. He could authorize the writing of a second will if the testator was dying while making his original will and died before it had been dictated to the end, provided that the full provisions of the will were known to witnesses beforehand. When, too, it was not possible to use the good offices of the bishop's court, recourse was had to the *ekdikos*. The clergy and monks of Tella who, in probably 448, preferred charges of conducting magic against their Bishop Sophronius, drew up the document in the presence of the *ekdikos* and deposited their sworn testimony in his custody.

The representative organ of the townspeople was the *boule*, or *curia*, the the city Council. Its members were drawn from the 'free men', well-known personages in the city; and it sat in conclave in the Town Hall. Edessa, like other Seleucid foundations, had known this institution from the earliest times, and the town Council of the Byzantine period was certainly the

[1] See pp. 15, 17, 20 f.

lineal descendant of that council of 'free men' who had assisted Abgar in the administration of his kingdom. The councillors, *curiales*, are called in fifth century Syriac documents by the term πολιτευόμενοι. The Governor, no doubt, kept a watchful eye on their activities. They were recognized as a convenient instrument of government. They were responsible, as we have observed, for the collection of taxes and they supervised the carrying out of the *sordida munera* by the poorer citizens—labour for building operations, the upkeep of the streets and sewers, the supply of watchmen, and the various public works which maintained the smooth running of the city. We do not know what was the number of councillors at Edessa; it may have been large, for other cities of the Empire had as many as six hundred.

The city Council was, however, too unwieldly for efficient administration. Executive power was vested in a small inner committee of *principales* or ἀξιωματικοί.[1] 'Those who are adorned with authority' they are called in a document of the fifth century, as opposed, no doubt, to 'those of lower [rank]', who must be the ordinary πολιτευόμενοι, or councillors. In some cities this select group of municipal administrators numbered ten or five. At Edessa, if we may judge from the practice of later times, there were twelve. They were sons of the most important families of Edessa. Some of their names are recorded in the time of Heraclius in the early seventh century. When, in anger, the Emperor expelled Bishop Isaiah from the Cathedral, the latter was followed into exile by the leading Monophysites of the town; the Roṣpaye (from Ruṣafa), the Tellmaḥraye (from the village of Tell-Maḥre),[2] the family of Qozma son of Arabi, and the family of Nalar.[3] Some persons of high rank at Edessa participated in the government of the city. In 489 a deputation that protested against the activities of Bishop Hiba, included among their spokesmen two persons with the title of Count, one Senator and two *magistriani*, provincial subordinates of the Master of the Divine Offices.

The order of *curiales* was hereditary. Membership of the *curia* might, we have noted, involve serious financial obligations. On the whole, however, the councillors, and certainly the *principales*, received privileges which outweighed the occasional disadvantages of their position. They were immune from the special taxes which occasionally were added to the indiction, and from the *sordida munera*. When the burden of taxation was lightened at the beginning of the sixth century, it was the city notables who were first to benefit. They rivalled each other in the ostentatious display of their riches. On Khusraw's arrival at Edessa after his expulsion from the throne, two nobles, Marinus and Iwannis Roṣpaya, competed for the honour of entertaining the young prince. Khusraw lodged in the mansion of Marinus. But Iwannis was not to be outdone. 'With vainglorious thoughts he wished

---

[1] Syriac, *rishane*.   [2] Near the river Balikh.   [3] Or Nalad; the name is obscure.

to show that he was richer than Marinus'. He invited Khusraw and the chief men and 'elders', that is, his fellow *curiales*, of Edessa to his house and exhibited his wealth of gold and silver, with what tragic sequel we shall see later.[1]

The notables, however, must have acted, for the most part, with concern for the general welfare of the city. In the famine of 499–500 they set up infirmaries for the sick and poor. They were usually consulted by the Governor before any action was taken that might have local repercussions. In the fourth century the assent of the city notables was sought before the order was given for the execution of the Christian martyrs. When Kawad demanded ransom from Edessa in 502, the request was referred to the city grandees. They withheld their consent to the demand declaring, 'Christ stands before our city', and the Byzantine general was emboldened to reject the Persian demand. During the siege of Amid by Kawad, too, the Persians terms for the surrender of the city were rejected by the Chief Councillor, the Governor, and the Steward. The order in which these dignitaries are mentioned is significant, but it should not surprise us. The outcome of the prolonged warfare between Byzantium and Persia depended on the loyalty to Byzantium of the city fortresses; in the last resort this depended on the will and energy of the citizens themselves, and on their leadership.

The ordinary people of Edessa seem to have accepted the decisions of their rulers for the most part without demur. In this they were encouraged by the example of the Church. Parish priests are enjoined by their superiors to show respect for the landowners.[2] So too, the chronicle of 'Joshua the Stylite', criticizes the 'administrators' of Edessa for participating in a pagan festival. But the writer adds discreetly, 'I do not choose to specify these sins distinctly, that I may not give an opportunity to those who like it of finding fault and saying of me that I speak against the notables'.

Nevertheless it was in the leaders of the church that the humble inhabitants of Edessa found their champions. The bishop was the spokesman of the needy and inarticulate. The biographer of Bishop Rabbula relates that he did not hesitate to reproach the rich of Edessa, who ground the poor, while they sat at ease in their magnificent houses. The family of Euphemia, a simple Edessan girl who had been abducted by a Gothic soldier, were too timid to accuse him before the military authorities. The Bishop of Edessa did so on their behalf; and when the man was sentenced to death he again intervened, and the sentence of death by burning was reduced to death by beheading! Barhadad, Bishop of Tella, interceded with the Byzantine commander, who returned by way of Edessa in 506 after concluding peace

---

[1] pp. 146, 154 below.   [2] See p. 136 below.

with the Persians. The general did not wish to enter the city because its inhabitants had, a little time previously, posted anonymous notices on the walls of the city complaining of ill-treatment by the army. Barhadad 'begged him not to allow resentment to get the better of him, nor to leave behind the feeling of vexation or annoyance in anybody's mind. [The general] readily acceded to his request.'[1]

When Edessans died in great numbers of hunger and plague, it was the bishop who led the funeral processions, accompanied by the Governor and notables. And when famine was at its height, Bishop Peter did not fear even to intervene directly with the Emperor, although, as he must have known, he was encroaching on the prerogative of the Governor of the province.

[He] set out to visit the Emperor [at Constantinople] to beg him to remit the tax. . . . However, . . . the money had [already] arrived. . . . In order not to send our father away empty-handed, [the Emperor] remitted two *folles* to the villagers . . .[2]

Five years later, the bishop came to the court on the same errand; but now he met with a less friendly reception:

The Emperor answered him harshly, and rebuked him for having neglected the charge of the poor at a time like this and having come up to him [at Constantinople]; for he said that God himself would have put it into his heart if it had been right, without persuasion from any man, to do a favour to the blessed city [of Edessa].[3]

Yet the bishop's journey was effective in spite of the Emperor's remonstrances, for, our historian continues:

whilst the bishop was still [in the capital], however, the Emperor sent remission [of tax] for all Mesopotamia by the hands of another without the [bishop's] being aware of it.[4]

In time of war against the Persians the bishop could be relied upon to strengthen resistance to the enemy; Bishop Barhadad of Tella, for example, in 503,

used to go around and visit [the defenders] of the city and pray for them, and bless them, commending their care and encouraging them, and sprinkling holy water on them and on the wall of the city. He also carried the Eucharist with him on his rounds in order to let them receive the mystery at their stations, lest for this reason any one of them should quit his post and come down from the wall.[4]

Barhadad did even more; he went out to speak to the Persian king Kawad, and persuaded him to raise the siege.[5] Other bishops showed the same

[1] 'Josh. St.'

[2] Ibid. The text becomes uncertain at this point.

[3] Ibid. A Novel of Justinian forbade bishops to absent themselves from their dioceses longer than one year, or to come to Constantinople without the authorization of their Metropolitan. The reissue of the regulation by successive emperors shows that it was little observed.

[4] Ibid.

[5] Procopius, describing this incident, remarks that Tella 'had neither a garrison of soldiers nor any other defence, but only the inhabitants who were miserable folk'.

courage. The Bishop of Sura on the Euphrates in 540 begged king Khusraw to spare his city, and the king agreed—though subsequently he seized the city by treachery.[1]

That the bishops should be the trusted allies of the central administration was already the policy of Constantine the Great. He gave wide powers to episcopal courts to try minor cases and to award prompt and cheap justice; their decisions, he ruled, were to be final and to be executed by the civil power. Subsequently this regulation was amended; the decisions of the bishop's court became binding only if both parties to the suit agreed beforehand to abide by them. Theodoret, in the fifth century, describes the work of Abraham, Bishop of Harran, a city which was still, we are informed, 'given to the frenzy of demons'. The bishop would spend the whole day reconciling litigants. Those who had intended to work injustice found that the other party to the suit, far from being hurt, left the court feeling that he had triumphed. The State also granted the prerogative of witnessing the manumission of slaves to the clergy, in the person of the bishop or priest in the city, and in the countryside to the bishop's representative, the *periodeutes*, or to the priest of the village parish. Emperor Justinian awarded bishops far-reaching rights of intervention in municipal administration. They were authorized to take part in the nomination of city functionaries, in the control of municipal finances, and in the upkeep of baths, public granaries, aqueducts and bridges.

Already, however, in the previous century bishops had been entrusted with works of construction involving much expense and a large labour force, at a vast distance from the capital. At Edessa Bishop Nona built a baptistry, a leper house, a shrine, monasteries, and towers and bridges; and he made the roads secure. Thomas of Amid supervised the building of Dara, in the reign of Anastasius. Bishop Peter of Edessa in 504–5 was given money by the Emperor to repair part of the wall, and the minister Urbicius gave him ten pounds of gold to build a church. At the same time Sergius, Bishop of Birtha (Birecik), who was under the authority of the Bishop of Edessa, had the wall of his city rebuilt at the expense of the Emperor. So common was this activity on the part of the bishops that the biographer of Rabbula remarks on the fact that this frugal bishop refrained from all building, except the construction of one church and the repair of another. The responsibilities and prestige of the bishops were, then, very high. At least two men were appointed to a diocese who had previously held the rank of Governor, Nona of Seleucia and his successor Mara.[2]

---

[1] It was through the entreaties of its bishop that the citadel of Aleppo was spared when the city itself had been destroyed by Khusraw in 540.

[2] There seem to be few parallels for this elsewhere in the Byzantine empire. Notable is the election of Ephraim, Count of the Orient, to the patriarchate of Antioch in the sixth century.

At times the easy co-operation between the State and the local ecclesiastical authority was ruptured because of doctrinal controversy. Emperors maintained their role as arbiters of the orthodoxy of their clergy. If the opinions of a bishop were called in question, he could no longer rely upon the support of the provincial governor or military commander.[1] In 448 Hiba of Edessa had been exonerated by his superior, the Patriarch of Antioch, from the charges brought against him by his fellow ecclesiastics, and the verdict was confirmed by an Imperial commission sitting at Tyre and Beirut. When he returned to Edessa, probably in April 449, the clamour of his vociferous opponents nevertheless continued unabated. Hiba then left the city to demand from the *magister militum* the support to which he was entitled. Far from obtaining this, he was arrested by the newly appointed Governor of Edessa, and he spent the next two years, he claimed later, in no fewer than twenty prisons before he was reinstated by the Council of Chalcedon. Much the same story was repeated in the following century. In 522 Bishop Paul of Edessa had been dismissed by the Emperor for being a supporter of the Monophysites; and he was taken out by force from the baptistry in which he had sought shelter. Asclepius was installed by the general at Edessa in his place. The new bishop was then able to persecute his enemies with all the vigour of the civil authority:

[he] was active and violent against the [Monophysite] believers; and many were banished by him and outraged with every kind of torture, or died under the harsh treatment inflicted on them by Liberius the Goth, a cruel Administrator who was called the 'bull-eater'[2]

It was the representatives of the State, both civil and military, who hounded the Jacobites, bishops as well as members of the lower orders of clergy and laymen. In the reign of Maurice about four hundred monks were slaughtered by the troops outside the walls of Edessa.

The principal charges brought against Bishop Hiba provide a vivid illustration of the power of a Metropolitan bishop in the fifth century. He was accused of diverting to his own use the major part of 1,500 *denarii* and other sums raised by public subscription for the ransom of captives, as well as two purses and a bag of, in all, 6,000 *denarii* deposited in the Treasury. Only 1,000 *denarii* had, it was alleged, been disbursed by Hiba. A valuable

---

[1] A bishop nevertheless exercised wide power of decision in ecclesiastical matters. Of Peter, Bishop of Edessa in the time of Anastasius, we are told that he 'added to the festivals of the year [at Edessa] that of Palm Sunday. He also established the custom of consecrating the water on the night immediately preceding the Feast of the Epiphany, and he prayed' (the word is uncertain) 'over the oil of unction on the Thursday [of Passion Week] before the whole people, besides regulating the other feasts.'

[2] '*Zach. Rh.*' The military were perhaps more lenient than the civil authorities. They insisted on Bishop Asclepius providing the expelled Monophysites with baggage animals. It was only, too, on the instructions of the Melkite bishop that Monophysites were put to death by impalement at Amid.

chalice donated to the church had disappeared. Hiba had received payment for the ordination of priests. He had sought the preferment to the see of Batnae of a deacon from whom he hoped to obtain certain magic formulae. When his plan was thwarted by an archdeacon, he had deposed his opponent, and subsequently he appointed his protégé as warden of the hospice of Edessa. He had ordained as *periodeutes* a person who was widely considered an adulterer and pederast, and those who objected were handed to the *archon* (here possibly the district judge) for summary punishment. He had appointed his nephew, Daniel, a young man of notoriously bad conduct, to the diocese of Harran, although its inhabitants were largely pagan and required the direction of a talented pastor who would influence them by the example of his virtue. He had permitted his brother and other relatives to enjoy the benefit of ecclesiastical revenues. He had allocated new wine of bad quality and in small quantity to the church for Holy Communion, while he and his associates maintained a stock of excellent wine for their own pleasure. He had enjoyed openly the diversions of the stadium and amphitheatre, and an associate of Hiba was thought by the people to have provided a circus specially to give pleasure to the bishop. In the list of accusations against Hiba—not always at the top, although popular clamour made much of it—was also the charge of heresy. Hiba was, it was asserted, a Nestorian, and had called Cyril of Alexandria a heretic. He had made statements of a scandalous nature at a meeting of his subordinate priests, at an interview with a lay notable of the town, and in a sermon from the pulpit to his congregation. His authorship of the letter to Mari the Persian was well-known.[1]

Charges were preferred against Daniel of Harran. He had maintained a liaison with a married woman of Edessa, and spent much time travelling with her outside his diocese. He had also, it was alleged, ordained priests as ill-famed as himself. He had given his mistress and her relatives money taken from the churches of Harran and Edessa, without any protest on the part of his uncle, and the woman, who had before been poor, practised usury with her ill-gotten wealth. He had tricked a deacon, who had acquired church property and wished to leave it to the poor; instead, Daniel gave the inheritance to his mistress. He allowed the trees in a wood belonging to the church of Edessa to be cut down for use in the building of her house. He had accepted, contrary to the canons, offerings on the altar from pagans and had given them absolution from their sins. Sophronius, Bishop of Tella, a cousin of Hiba, had, it was insinuated, also been appointed to his see through nepotism. He was accused of practising magic, and his son was in the habit of consorting with Jews. Somewhat as an afterthought, Sophronius was charged with holding Dyophysite views.

Some of the accusations against Hiba may have been unfounded. It should

[1] See p. 93 above.

be recognized, however, that the temptations that faced an ambitious and easy-living Bishop of Edessa were great indeed. The Church disposed of considerable wealth, the major part derived from the gifts and bequests of the devout, both rich and poor, and from the property of clerics who died intestate or donated their wealth to the church in their lifetime.[1] Bishop Rabbula opposed luxury. He insisted that the altar vessels of silver and gold should be sold and the proceeds given to the poor; they were replaced by vessels of earthenware. Only those church vessels that had been consecrated as memorials to the dead were retained. Other Bishops of Edessa, however, welcomed gifts. In 437–8 a great silver table weighing 720 pounds was presented to the Old church; four years later, the bones of St. Thomas were enshrined in a silver chapel. Under Hiba, a chalice, studded with jewels and of great value, was given to the Church. The silver vessels, which Hiba had allegedly melted down, apart from those which he was accused of taking for his own table, were sold at a weight of 200 pounds. A wealthy priest gave money to endow those churches that had no revenue. The Church received large legacies. There was so much money in the Treasury that Bishop Hiba (we are told) was able to abstract two purses and a bag with silver to the value of about 6,000 *denarii*. During a plague of boils at Edessa in 496–7 a silver litter was donated on account of the 'seemly zeal' of the bishop, one congregant giving as much as 100 *denarii*. Shortly afterwards a priest provided copper plating for the door of the men's aisle in the Great church.

The church, it is true, had high expenses. It paid tax on its lands, although it was exempt from any additional levies. It had to maintain its buildings, to pay the stipends of the clergy, to provide for the sick, widows and orphans, the poor, and strangers,[2] and to expend money on the ransom of captives. But frequently it received donations for these specific purposes, and not only from rich parishioners. In the time of Hiba a poor deacon who had grown rich, it was hinted, by the improper acquisition of church property, bequeathed his money to the poor. An appeal by the bishop in the Cathedral for money for the ransom of prisoners yielded about 500 pounds of silver (that is, 1,500 *nummi*). Even women and widows and orphans offered about 50 or 100 *nummi*. A list of the loot taken from the churches of Edessa by Khusraw II, after he occupied the city in 609, gives an impression of the wealth that the Church had amassed. It comprised the treasure of the various shrines, stone tables, columns of marble, windows of gold and silver, silver plating in the chapel[3], on the altar, on the four columns, and the columns in front of the altar, and the throne in the middle of the church,—

---

[1] As did Bishop Rabbula, who was a wealthy landowner to the west of the Euphrates, before he became a priest.

[2] It was perhaps in connection with alms for the poor that the 'City deacon' visited the episcopal palace in about 448 to obtain the bishop's signature on an alms ticket.

[3] Greek, ναός.

totalling in all a weight of about 120,000 pounds. This was not all. Heraclius confiscated the property of the Monophysite church, donated, we are told, by the rich families of the city. It consisted not only of gold and silver but also of gardens and mills and shops and baths. With careful husbandry the wealth of the church had grown fast. We should not forget, either, that by a Code of Leo in 472 the clergy were exempt from the payment of taxes and from the family obligations broadly covered by the *patria potestas*.

An unscrupulous bishop could amass much wealth in a short time. We need not accept the malicious accusations that Hiba had received payment for the ordination of priests, or that Daniel accepted the offerings of pagans who wished to atone for their sins. There is no reason, however, why Hiba should not have appointed members of his own family, or of his own circle of associates, to vacant bishoprics and other posts in Osrhoene, or have given church revenues into the keeping of his brother and others of his relatives. Nepotism was regrettable but it was not a sin. A bishop was free to dispose as he wished of the ecclesiastical property in his province. Domnus of Antioch, therefore, ruled correctly that no blame attached to Hiba on this score. There was a Treasurer of the Church at Edessa and a Steward (*logothetes* or *oeconomos*; Syriac, *rabbaita*) in charge of Church estates. But the responsibility for disposing of them lay with the bishop himself, after consultation, when this seemed fitting, with his Patriarch. Church Councils reiterated that ecclesiastical funds should be administered by a cleric especially nominated to the post, but they could not interfere with a bishop's powers unless he acted with blatant indiscretion. In precisely the same way, Councils condemned simony, but could not wholly prevent its appearance in some form or another.

The bishop's authority over his own subordinates was also complete. He had the power to suspend or excommunicate a recalcitrant priest. There was a safeguard against arbitrary action by the bishop in that priests at loggerheads with their superior had the right of appeal to the tribunal of the Patriarch, or even to the Emperor himself, and the right was frequently exercised. Hiba had evidently been sorely tried by the Monophysite opposition in his province; perhaps he lacked the influence or the capacity of his equally autocratic predecessor Rabbula. He accepted the somewhat humiliating advice of the Imperial commission not to discriminate against a priest or monk of whose actions he disapproved and to consult the Patriarch before taking any drastic steps against his opponents. But the Council of Chalcedon drew a different moral from the Hiba affair. They enacted regulations against secret societies and brotherhoods of priests and monks, in order to avoid a repetition elsewhere of the plots against the bishop of Edessa—in other words, they upheld the overriding authority of the bishops.

The jurisdiction of the Bishop of Edessa extended throughout the province of Osrhoene. He controlled the neighbouring sees, of which the most important were Harran and Callinicos to the south, Batnae (including Serug) and Birtha to the west, Tella and Resaina to the east.[1] Hiba claimed at the Council of Chalcedon that his clergy at Edessa numbered two hundred or more. The staff of the Cathedral, who signed the document in his support, consisted of seventeen priests, thirty-seven deacons, thirteen sub-deacons, and one lector.[2] Reference has already been made to the Steward, probably the most important local official in the Church after the bishop himself. The post was held by a prominent townsman; we have observed that at Amid he stood directly below the Governor. Occasionally a *rabbaita*, who was normally a *bar qeyama*, would succeed to the office of bishop. In the famine of 500–1, the two Stewards of the Great Church of Edessa, of whom one later became Bishop of Harran, set up an infirmary in buildings adjoining the church. Other dignitaries in the city were the *xenodochos*, the warden in charge of the hospice, and sometimes chief priests and archdeacons; there were also deaconesses. Prominent among the lower ranks of church officials were the vergers and the scribes. Rabbula provided for the latter in his will, Sophronius evidently used the scribes of Tella to prepare his astrological calculations, while Jacob of Serug is reported to have employed seventy secretaries to copy his poetic compositions.

Of the conduct of the affairs of a bishopric in Osrhoene we learn little. A bishop resided in his official palace, and when he entertained he did so in the banqueting hall, or *triclinium*. He would preach in the pulpit of the Cathedral. It was the bishop, strangely enough, who provided wine at Edessa for Holy Communion at the feast of the Holy Martyrs. The Bishop of Edessa was expected to be present in the city at Easter. It was then that he assembled the clergy of the city, gave them small presents in honour of the festival and delivered an address. The bishop was evidently regarded with proper deference. Even Hiba's opponents claimed that they would have respected his rank whatever his conduct, but for his heretical opinions. The uproar that broke out in the Cathedral at Edessa one Sunday was in the absence of the bishop. A bishop could not normally be reduced from his rank unless he had abused his position. Nona, who had acted as Bishop of Edessa during the exile of Hiba, retained his status when the latter was reinstated, though no see was vacant at the time, and Nona was placed at the disposal of the Patriarch of Antioch. A bishop might, however, resign. The Monophysites

---

[1] Others were Circesion, Tell-Maḥre, Himeria (Greek, Himerion), Dausara, Nea Valentia, Marcoupolis (Charax Sidou, or Haikla deṢida; on these names see U. Monneret de Villard, *Rendiconti . . . dei Lincei*, Serie ottava, vi, 1951, 76 ff.), Ma'ratha, and perhaps a bishopric of the Beduins (Syriac, Ṭayyaye).

[2] His opponents mustered fifty signatures for one of their letters of protest, but of these eleven were the names of monks, the rest were ten priests, twenty deacons, and nine sub-deacons.

of Edessa who demonstrated against Hiba expressed surprise that he had not, in view of his Nestorian leanings, himself resigned from his office. Daniel of Harran is reported to have admitted his unworthiness for a bishopric, when he was reproached face to face by his fellow ecclesiastics, and to have submitted his resignation in writing. His letter would normally have been passed to a Synod for consideration. In fact no action was taken; the see, which had been occupied by a certain John before the Council of Chalcedon, then reverted to Daniel.

At Edessa, as elsewhere in the East, Christianity took a firm hold in the countryside as well as—indeed, possibly earlier than—in the cities. The work of the parish priests of the diocese was controlled by the bishop. In the villages the place of the bishop and his presbyter in the city was taken by the *periodeutes* and his presbyter, and on certain occasions by the presbyter, deacons, and 'old men', or lay elders. The clearest description of the work of the parish priests is to be found in a group of rules governing the actions of priests and *benai qeyama*; the priests here are clearly parish priests. These rules are ascribed, probably correctly, to Rabbula in the fifth century; they merit summary here since they evidently had influence on the general conduct of Edessan society. Priests were instructed to avoid the company of women, not to take bribes or enforced 'gifts' from laymen, and not to demand interest or discount or to give financial security. Priests were adjured to attend to the needs of monasteries; they were to build churches where there were none, to keep them white and with well constructed apses and courts. In every church there was to be a place of rest. Priests were to lodge only in the church hospice or in a monastery, not in an inn, for that was the haunt of loose-living soldiery and prostitutes in their special garb.[1] They were not permitted to eat meat or drink wine unless they were unwell, and then only in moderation. They were obliged to attend church services regularly, and to be diligent in fasting and prayer. They were to avoid involvement in lawsuits, particularly in the city. They were not to leave their church to travel to distant places, even on the business of the village or the Church, without specific permission. They were required to reside in the church and to bequeath their property to the Church. They were ordered not to condone adultery in any way. They were forbidden to accept employment from laymen, or to act as guardians. A copy of the Separate Gospels (that is, not the Diatessaron) was to be in their church. They were warned to have no association with heretics or with demon-worshippers. They were recommended

---

[1] It was at an inn outside Edessa that, according to the traditional account, the martyrs were detained by the police, at the beginning of the fourth century, before being brought to trial. In the middle of the fifth century priests conducting Holy Communion at the feast of the Holy Martyrs at Edessa sent hastily to the local inn for additional wine, and complained later that it was fresh and bad.

[to] care for the poor and seek the cause of the oppressed without showing favour. . . . [They were to] hold all landowners in the respect that is their due without showing them favour or oppressing the poor.

Attached to the priests were the *benai qeyama* and *benath qeyama*, 'children of the Covenant', both men and women. For their welfare the priests were to be especially solicitous. The *benai qeyama* in this region at this time were to observe many of the rules prescribed for the parish priest. They were to be abstemious and chaste, to live only with their families or with other *benai qeyama*, not to live alone and not to attend meetings without deaconesses in the case of women, priests in the case of men. The Steward was to be appointed from among the *benai qeyama*; it was proper to appoint a layman to this post only if no suitable *bar qeyama* was available. The status and qualifications of *benai qeyama* varied probably from region to region and from period to period in eastern Christendom. From these regulations it is evident that at Edessa at this time, in, that is, the early fifth century— although the rules may well be based on earlier practice—these persons stood in some manner between laymen and priests. They were, indeed, closer to the latter, because they accepted a rigorous ecclesiastical discipline; together with priests they could be termed 'children of the Church'. They were celibate. They did not, however, take vows of poverty, and, while not permitted to accept certain types of employment from laymen, they may have retained the use of their own property.

The leading citizens of Edessa were landed gentry. It was from their number that were drawn the members of the Town Council; a document of 449 writes of 'the *curiales* and the rest of the [land]-owners'. But the occupation from which wealth might be acquired most rapidly was that of merchant. The Roman authorities were careful both to control and to encourage caravan traffic between Persia and the Empire; in the later Roman Empire a customs duty of $12\frac{1}{2}$ per cent was levied on imports and exports. Under Diocletian a principal trade route to Persia was directed through Nisibis, on the border of Roman territory. When the frontiers between the two countries ran through the middle of Mesopotamia with the treaty of 363, Nisibis retained its function as a customs post, but now on the Persian side; the customs post of the Byzantines was at Callinicos at the beginning of the fifth century, and in 562 at Dara. Edessa's situation on the highway to Nisibis was a source of considerable profit to its citizens. The distinction of the two cities as centres of commerce is commented upon in a description of Mesopotamia, written perhaps a decade before the treaty of 363. The 'excellent folk' of Nisibis were, we are informed,

remarkably astute in business and well supplied, and exceptionally rich and adorned with all [sorts of] commodities. For they themselves receive goods from Persia, sell them throughout Roman territory and then buy and transport [other goods] in exchange. . . .

The cities [of Mesopotamia] are in a ferment with business operations, which they transact successfully throughout the province. Next is Edessa of Osrhoene, itself a magnificent city.[1]

The chief single article of trade was silk. It commanded notoriously high prices at Rome. Some Romans, it is true, regarded its use as effeminate; Emperor Aurelian neither wore silk himself nor permitted his wife to do so. In the following century, however, when Constantinople had become the capital of the Eastern Empire, the demand there for silk was insatiable. The austere Julian expressed disapproval of its use, but to little effect. Ammian describes the activity of merchants at Batnae in this period:

[Batnae was] filled with wealthy traders, when, at the yearly festival near the beginning of the month of September, a great crowd of every condition would gather for the fair, to traffic in the merchandise sent from India and China and in other articles brought there regularly in great abundance by land and sea.

The Latin term here for China, *Seres*, refers particularly to its silk products. Batnae was the scene of this fair because it was the last halt on the caravan route before crossing the Euphrates and leaving Mesopotamia. But Batnae was dependent on Edessa, and Edessa, as the administrative headquarters of the region, must have been even more flourishing as a mercantile centre.

In the time of Justinian a decline must have set in in the prosperity of the merchants of Edessa. The nobles of Constantinople still 'found satisfaction in making a show of [silken] finery through the lavish expenditure of their money—or ... felt obliged to do so.'[2] Justinian tried to divert the silk trade from the Persian route with the help of the ruler of Ethiopia, but without success. A silk industry was created near Constantinople itself—through, it is related, the enterprise of two monks from Central Asia who smuggled the eggs of silk worms in hollow sticks to the West between 552 and 554; there they were successfully reared on mulberry leaves. But the native product satisfied only part of the demand in the capital. Silk continued to be brought overland from the East through Edessa, and it no doubt continued to command high prices. Now, however, the road had grown unsafe, principally owing to the blackmail of marauding Beduins, and the caravans may have become less frequent.

There are few allusions to merchants in the local literature of this period. Writers considered their methods to be dishonest. John of Ephesus writes of two brothers who were commercial travellers, carrying merchandise between Constantinople and Persia. They abstained, he remarks significantly, 'from the evil practices which the traders of the world are wont to follow', from bargaining, 'and from oaths of all kinds and from lying and extortion'.[3] The brothers could not have grown rich by their occupation. At first they were

---

[1] *Liber Junioris philosophi* (Geog. graec. min., II. 517, § 22).
[2] Procopius, *Anecdota*.   [3] John Ephes., *Lives*.

paid five or six *denarii* a year, when they began to bring the commodity by caravan they received twenty *denarii*, and after twenty years service their salary was no higher than thirty *denarii* a year. They regarded this, however, as sufficient to set up business on their own at Amid, and later at Melitene. Two centuries earlier, commercial travellers cannot have been more prosperous. A 'wealthy merchant' of Mesopotamia, Antoninus, renounced his occupation in order to enter the service of the *dux* as a clerk, and eventually he became a *protector*, a soldier in the Guards. If he changed his profession in order to better his financial circumstances his income as merchant must have been modest.

An unflattering picture of the morals of commercial travellers is drawn in an anonymous tale of a pagan merchant from Paddana near Harran; the story cannot be dated, but evidently the original was Syriac and must be pre-Islamic. The merchant undertook to bring from the monastery of Abraham at Harran a piece of the stone which the patriarch Jacob rolled from the top of the well at his meeting with Rachel, for this, it was thought, would cure the sterility of the wife of a business acquaintance of his at Constantinople. Returning to the capital, the merchant was asked to produce the precious talisman; but he had forgotten the errand with which he had been charged. He did not confess his negligence. He 'went forth outside the city, and found a stone and broke off a little from it and wrapped it in a clear piece of silk and put it inside a bag, and gave it to the woman'. That the story has a happy ending, for the woman conceived and bore a child, is to be ascribed to the power of faith, not to the integrity of the merchant. The latter, we are told, exclaimed, 'If a bit of common stone through the woman's faith can give her a son, how much more [remarkable would have been the result] if I had brought some of that very stone for which she asked!'[1]

We have discussed already the special regard of Edessans for healing. The status of physicians was high. Under Byzantine law physicians, like teachers, both in cities and in the countryside, were exempt from the payment of *collatio lustralis* and from the onerous obligation of acting as guardians to orphans. 'Physicians', states the code, 'heal bodies and the learned [heal] souls.' The fact that physicians were occupied with secular, not religious, study led some of the clergy to view their profession with suspicion. Students at the theological academy of Nisibis were forbidden to lodge with physicians in the town. Significantly, too, the 'city physician' of Tella was one of those who were alleged to have compiled books on astrology for the use of Bishop Sophronius. Nevertheless, we read in Procopius of a certain Stephen, a native of Edessa, ' a physician of marked learning, among those of his time at any rate, who also had cured the Persian king Kawad . . . when ill, and had been made master of great wealth by him.'[2] Stephen was sent by the

[1] Burkitt, *Euphemia and the Goth.*   [2] Procopius, *Wars.*

Byzantines to persuade Khusraw to withdraw from his siege of Edessa in 544. The physician claimed that he had 'fostered [Khusraw] from childhood and had advised [his] father to appoint [him] his successor on the throne'.[1]

Other professions practised by Edessans in the fifth century included the civil service. High in the list of a deputation at Edessa in 449, which submitted to the Governor a petition against Bishop Hiba, were ταξεῶται, officials in the provincial administration, and *palatini*, officials of the Imperial administration stationed in the province. Perhaps of less consequence, since they appear lower in the lists, were a *princeps*, the civil servant in charge of the *officion*, and a *scholasticos*, possibly a barrister. At a later date Edessans reached positions of distinction in the Imperial service. A certain Procopius of Edessa, 'a man of learning', became Governor of Nablus in Palestine in the reign of Anastasius. Sergius of Edessa, a 'trained speaker and exceedingly clever', was Byzantine envoy to Khusraw in 543. In 544–5 he went a second time to the Persian court and arranged a treaty for five years.

Craftsmen were already a recognized order of society at Edessa under the monarchy, and this was the case also in the fifth century. After the flood of 201, they had been forbidden to erect booths by the side of the river without express permission; in 496–7 orders were given by the Governor for the raised platforms built by the artisans in the porticoes to be removed. The tax of the *chrysargyron* (or *collatio lustralis*) paid by the artisans and other *negotiatores* was abolished throughout the Empire in May 498. At Edessa,

the whole city rejoiced and they all, both small and great, put on white garments, and carried lighted tapers and censers of burning incense and went forth with psalms and hymns, giving thanks to God and praising the Emperor, to the shrine of St. Sergius and St. Simeon, where they celebrated the Eucharist. Then they re-entered the city and kept a glad and merry festival during the whole week; and they enacted that they should celebrate this festival every year. All the artisans were reclining and disporting themselves, bathing, and feasting in the courtyards of the churches[2] and in all the porticoes of the city.[3]

That the artisans of Edessa were prosperous at this period is shown by the sum at which the *chrysargyron* was assessed, 140 pounds of gold every four years.

Craftsmen and shopkeepers were organized in guilds; and the exercise of certain processes may also have been restricted to authorized persons.[4] Where the control of occupations was so rigid, we realize how serious was the threat of the Melkite Patriarch of Antioch in 536–7, that no man in the great cities of Byzantine Mesopotamia would be allowed to practise his

---

[1] Khusraw did not, however, accept Stephen's plea.

[2] Reading plur., rather than sing., 'the courtyard of the [Great] Church' as Wright, *Chronicle of Joshua the Stylite*, loc. cit.

[3] 'Josh. St.'

[4] Cf. the monopoly apparently exercised by Aggai, a craftsman in silk before he became bishop, already in the Addai story; pp. 79 f. above.

calling unless he accepted the Synod of Chalcedon. Other occupations were of more menial status. Side by side with the category of craftsmen in the fifth century was a category of 'those who [are employed] in handicrafts'. The latter may have been apprentices or untrained workers, and no doubt they were not members of a guild. It is probably of significance that the craftsmen, like the clergy and the city Councillors, signed their names on the petition to the Governor against Hiba; but 'those who [are employed] in handicrafts', like 'those whose occupation is in [agricultural] work', merely 'affixed their hands', that is, we may assume, appended their marks. There were also domestic servants at Edessa. A hagiography of the sixth century relates that a holy man employed in a household was paid 100 *nummi* and a daily ration of one loaf of bread; he gave the money to the poor, and on Sundays he bought fruit, which he distributed to the people in the hospice.

The baking of bread was a particularly humble task, close to actual servitude. It was normally the function of women.[1] It was also performed on occasion by special order of the Governor or the military commissary-general. In the famine of 499–500, the Governor's deputy

saw that the bakers were not sufficient to make bread for the market, because of the multitude of country people of whom the city was full and because of the poor who had no bread in their houses. He gave order that everyone who wished might make bread and sell it on the market. And there came Jewish women, to whom he gave wheat from the public granary, and they made bread for the market.[2]

During the Persian advance into the area of Tella, Harran, and Edessa in 503, the commissary-general was stationed at Edessa to organize the provisioning of the Byzantine troops. 'As the bakers were not able to make enough bread, he ordered that wheat should be supplied to all the houses of Edessa and that they should make soldiers' biscuits[3] at their own cost.'[3] On this occasion the Edessans baked 630,000 *modii* of bread for the army. In May 504 Edessans were again given wheat to bake at their expense; and they produced 850,000 *modii*. In the following year they baked, in the courtyards of their houses, 630,000 *modii*, 'besides what the villagers baked throughout the whole countryside, and the bakers, both strangers and natives'—enough rations, it has been calculated, to feed an army of some 40,000 men for six months.

Slavery was no doubt a feature of Edessan society, but, apart from the sale of a slave-girl of Edessa in 243, we have little direct evidence for it. The regulation of pre-Christian Roman law that a slave-girl might be given as a pledge for the repayment of a loan and her work regarded as interest on the

---

[1] At Amid in 504–5 the Persian garrison suffered terribly from lack of food; they threw the male population into the amphitheatre to die of hunger. But they fed the women 'because they used them to satisfy their lust and because they required them to grind and bake for them', 'Zach. Rh.'. Later the Persian soldiers were forced to do this work themselves.

[2] 'Josh. St.'

[3] *Buccellatum*.

capital remained valid in Byzantine Mesopotamia.[1] The abduction of a free person into slavery was punishable by death. This law is well illustrated by the story of the Edessan girl, Euphemia, written possibly in the fifth century. The girl had been persuaded to marry a Gothic soldier only to find, when they were far from her home, that he was already married. Her husband 'stripped off her rich clothing . . . and unloosed the gold from her . . . , and clothed her in the costume of a slave-girl'. Miraculously, she was transported by night to Edessa. The Goth who had wronged her was later denounced and put to death because he was 'contemptuous of the pure laws of the Romans . . . , and had given to subjection and bridled a free person with the yoke of slavery'.[2]

Some townsmen at Edessa were, we have seen, engaged in agricultural work, presumably in the orchards and vineyards which lay near the city, as at modern Urfa. At harvest time they worked in the villages and on large estates as casual labour; when Kawad's army overran this area at the beginning of the sixth century, it captured not only peasants, but city folk from Edessa and Harran who had come to help with the vintage. In the countryside outside the city, farming was carried on on a large scale, and agriculture provided Edessa with its staple source of livelihood. The plain at the foot of the hills of Edessa, to the south and east, is described by a chronicler of this period as 'a fertile land'. It was well-watered and produced abundant crops of cereals, vegetables, and fruit. It contained numerous farms and villages. The leaders of these communities were lay elders; law codes recognize the status of these 'old men who administer the villages'. Together with the priests, and on occasion also the deacons, they had the duty of opening a will in the presence of the heirs, and then certifying it for deposit in the archives of the local church.

The countryman was either an independent farmer, *akkara*, or an agricultural labourer, *pallaḥa*. The livelihood of the farmers was often precarious, and we may dismiss as empty rhetoric the verse of the fifth century Syriac poet:

> The farmer is more at ease than the merchant,
> And he who works the land despises the king.[3]

When his cattle died of disease or were stolen or requisitioned, when his harvests failed because of bad weather or war or brigandage, the smallholder had no reserves of capital to meet the demands of the tax-collector. He became entangled in debt. Rapacious creditors foreclosed before payment

---

[1] If, however, the law continues, a slave-girl who had been given as a pledge in this way were to bear children, the latter would be regarded as the property of her own master; 'a woman', it is declared, 'is not like the earth'.

The regulations concerning runaway or sick slaves, p. 22 above, were still enforced during this period.

[2] Burkitt, op. cit.

[3] Isaac of Antioch.

had fallen due, or even demanded a further repayment on loans that had already been settled in full. Against such injustice hermits and holy ascetics living in the villages protested in vain. The free peasants were bought out by absentee landlords who lived in the city and merely visited their estates from time to time to supervise their condition and doubtless to collect their revenues. On the rural population fell here, as elsewhere in the Empire, a heavier burden of taxation than on the townspeople, in money, in kind, and in manpower. The levies were exacted without mercy. In 499-500 there was severe famine at Edessa. Nevertheless, the Governor sent the capitation tax in full to Constantinople after, we are told, 'he had laid hold of the land-owners and extorted it from them by the use of great pressure'.[1] We can imagine the degree of pressure which the landowners in their turn applied to their tenants. The remission of no more than two *folles*, that was granted by the Emperor in the same year, on the personal intervention of the Bishop of Edessa, in some measure lightened the load on the villagers. The villages had become chattels to be sold or conveyed at the will of their masters. The ownership of villages was a passport to influence in the city; we know that landowners disapproved of the sale of estates in their vicinity to persons from other districts.

Peasants brought their produce to sell in the market outside the city gate, and there, no doubt, they purchased the manufactured articles that were not obtainable in the villages. Sometimes they were roughly handled. A Christian historian even praises the Persian garrison for protecting the countryfolk at the gate of Amid. The harsh treatment of peasants by the military was regarded as a matter of course. We are told, however, that Justinian's general Belisarius was an exception, for when he commanded the Byzantine army in Mesopotamia he 'was not greedy after bribes and was kind to the peasants and did not allow the army to injure them'.[2] But church-men were little better than the soldiery. In the fifth century, the village priest was enjoined to act with kindness to the poor, but he was also in-structed to behave with deference to the squire who owned the villages. It is, indeed, a matter for comment that Asclepius, Bishop of Edessa, 'was kind to the peasants and was gentle towards them'.[2] The status of the agricultural labourer is clearly illustrated by a law code of this period. Anyone, it declares, who abducted a labourer was himself to be reduced to that condition, exactly as the man who abducted a slave was himself to be enslaved—unless he was an important personage, in which case the punishment was exile. The position of the agricultural serf was indeed little higher than that of a slave.

The region beyond the villages and the cultivated land outside the city was occupied by the partially nomadic 'Arab, as in the days of the monarchy. It extended from the Tektek mountains, within sight of the plains outside

[1] 'Josh. St.'   [2] 'Zach. Rh.'

Edessa, to the approaches of Nisibis, from Amid in the north to Thannurios in the south. After the treaty of 363 this was a sensitive area, for
through it passed the Byzantine–Persian frontier. By the Byzantine authorities, the ʿArab were not unfavourably regarded. They were, however, more
mobile than the agricultural population, for the latter were permanently
attached to the estates on which they were registered.[1] The government,
therefore, sought to control the movements of the ʿArab, to encourage them
to settle down on the land, and thereby to acquire a stake in the maintenance
of peaceful conditions. Anastasius fortified the village of Dara both for his own
troops, and 'to guard the country of the ʿArbaye from the inroads of Persians
and Beduins'.[2] Later Justinian built Thannurios, 'as a place of refuge in the
desert for a military force to be stationed, to protect ʿArab against the
marauding bands of Beduins'.

Of the Beduins themselves Ammian writes from personal observation:

> None ever grasped a plough handle or cultivated a tree, none sought a living by
> tilling the soil. They roved continually over wide and extensive tracks without a home,
> without dwellings or laws. . . . I have seen many of them who were wholly unacquainted
> with grain and wine.

The monk Malka, who fell into their hands, described to St. Jerome his
experiences among them:

> Ishmaelites, mounted on horses and camels, bands around their long hair, their
> bodies half-naked, wearing cloaks, quivers hanging from their shoulders and their bows
> unstrung, with long spears in their hands—for they had not come to fight but in search
> of booty.[3]

They were masters of the interior. They roamed freely as far west as the
shrine of Ruṣafa beyond the Euphrates. The restraints that they recognized
were internecine feuds between tribes, not the laws of Byzantium or Persia.
The ordinary citizen of Edessa need not have come into direct contact with
the Beduins unless he ventured far from the city, but he must always have
been conscious of their distant menace. No solitary wayfarer was safe; to
wander from the road was to invite almost certain destruction, for the desert
steppes were known only to the nomads.[4] Even large caravans were sometimes
waylaid by Beduins, their merchandise looted, and the travellers themselves
killed or sold into slavery. There was reason for the deep concern of Edessans
in the middle of the fifth century, who had subscribed freely to Church
funds for the ransom of captives, and were told that Bishop Hiba had donated
only 1,000 *denarii* for the purpose. Monks and nuns had been seized by the

---

[1] See pp. 120 f. above.　　[2] 'Zach. Rh.'.
[3] Jerome, *Vita Malchi*, composed in about
390–1.
[4] In June 504 the Byzantine general Con-

stantine, who had defected to the Persians, fled
back to his former allegiance to the West, with
his two wives and retinue, across the desert
route. The journey took fourteen days.

Beduins. The former, it was reported, 'were compelled to serve idols or whatever the barbarian Beduins worship, the nuns to become prostitutes and to stand in the public places. For such was the custom of the barbarians.'[1]

The long wars and the unsettled conditions in Mesopotamia enabled the Beduins to play an important role in the history of this time. 'Joshua the Stylite' rightly declares that 'to the Beduins on both sides this war was a source of much profit and they wrought their will upon both kingdoms'. Already Emperor Constantius had turned the 'marauding' Beduins against the Persians, presumably enrolling them as *foederati*. When, a few years later, Julian arrived in Mesopotamia, 'the princes of the Beduin nations as suppliants on bended knees presented [him] with a golden crown . . . and were gladly received since they were adept at guerilla warfare'.[2] But when the young Emperor was killed, the nomad mercenaries became hostile to the Romans, who could not meet their demand for gold, and they harrassed Jovian's withdrawal. In Persian territory in the early part of the reign of Kawad, the Beduins, eager for loot, took advantage of the unrest to carry out raids freely wherever they wished. Kawad announced his intention of attacking Byzantium, and the Beduins 'flocked to him with great alacrity'.[3] Later the Persians reduced this threat to ordered government by concentrating authority in a single hand. The ruler of Ḥira, Mundhir, received the title of king and 'ruled alone over all the Beduins in Persia'. The choice of the Persians was fortunate. Mundhir was 'most discreet, well experienced in matters of warfare, thoroughly faithful to the Persians and unusually energetic'.[4] For fifty years he held Byzantine Mesopotamia in fear; 'he plundered the whole country, pillaging one place after another, burning the buildings in his track, and taking captive the population in tens of thousands in each raid',[4] killing most and selling the rest. He moved so rapidly that 'he would fall upon his pursuers while they were still unprepared . . . and would destroy them with no trouble'.[5]

The Byzantines then took a leaf out of the book of the Persians. They, too, nominated an overlord over their Beduins, Ḥarith son of Gabala, ruler of Ghassan, 'and bestowed upon him the dignity of king', more precisely, the titles of phylarch and patrician. Ḥarith was not as successful a warrior as Mundhir, though he had some victories. But he, too, certainly struck terror into the hearts of his Byzantine paymasters. For he was as ready to fight against them, claims Procopius, as against the Persians. At Constantinople itself, the warders of the demented Emperor Justin II had only to shout, 'Ḥarith son of Gabala has come to fetch you', and the wretched man would run cowering for shelter under his bed.[5] In time, the menace of the Beduins

---

[1] J.-P. Martin, *RSE* xxx, 1875, 22 ff.; Syriac text in British Museum MS Add. 14530, fol. 41b.
[2] Ammian. On the golden crown, see p. 111, n. 1 above.
[3] *'Josh. St.'*
[4] Procopius, *Wars.*
[5] John Ephes., *History.*

and the devastation which they caused became intolerable to the rulers of
Byzantium and Persia alike. Sometimes the representatives of both Empires
insisted forcibly on respect for the law. In 504–5, the Persian general at
Nisibis put to death sheikhs in his area whose tribesmen had crossed the
frontier and plundered two villages in Byzantine territory. In the same year
the Byzantines executed four Beduin leaders who had invaded Persian
Mesopotamia and enslaved the inhabitants of a hamlet. But more drastic
action was required, and against more influential persons. Khusraw II
removed the Beduin chieftain Nuʿman by poison. Emperor Tiberius detained Mundhir, son of Ḥarith, at Constantinople. In anger Mundhir's
sons laid waste, and looted, and took captive all that they could find, so that
'all the region of the East was terrified . . . and fled to the cities and did not
dare to show themselves before them'. The Byzantines later divided the
kingdom of the western Beduins among fifteen princes, and most of these
then allied themselves, we are told, to the Persians. The triumph of the
Beduins was yet to come, with the emergence of Islam and the Arab conquest of Mesopotamia; and then it was decisive.

To the peaceful Edessans and the countryfolk around the city, came
stories of the heathen Beduins that sent a thrill of horror through their
hearers. The Beduins offered sacrifices and libations to the planets. One
chieftain, it was said, seized four hundred virgins at Emesa and slew them
in one day in honour of ʿUzzai (Venus). Shortly after 545 the Beduin Mundhir, fighting for the Persians, even sacrificed the son of his enemy Ḥarith to
this goddess. True, these pagans observed the truce of two months each year
at the spring equinox. More important, Christianity penetrated the royal
household of the Beduin township of Ḥira in the reign of Khusraw II. In the
West, some Beduin leaders were fervent Monophysites who had far-reaching
influence on the course of events in the Church. Ḥarith son of Gabala did
not fear to upbraid the Patriarch Ephraim of Amid. He prefaced his argument
with the words 'I am a barbarian and a soldier, and I cannot read the Holy
Scriptures'; the Tome of Leo, on which were based the rulings of the
Council of Chalcedon, he declared to be an 'infested rat'.[1] It was he who
encouraged Empress Theodora to restore the declining fortunes of his
denomination, and it was at his request that Jacob Burdʿaya was appointed
to the see of Edessa. His grandson Nuʿman refused to abandon his Monophysite faith, even at the court of Emperor Maurice, a fanatical Melkite,[2] and
he sought to reconcile the dissident groups into which the Monophysites
had broken.

Of the architecture of buildings at Edessa at this period we know little.
Houses were built around a central courtyard, and the upper floor was

---

[1] Mich. Syr.   [2] But see p. 99 n. 1 above.

reached by an outside staircase, as at Urfa today.[1] The roofs were flat.
Houses were sometimes so close to one another that it was possible to jump
from roof to roof, as did the Byzantine general when he escaped from his
mutinous Gothic soldiers in 505–6. The more substantial buildings were of
brick or of stone plastered with lime; the huts of the poorer townsfolk were
made of clay. Wood for building was evidently expensive. One of the principal charges against Daniel, Bishop of Harran, in 448–9 was his alleged
misappropriation of a forest belonging to the Church of Edessa, and the use
of its wood for a building for his mistress at Edessa.

Edessa was certainly 'more rustic than many [cities]', as St. John Chrysostom remarked in the latter half of the fourth century. Nevertheless, the
rich of Edessa lived in conditions of luxury. John son of Basil, 'the most
illustrious of all the inhabitants of Edessa in birth and wealth', was sent by
the Byzantine general Belisarius in 542 as hostage to Khusraw, but 'much
against his will'. Later John's grandmother offered to release him from the
Persians for the immense ransom of 2,000 pounds of silver. Justinian refused
to allow this money to be paid to the Persians; he had, if we may trust
Procopius, a different destination for it. 'Not much later . . . John fell sick
and died, and the magistrate in charge of the city . . . stated that a short time
previously John had written to him as a friend that it was his wish that his
estate should go to the Emperor.'

It was, however, the wealth of the Roṣpaye, one of the leading families of
Edessa, that became a legend in the city. They owned villages and gardens
and mills and shops. When Khusraw II fled from Persia to Edessa to seek the
help of Byzantium, the leading citizens Marinus and Iwannis Roṣpaya, as we
have already observed, showed the prince great respect.[2] Khusraw admired
from outside the beauties of Iwannis's palace and desired to enter. Iwannis
was carried away by pride; he invited to his entertainment not only Khusraw
but all the nobles of the city. In order to demonstrate that he was richer than
Marinus, he displayed his treasure of gold and silver tables and trays and
chargers, dessert dishes, spoons, and saucers. His cups and wine goblets,
his pots and jugs and carafes and bowls and other vessels were all of silver.
There was more that he did not show. When the Roṣpaya treasure was
discovered nearly 300 years later, in the reign of Harun al-Rashid, there
were other 'princely articles'—snakes and scorpions of silver filled with
elixir, and plate and coins. The house of Iwannis's rival Marinus, which
stood beside the fish-pools, must have had its wonders also. It was there that
the unhappy Melkite bishop, Severus, was brought to the Byzantine general
Narseh in about 603 for summary trial, to be led away surreptitiously and
stoned outside the city walls. There too, some fifteen years later, Heraclius
resided after his recapture of Edessa.[3]

---

[1] See the photograph on Pl. 35.   [2] See pp. 126 f. above.   [3] See p. 114 above.

Syriac chroniclers had little patience for the luxuries of the rich; they were men of the Church, simple and sincere pastors, concerned for the well-being of all their flock. The poor of the city were neglected and some-times without shelter, and our writers castigate the wealthy citizens. In the biography of Euphemia of Amid, that noble woman inquires:

Is it well that you yourselves sit thus while slaves stand and wait upon you? You enjoy a variety of tastes in dainty foods and wine, while God (in the shape of the poor and persecuted) is buffeted in the street and swarms with lice and faints with hunger?[1]

Decent folk dressed in wool, cleanly and simply. John of Tella advises devout laymen whose children were to become *benai qeyama* to clothe them in 'comely robes', and not to allow them to become 'luxurious in white cotton garments'. The poor, however, had to be content with rags, and St. Ephraim and later Jacob Burd'aya wore rags as a sign of their fellowship and sympathy.[2] Ordinary citizens ate a diet of bread, usually of barley rather than wheat, meat, chickens, eggs, and wine: the needy were satisfied with a fare of chickpeas, beans, lentils, and raisins. Prices were subject to violent fluctua-tion if the harvest was particularly good or bad. In a normal year a *solidus* bought about 30 *modii* of wheat and 50 *modii* of barley. When, however, the crops had failed, the situation could not be easily remedied by the import of additional supplies; transport was expensive, and the corn in the public granary was intended for use only in an emergency. At such a time a *solidus* bought only 4 to 6 *modii* of wheat and 6 to 10 *modii* of barley.

At Edessa, the poor probably lived always on the verge of starvation. The plight of the homeless in the severity of winter was pitiable. In 499–500 locusts devoured the crops; a year later there was famine. The country people came into the town; the old and sick, and women, children, and infants abandoned the villages to eke out a livelihood by begging in the streets of Edessa. Grain was released from the public stores by the Governor's deputy, and bread was put on sale in the market. But its price was beyond the means of the poor:

Those who were left in the villages were eating bitter vetches, and others were frying the withered fallen grapes. . . . And those who were in the city were wandering about the streets, picking up the stalks and leaves of vegetables, all filthy with mud, and eating them. They were sleeping in the porticoes and streets, and wailing by night and day from the pangs of hunger. . . . The whole city was full of them, and they began to die in the porticoes and streets.[3]

The Governor of Edessa sealed the wretched people on their necks with leaden seals and gave each of them a pound of bread a day. This was too little to

---

[1] John Ephes., *Lives.*

[2] Rabbula wore a hair-shirt and clean mantle; when conducting a service he wore also a vestment or cloak in winter, but a long sleeveless tunic in summer. We are told that when a monk acted as priest in a town or village, he was required to put white garments over his monastic robe so that the 'monastic calling should not be despised in the secular world': A. Vööbus, *Syriac and Arabic Documents*, 90.

[3] '*Josh. St.*'

alleviate their starvation, and they were wasted with hunger. In the following winter,

the pestilence became worse . . . when there began to be frost and ice, because they passed the nights in the porticoes and streets. Children and babes were crying in every street. Of some the mothers were dead; others had been deserted by their mothers— they had run away from them, because when they asked for something to eat they had nothing to give them. The dead lay exposed in every street.[1]

There was one work of mercy which mitigated to some degree the misery of the poor—the liberal establishment of hospices and infirmaries. Edessa, we have seen in an earlier chapter, had won a reputation for its acts of healing.[2] The biographer of St. Ephraim tells us how in 373, a month before he died, the old man was commissioned to supervise, with the help of a Steward and agent, the care of the poor during the great famine of that year; he was the only citizen of Edessa to whom the rich would entrust their donations. The streets were cordoned off and in the empty space were laid about three hundred beds; some served as biers for burial, others as couches for strangers, and for the needy of the city and the villages. About fifty years later Bishop Rabbula set up permanent hospices, one for men and one for women. He endowed them with a generous income. The beds, we are assured, were clean and soft, and there was a diligent and kindly staff of God-fearing men and women.

These hospices were not for any stranger, but for the sick and dying.[3] It was, according to legend, at an Edessan hospice of this sort that the 'man of God', the mysterious stranger whom some accounts name as Alexius, passed his last hours.[4] At his death he was carried out on a bier and buried in the hospice cemetery. The anonymous martyrologist maintains that it was the miracle at the demise of St. Alexius, when the body of the holy man inexplicably vanished, that inspired Rabbula's zeal for the needy, for widows and orphans, and strangers from distant countries. Near the site of the well called in later times after the prophet Job, with its healing waters,[5] were founded the shrines of St. Cosmas and St. Damian, the martyr-physicians. Also in that district, outside the south wall, was the infirmary for lepers endowed by Bishop Nona in about 460. In the great famine and plague of Edessa in 500–1, the infirmary buildings could not contain the large number of the sick; part of the basilica and streets of the city were blocked up, and straw and mats laid down to receive the sick. The nobles of the city, and even the Byzantine soldiery stationed at Edessa, set up infirmaries for the populace at their own expense. The baths under the Church of the Apostles beside the Great gate in the east of the city was also used for the accommodation of invalids.

[1] 'Josh. St.'   [2] See p. 71 above.
[3] It is significant that in the Greek version of a hagiographical tract the Syriac *xenodo-* *chaion*, hospice, is rendered by νοσοκομεῖον, infirmary.
[4] See p. 173 below.   [5] Cf. pp. 72, 250.

The monks in their monasteries were the source of learning and instruction. John of Tella prescribes in his rules of conduct that:

children who are to become *benai qeyama* shall be sent to the monasteries to read books to learn in them pious behaviour. For if, for the sake of instruction for this world, many send their children to far-off countries, how much more fitting is it for those who have set aside and offered their children to God to send them to holy monasteries for the sake of spiritual wisdom.

In the cities the schools were apparently within the walls, even though the monastery to which the school was attached may have been outside the town. The only brief reference to schooling at Edessa is of the time of Rabbula. The bishop evidently visited a school there, that was attended by the sons of nobles, twice a month; children of pagans were called to him and instructed by him in 'the word of truth'. An account of a village school in the neighbourhood of Amid would, however, no doubt apply equally to the region of Edessa:

The blessed [monks] . . . chose for themselves to teach boys. This they did out of the window since a seat was placed inside the window and hours were fixed for the boys to come, that is, in the morning and in the evening; and when they had taught one class to read the Psalms and the Scriptures, and these had withdrawn, another came in of little infants, thirty of them; and they would learn and go to their homes, for it was a populous village. And so the old men continued to do until the time of their end; and the boy pupils supplied their needs.[1]

In another school, boys and girls were taught together. A teacher made tablets for the children, and wrote for them; and they copied the writing. School education, then, was largely restricted to memorizing the Psalms and Gospels and the art of writing. In the reign of Valens, Protogenes of Edessa, who later became Bishop of Harran, set up a boys' school during his exile in Egypt. He instructed his pupils 'not only in the art of swift penmanship . . . but also in the Psalms . . . and the most important articles of the Apostolic faith'.[2]

Neither rod nor child was spared. When the chronicler of the sixth century describes the persecution of their opponents by the Arians, he reflects the practices of his own time. 'Men', he writes, 'were dragged to church like children to school with blows on the face and pulling at their clothes . . .'.[3] And Isaac of Antioch, inveighing against the remissness of copyists, declares:

Perchance a venerable man may take up [your] book to instruct the pupils therefrom, but caught [unawares] by the mistakes, he is covered in confusion—and the fault is yours.

The pupil, however, would suffer worse than confusion for a similar error, for our poet continues:

Or the boy may take up the book in the presence of his teacher to read therefrom; the teacher rises and thrashes the pupil because he makes the mistakes caused by your negligence.

[1] John Ephes., op. cit.
[2] Theodoret, *Ecclesiastical History*.
[3] Barḥadbeshabba ʿArbaya, *History*, ed. Nau (*PO*), i, 65.

It is not surprising that the standard of education at schools was low: so too was the salary of the teachers. Under Diocletian the primary school teacher received no more than 50 *denarii* a month for each pupil, while a craftsman would be paid 50 to 60 *denarii* a day in addition to his keep.

An intelligent youth at Edessa might, however, gain entrance to one of the academies of the city or to one of the more celebrated monasteries in the region. In the middle of the fifth century there were three institutions at Edessa, the School of the Armenians, that of the Persians, and that of the Syrians—each named, presumably, after the ethnic affiliation of the members of the staff. The brilliance of its teachers brought the School of the Persians more than local fame.[1] The first Principal whose name is recorded was a certain Qiyore in the earlier part of the fifth century. At that time the School was evidently small; the Principal was himself in charge not only of exegesis but also of recitation, pronunciation, and homiletics. A generation later, when Narseh was Principal, the staff was increased; lecturers were appointed to teach recitation, pronunciation and grammar, homiletics, and writing, the Principal himself holding the chair in exegesis. Studies were based on the commentaries of St. Ephraim, and later the works of Theodore of Mopsuestia were used, as well as translations into Syriac of Greek philosophy. We may suppose that the curriculum included also secular subjects, history, rhetoric, and some fields of natural science.

The system of instruction in the School of the Persians at Edessa, before its closure in 489, must have resembled in no small degree that of the academy of Nisibis which was largely staffed by lecturers expelled from Edessa. The statutes of the college of Nisibis,[2] promulgated in 496, are still extant. At one time it had, we are told, no fewer than eight hundred students. Administrative and disciplinary matters were delegated by the Principal (*Rabban*) and his colleagues to the Bursar (*Rabbaita*). Lecturers were not permitted to engage in trade or handicrafts, or to be negligent in their teaching duties. Students were required to pass a preliminary examination. The course of study lasted three years. The college was residential, and students were allowed to live in the city only if no accommodation was available in the college hostel. Attendance at classes, which began with cock-crow and ended with the evening psalms, was compulsory. The annual vacation was from August to October; and during this period the students were permitted to take paid employment but only outside Nisibis, evidently in order not to compete with residents of the town. Students were required to be unmarried. Discipline was strict, and breaches were punished by expulsion. Students were forbidden to frequent taverns or to attend outdoor wine

---

[1] See p. 95.

[2] The Christian academy of Nisibis was evidently modelled not only on the Christian academy of Edessa, but also on the Jewish academy of Nisibis itself.

parties, to read secular books, to beg, or to be untidy in their appearance. The borrowing of books from the college library was severely controlled; borrowers were forbidden to write their names in books. Students were discouraged as far as possible from crossing the frontiers into Byzantine territory.

For all their monopoly of education, there were not a few priests who themselves remained illiterate, and Isaac of Antioch castigates these backward monks. The monks of the Monastery of the Orientals at Edessa, for example, could not even sign their names; they were asked to 'anathematize the Synod of Chalcedon, each one making a mark with his thumb'. And when John of Tella, in his campaign to revive the Monophysite Church, ordained priests in great numbers, 'he subjected all of them to a careful examination and test in reading the Scriptures, in reciting the Psalms and in their ability to write their names and signatures. He did not admit anyone who did not sign his name.' But even this not very severe examination was not rigidly applied, for the writer adds; 'If any candidate was unable to sign his name, [John] would bid him learn and his companion would sign for him.' John of Ephesus relates that, when he and seventy others came to John of Tella to be ordained as Monophysite priests, the latter saw that they 'read and wrote with confidence'. He accepted them without hesitation, saying, 'I am satisfied with you, my sons, and lo! I adjure you, "Pray and cease not" '.

One feature of education in western Mesopotamia served to accentuate the isolation of the country from the rest of Christendom. The language of instruction was Syriac. This, strangely enough, aroused the envy of contemporary educationists in the West. Western academies, in which Greek and Latin were employed, faced the embarrassment of assimilating the new studies of the Bible and divinity to pagan rhetoric, philosophy, and belles-lettres. In Syriac-speaking Schools, theology could be studied in all its aspects. Junilius mentions his meeting with a Persian who had studied at the Schools of the Syrians where 'divine law is taught systematically by rule by public professors as we teach grammar and rhetoric in secular studies'. Cassiodorus in the sixth century set up a theological college in the West in imitation of those of Edessa and Nisibis, but it did not survive his death.

This view of the advantage of Syriac as a medium for a broad training in theology was not shared by young men of Osrhoene eager to gain some acquaintance with the culture of the outside world. After the monarchy, as during it, study at foreign universities, like those of Antioch or Alexandria or Beirut, was an essential part of the upbringing of the sons of patrician families. The poet has this in mind when he writes:

the sons of slave-women lead a pleasant life in their master's home, as though they were its heirs—while their master is abroad, seeking a knowledge of letters, wandering from town to town in great discomfort.[1]

[1] Isaac of Antioch.

These youths would return from their journeys with a sound knowledge of Greek, and this in western Mesopotamia was the mark of the educated man.

But these educated persons were few, and the ordinary folk had no Greek. The captive general could shout in Greek to his Byzantine commander on the battlements of Tella, in 503, certain that his words would not be understood by the local people. Daniel the Stylite who came from the neighbourhood of Samosata spoke only Syriac. When the Monophysite monk Ze'ora went to Constantinople he took with him the cultured Tribunus as interpreter. Even an educated man in Osrhoene could be content with Syriac. According to Theodoret, Abraham, an influential bishop of Harran, also knew no Greek. Uranius, Bishop of Himeria in Osrhoene, required the services of an interpreter at Church Councils where he played an important role in the trials of Hiba of Edessa. Of the sixty-four priests, deacons, sub-deacons, and lectors of Edessa who signed a document in favour of Hiba at the Council of Chalcedon, as many as twenty (including a physician who was a deacon) could not write their names in a language other than Syriac. In foreign lands, men and women of Osrhoene were lonely and helpless. Euphemia, the girl of Edessa who had left the country with her Gothic husband, was, we are told, 'longing for someone to speak Syriac with her'; and even Mara, the learned Bishop of Amid, in exile at Alexandria, was happy to come across a fellow-countryman who spoke his native tongue.

The status of women at Edessa under the kings has been touched upon briefly in an earlier chapter.[1] In this respect there was evidently little change in the period following the monarchy. It was governed by the laws current in other areas of the Byzantine empire. Orphaned girls were under the care of a guardian, usually the brother of their deceased father, until the age of twelve,[2] and they attained their majority at the age of fifteen. Girls might be betrothed at the age of ten, at any rate in the villages; until their betrothal, they were carefully shielded from strangers. The betrothal was marked by a dowry contract in writing. Often, we learn from the law codes of the fourth or early fifth century, this was replaced by a public ceremony at which the bride was crowned, songs were sung in honour of Virginity, and trilling women escorted the bride from the home of her parents.

After marriage, women were engaged in the duties of the household, among them weaving; a man, on the other hand, undertook marriage 'for the sake of the security of the house'. Local law codes prescribed that a man could divorce his wife on the ground of adultery or because she had gone, without her husband's consent, to a house not her own, or to the theatre 'to see unseemly things'. A wife could divorce her husband only if two or three male witnesses were available to testify that he had robbed or used witch-

[1] See p. 38 above.   [2] Boys remained wards to the age of 14.

craft or raised an iron weapon against her, or brought a prostitute into their home. The wife was released from her conjugal obligations if her husband had deserted her without maintenance for seven years,[1] or had granted her maintenance but deserted her for fifteen years. Girls inherited equally with boys, if their father had died intestate; if there were only daughters, these were then the sole heirs. A minimum of three uncias was to be bequeathed to each daughter. Where there were neither children nor wife of a man who had died intestate, male heirs had precedence over female.[2]

Women went veiled—to go unveiled was to appear 'like a mad woman'.[3] The wife of a notable of Nisibis approached the Persian king in 359 'covered as far as her very lips with a black veil'.[4] Euphemia of Amid in the sixth century would tend the sick and infirm only 'if her head covering was in its place'.[5] Euphemia and her daughter, 'because they were fine and excellent workers, would weave two pounds of goat's wool yarn for one *denarius* which she received from the great ladies of the city'. We have one other example of women working for hire: in the region of Amid a poor woman taught drawing to other women. Two of her pupils acquired skill in the art under her but refused to pay for their lessons; she had recourse to the intervention of a holy man who struck them with sickness and released them only when they had paid their debt.

Priests affected to regard women with contempt. We may note the tone of Ephraim's comment on the incident that befell him when, according to his biographer, he approached Edessa for the first time. On the banks of the river Daiṣan he saw women washing clothes in the river. One of them looked at him for a long time, and Ephraim rebuked her shamelessness:

She, however, replied . . . , 'It is for you to look at the ground, for you are [taken] from it; it is for me to look at you because I am taken from you'. He was amazed at the reply and recognised the wisdom of the woman . . . and said, 'If the women of the city are so wise, how much wiser must be its menfolk and even its sons'.[6]

But the rough Monophysite propagandist, Simeon of Beth Arsham, did not regard it as unfitting to ask Empress Theodora to intervene on behalf of his

---

[1] For ten years, if he had been taken prisoner.

[2] We should probably not regard seriously the allegation in a Novel of Justinian dated 535–6 that incestuous marriages had taken place among the 'rustic populace' of Osrhoene and Mesopotamia. The Novel itself declares the 'rumour' to be not wholly worthy of credit; if such marriages had occurred this must have been under the influence of the 'neighbouring peoples' of Persia where these unions were permitted. Justinian decrees that past offences should be condoned but that further offences should be punished with all severity. This Novel was re-enacted by Justin II in 566.

[3] Moberg, *The Book of the Himyarites*, Ch. XXII.

[4] Ammian.

[5] John Ephes., *Lives*. Of two saintly Syrian women, Theodoret reports that they were veiled down to the waist. The Maphrian Marutha (died 649) instructed God-fearing women of the Jacobite community in Persia to plait their hair and wear a veil.

[6] This story, which appears in the Syriac biography of St. Ephraim, is related in abbreviated form in the Greek panegyric to that saint ascribed to Gregory of Nyssa. But it appears also in the biography of Jacob of Nisibis.

fellow-sectarians by writing to the Queen of Persia. Christianity, indeed, had given women a degree of self-assurance. The daughter of the martyr Shmona was among those who went out to mourn him, and both women and men attended his interment; so, too, women as well as men sympathizers were present at the execution of Ḥabbib. Rabbula was greatly influenced by his Christian mother. Mara, who was Governor, Steward, and later Bishop of Amid, was educated by his two unmarried sisters. Ephraim of Amid, the clever Patriarch of Antioch, was won over to Melkite doctrines by books belonging to his mother. The Monophysites of Edessa campaigning in 449 against their bishop Hiba were willing to permit women to be counted among their number.

Rich women of noble birth were little affected by inferiority in legal status. The sister of the king of Ḥira was celebrated for the liberality of her patronage towards the Nestorians. The same king was encouraged by the brave words of his wife to face the enmity of the king of Persia, 'It is better to die with the name of king'. The grandmother of John son of Basil, the noble of Edessa, could dispose of 2,000 pounds of silver. And the wife of Iwannis Roṣpaya was the proud mistress of her actions in her own house. When Khusraw II, as we have seen, was being lavishly entertained by Iwannis in his mansion at Edessa, he called his host:

[Khusraw] said to him, 'We have been greatly honoured by you. But there is a custom in Persia that when kings condescend to enter the house of one of the princes, the wife of the prince must come forward and fill a cup which the king drinks from her hand . . . If you wish to do me full honour complete it in this way . . .' Hearing this Iwannis was confused. He did not wish to reply to Khusraw or to offend him, and left the matter for his wife to settle, because he had confidence in his wife's wisdom. He conveyed to his wife, through a young girl, what Khusraw had said. Now . . . she despised Khusraw in her mind; but she answered, 'You are great, in our eyes, O King, but the custom that prevails and is current among Byzantines does not permit a noble woman to present wine to a man'. Khusraw, on hearing this, was silent.

When the banquet was over . . . the wife of Roṣpaya was slandered to Khusraw. It was alleged that [Iwannis's wife] had said, 'How should I go out to meet this lousy fellow who has been expelled from his country?' Khusraw . . . then swore by his gods, 'If ever I have rule over this country I shall not leave this woman in peace because of the affront to which she submitted me; but I shall make her a stranger to her country and I shall have her flesh devoured by lice'. And so, when Khusraw occupied Edessa he sent and took this woman and he made her go to Persia with her son Sergius who was the sole heir left of the Roṣpaye. He threw the woman into prison, and ordered that no water should be cast on her or bath, and that her clothes should not be washed or changed, and that she should be given bread and water to keep her alive. And so this honourable woman came to be tormented by lice and perished very cruelly.[1]

Edessa stood far from the Imperial capital and in a region that, for all its

---

[1] *Chr. ad* 1234. Sergius was later permitted to return to Edessa; see p. 203 below.

fertility, was comparatively poor in material resources. It was neglected by
the central administration; to them its importance lay mainly in its strategic
position near the borders of Persia. Its population, then, suffered the more
acutely from natural disasters and recovered the more slowly. There was a land-
slide in October 499 which made a great breach in the walls to the south
of the East gate and caused much public alarm. In 494–5 and again two
years later, there was a widespread plague of boils and tumours and many
Edessans lost their sight. In May 499 a swarm of locusts laid their eggs in
Osrhoene, and in the next year the people 'imagined . . . that the very air
was vomiting [locusts] . . . and that they were descending from the sky. When
they were only able to crawl, they devoured and consumed all the territory . . .
of Resaina and Tella and Edessa.'[1] Destruction of the crops led to famine;
as many as one hundred and thirty persons died in a single day, and the
scenes of horror on this occasion are graphically described by 'Joshua the
Stylite'.[2]

Half a century later another famine throughout Mesopotamia lasted some
eight years. It was followed by an outbreak of bubonic plague which swept
across the Eastern Empire from Egypt to Palestine and Syria, and into
Persia. In Mesopotamia there were rumours of invasion and war. People
wandered in frenzy. John of Ephesus relates how they began to bleat and
bark and bite and scream and swear blasphemously, attacking pious worshippers in the churches; they knelt and jumped and stood on each other's
shoulders. The remedy, we are assured, was discovered to be the avoidance
of oil with bread and abstinence from wine, and the people recovered. In
504–5 when the wars had come to an end, another calamity befell the
Edessans:

> Wild beasts became very ferocious. . . . They had acquired a taste for human flesh;
> and . . . they entered the villages and carried off children, . . . and also fell upon single
> men on the roads. . . . People became so fearful that at the time of threshing not a man
> in the whole countryside would pass the night on his threshing-floor without a hut for
> fear of the beasts of prey. But by the help of the Lord . . . some of them fell into the
> hands of villagers, who stabbed them and sent their dead carcases to Edessa; and others
> were caught by huntsmen, who bound them and brought them [thither] alive . . .[3]

In the following years hunts of wild boars were organized by the Byzantine
general. More than forty were caught in a single day, and some were sent,
alive or dead, to Edessa.

These misfortunes were common to other areas of Mesopotamia. But
Edessa had its own source of calamity. It was at the mercy of the river
Daiṣan (Greek, Scirtos), the 'leaping' river, which at least once in each
century overflowed its banks and caused widespread havoc in lives and

---

[1] 'Josh. St'.   [2] See pp. 147 f.   [3] 'Josh. St.'

property. The flood of 201[1] was repeated in the spring of 303. We have a vivid account of another flood in April 413, when the river rose and found the exit to the east of the city blocked. The waters accumulated in the city and flowed through the streets. Houses of brick and huts of clay collapsed upon their occupants; dwellings that were reinforced with stone and lime withstood the pressure of the water, especially if they were built on the slope of the hills, but even here persons surprised in the lower storeys were drowned. Portions of the city wall, houses and timber and bodies and domestic articles were swept into the plain and down the Gullab to the Balikh and thence to the river Euphrates. In April 525 the disaster recurred on an even more serious scale. It took place in the evening when many were asleep, some were bathing in the public baths and others were at supper. We are told that on this occasion 30,000 people died; Procopius states that one third of the population perished, and that the finest buildings were completely destroyed. Bishop Asclepius and the city Administrator fled to Antioch. Engineers were sent from Constantinople by the Emperor to construct a dam and to change the course of the river. Justinian was determined to 'preserve the benefit that the city gained from the river, but also to free the city from the fear of it'; at the same time, the city walls were restored. As a tribute to its benefactor the city was renamed Justinopolis. But the Daiṣan had not been tamed. The dam fell into disrepair, and again and again Edessa was at the mercy of its flood waters.[2]

The misfortunes caused by human agency were, however, more to be dreaded than the vagaries of nature. The wars of the third, fourth, sixth, and seventh centuries wrought wholesale destruction. Entire villages were laid waste. In 359, for example, the Byzantines ordered 'all the plains to be set on fire to prevent the enemy from getting supplies. . . . From the very banks of the Tigris all the way to the Euphrates not a green thing was to be seen.'[3] In the winter of 502 the Beduins of Ḥira came as far as Edessa, 'laying waste and plundering and taking prisoner all the villagers'. The number of persons carried into captivity was 18,500,

besides those who were killed and besides the cattle and property and the spoil of all kinds. The reason that all these people were found in the villages was its being the time of the vintage, for not only did the villagers go out to the vintage but also many of the Harranians and Edessans went out and were taken prisoner.[4]

In 577, too, the Persian general

burned and laid waste and devastated all the region of Osrhoene, each man going about in the region confidently and without fear as though dwelling in his own house. . . . They did not leave a house standing wherever they passed. . . . They drove off all the cattle and captives . . . , and fled from Edessan territory.[5]

---

[1] See p. 24 above.   [2] Cf. pp. 187 f., 203 f. below.   [3] Ammian.
[4] 'Josh. St.'   [5] John Ephes., *History*.

Thousands of peasants were carried off. The more fortunate of the villagers took refuge in Edessa itself; behind the security of its walls, they watched helplessly while the enemy destroyed their crops and set fire to their homesteads. Usually the country people were received by the townspeople at such a time with sympathy, and were lodged in the hospices and infirmaries. We read, indeed, that in 500–1, 'a report had gone forth throughout the countryside of Edessa that the people of Edessa took good care of those who were in want; and for this reason a countless multitude of people entered the city.'[1] The kindness of the Edessans was rewarded. Two years later the Persian king Kawad laid siege to their city; it was the villagers who sallied out and threw him and his host into retreat. The Byzantine general thanked them in public and gave them a reward of 300 *denarii*.

The fear of sudden attack made it necessary to keep the defences of the city in a state of preparedness. In November 502, the city was menaced by a Persian invasion.

Edessa was closed and guarded, and ditches were dug and the walls repaired; the gates of the city were stopped up with blocks of stone, because they had fallen into decay. The citizens were going to put up new ones, and to make bars for the sluices of the river, lest anyone should enter thereby. But they could not find iron enough for the work, and an order was issued that every house[2] in Edessa should furnish ten pounds of iron. When this was done, the work was finished.[3]

When Kawad's army encamped near the city in September 503,

[the Edessans] pulled down all the convents and inns that were close to the wall, and burned the village of Kephar Ṣelem, also called Negbath. They cut down all the hedges of the gardens and parks that were around, and felled the trees that were in them. They brought in the bones of all the martyrs [from the shrines] which were around the city; and set up engines on the wall, and tied coverings of hair cloth over the battlements.[3]

We are fortunate in having a contemporary account of the siege of Edessa in 503. Negotiations between the opposing commanders broke down.

We saw the words of Christ and his promises to Abgar really fulfilled. For Kawad . . . came and encamped against Edessa . . . [on the south, the east, and the north of the city]. This whole host without number surrounded Edessa in one day, besides the pickets which it had left on the hills and rising ground. In fact the whole plain was full of them. The gates of the city were all standing open, but the Persians were unable to enter it because of the blessing of Christ. On the contrary, fear fell upon them, and they remained at their posts, no one fighting with them, from morning till towards the ninth hour. Then some went forth from the city and fought with them; and they slew many Persians, but of them there fell but one man. Women too were bearing water, and carrying it outside the walls, that those who were fighting might drink; and little boys were throwing stones with slings. Then a few people who had gone out of the city drove them

---

[1] 'Josh. St.'   [2] Or 'courtyard'.   [3] 'Josh. St.'

away and repulsed them far from the wall, for they were not further off it than about a bowshot; and they went and encamped beside the village Qubbe.[1]

Kawad demanded hostages and a ransom was agreed upon. The king, however, required a quantity of gold to be handed over without delay. The Byzantine general, on the advice of the grandees of Edessa, refused.

Then Kawad became furious, and armed the elephants that were with him, and set out . . . and came again to fight with Edessa. . . . He surrounded the city on all sides, more than on the former occasion, all its gates being open. [The Byzantine soldiers were ordered] not to fight with him, that no falsehood might appear on his part; but some few of the villagers who were in the city went out against him with slings, and smote many of his mail-clad warriors, whilst of themselves not one fell. His legions were daring enough to try to enter the city; but when they came near its gates, like an upraised mound of earth, they were humbled and repressed and turned back. Because, however, of the swiftness of the charge of their cavalry, the slingers became mixed up among them; and though the Persians were shooting arrows, and the Huns were brandishing maces, and the Beduins were levelling spears at them, they were unable to harm a single one of them. . . . After they saw that they were able neither to enter the city nor to harm the unarmed men who were mixed up with them . . . ,[1]

the Persians withdrew, setting fire to shrines and monasteries outside the city walls.

Procopius describes the siege of Edessa by Kawad's son, Khusraw I, forty years later. The Persian king had already been obliged through sickness to desist from an onslaught on the city, and had fallen 'into a great dejection at being worsted by the God of the Christians'. He returned to the attack in 544. An assault by his Hun mercenaries on the northern wall of the city failed. Khusraw withdrew and opened negotiations. Four envoys from Edessa admitted that they 'would choose peace rather than the dangers of war'; but Khusraw's terms were so high that it was felt preferable to defy his power. The Persians then began to construct siege-works to the south and east of the city. Sorties by the garrison failed to interrupt the work, and plans for a peaceful settlement were met by a demand for either 50,000 pounds of gold or the entire wealth of the city. The Byzantine garrison determined to resist; they constructed a mine underneath the embankment thrown up by the Persians and completely destroyed it. An attempt by the Persians to scale the Citadel wall by night was thwarted by a villager who roused the sleeping guards to beat off the attackers. A Persian attack on the East gate had no greater success.

The arrival of an envoy from Constantinople to mediate between the two forces led Khusraw to make a last bid to storm the city.

At every gate he stationed some of the commanders and a part of the army, encircling the whole wall in this way, and he brought up ladders and war-engines against it. And

---

[1] 'Josh. St.'

in the rear he placed all the Beduins[1] with some of the Persians, not in order to assault the circuit wall, but in order that, when the city was captured, they might gather in the fugitives and catch them as in a drag-net. . . . The fighting began early in the morning, and at first the Persians had the advantage. For they were in great numbers and fighting against a very small force, since most of the Byzantines had not heard what was going on and were utterly unprepared. But as the conflict advanced the city became full of confusion and tumult and the whole population, even women and little children, were going up on to the wall. Now those who were of military age together with the soldiers were repelling the enemy most vigorously, and many of the countryfolk made a remarkable show of valorous deeds against the barbarians. Meanwhile the women and little children, and the aged also, were gathering stones for the fighters and assisting them in other ways. Some also filled numerous basins with olive oil, and after heating them over fires a sufficient time everywhere along the wall, they sprinkled the fiercely boiling oil upon the enemy who were assailing the circuit wall, using a sort of whisk for the purpose, and in this way harrassed them still more.

In 'a passion of anger' Khusraw threw all his forces against the city:

The [Persian] soldiers with much shouting and tumult brought up the towers and the other engines of war to the wall and set the ladders against it in order to capture the city with one mighty rush. But since the Byzantines were hurling great numbers of missiles and exerting all their strength to drive them off, the barbarians were turned back by force; and as Khusraw withdrew, the Byzantines taunted him, inviting him to come and storm the wall.

Only at the North gate, which was lightly defended, did the Persian attack have momentary success, but here too it was beaten off. The assault on the wall ended in the late afternoon. Two days later the Persians made an onslaught on the South gate, but they can scarcely have been surprised that this limited operation was decisively repelled. At a conference between the commanders of both sides, Khusraw received 500 pounds of gold and gave 'in writing the promise not to inflict any further injury upon the Byzantines; afterwards, setting fire to all his defences, he returned homeward with his whole army'.

The Edessans, then, had experience of the trials of warfare; they always welcomed the return of peace. In 506, for example,

the people of the city rejoiced in the peace that was made and exulted in the immunity which they would henceforth enjoy. . . . Dancing for joy at the hope of the good things which they expected to befall [them], and lauding God who in his goodness had cast peace over the two kingdoms, they escorted [the Byzantine commander] as he set forth, with songs of praise that befitted him and [the Emperor] who had sent him.[2]

Nor did they lose compassion for others who had suffered from the horrors of war. When Khusraw I wished to sell the captives he had taken at Antioch,

the citizens of Edessa . . . displayed an unheard-of zeal. For there was not a person who did not bring ransom for the captives, and deposit it in the sanctuary according to the

---

[1] Procopius has 'Saracens', that is, Ṭayyaye.   [2] 'Josh. St.'

measure of his possessions. And there were some who even exceeded their proportionate amount in so doing. For the prostitutes took off all the ornaments which they wore on their persons and threw them down there, and any farmer who was in want of plate or of money but who had an ass or a sheep, brought this to the sanctuary with great zeal. So there was collected an exceedingly great amount of gold and silver and money in other forms.[1]

None of this, however, reached Khusraw. The Byzantine commander prevented the transaction—it is suggested that he purloined the money—and Khusraw returned to Persia with his captives.

Enemies in war were not the only danger that Edessans had to face. In 395–6, in 515, and again in 531 the dreaded Huns swept over the frontiers into Byzantine Mesopotamia and left behind a trail of disaster before they were forced to withdraw. The terror which they inspired is shown by the visions of an anchorite.

Apparitions would often come and cry, 'Flee! flee! Behold, the land is full of Huns!' And Huns appeared to me in various fearful shapes, riding on horses, with swords drawn and flashing. And they came up to the gate crying in a barbaric language and in an excited state, with arrows fitted to their bows. And I would say, '. . . I do not care; and if you are in truth barbarians and have received power to kill, I do not fear death. . . .' While I was saying these words, all the hosts of the Huns went up upon these rocks thus . . . , crying, 'This man has conquered'.[2]

It was, however, the burden of the numerous Byzantine forces quartered in the region that lay most heavily on the people of Edessa and its environs. The first charge upon the administration was the maintenance of military security, not the welfare of the citizens. The latter were under a legal obligation to supply the soldiers with accommodation and food and water, at their own cost.[3] In 499–500, when the Emperor reduced the capitation-tax on villagers by two *folles*, he also freed the townspeople from the task of drawing water for the soldiers. The presence of the army certainly assured the Edessans of some employment, but for this they evidently received little remuneration. An exception seems to have been the construction of Dara by Anastasius. Anxious to forestall the objections of the Persians to this contravention of the treaty between the two countries, he collected rapidly a large labour force by offering 4 carats a day for each labourer and 8 carats for a man with a donkey. But normally Edessans were conscripted to perform *sordida munera* which in wartime proved dangerous and arduous. They erected the siege-works around their own city. In 504–5 they were

[1] Procopius, *Wars.*

[2] John Ephes., *Lives.* A poem on the invasion of the Huns in 395–6 was written by Cyrillona; he has been identified with a Qiyore, who was director of the School of the Persians at Edessa, but the identification is not proved; Wright,

Short History of Syriac Literature, 40 f. The Edessan ʿAbsamya, nephew of St. Ephraim, composed discourses on Hun raids in 397 or 404.

[3] See, for example, *Cod. Theod.*, xii, 10.

required to carry provisions to the camps at Amid; how much they suffered in this enterprise, we are told, only those who engaged in it could tell, and most of them died on the way with their pack-animals.

Static units of the *limitanei* were stationed in forts, mostly in the villages or open country; if they were stationed in the cities, they were probably in barracks. But the field army, when it was not under canvas at the front, was frequently billeted in the town. The soldiers lived for the most part in private house and inns, and only physicians, teachers, clergy, and some categories of craftsmen were exempt from the obligation of providing accommodation for them. The requisitioning of rooms and provisions for these troops was in the hands of the notables of the city, and this was a source of friction between them and the common people. The notables took advantage of their privilege.

[They] stretched out their hands for bribes; they took them from everyone and spared nobody. After a few days they sent other [soldiers] to those upon whom they had quartered some in the first instance. [Soldiers] were billeted even upon priests and deacons, though these had been exempted from this [duty] by the Emperor.[1]

When the whole Byzantine army was stationed at Edessa in April 506 and remained there for five months, troops were billeted also in the villages and in the monasteries around the city, and even upon the solitaries who lived in the hills outside the walls of Edessa.

In 505–6 the Emperor decreed the remission of the capitation tax. The landowners were delighted, but the populace maintained that the landowners who had benefited by the decree should now provide accommodation for the troops. The prefect of the city acquiesced. Although a householder was legally obliged to give soldiers only bare accommodation up to one-third of the house, soldiers evidently demanded bedding, wood, and oil also. The city grandees then appealed to the general; they required him to allocate rations by the month to each soldier, 'lest when they enter the houses of wealthy people, they plunder them as they had plundered the common people'. This request in turn was granted, and the monthly ration was fixed at one measure of oil, 200 pounds of wood, and bed and bedding for every two soldiers. Now, however, the soldiers mutinied. The general barely escaped with his life, and the order concerning soldiers' rations remained a dead letter; '[The general] said nothing [more] to the troops; so they remained where they were billeted, behaving exactly as they pleased, for there was none to check them or restrain or admonish them.'[1]

In this atmosphere of intrigue and in the absence of decisive authority, it was inevitably the poor who suffered most. Their sense of grievance was heightened by the comparative luxury in which the soldiers lived. The soldiers ate wheaten bread, which was beyond the reach of the ordinary

---

[1] '*Josh. St.*'

citizen, baked by the townspeople in their houses and by villagers throughout the countryside, as well as by bakers, both foreign and native:

To the Byzantine troops nothing was lacking; everything was supplied to them at the right time, and sent down with great care by order of the Emperor. Indeed, the things that were sold in the camps were more abundant than in the city, whether meat or drink or shoes or clothing.[1]

When the winter set in, the soldiers deserted their camps for the warmth and comfort of the cities.

The soldiers bullied the citizens and the countryfolk; even Rabbula had to exert his authority to insist on respect from the soldiers for the priestly cloth. A chronicler writes bitterly:

Those who came to our aid under the name of deliverers ... plundered almost as much as enemies. Many poor people they turned out of their beds and slept in them, whilst their owners lay on the ground in cold weather. Others they drove out of their own houses, and went in and dwelt in them. The beasts of burden of some they carried off by force as if [these] were spoil of war; the clothes of others they stripped off their persons and took away. Some they beat violently for a mere trifle, with others they quarrelled in the streets and reviled for a small cause. They openly plundered everyone's little [stock of] provisions and the stores that a few had in the villages and cities. Many they fell upon in the highways. Because the houses and inns of the city [of Edessa] were not sufficient for them, they lodged with the artisans in their booths. Before the eyes of everyone they violated women in the streets and houses. From old women and widows and poor women, they took oil, wood, salt, and other things, and kept them from their work to wait on them. In short, they harassed everyone, both great and small, and there was not a person left who did not suffer some harm from them.[1]

Many of the mercenaries were Goths, some of them of high rank. Edessans regarded them as barbarians; they were angered by the manner in which the Goths flaunted their gold[2] and by their general behaviour:

Since [the Gothic soldiers] did not live at their own expense from the very first day they came, they became so gluttonous in their eating and drinking that some of them, who had regaled themselves on the tops of the houses, went forth by night, quite stupefied by too much wine, and stepped out into empty space, and so fell headlong down, and departed this life by an evil end. Others, as they were sitting and drinking, sank into slumber and fell from the house-tops and died on the spot. Others again suffered agonies on their beds from eating too much. Some poured boiling water into the ears of those who waited upon them for trifling faults. Others went into a garden to take vegetables, and when the gardener arose to prevent them from taking them, they slew him with an arrow and his blood was not avenged. Others still, as their wickedness increased and there was none to check them, since those on whom they were quartered behaved with great discretion and did everything exactly as they wished, because they were given no opportunity for doing them harm were overcome by their own rage and slew one another.

---

[1] 'Josh. St.'
[2] Burkitt, op. cit. The writer of 'Euphemia'

gives its date as 396, but the text cannot have been set down before about 430.

That there were among them others who lived decently is [obvious] . . . , for it is impossible that in a large army like this there should not be some such persons found. The wickedness of the bad, however, went so far in evil-doing that those too who were ill-disposed among the Edessans dared to do something unseemly—they wrote down on sheets of paper complaints against the general and fastened them up secretly in the places of the city used [for public notices].[1]

The histories expatiate on the misfortunes of the people of Edessa. But it should not be supposed that life there was one of unrelieved fear and poverty. The Edessans were always willing to find an occasion for celebrations, at the declaration of peace, on the remission of taxes, or at the pagan spring festival. They went in procession wearing festive white garments, carrying torches and censers; they decorated their city with candles along the river bank and in the streets and on the public buildings; they lolled and feasted in the open air, in the porticoes and courtyards. The anonymous author of the *Romance of Julian*, probably an Edessan writing in the early sixth century, no doubt reflects the practice of his own time when he describes the decoration of the city after the return of the pious Emperor Jovian. The streets and gates were hung with cloth of variegated colours, and lamps and candles were suspended from cords in the streets and porticoes. Outside the gate a great canopy was set on pillars with capitals of gold and silver and on top a golden cross.

In an earlier chapter it has been suggested that Edessans were fond of music and poetry. Dancing was also a popular pastime. The 'barbaric dance' that Trajan had witnessed on his visit to Edessa[2] was presented also to the Byzantine general Sabinianus, when he was stationed at Edessa in 359, preparing to ward off a Persian invasion of Mesopotamia. In the open air, presumably to the south-west of the city, 'amid the tombs . . . , with the wantonness of a life free from care, in complete inaction [the general] was entertained by his soldiers in a pyrrhic dance, in which music accompanied the gestures of the performers.'[3] It was no doubt later that the theatre was built at Edessa. We know that, in the late fifth century, it stood on the river bank in the east quarter of the city. Here the spring festival was celebrated by a public display of dancing, until this was prohibited by the decree of Anastasius in 502. The actor seems to have danced on a stone stage; he wore sandals to which were affixed metal plates that resounded as he struck the floor. There was also apparently a board which was beaten with a small piece of wood. The mummer, dressed in special robes, was surrounded by a chorus. Female roles were played by men in women's costumes with padded breasts.[4]

Built probably at an earlier date—for legend even ascribed it to Emperor

---

[1] 'Josh. St.'   [2] See p. 13 above.   [3] Ammian.
[4] See especially Jacob of Serug, 'On Spectacles of the Theatre'.

Augustus—was a hippodrome; it lay to the north-west of the city, immediately south of a small hill and no doubt outside the city walls.[1] This is to be identified with (or perhaps it lay beside) the place later called the amphitheatre or stadium. Here, it may be presumed, criminals were thrown to the wild animals. The mob at Edessa who screamed against their Dyophysite bishop Hiba in 448 or 449, demanded that 'the haters of the Messiah should be sent to the hunt[2] and the brood of the impure to the stadium'. Hiba was called the 'jockey bishop'; one of his protégés was said to have arranged a circus for him. The function of the stadium may have changed after August 499, when the hunting of wild beasts in the amphitheatre was forbidden throughout the Byzantine Empire by Emperor Anastasius, though the prohibition was revoked shortly afterwards.

Most popular at Edessa, however, were the public baths, one for winter and one for summer. In May 498, the two colonnades and probably the *tepidarium*[3] of a new summer bath-house fell down a few days before the building was to have been opened. Only two of the workmen were killed as they ran to the door of the cold-water bathroom[4] and revolved the door from opposite sides, each man trying to get out first. The building was finally completed in 504–5. There were colonnades also in front of the winter baths; these were used in the famine of 500–1 as a temporary infirmary. There was a bath under the Church of the Apostles by the Great gate to the east of the city, and another public bath was beside the public granary.

The pious, both pagan and Christian, were at one in strong disapproval of these entertainments, although their disapproval was half-hearted in respect of the baths. The law codes prescribed that no man should adopt as his heirs 'those who serve in the theatre, the hippodrome, or the stadium or mimes, prostitutes, charioteers, *ludarii*.' When Julian organized a pagan priesthood in the provinces and cities of the Empire he instructed its members:

[to avoid] the licentious theatrical shows of the present day.... Leave them [he adjured] to the crowd. . . . Let no priest enter a theatre or have an actor or charioteer for his friend. . . . With regard to the hunting shows with dogs which are performed at cities inside the theatre, need I say that not only priests but even the sons of priests must keep away from them.[5]

At Edessa Rabbula forbade attendance at circuses: 'Far be it that in the city of believers men who eat the body of God in faith and drink his blood should see the flesh of men eaten wickedly by evil beasts in sport.'[6] So too John of Ephesus, like his Monophysite leader, Severus of Antioch, deplored the circuses and mimes; and 'Joshua the Stylite' ascribed the calamities which

---

[1] See Pl. 37.

[2] Greek, κυνήγιον.

[3] The text is difficult; we should perhaps translate 'urinal'.

[4] The meaning of the Syriac word is doubtful.

[5] Julian, 'Epistle to a Priest'.

[6] *Life of Rabbula.*

Edessans suffered in his time to their patronage of the spring festival with its pagan undertones. In the sixth century Jacob of Serug writes:

The fruits [of the theatre] are . . . dancing, sport and music, the miming of lying tales, teaching which destroys the mind, poems which are not true, troublesome and confused sounds, melodies to attract children, ordered and captivating songs, skilful chants, lying canticles [composed] according to the folly invented by the Greeks.[1]

Edessa was the home of classical Syriac, and its inhabitants are credited with having spoken and written the language in its most perfect form.[2] The scribes of the monasteries of Edessa copied important manuscripts. Students came there to be instructed in the art of calligraphy and the science of correct copying, like Marutha of Tagrith and his biographer Denha at the beginning of the seventh century; the former was to become Maphrian, head of the Jacobite Church in the East, the latter his successor. From an early date the work of translation into Syriac occupied the foremost scholars of Edessa. Their principal care was, of course, the rendering into Syriac of the Bible. We cannot, with any degree of certainty, associate Tatian's Diatessaron with Edessa; but Adiabene, from where Tatian originated, and where the Diatessaron may have been written, had close ties with the Christian community of Edessa. The Separate Gospels (*Evangelion daMepharreshe* or Tetraevangelion), and various books of the Peshitta and other Syriac versions of the Bible may well have been composed at Edessa. The desire of Christians for a standard form of Bible text in Syriac doubtless arose out of the theological controversies conducted in a largely Hellenistic environment, and from the need for the clear expression of accepted dogma. Certainly the Peshitta, the work of several hands, displays at points close reliance on the Greek version. Philoxenus of Mabbog, who was born in Beth Garmai but studied at Edessa, provided the stimulus for a new translation of the Greek Bible into Syriac in about 508. A Syriac version of the whole of the Old Testament, and possibly of the New Testament, is said to have been produced by the Nestorian Catholicus, Maraba I, in the middle of the sixth century; he had mastered Greek at Edessa.

Theological treatises were eagerly translated from Greek into Syriac at Edessa. The ecclesiastical histories of Eusebius and the writings of Clement and of Titus of Bostra must have been translated in the lifetime of these authors or shortly afterwards. Texts of these works appear in Edessan manuscripts dated 411 and 462, and they had probably already passed through the hands of successive scribes. The translators of Aristotle, who had great influence on Syrian philosophy and theology, Probus for the Nestorians and

---

[1] Jacob of Serug, op. cit.

[2] Dionysius of Tell-Maḥre, in Mich. Syr., writes, 'The root and base of the Syriac language, that is, Aramaic, is Edessa'. A century earlier Jacob of Edessa had referred to 'this Mesopotamian or Edessene or, to be more precise, Syriac language'.

Sergius of Resaina for the Monophysites, were not from Edessa; but the Schools of Edessa and the neighbourhood were responsible for rendering into Syriac the works of Diodorus of Tarsus, Theodore of Mopsuestia (these two already before 435), Nestorius, Paul of Samosata, Severus of Antioch, and many other Greek authors. Rabbula translated the tracts of Cyril of Alexandria at Cyril's own request. Especially active was the School of the Persians before its closure in 489. Not only were Greek theological works put into Syriac but original writings were composed in prose and poetry. Notable was the work of Narseh and his fellow Nestorian, Ma'na. The scholars of Edessa were in constant contact both with those of neighbouring Harran and Tella, and also with those of Antioch and Cyrrhus.[1]

The reverse process, the translation of Syriac into other languages, commenced at an early date. The famous story of the Seven Sleepers of Ephesus may have been composed originally in Syriac and then translated into Greek; such was almost certainly the case with the early *Acts of Thomas*. The works of St. Ephraim were, as we have remarked, translated into several languages, including Greek, shortly after his death. St. Jerome may have known Syriac, for he received the story of the adventures of Malchus (Malka) during his captivity among the Beduins, direct from that monk. The chronicler Sozomen derived his account of the persecution of the Christians in Persia from Oriental sources, probably Syriac. Theodoret turned some Aramaic martyrologies into Greek and knew the *Life* of St. Ephraim. Syriac was translated into Persian also, notably by Ma'na.[2]

There is, however, no evidence that original literary work at Edessa in this period was composed in any language other than Syriac. Extracts from historical writings have already been given. We have observed the moving simplicity of some of the early martyrologies of Edessa and the straightforward narrative of the *Doctrine of Addai*.[3] The chronicle attributed to 'Joshua the Stylite' was written in about 507 by a monk of the monastery of Zuqnin, near Amid, who was resident at Edessa; and it provides excellent material for the history of this period, written in a homely style.[4] The *Chronicle of Edessa*, by an anonymous writer or compiler, was completed in about 540, but in its present form it is little more than a bare outline of events.[5]

Edessa cannot claim John of Ephesus, the eminent Syriac historian of the sixth century. The short 'biography' of Euphemia, the Edessan girl

[1] Some literary activity may be ascribed to Bishop Aitallaha. All, however, that has survived of the bishop's writings are fragments translated into Armenian.

[2] On the other hand, Eusebius, Bishop of Emesa (died before 359), who was a native of Edessa, is remembered for theological writings in Greek, later translated into Syriac. He spent some years in Palestine and at Antioch before receiving preferment to the see of Emesa.

[3] See pp. 83-6; 76, 78-81 above.

[4] See the extracts on pp. 106, 123, 128, 139 f. 147 f., 155-9, 161-3.

[5] The account of the flood of A.D. 201 shows, however, that sections of the Chronicle may originally have been at greater length; see p. 24 above.

abducted by a Gothic soldier, and miraculously transported home by the intervention of the martyrs, was, however, almost certainly composed there.[1] We should probably ascribe to an Edessan the authorship of the tripartite 'historical' writings on Constantine, Eusebius of Rome, and Jovian, the so-called *Romance of Julian*; the work was composed by an anonymous monk, doubtless between 502 and 532. It contains gross exaggerations and distortion of fact, but the style of its Syriac is admirable.[2]

The most celebrated poet of Edessa in the Byzantine period was St. Ephraim. His literary work has been discussed and excerpts have been cited in an earlier chapter.[3] Here we touch briefly on an aspect of his writings that has been rarely noted, its scientific bent. A few illustrations must suffice:

When [the stomach] does not disgorge there comes evidence of [food's] heaviness and coldness. . . . If it does not digest, it does not liquefy, and if it does not liquefy, [the stomach] does not disgorge. . . . For coldness shuts up the food heavily . . .

A line has not any substance, as a horse has substance. . . . When artists portray the likeness of bodies which they perceive, they cannot add or subtract anything, and when they portray the likeness of substances which they do not perceive, they portray them in their proper colours and shapes. . . . But in the case of a line, [the artist] adds and subtracts anything that he wishes . . . and he is not blamed.

That thou mayest learn well how tubes concentrate scattered things and propel them, consider also fire-hoses, and see to what a height they propel and scatter the unstable water. Consider moreover aqueducts and see how water is collected in cisterns and pipes and [then] ascends and does service on heights that are difficult of access. . . . See that when [air] is concentrated in the furnace of a blacksmith or the fire-place of a goldsmith its blast goes forth strongly because of its concentration. . . . Again make an experiment for thyself—if thou openest thy mouth wide and criest, thy voice wanders and is weak, but if thou compressest thy lips a little on the outer side and makest with them as it were a spacious hollow on the inner side, thy voice is concentrated and increaseth, especially if thou art looking downward and not upward. Again, observe a carpenter—that when he considers the straightness of the wood . . . , he closes half his eye that he may concentrate [his sight] against the straightness of the wood.

When a man looks in the direction of the sun, if he does not place his hand above his eyes and shelter them, their sight is not concentrated [to look] steadily. . . . When a man looks into a basin of pure water, he sees, in the collected water below, the colour of the sky and likewise a bird if it happens to fly over the aforesaid basin.

Rays do not go forth from unpolished bodies or from substances that do not glitter, as they go forth from polished objects or from substances that glitter. As everything which falls into a mirror is . . . thought to belong to the mirror, although it does not belong to it, so also those rays were thought to belong to the mirror, although they did not belong to it. . . . When hard substances strike against one another a sound is engendered from between them—and it was not the case that that sound was within them and was inaudible, for it is their nature to engender a sound by striking together . . .

This scientific quality in Ephraim's writings gives a touch of apparent

[1] See p. 141.
[2] Another *Romance of Julian* was composed probably later in the sixth century.
[3] pp. 88–90 above.

dogmatism to his theological arguments. But it lends them also a matter-of-fact colouring which was attractive to the ordinary Edessan. The inclination towards science was characteristic already of Bardaiṣan, who was at the same time probably a greater poet than Ephraim; it underlay the systems devised by the cosmologists. Most important, it had, for all its naïveté, far-reaching influence upon the work of later writers in both Syriac and Arabic. In Ephraim's work we may detect that spirit of inquiry which made of Syriac-speakers ready vehicles for the transmission of Greek philosophy and science.

Another Syriac poet, the celebrated Isaac of Antioch, was a native of Amid; but he passed his early years at Edessa and studied under a pupil of St. Ephraim. Subsequently he went to Antioch and died there in about 460. His voluminous works were highly admired by his contemporaries; to the modern reader they appear somewhat artificial and tedious. Nevertheless, although his declamations against heathen worship may lack fire, they are not wanting in sincerity. Isaac's two homilies on Beth Ḥur, which was sacked by the Persian Beduins in about 457, present an interesting picture of Byzantine Mesopotamia at that time:

Why does our foolish generation haste to clamour at our chastisement, sitting in judgement on their Judge; and wherefore do they claim [vengeance] at his hand? 'Behold', they cry, 'captives and exiles with spoil of worldly wealth—Beduins that fouled the land have borne them far away. Crushed are the houses of men, when [Beduins] crossed the peaceful frontier—furies, wild asses, Ishmaelites, slaughtering good and bad alike . . .' But truly [Beth Ḥur] was a shoot that grew from the vine of perdition, a [new] Harran that arose in our land; and rightly the despoiler tore up her roots . . .

The Persians spared her not, for with them she served the sun; the Beduins left her not, for with them she sacrificed to 'Uzzai. She made herself like a harlot that is buffeted for the sake of riches, that has wily paramours for abundance of jewels. She was the rendezvous of the wanton, of gluttons and of thieves, of the servant fleeing from his master, the son rebelling against his father . . .

Diviners were in her that claimed knowledge of hidden things—but they foretold not that her own fate was to go into the hands of marauders. The tyrant there, chief of the city's heathens—his trust was in divination, yet the wrath swept him away utterly. Their wives, the priestesses, became spoil in the house of strangers, their virgin daughters were violated in the rite of Balthi . . .

But the wrongs of Beth Ḥur were avenged:

Pause awhile and be amazed how the despoilers have perished, with the spoils which they despoiled, at the hands of the Persians on our frontiers. Many came together from the fortress of Nisibis; in a trice there perished the force that came to our frontier. . . . Those who were enriched at our hands are made poor; those who despoiled are now a spoil. By war and pestilence Justice has ended them.

Isaac castigates hypocritical ascetics, those whom Emperor Julian a century earlier had called, 'for the most part men who by making small sacrifices gain much, . . . on specious pretexts levying tribute which they call alms—whatever that means'[1]:

> Let us come now to the chaste order of ascetics, who excel in their long hair, and are honoured for their garb. . . . Servants who have left obedience to their masters, sons who neglect their rightful duty to their father, they grow their hair, contrary to the discipline of their teaching, thinking they can cover their abandoned morals with their long hair. They wander through the cities to collect alms, they are laughed at by nobles and scoffed at by their servants; . . . under various pretexts of justice greedily they multiply and amass money. . . . Everywhere they create a scandal in the houses of hucksters and merchants. . . . They play the anchorite with perfumes and uncleanness, they gorge themselves with food and wine. With [their] scrip and [their] hair they make show of sanctity—but they commit adultery and theft. . . . They have broken the yoke of teachers, and ceased from any kind of work, eager only for the hospice board; they will not stay in chaste and holy monasteries, for they have learnt no Psalms nor can they meditate on the Scriptures. . . . They disturb the watchful, sober monks by their debauchery and somnolence. . . . They are eager for the comfort of their bellies, and pass from monastery to monastery, seeking always new repasts, as strangers . . . , that by this pretext they can indulge their gluttony and drunkenness.

A poem by Isaac entitled 'On the Power of the Devil to Tempt Man' seems to have been written at Edessa itself. He rebukes the superstitious women of the city:

> Their faith is not great, their error is mighty; they go to be anointed by the recluse, but not as if he were a man of truth. 'Whether he uses magic or incantations', they say, 'to me will he give healing.' Though he be a haughty fool with foolish women flocking to him, in another guise they run to his gate without love. 'Whatever it may be', they say, 'for my ailment something will he devise; with the book of exorcism, with libations, he will remove the devil from my son.'

Isaac writes scathingly of the reverence shown at Edessa to the shrine of St. Thomas:

> . . . Crooked are his voices, they make us wander from the holy place. Greatly we despise the Church, truly we scorn its oaths. The man who swears and adjures by the Church—we have no respect for his oath. One seeks to swear by the Church, but he that adjures him has no respect for it. 'If by the shrine of the Apostle Thomas you swear not' [he cries] 'I shall not hold [your oath] true.' [Thomas] they hold dearer than his Lord, because the demons have mourned [by his tomb]. If one swears by the Church —it is in haste; by the Apostle's shrine he lingers.

Yet Isaac condones this cult of a saint:

> Have you not seen a king's court? Before him no man is beaten; but the generals that stand before him—it is they that chastise the rebellious. In the Church, Christ is like the king, and the Apostle is like the general. The royal house demands repose, but there is tumult in the general's house. So Christ in this way glorifies his churches by repose.

[1] 'Oration to the Cynic Heraclius'.

Jacob of Serug had closer ties with Edessa. He was born, the son of a priest, in 451 at Serug, forty kilometres south-west of Edessa. He studied the Scriptures at Edessa between about 469 and 473, and remarks that he came 'by chance upon one of the writings of Diodorus [of Tarsus] and found in it a host of opinions and ideas contrary to the truth'. Jacob was *periodeutes* in the region of Serug, and became Bishop of Batnae in 519 at the age of sixty-seven or sixty-eight. He led a life of quiet study and spent all his days near his native town, but he took an active part in the local events of his time. Several of his letters have survived and are of considerable interest. The immense number of metrical compositions ascribed to him—he is said to have dictated his 760 poems to seventy amanuenses—won for him the title of 'Flute of the Holy Spirit and Harp of the believing Church'. It is related that in 521 he was summoned to Edessa by Bishop Paul. Jacob, a devout Monophysite,[1] obeyed the call reluctantly, fearing that Paul would ask him to accept the Council of Chalcedon. According to tradition, Jacob reached the Monastery of the Persians, six miles from Edessa, and there received a vision that he would die in two days. He returned to Batnae, set his church in order and died at the time foretold in his dream.

Among Jacob's letters is one about Edessa reminding its citizens of the legendary promise by Jesus that it would never be captured by an enemy. Jacob's letter was written when Amid had fallen to Kawad in 503, and we know from the chronicle of 'Joshua the Stylite' that it encouraged the people not to flee in terror before the Persians. In a letter to a certain Count Bassus, Jacob praises his loyalty to Monophysitism. Evidently Bassus was a leader of Edessa, since Jacob calls him a 'good heir of Abgar the Parthian', and continues, 'As you have inherited his city, so also you have inherited his faith; you have arisen like a brave warrior, and displayed the truth of your faith, with [Bishop] Paul the pastor and confessor.'

There is a fine letter, written between 514 and 518, from Jacob to the monks of the monastery of St. Bassus near Apamea:

Affection is like gold, but Faith is like a pearl. . . . Whence do you come, O pearl? . . . You surpass the mysteries of light. . . . You are clothed in beauty and splendour. . . . Merchants desire you, for they are never satisfied by looking upon you . . . .

The precious stone replies, 'I am the daughter of light; in me is its image formed. Leaving the heights, I descended to the depths of the abyss, and touched it. I am the moisture of the firmament; I was born in the great womb. Lightning ran before me, thunder is my companion; clouds escorted me in their courses and the winds carried and brought me, I am covered in the mists of light. I went down from the house of my father, the sea longed to meet me and received me, the deep embraced me in its belly. I washed in the waters and my beauties were not spoilt, the womb of darkness bore me and my brightness was not covered.'

---

[1] Peeters, however, claims that Jacob was a Chalcedonian, but his arguments are scarcely convincing.

In a letter to Paul of Edessa, Jacob congratulates the bishop on being restored to his see by the Emperor:

If you had not been persecuted your beauty would not have appeared, and if you had not been insulted great honour would not have befallen you. . . . Now, my lord, there is joy in all the land, and the little flock is glad because the shepherd has returned to his fold, and all the churches are bright with torches of fire and with spiritual hymns. And all the congregations pray with all their heart for the believing Emperor and for your holiness. . . . It is fitting that through the priest of Edessa the faith of our Emperor should arise like the sun in the world, for Edessa is the first betrothed of Christ, and it is fitting that she should be the first-born full of virtue at all times. . .

Jacob's discourse 'On the Fall of the Idols' has special interest for students of paganism in this period, although allowance must be made for poetic hyperbole, in his description:

A great light appeared in the world in the days of our Lord, and with its appearance brought joy to regions that were in gloom. At the rays of the Father the shadows saw that they were dismissed; they feared Him, they swallowed each other, passed away and were removed. The fair Sun of righteousness from Golgotha appeared in the world and drove forth the night of idolatry.

[Satan] set Apollo and other idols in Antioch and in Edessa he set up Nabu and Bel and many [more]. He led Harran astray through Sin and Be'elshamin and Bar Nemre and Mar(i) of his dogs and Tar'atha [and] Gedlath the goddesses.[1] Mabbog he made a city of priests of goddesses. On the tops of the hills [Satan] built palaces to the goddesses, and on the high places [erected] painted temples to idols. . . . On one hill were slaughtered sacrifices to Ares, on another was built an altar to Hermes; one valley was called the [vale] of Heracles, and another high place [was called] . . . by the name of 'the house of the gods'. There was no hill that was not moist with the blood of sacrifices and no high place that was empty of libations; youths in multitudes were given as sacrifices and maidens slaughtered to female idols . . . , to the Sun and the Moon and to the star of Venus and to the luminaries. . . . And the gods had a lofty seat of renown and images were erected on heroic pillars, and priests were dressed in fine spun linen and goodly robes.

When light appeared with the coming of Christianity, the temples were cast down:

On the tops of hills he set monasteries in place of the houses of demons, and on the height, he built shrines instead of temples. . . . [Satan] went to Edessa and found in it great labour. Its king became a worker for the church and built it. The Apostle Addai stood in it like a builder, and King Abgar wore his crown and built with him. . . .

Jacob warns that only love of gold would enable Satan to restore the reign of idolatry.

More valuable for the study of Edessa is a long homily entitled 'On the

---

[1] On these deities see p. 50 above.

Burial of Strangers'.[1] It reflects not only the loneliness of a wandering student, but also Jacob's own dislike, as a quiet country priest, for the bustle and unfriendliness of the town:

One day when I was passing through the worldly streets, the sound of groans full of pain fell upon my ears. I turned and saw a poor man, a stranger to the place, lying stretched out tortured by sickness. I stopped to hear the plaintive words he spoke, about his exile and the woes stored up in it. He began to weep and made the passers-by weep with him, and by the variety and sweetness of his words, he held me where I stood. With grievous sighs, he made his plaint, recounting what he had endured from his exile. '. . . I left the house of my own folk, hoping to return, to come back well in spirit and body. . . . But now grievous pain and sickness torture me, and they beat upon me at every hour—waves charged with death. . . . No man asks to know my griefs and sickness. . . . Each one passes by in haste, no one stops beside me; they hasten their steps deliberately that they may not see me. Day passes, night comes to flagellate me; it brings darkness, it isolates me, it makes gloomy the walls of the streets. . . . There is no light, no company . . . I am a stranger to the world and its consolations. O exile . . . , on thy roads are persecution and travail, vexation, hunger and thirst, fatigue, disgrace, and threats. Harsh looks and words pierce like arrows, like spear-points cruelly they wound my heart. . . .'

. . . His end approached when he would be gathered [in death]. . . . He looked on all sides—there was none to help him; his eyes wandered to and fro—there was none to rescue him. His tears fell pitifully on his pillow, his face was covered with dust—there was none to wipe it. . . . His lips stammered, [calling] on his dearly-loved mother to come and bewail him. . . . He called on his father to see his dear son on the dung-heap rolling in the dust. 'O mother . . . , where is your love full of tenderness . . . , where your voice with its caresses? See, I call you that I may have your consolation—and you hear not. . . . If I could but see you now, [leaning] over my face, wiping away in grief the dust around my eyes. . . . If I could but behold my friends, my neighbours, my family, fellow-students, comrades, and all my relatives! . . . Now my fingers weaken and tremble. O death, pause awhile if this may be; perchance someone may come to escort me and to bury me. . . . Let those whose son is on a journey weep for me, let those whose son is in exile weep for me, let those also weep for me whose loved ones have died by the road-side and in places of exile, and those whose hearts are afflicted . . . as my parents' hearts are afflicted. . . . Now I deliver to you my poor soul, receive it in pity, Lord, according to your bounty. . . . May you release me from the anguish and torture [of the road], may I fly and with angels cross the abyss of Hell. . . . Shield me with your right hand against Gehenna, console me for the anguish here and yonder.'

. . . And he joined his hands and bowed his head and received death. Like a flower, his beauty faded and his voice was no more. Blessed be He who pardoned him . . . and gave him rest from his toil. . . .

The triumph of orthodox Christianity at Edessa was, as we have seen, the reward of diligence and endurance that had lasted many years; it had been marked by at least three martyrdoms.[2] By the fourth century the city

---

[1] There is no need to doubt the ascription of this homily to Jacob of Serug, or to assert that it describes not Edessa but Antioch (as Peeters).

[2] See pp. 82 ff. above.

had become famous for the legend of the 'letter', in which Jesus promised that no enemy—later the phrase is 'no barbarian'[1]—would ever become master of Edessa. Its shrines were the goal of pilgrims from Mesopotamia, from Persia and Syria and Asia Minor, even from the Far East and from Europe. Some came for a brief visit like the abbess Egeria of Aquitania;[2] some came to study, like the 'stranger' in the poem of Jacob of Serug. Others came to pray. The celebrated legend of the 'man of God', Alexius, relates how a wealthy young man—writers hint that he was the son of Emperor Theodosius II—left Rome secretly on the eve of his marriage:

The blessed man . . . traversed the countries as a beggar, and went to the city of the Parthians called Edessa. There he remained, [living the life of] a beggar until his death. This was the way of life of the blessed man at Edessa. In the daytime he was constantly in the church and the martyrs' shrines, taking nothing from any man. He even wished to deprive himself of food by day in order to maintain his fast until evening. When evening came, he stood by the door of the church with outstretched hands, and received alms from those who entered the church. When he had received from them enough for all his needs, he closed his hand [and would] receive no more. His ration of food was ten measures of bread and two of vegetables; and if by chance he received more, straightway he gave it to another and gave alms out of his alms. . . . He did not keep himself apart from the poor in his dwelling. But when night arrived, while all the poor beside him were asleep he rose and placed his arms in the form of a cross by the wall or by the pillar, and prayed. With the first who gathered at the church for prayer he would enter until morning. So he fulfilled all his days.[3]

The Edessans collected sacred relics with the same zeal that modern museums collect Old Masters, and for much the same reasons—to stimulate the pride of the citizens in their city and to maintain the stream of visitors. This faith in the efficacy of relics may, of course, be matched elsewhere in the Near East. The remains of Jacob of Nisibis who died in 337–8 were preserved within the walls of his city, and St. Ephraim declares that it was their sanctity that gave Nisibis divine protection against the onslaught of the Persian unbelievers. The sophisticated citizens of Antioch refused to part with the body of St. Simeon the Stylite because it was 'a rampart, a fortress, for this city'. Nowhere, however, was greater satisfaction taken in sacred relics than at the capital of the Empire, Constantinople. Its churches and shrines acquired in the course of time the true Cross, the crown of thorns, the robe and mantle and girdle of the Virgin Mary, the head of St. John the Baptist, the bodies of St. Stephen, St. Timothy, St. Andrew, and St. Luke and a host of miscellaneous objects which were revered by pilgrims from all

---

[1] A later chronicle has, 'no Assyrian'.
[2] See pp. 176 f., 183 below.
[3] The story of Alexius is echoed in a hagiographical text of the sixth century which relates the acts of an Italian bishop named Paul who travelled to Edessa as a pilgrim in the time of Bishop Rabbula. There he took vows of poverty; after working as a simple labourer in the city, he wandered to Sinai and Nisibis, encountering many fanciful adventures on the way: he then mysteriously disappeared.

Christendom.[1] The hunger of the people of Constantinople for relics was avid and in the tenth century its rulers transferred to their own custody the sacred treasures of Edessa, the portrait and the letter of Jesus.[2]

At first the holy relics of Edessa were preserved outside the city, exactly as the citizens themselves were buried in cemeteries outside the walls. Roman law forbade interment inside a town, and this rule was observed until about 350. At Edessa a shrine was erected near the walls at the place of execution of the three martyrs, Shmona, Gurya, and Ḥabbib; beside it arose a monastery whose monks performed the daily service at the shrine. But when Edessa was threatened by the Persians in 503, the citizens brought 'the bones of all the martyrs which were around the city' into the Church of the Confessors which had been built inside the walls by the North gate.[3] The bones of Addai the evangelist and of King Abgar had been buried in the tomb of the royal family, presumably outside the city walls. They also were in time moved to be housed in churches within the city.[4] The shrines of St. Cosmas and St. Damian outside the city to the south were reputed to contain the bodies of those physician-martyrs. These may have remained outside (except when the presence of an enemy threatened them with desecration), because nearby were hospice buildings. At a later time, however, it seems to have become the practice to instal newly-acquired relics directly in churches inside the city. St. Ephraim appears to refer to bones of St. John preserved in the city,[5] perhaps in the Great baptistry built in 369–70.

The most deeply venerated relic of Edessa, second only to the letter and portrait of Jesus, was the 'treasure' of the body of St. Thomas, Apostle of the East, who was credited by legend with having dispatched Addai to Edessa on the orders of Jesus himself.[6] The body is said to have been brought by a merchant from India, where Thomas had suffered martyrdom. This translation presumably took place at an early date. A passage at the end of the *Acts of Thomas* declares that 'one of the brethren had taken [the bones of St. Thomas] away secretly and conveyed them to the West'.[7] These words

---

[1] Even the swaddling clothes of Jesus, the bread given by Jesus to Judas, the rod of Moses, the cloak of Elijah, and four of the trumpets which brought down the walls of Jericho.   [2] See pp. 215 f. below.

[3] The shrine built by Bishop Abraham (p. 182) must have been the church, not the martyry outside the walls; otherwise we would have no reference in the chronicles to the construction of this important edifice beside the North gate.

[4] See pp. 184, 249.

[5] St. Ephraim, 'Carmina Nisibena' xxxiii, 'Through the bones of John, some of which are in our place, the prophets have come to our place'.

[6] The Monophysites of Edessa, in their complaints to the Byzantine Governor against Bishop Hiba in 449, declare that their city was 'glorious in faith—first because of the blessing with which it was blessed by the Creator of heaven and earth . . . , next because it was worthy of the treasure of the bones of the Apostle Thomas who was the first to acknowledge that our Saviour is the Lord God . . .'.

[7] Another version has, '. . . . conveyed them to Mesopotamia'. Monneret de Villard, *Rendic. Lincei*, 1951, 77 ff., maintains that the body of St. Thomas was brought first to Batnae and later to Edessa, but he has scarcely proved this hypothesis.

may, it is true, be an interpolation, but already in the fourth century Rufinus of Aquileia calls Edessa 'a city of believers in Mesopotamia, adorned with the relics of [the Apostle] Thomas'.[1] In a striking passage, St. Ephraim at about the same time writes:

The devil wailed, 'Whither now may I flee from the righteous? I stirred up Death that I might slay the Apostles, so that, by their death, I might escape their torment. Now I am tormented yet more cruelly. The Apostle whom I slew in India has come before me to Edessa. Here he is altogether, and there; I went there—he was there; I found him both here and there and I am saddened. . . . That merchant bore his bones—or rather they bore him. . . . The coffin of Thomas has slain me; the hidden strength in it tortures me. . . . His great treasure has increased my poverty. His treasure was opened in Edessa, and by [its] help the great city has been enriched'.[2]

The shrine of St. Thomas lay in the open country outside the walls to the west of Edessa. It was there that the opponents of Arianism assembled under Bishop Barsai in about 372, in defiance of Emperor Valens and his officers. The story has it that the Arian Emperor ordered a general massacre of the citizens. A simple woman was seen by the commander running with her children to the shrine to accept martyrdom. So moved was he by this sight that he prevailed upon the Emperor to content himself with the expulsion of the Bishop of Edessa and the principal orthodox clergy. Ephraim writes of the incident:

The doors of houses stand open; [the city] has left them and gone forth with her pastor to the moat to die rather than forswear her faith. 'Let the city, villages,[3] buildings and houses [the inhabitants cry] be given to the Emperor; our goods and gold we shall leave; we shall not forswear our faith.' . . . May Christ bless her inhabitants—Edessa whose name is her pride. The name of her Apostle is her glory, the city that is mistress of her fellows, the city that is the shadow of the heavenly Jerusalem.[4]

In August 394 the remains of St. Thomas were transferred from the martyry outside the walls to 'his own great shrine' inside the city.[5] We know from a trustworthy source that this church was in the south-west quarter of Edessa, probably, that is, in the same direction as the martyry outside the wall.[6] The coffin of the Apostle was placed 'at the beginning of the north portico of the church on the west side of the portico'. In 441–2 a general named Anatolus donated a silver chapel[7] for the Apostle's remains.

---

[1] There is a story that Emperor Alexander Severus was asked by the Edessans, when he had defeated the Persians, to demand the return of the bones of St. Thomas, that is, in 232. There is, however, no historical justification for the story.

[2] Op. cit. xlii.   [3] Or 'wall'.

[4] *Life of St. Ephraim.*

[5] In the biography of St. Ephraim, that saint is said to have miraculously healed an epileptic at the 'door of the church of St. Thomas in the city'. This would imply that the Church of St. Thomas was built before 373. But we should not place too much reliance on the historical value of this type of literature.

[6] In the same way, the church of Shmona, Gurya, and Ḥabbib was situated in the north of the city in the same direction as their martyry outside the walls.

[7] Greek ναός.

The Aquitanian abbess Egeria visited Edessa principally to pray at the shrine of St. Thomas, and there she recited certain prayers including the words of the Apostle. She makes no mention of Addai (or Thaddaeus) as the emissary of St. Thomas and evidently she regarded St. Thomas as himself the evangelist of Edessa. We have observed how readily Addai could be identified with St. Thomas, not only by foreigners unfamiliar with the Addai-Abgar legend but even by Edessans.[1] Isaac of Antioch remarks that the people of Edessa set greater store by oaths taken by the shrine of St. Thomas than by oaths taken by the Church, and the poet is lenient in his reproaches.[2] Towards the end of the sixth century, Gregory of Tours appears to describe in exaggerated language an annual celebration at Edessa to the memory of St. Thomas. In the fifth month, that is, in February or March, great crowds assembled to pay their vows and to hold a market. For thirty days they were permitted to buy and sell without the payment of taxes:

Among the people no discord arises, no fly settles on dead meat, none that is thirsty lacks drink. On other days water is drawn from the wells from a depth of a hundred feet, now if one digs a little one finds clear water springing up in abundance. There is no doubt that this is bestowed by the merit of the Apostle. When the days of the festival have run their course, taxes are again imposed on the public, the flies that had come to an end appear, the waters that were near to the ground are swallowed up. Thereupon . . . the rains cleanse all the hall of the church of dirt and different forms of filth deposited during the festival so that one would think that it had not been trodden [by foot].[3]

Pilgrims to Edessa, like pilgrims elsewhere, were taken on a tour of the principal sights. Egeria describes her visit, probably in the middle of the fifth century,[4] with artless pleasure, and relates the stories, with which pilgrims were edified:

And since the holy bishop of that city, a truly religious man and a monk and confessor, took me willingly and said to me, 'Since I see, daughter, that you have for the sake of religion imposed much labour on yourself, to come from very distant lands to this place—then, if you will, we shall show you whatever places here it is pleasing for Christians to see. . . .

The bishop conducted the abbess around the palace of Abgar with its shining statues of Abgar and 'his son Magnus',[5] and the pools full of fish of such size, so gleaming and succulent that Egeria had never seen the like. He recounted the correspondence of Abgar with Jesus. Shortly after the arrival of the 'letter from Jesus', declared the bishop, a Persian army surrounded Edessa,

---

[1] See p. 66 above.

[2] Cf. p. 169 above.

[3] *Liber gloria martyrum*, Ch. xxxii. Monneret de Villard associated this annual holiday at Edessa with the annual fair at Batnae described by Ammian, p. 137 above. Certainly it bears close similarity to the pattern of spring festivals in the Near East, surviving to the present day

and partially reflected in Islam (with adjustments arising from the change from a solar to a lunar calendar). For miracles ascribed to celebrations of festivals of St. Thomas at Rome and in India, see P. Devos, *Anal. Boll.*, lxvi, 1948, 3.

[4] See p. 183 n. 4 below.

[5] See p. 33.

and Abgar, raising aloft the precious letter, invoked its help for his city. The Persians were straightway enveloped in darkness, and they could not approach within three miles of the city. After remaining inactive for several months, they decided to reduce the city by cutting off its water supply. The bishop explained:

that mount which you see, daughter, above the city, at that time supplied water to the city. So, seeing this, the Persians turned aside the water from the city and made a diversion for it towards the place where they were encamped. Thereupon, on that day and in that hour in which the Persians turned aside the waters, immediately these springs which you see in this place burst forth of their own accord at the command of God; from that day to this, these springs have remained by the grace of God. But the water which the Persians had turned aside was dried up on that day, so that they themselves had nothing to drink for even one hour as can be seen to this very day; thereafter and to this day no moisture at all has ever appeared there. So by the command of God who had promised that this would come to pass, they were forced to return to their own country—that is, Persia.

The bishop then took Egeria to the gate through which, tradition had it, the 'letter of Jesus' had been brought to Edessa; there he prayed, recited the letter and prayed again. They visited the palace on the Citadel mount and 'other places', and Egeria received from the bishop a copy of the Abgar–Jesus letters to take to her own country.

That much of the patter of the bishop cicerone is nonsense is evident to anyone acquainted with Urfa, although we should perhaps make allowance for difficulties of communication between Egeria, who used Latin, and her guide, who may have spoken Syriac and some Greek. The water supply could not have come from the limestone crag on which the Citadel is built, and the springs that supply the fish-pools are obviously ancient.[1] The bishop maintains that Abgar's palace stood on the mount and that subsequently his son lived in a palace by the pools.[2] This is contrary to the account of the *Chronicle of Edessa* (given in an earlier chapter),[3] which is undoubtedly correct. Now, we need not expect the bishop to have consulted the records of the city; but equally we need not assume that the old wives' tales of miracles were manufactured solely for the edification of pilgrims. The Edessans, always endowed with a gift of imaginative story-telling, doubtless believed these tales themselves. At a later date, it is true, sectarian animosities and

---

[1] Indeed, Egeria herself remarks, 'The city has no water inside it now except what comes out from the palace which is like a great silver stream'. It should be remembered that she visited Edessa in May when the level of the river Daişan is usually low.

[2] 'The holy bishop related that where these springs burst forth [or, came from the rock] had been previously an open space inside the city below the palace of Abgar. The palace of Abgar had been placed on, as it were, higher ground, as appears even now as you see. For at that time it was the practice for palaces whenever they were constructed, to be always on higher ground. But after these springs burst forth in that place Abgar himself made this palace for his son . . . so that these springs would be enclosed within the palace.' See also the discussion on p. 17 above.

[3] See pp. 24 f. above.

that truculence, for which Edessans are rebuked by chroniclers throughout the centuries, had strange results. There was not one but three portraits of Jesus, one for each of the principal sects, Jacobites, Melkites, and Nestorians, and each was claimed as genuine;[1] and there were more than three 'authentic' 'letters of Jesus'.[2] Such was the power of belief. But the faith of the Edessans was deep and sincere. It was put to the most severe test in 503. The contemporary chronicle of 'Joshua the Stylite' points out that, 'those who were far away from this [threat of capture by the Persians] were tortured by fear for their own lives by their lack of faith, for they thought that the enemy would make himself master of Edessa too, as he had of other cities'. The Edessans themselves did not waver. The gates of the city were left open and undefended in the face of the Persian army, and the Persians withdrew in confusion.

Faith, of course, degenerated also into superstition. Euphemia, the Edessan girl abducted by a Gothic soldier, believed that the martyr-confessors of Edessa, on whose tomb the Goth had sworn to treat her kindly, would avenge her. Far from her own city, she prayed for help. And, we are told:

by the divine power that resides in the bones of the holy martyrs and confessors to whom she had called and in whom she had taken refuge, in that very night she found herself on the hill [outside Edessa] by the side of the shrine of the holy martyrs and confessors.

Such stories are not peculiar to Edessa. Nor are the everyday practices which were rooted in superstition. The wearing of white, for example, was a symbol of gladness and confidence. In the *Romance of Julian*, the Jews of Edessa go to meet Julian dressed in white, and the Christians put on white garments to welcome Jovian, their protector. Significantly, the mother of the martyred Ḥabbib was dressed in white when she accompanied her son at his execution. During an eclipse of the sun in October 499, on the other hand, clergy and laymen at Edessa went in procession through 'all the streets of the city, carrying crosses, with psalms and hymns, clad in black garments of humiliation.'[3] In the ecclesiastical regulations ascribed to Rabbula, the village priest is instructed to keep his church painted white.

It is with thinly veiled sarcasm that 'Joshua the Stylite' writes:

by order [of the Governor in 497–8] all the porticoes of [Edessa] were whitewashed, whereat persons of experience were much annoyed, for they said that it was a sign . . . of evils that were to befall [the city].

This writer was not himself so gullible. He repeats the letter of the people of Zeugma in March 504 recounting that a goose had laid a marvellous egg, on which was written in Greek characters the legend, 'The Greeks shall conquer'. But he prefaces this story with the words, 'that it may not be thought that I say anything on my own authority or that I have hearkened to or believed a false rumour, I quote the very words of the letter that came to us.'

---

[1] See p. 216 below.   [2] Cf. p. 219 below.   [3] '*Josh. St.*'

Nevertheless, we can hardly doubt that Joshua himself believed the 'sign' that followed the celebration of the heathen spring festival at Edessa in 496.

The symbol of the Cross, which the statue of the blessed Emperor Constantine held in its hand, receded from the hand of the statue about one cubit, and remained thus during the Friday and Saturday until evening. On the Sunday the symbol came of its own accord and drew nigh to its place, and the statue took it in its hand as it had held it before. By means of this sign the discreet understood that the thing that had been done was very far removed from what was pleasing unto God.

Superstitious practices were associated with *ḥanana*, the mystic property to be found in sacred persons and things. It was not only the remains of martyrs, saints, hermits, and stylites that were collected with loving care; but anything that had come into contact with them in their lifetime or even long after their death—the dust trodden by their feet, their clothing, and even their spittle—conveyed an innate quality of the divine.[1] The devout came to the shrine to buy recipes for good health or good fortune, or to pass the night there. A poor boy out of his wits would be led to the 'holy places' to be smeared with sanctified oil, and would recover his sanity. The sick were visited by ascetics, who prayed over their bed, breathed upon them, and made over them the sign of the cross.[2] These practices were common among the simple and uneducated, as they are to the present day.[3]

More surprising is the extent to which magic was current among Christian clerics of high rank in Osrhoene, who were ready to scoff at the pagan rites of Harran, 'the city of heathens,'[4] or of the Beduins. We need not regard seriously the accusations brought against Bishop Hiba in 449 by his enemies at Edessa. He was said to consort with those who exercised the arts of incantation. The mob screamed against him, 'Musraya the magician has triumphed [with Hiba]! . . . No one wants [Hiba] the magician.' Hiba, it was alleged, had endeavoured to secure the see of Batnae for a protégé who was in contact with a magician. His nominee failed to obtain the post, but was appointed by him to the wardenship of a hospice, and in return (it was insinuated) the bishop was rewarded with formulae of sorcery.

These allegations may have been malicious slander. But we can scarcely dismiss so lightly the account of the magic rites practised by Sophronius, Bishop of Tella and cousin of Hiba, in probably 448:

He participated in the table of devils,[5] of the abominable calculations [of astrology], of the motions of the stars, of error and of divination, and of pagan prognostications! . . . He devoted himself to all these wicked things.

[1] In 'Zach. Rh.' we are told, on the other hand, that churchmen at Amid, who had invented a process of drying wine by placing it in the sun for seven years, would 'put a little of it into water so as to make a mixture which when drunk afforded the sweetness and flavour of wine'. They concealed this self-indulgence from their flock by 'telling the ignorant that (the powdered wine) was *ḥanana*', made, that is, from the ashes of a saint.

[2] Ephraim, 'Against Heresies' xlvi.

[3] See pp. 104 f.

[4] Lit., 'Hellenes'.

[5] 1 Cor. 10:21.

Once, on his travels Sophronius, we are told, lost a sum of gold. He suspected some persons and made them swear on the Gospel. Dissatisfied with the result, he then submitted them to a magic ordeal, forcing them to eat bread and cheese. Still he did not find the gold, so 'he made a divining cup, saying, "The gold is in the possession of such and such a person whose name is so and so and who is dressed in such and such a way."' Sophronius's accusers evidently had as much faith as he in these rituals, for they add, 'Many times the devils, seeking to confirm him in error, made known the thief to him, not because they sought to convict [the thief] but because they were eager to plunge the bishop into perdition.'

On another occasion Sophronius took a lad,

[and] brought him alone into his bedchamber together with a deacon Abraham, a relative of his. Having placed a table in the middle, they put under the table incense destined for the demons, but upon the table a phial in which were oil and water. He then placed the lad in a state of nudity at the side of the table, and the whole was covered with clean linen. Then the deacon began whispering words, which the Bishop formulated for him from his wicked divining art. They questioned the lad saying to him, 'What do you see in the phial?' and he said, 'I see flames of fire going up out of it.' Again after a little while he questioned him saying, 'What do you see now?' and he said, 'I see a man sitting on a throne of gold and clad in purple, with a crown upon his head.' Then they dug [outside] the door and made a deep hole which they filled with oil and water, and they made the lad stand there. They said to him, 'What do you see in the hole?' and he said, 'I see Ḥabbib, the bishop's son, proceeding on the road'—for he had gone on a journey to Constantinople—'and I see him', the lad continued, 'sitting on a black mule and blindfolded, and behind him two men on foot.' Then they brought an egg, and when they had opened it they threw away the white of the egg and left the yolk; and they said to the lad, 'What do you perceive in the egg?' and he said, 'I perceive Ḥabbib coming on the road on horseback; he has put a collar around his neck, and before him are going two men.' And on the next day the bishop's son arrived from Constantinople just as his father had divined.

The accusers of Sophronius described too the books of astrology written down, at his request, by men and women of his church and by the local town physician. 'He carried a sphere of brass, moreover, for his evil divination, and related to his friends all that he saw in it.' To the members of the Council of Chalcedon, however, these stories of witchcraft were either unimportant or of everyday occurrence. They decreed that Sophronius should stand trial before the provincial Synod only if he had expressed Nestorian opinions; they made no mention of his alleged practice of magic.

Towards the end of the monarchy, the *Chronicle of Edessa* already writes proudly of the 'charming and beautiful buildings' of the city.[1] In the following four centuries the increase in number and magnificence of the buildings of Edessa kept pace with its importance as administrative centre of the

[1] p. 24 above.

province, as military headquarters, and as the seat of the principal Syriac-speaking diocese of the Church. Most of our chronicles are written by churchmen and it is therefore the construction of new churches and monasteries that receive closest attention.[1]

Of the buildings from the close of the kingdom, we have located the site of the winter palace on Beth Tabara (the 'wide space of 'Awida son of 'Abednaḥad') as the present Citadel area, and of the summer palace as the area around the fish-pools.[2] The mansions of the nobles were situated probably on the high ground east of the Citadel and adjoining the High Street in the district called Beth Saḥraye.[3] The 'Church of the Christians', destroyed in the floods of 201, must have lain on low ground, probably on the site of the present Makam Ibrahim.[4] A late tradition has it that this church, 'above the spring of water to the west of the city', was formerly a heathen temple built in the time of Seleucus. The eastern wall was broken down and the building extended on that side to form an apse in which was set the altar.[5] The church, dedicated to the Saviour (like the Lateran church at Rome), was beautifully decorated; in the middle were great columns of marble. Legend had it that Addai officiated here in the presence of Abgar and all the people.

During the persecution of the Christians the 'Church of the Christians' may have fallen into disuse, and it may have been damaged in the floods of 303. It was probably in 313, immediately after the Edict of Toleration of Milan, that Bishop Qona[6] laid the foundations of the Cathedral church, possibly on the site of the old 'Church of the Christians'. The building was completed by his successor Sa'ad.[7] It was extended by Bishop Aitallaha in 327–8[8] by an addition on the east side; the entrance, as usual in Edessan churches, was from the west.[9]

---

[1] We hear only fortuitously of statues with which the city was embellished. Besides the statues of Abgar and his family, there was a bronze figure of Constantius, which the Edessans in the lifetime of that Emperor broke with rods. At the end of the fifth century a statue of Constantine the Great stood in the city, p. 179 above.

[2] See plan I.

[3] On Beth Saḥraye and the High Street, see p. 26 above. It is unlikely that the latter should be rendered 'Corn market' as suggested cautiously by Wright, *The Chronicle of Joshua the Stylite*, 18 n.

[4] See p. 26 above and the key to Plan I. It is assumed that the present-day mosques have been erected on the site of churches, synagogues, or other buildings of a public character. This may not, however, always have been the case; on occasion churches and mosques were deliberately converted to secular uses, see pp. 249 f.

The attempt to locate churches in the key to Plan I must therefore be regarded with reserve. It is nevertheless based as far as possible on information derived from local chronicles and from personal observation at Urfa itself.

[5] This may be an echo of the reconstruction of the church by Bishop Aitallaha, below on this page.

[6] Also called Qora (that is, Cyrus, perhaps by confusion with later bishops of this name, pp. 95, 182) or Yona.

[7] Or, Sha'd. The name is given also as Sa'duth (Sha'duth), or Sha'utha or Shabruth.

[8] Other sources date this event as 324–5 or 331–2.

[9] This is not to be confused (as by, for

The next church to be erected was, appropriately enough, the 'house' in honour of the martyrs of Edessa, Shmona, Gurya, and Ḥabbib; and it was Bishop Abraham who carried out this work, after 345. There was already a shrine at the burial place of the martyrs on the 'Watchmen's Hill' (also given the strange name of 'the height called Beth Alah Qiqla'[1]) to the north of the city, and services were conducted regularly in the shrine by the brethren of the monastery attached to it. The church, however, was inside the walls near the North gate;[2] it was here that the bones of the martyrs were deposited for safety when Edessa was threatened by an enemy.[3] The northern basilica of the church was exposed to attack by hostile *ballistae*, and it was damaged by the Persians besieging the city in 503, and again in about 580.

In 369-70 Bishop Barsai built the Great baptistry, perhaps, as some scholars have maintained, as an extension of the Cathedral; the epithet 'Great' evidently indicates that at the time of the chronicler, in the sixth century, there were more than one baptistry at Edessa. Ten years later, in about 379,[4] Bishop Walagash (Eulogius) built a church in honour of Daniel; in the sixth century it was called after Dometius, either the physician (famous for his ability to heal sciatica) or the martyr of that name.

In August 394 the coffin of the Apostle Thomas[5] was transferred by Bishop Qora (Cyrus) to a church built in the south-west corner of the city, probably, that is, immediately north of the fish-pools. The apse was in the east, as in the Cathedral church.[6] Bishop Diogenes after 408[7] began to construct the church of the martyr Barlaha, which evidently became one of the most important shrines of the city. It stood near the South gate, called by Procopius the Barlaos gate after the church. The shrine of Barlaha was celebrated for the fine linen, perhaps linen shrouds, that Bishop Hiba was accused in 448 of having appropriated for his own use. In it were buried three bishops of Edessa, Nona (died 460-1), Asclepius (in September 525; he had died at Antioch three months earlier), and Andrew (died December 532). In the middle of the city a synagogue[8] was converted by Bishop Rabbula (died 435 or 436) into the Church of St. Stephen. This work was carried out at the order, that is, at the expense, of the Emperor, and apparently early in the bishop's reign.

example, Baumstark) with the Melkite cathedral built under Amazonius; see p. 189 below.

[1] Lit., 'place of the god of the dunghill'. The name may be referred to in the *Testament of St. Ephraim*, 'Leave [Ephraim's dead body], cast [it] on the dunghill, for it cannot be conscious of honour; for the wealthy wealth is fitting, and for the poor the dunghill'. There may be a reminiscence of the ancient name in the modern name Külaflı Tepe, whose location is indicated on Plan II. The conjecture of

Peeters, *Anal. Boll.*, lviii, 1940, 110 ff., that the martyrs were executed to the south-west of the fish-pools should be rejected.

[2] See p. 174 n. 3 above.

[3] Cf. p. 174 above.

[4] According to another source, 376-7.

[5] See p. 174 above.　　　[6] See p. 181 above.

[7] After 410, according to another source.

[8] There seems little reason to follow Hallier and amend the text to 'meeting-place of the 'Udaye'.

Rabbula disliked extravagance and imposed a ban on building. Apart from the reconstruction of the church of St. Stephen, he had done no more than carry out essential repairs to 'a portion of the north wall of the nave[1] of the church of his city', presumably the Cathedral church, which had fallen into disrepair. Under his successors a reaction set in; the pace of building quickened. In 437–8 the Cathedral church, itself now called the 'Old church', received a great silver altar weighing 720 pounds; and four years later Anatolus had a silver chapel erected for the remains of St. Thomas.[2] Hiba himself, who succeeded Rabbula as Bishop of Edessa in 435, and whose lavish tastes antagonized many of his fellow Edessans, founded the church of the Twelve Apostles in the eastern quarter of the city. A chronicler declares that 'for its splendour and remarkable proportions[3] it had no equal in the world'. It was popularly called the 'New church', by others the 'Great church'. If we regard its novelty as lying in the shape of its architecture we may fix the date of the visit to Edessa of Egeria of Aquitania as shortly after its completion. After mentioning the 'church and martyry of St. Thomas', the abbess continues, 'But a church that is there is immense and very beautiful and [constructed] in a new shape and truly worthy to be the house of God.'[4]

The 'new' architecture of the Church of the Twelve Apostles was, how-ever, no isolated phenomenon. Hiba built also the Church of the martyr Sergius outside the East gate on the same model. It was later called the Church of St. Sergius and St. Simeon (after Simeon Stylites the Elder), and here a public service was held to celebrate the abolition of the tax of the

---

[1] Syriac *haikla*, perhaps simply 'shrine'.

[2] On these gifts see p. 132.

[3] Or 'cells'; lit., 'divisions'.

[4] Egeria (a variant of the name is Aetheria) came from, probably, south Gaul and was, more precisely, a *sanctimonialis* rather than an abbess. There has been much controversy about the date of her journey; suggestions have ranged from the end of the fourth to the beginning of the sixth century. It must have preceded the sixth century because, (i) Egeria writes that Harran was 'wholly pagan' in her time, but this was no longer the case in the time of Bishop Daniel (c. 448); (ii) she does not mention the portrait of Jesus at Edessa which was celebrated in the West towards the end of the sixth century; (iii) she was shown the palace of Abgar at Edessa,—but there is no reference to the palace in 'Josh. St.' (who knew Edessa well) at the end of the fifth century (iv) she makes no mention of St. Addai although his remains were transferred to the Church of St. John and his name added to the title of that church by the end of the fifth century. On the other hand, (i) she clearly wrote after 363 when the frontier between Byzantium and Persia ran through the middle of Mesopotamia; (ii) the topography of Jerusalem described by Egeria requires a date before 460; (iii) references to the liturgy by Egeria make a date after the middle of the fifth century improbable. That Egeria does not mention St. Simeon Stylites (390–459) is not surprising; the holy man discouraged visits from women. The most factual detail given by Egeria of her visit to Edessa, the church constructed 'in a new shape', fits more exactly the Church of the Twelve Apostles than that of St. Thomas built in about 394 (which is not described in this manner), or the Melkite Cathedral of Amazonius in the sixth century, whose con-struction followed the floods of 525, and was accompanied by much other building activity at Edessa to which Egeria makes no reference. We may therefore reasonably assign Egeria's visit to Edessa to the middle of the fifth century.

chrysargyron in 497–8.[1] The church of Saints Sergius and Simeon was, like the northern basilica of the Church of the Confessors near the North gate, a target for the destructive malice of enemies who failed to capture Edessa. The retreating Persians burnt it in September 503 and again in about 580.[2] This church of St. Sergius is not to be confused with another church dedicated to the same saint but situated inside the walls, slightly south of the Church of the Twelve Apostles. The second Church of St. Sergius was built after the pattern of the Church of St. Thomas.

Bishop Nona replaced Hiba at Edessa in 448 during the interlude of his suspension from the diocese; and later Nona returned to Edessa after the death of Hiba in 457. Nona was even more celebrated than his predecessor, for his achievements as builder. During his first period as Bishop of Edessa, Nona constructed the chapel of the 'Church', presumably this is the Cathedral of Qona. During his second occupation of the see, Nona is said to have built monasteries and towers and bridges. His greatest memorial was, however, the Church of St. John the Baptist, a fine edifice with thirty-two columns of red marble. In it, before the end of the fifth century, were deposited the remains of the evangelist Addai, removed, it may be supposed, from the ornamental royal tomb where they had originally been placed.[3] (We learn from a late chronicle that King Abgar's remains also had been transferred inside the city.)[4] The Church of St. John the Baptist stood in the western quarter of the city, evidently a little north of the basilica beside the winter baths, which themselves (as was recently discovered) stood north of the fish-pools.[5] In this basilica, the Roman Governor of Edessa presided over the trial of the martyrs Shmona and Gurya.[6] During the famine of 500–1 the basilica was blocked up, and straw and mats were laid down for the sick and poor.[7] But the area was still a place for dispensing justice. In 496–7 the Byzantine governor sat, we are told, in the Church of St. John, now named also after St. Addai, to settle law suits and to redress the wrongs of the oppressed.[8]

Bishop Nona built also 'the infirmary of the house of poor lepers outside the gate of Beth Shemesh', that is the South gate; in this 'infirmary of the poor', he built a martyry to St. Cosmas and St. Damian. From a later document it appears that there were separate shrines to Cosmas and Damian the former in the plain to the south of the city, the latter on the summit of a crag near the city. Each is said to have contained the remains of the martyr-physician to whom it was dedicated. Since these saints were associated with

---

[1] See p. 139 above.

[2] It was demolished by foreign attack also in the Moslem period; pp. 194, 221. The shrine is to be identified with a mosque and place of pilgrimage east of the walls, where Christian Syriac inscriptions were recorded by the present writer in 1966, p. 257 below; see Circis Peyamber on Plan II.   [3] Cf. p. 80 above.

[4] See p. 249 below.

[5] See p. 32 n. 1 above.

[6] See p. 83 above.   [7] Cf. p. 148 above.

[8] See p. 123 above.

healing, it is reasonable to suppose that the shrine of Cosmas stood near the 'well of Job', and that the leper house stood in the present-day Eyüp Mahallesi somewhat nearer the South gate. After 504–5 a martyry was built to the Virgin Mary, with money contributed by Urbicius, the Emperor's minister. This may well have been erected on the site of the School of the Persians, closed in 489 by Imperial decree.[1] The dedication of a shrine to the Mother of God must have seemed to the Monophysites a decisive riposte to the theologians who had propagated the Dyophysite doctrines of Nestorius on this very spot.[2] In this place a monastery of the Mother of God was still standing in the thirteenth century.

The churches that we have enumerated so far were certainly completed before the flood of 525. Our information on other features of the city before that date is sparse. There were four gates, at approximately the cardinal points of the compass. Three are named before 525, the West gate (Gate of Arches or Vaults),[3] the East or Great gate, and in the south the Gate of Beth Shemesh. These were road-gates, not water-gates. They are not, then, to be confused with the gate near the sluices, also in the west, through which the river flowed into the city,[4] or the 'gates with eight sluices' in the eastern wall, through which the river left the city, augmented by the water of the springs that arose near the fish-pools. These gates were closed with large plated iron bars reinforced with bolts; the system described in the account of the flood of 201 was still the same at the time of Kawad's attack on Edessa in 503.[5]

Allusion has been made to the three main cemetery areas outside the city walls.[6] In the early sixth century the hospice had its own cemetery, presumably beside the hospice buildings outside the South gate, and this was used for the burial of strangers.[7] The 'Church cemetery', was evidently intended for the interment of citizens; we need not assume from its name that the cemetery stood inside or beside the Cathedral church,[8] for it could have been the area around the shrine of the Martyrs on Watchmen's Hill outside the walls to the north. The 'old graves beside the church of (Bishop) Qona'[9] may be the tombs to the south of the city (that is, near the cave of the Family

---

[1] See p. 95 above.

[2] See the key to Plan I.

[3] It is uncertain whether Syriac *kappe* refers to the vaults of the caves in the rock at the foot of this section of the wall, or to the arches of the gate itself, or to some feature of the control system of the river outside the west wall (cf. p. 188 below). There is, however, no reason for reading *kephe* (with the omission of the *alaph*), 'stones', for *kappe*. The reconstruction of the relative positions of the gates of Edessa by Wright, Burkitt, and others must now be rejected in the light of information found in

documents recovered since the time of those scholars. See Plan I and Pl. 6a.

[4] It is probably this that is called at a later period the 'Water-gate'.

[5] See pp. 24, 157 and Pl. 8 *a*, *b* above.

[6] See p. 27 above.

[7] Here was buried the 'man of God' called St. Alexius, according to legend; see also the extract from the poem by Jacob of Serug, p. 172 above.

[8] Later, however, bishops and others were buried in churches within the walls; pp. 182, 249.

[9] Cf. p. 124 above.

Portrait mosaic), if our location of this church is correct. This was probably the cemetery made by Bishop Aitallaha.[1] When these graves were not sufficient to bury the dead during the terrible famine of 500–1, 'any ancient grave' was opened up to receive the dead. The allusion here is probably to pagan graves to the west of the city. In a martyrology a certain 'Abshelama son of Abgar is said to have constructed a cemetery here; it may have extended as far as Kırk Mağara to the south.[2] Except in emergencies as in that of 500–1, use of the western cemetery was evidently discontinued by the middle of the fifth century. This explains why, at probably that period, Egeria could write that 'no dead body is taken out through that gate [by which the 'letter of Jesus' was brought to Abgar]', which we may assume was the West gate.[3] The only Christian grave inscriptions in Greek that belong to this epoch of the city's history have been found either in the northern cemetery or to the north-west, near the tomb of St. Ephraim.[4]

In 496–7 the Governor of Edessa built what was perhaps a covered walk beside the West gate.[5] An important public building was the Town Hall.[6] Others were the baths, hospice, infirmaries, and the government granary.[7] Aqueducts from Tell Zema and Mawdud brought water to the city from

[1] Probably in 324–5, certainly before 332.

[2] See p. 85 above and Plans I and II.

[3] A copy of the 'letter' from Jesus to Abgar found on a stone at Kırk Mağara may well pre-date Egeria's visit; p. 75 cf. p. 183.

[4] Two were published by Sachau in 1882. One was discovered in the north-west of the city; it is slightly broken and reads,

ΑΝΕΠΑΕΝ
ΕΥΔΟΚΙΑΜΕΝΙ
ΠΠΟΥΗΙΟΥΗΡΑ
ΚΥΡΙΑΚΕ

This may be rendered, 'There passed away Eudocia (daughter) of Menippos . . . on Sunday(?).' The second is complete and lay at the entrance to a cave near the Monastery of Sergius to the west of the walls. It reads,

ΕΙΣ ΘΕΟΣ ΚΕ
Α ΧΡΙΣΤΟΣ Α
+ ΑΜΕΑΣ ΚΑ ΟΥΜΘΑ +
ΑΔΕΛΦΑΣ ΕΦΗΚΑΝ Τ
ΟΥΤΑ ΜΝΗΜΙΑ ΝΤωΤ[Γ]ΕΝ
+ ω ΑΥΤΟΣ ΑΣΚΛΗΠΙΣ ΜΑΘΑ +

It may be rendered, 'One God and 1 Christ 1. Ameas and . . . sisters. These memorials were set up (ἔφηκαν for ἔθηκαν) . . . (by) Asclepius himself (and) Matha.' The opening formula of this inscription is found also on another, hitherto unpublished, inscription found by Professor D. S. Rice in the Şehitlik Mahallesi in 1956. It states: εἱϲ θεοϲ (two vertical strokes

follow, perhaps part of a cross) φιλοκαλια κυριακος, and may be interpreted, 'One God. Philocalia [and] Cyriacus (or, Cyriacus [to] Philocalia)'. A further Greek inscription, to be assigned, according to Chapot, to the fifth or sixth century, found on the lintel of a house in the west of Urfa, may not be in its original position. It reads; '[For the victo]ry and safety of the r[ul]e[r]'. Also probably moved from its place is a stone slab, in the shape of a bath, engraved with a cross which in 1966 lay outside the south-west section of the wall. All the Greek inscriptions described here are now missing; the same is true also of a great stone inscribed simply with a cross which was in the Şehitlik Mahallesi in 1956. It should be added that a dated Christian tomb inscription in Syriac at a short distance south-west of Urfa was published by Sachau in 1882. It reads; 'In the month of former Teshrin in the year 805 (October 493, unless we read the date 850, that is, A.D. 538) the tomb was completed in the days of Mar Elias the archimandrite and Mar Abraham the deacon and Mar John the deacon with the rest who were with th[em]. Praise be to him who resurrects us. +Amen+'

[5] The meaning of the Syriac term is uncertain; it may denote 'rampart' or 'warm baths'.

[6] If this is the correct interpretation of ἀντίφορος.

[7] For other buildings, including the hippodrome, see pp. 163 f. above.

twenty-five springs. The city walls and the Governor's *praetorion* were restored by the Emperor through the agency of the Governor in 504–5. Outside the city were inns, probably south of the Harran gate not far from the hospice, which were frequented by soldiers and prostitutes, and where wine was on sale to the public. To the east of the walls lay orchards and gardens in the low-lying land at the edge of the Harran plain, irrigated no doubt (as at the present time) by the water that came through the sluices on that side of the city. For an enemy, attack from this direction was, of course, easiest; and trees and gardens were cut down by the citizens when it became necessary to deprive a hostile force of wood and of places for ambush.

We have referred already to the flood of 525; it caused heavy loss in life and the destruction of the chief buildings in the city. This event proved a turning-point in the architectural development of Edessa. For the first time, so far as we know, an attempt was made by the central government to prevent the recurrence of such a disaster:[1]

[The flooded river had] levelled to the ground a large part of the outer wall and the *peribolos*.[2] . . . [Justinian] made effective provision that such a calamity should not occur again. For he succeeded in making a new channel for the river in front of the *peribolos*, circumventing it by the following device. The land on the right of the river was formerly both flat and low, while on the left stood a steep hill which did not permit the stream to turn aside at all or to deviate from its customary course, but drove it against the city by sheer force. On the right there was nothing to check it when it rushed straight towards the city. So he cut down this whole hill, and, while making the land on the left of the hill hollow and deeper than its own [the river's] bed, on the right he set up a huge wall of stones, each a load for a waggon, so that as long as the river flowed with its usual temperate stream the city would never be deprived of its benefit. But whenever by any chance [the river] rose to a great height and overflowed, a moderate portion of it would flow as usual into the city, while the remainder of the stream would pass under constraint into the channel devised by Justinian and be led away behind the hippodrome which is not far away, thus being vanquished, contrary to all expectations, by human skill and foresight.[3]

Justinian's dam to the north-west of the city conducted the river by an artificial channel outside the north and east walls of the city. When the river rises to an exceptional height, the excess waters pass over the dam on the southern or right bank of the river and follow the old course of the wadi bed southwards alongside the west walls. By this feat of engineering the city was spared the floods which had caused disaster in November 201, May 303, March 413, and April 525, when the whole force of the river water was driven against the west wall. Justinian's system remains to the present day.[4]

---

[1] The programme of building at Edessa was opened in the reign of Emperor Justin (died 527), but the guiding authority was certainly that of his successor Justinian.

[2] The covered walk between the outer wall and the main wall.

[3] Procopius, *Buildings*.

[4] Pl. 7 and 4b; see the location on Plan II.

But during the centuries it was allowed to fall into disrepair. A late anonymous chronicler—attributing the original work to Seleucus and Nimrod and its renovation to Addai!—declares:

[Addai] saw the wadi through which the flood came continually and entered and broke down [the wall] on the west side of the city and entered and laid waste many houses and destroyed all the buildings which lay in its path. For the path and exit which had been constructed by Seleucus and Nimrod had been built again before this time of stones[1] and great wide arches of two storeys and three paths,[2] and through them the flood passed and caused no damage. But it became filled with sand and reeds and stubble that had been swept down during many years. The Apostle was zealous and with the zeal and help and care of King Abgar a great dam was made of mighty stones at the head of the wadi outside the west wall of the city called the wadi of the Stadium. He placed piles along the length and breadth with mighty stones, and put on them moist lime and mortar and dug in the earth until the ditch joined[3] the moat that went around the city outside the wall along the whole northern side of the city. So from that time the city was saved from being violently swept away until the dam was spoilt and the earth raised, and from time to time the water went up over the dam.[4]

Even the renovation ascribed by this writer to Addai did not prevent floods; we shall return to this later.

Justinian's engineers also adjusted the course through the city of the bed of the river and of the spring waters that joined it. This, too, still survives in present-day Urfa.[5]

[The Emperor] compelled the river to follow a practically straight course after it comes inside the city, and above it he raised a structure resting on either bank so that it could not be diverted from its route; he thus not only preserved the benefit which the city gained from the river, but also freed the city from the fear of it.[6]

At the same time the main wall, the *peribolos*, and the outer wall of Edessa were rebuilt and strengthened. In particular, the wall around the Citadel in the south-west of the city was made more effective.

A certain section of the *peribolos* of Edessa contains a fort outside which rose a hill, which stood very close by and commanded the city spread beneath it. The inhabitants of early times, perceiving that this hill constituted a threat to the ramparts on top of the wall, had brought it inside the *peribolos*, so that it might not render the city vulnerable. But by this they caused the city to be actually much more vulnerable, for a very small cross-wall, lying on the exposed ground, was an easy thing to capture even for children playing at storming a wall. Therefore, after this had been torn down, another wall was built on the crest of the hill, the work of the Emperor Justinian, which did not have to fear any attack from a higher position, and this descended along the slope as far as the level ground at either end and was joined to the *peribolos*.[6]

---

[1] Syriac *ke'phe*; perhaps this should be *kappe*, the 'vaults' from which the West gate may have received its name, p. 185 n. 3.

[2] The meaning is obscure; is the reference to aqueducts?

[3] Lit., 'was mingled with . . .'

[4] *Chr. ad 1234.*

[5] See photograph on Pl. 11.

[6] Procopius, op. cit.; Pl. 4*a*.

The flood of 525 had demolished the Town Hall and the 'Church of the Christians'; through the liberality of Justinian both were restored. The 'Church of the Christians' is probably, we have suggested, to be identified with the Cathedral built by Qona and completed by Bishops Saʿad and Aitallaha, and situated near the present-day Makam Ibrahim. The Christians of Edessa were by now divided into two factions; the Monophysites, revived by Jacob Burdʿaya and dubbed the 'Jacobites' after him, and the Chalcedonians, supported by the Court at Constantinople and therefore named the 'Melkites'.[1] Each party had its own leader. The Cathedral church had evidently passed into Melkite hands; certainly the construction of the new church was entrusted by the Emperor to the Melkite bishop Amazonius (or Amidonius). It stood probably in the same place as the church of Qona by the spring of water.[2] It was called Hagia Sophia after the famous church of that name in the capital, and it is said to have been beautiful beyond description, with its gold plating and glass and marble. Among its treasures was the sacred portrait of Jesus; we may recall that the church stood near the site of Abgar's palace and that it was there, according to the *Doctrine of Addai*, that the king had deposited the painting of Ḥannan.[3] A well-known hymn portrays the church of Amazonius in effusive terms:[4]

> ... It is indeed wonderful—like the vast world in miniature, not in dimensions but in shape. Waters surround it as the sea [surrounds the world]. Lo, its roof is extended like the heavens, without columns, vaulted and pressed firm, ornamented moreover with gilded mosaics like the firmament with bright stars. Its lofty cupola is made like the heavens' heavens; like a helmet its upper part is firmly placed upon its lower part. [As for] the splendour of its broad arches—they are fashioned like the four corners of the world. In the variety of their colours too they resemble the glorious [rain]bow of the clouds. Other arches surround it like the copings that project from the hills—on them, in them, and by them all its roof is bound to the vaults. Its marble bears the impress of the portrait [of Jesus, made] without [mortal] hands, and its walls are overlaid harmoniously. By its splendour, polished and white, is gathered in it light like [the light of] the sun. On its plating they have set lead, that it should not be spoilt by torrents of rain; there is no wood at all in its roof, which is all as though molten from stone. It is surrounded by glorious courtyards, with two porticoes formed by columns that represent the tribes of Israel. ... On every side it has an identical façade, for the type of the three [façades] is uniform; on its altar glows a single light through the three open windows. ... The light of the three sides is strengthened by many windows. ... In its midst is set the platform. ... The pillar that is in the place of the platform ... —above it is fixed a cross of light like our Lord between the robbers. In it too lie open five gates. ... Ten pillars bearing the cherub of the sanctuary are formed like the ten Apostles who fled at the time that our Saviour was crucified. The structure of the nine steps set in its

---

[1] See p. 96 above.   [2] Plan I.   from this hymn, see Kirsten, art. 'Edessa', in
[3] See p. 76 above.   *Reallexikon für Antike und Christentum* and the
[4] For the conclusions concerning the church   bibliography there.
architecture of the period which may be drawn

sanctuary and the throne represent too the throne of the Messiah and the nine orders of angels. Exalted are the mysteries of this shrine . . .

We have a list of other churches and monasteries, some evidently Monophysite, the rest Melkite. At what time they were built we cannot tell; a number may well have been constructed before the flood of 525. The Monophysite churches in the city included one dedicated to Theodore, near the Citadel, another to Cyriacus north-east of the Church of the Confessors, and perhaps the Bishop's monastery of the Mother of God. There were five churches belonging to Melkites in the city in addition to the church of Amazonius: one dedicated to the Cross (later dedicated to St. Theodore whose head was deposited there),[1] opposite it one to the Mother of God, another to the Mother of God north of the Church of St. Stephen, and in the south of the city a Church to the martyr George and another to the Archangel Michael.[2]

There are no more than a few passing allusions to buildings at Edessa after the large-scale constructions of Justinian. Procopius, who mentions the 'Gate of Barlaos' (South gate), and the 'Great gate' (East gate), also mentions the Tripurgia, a building of three towers, near the 'Gate of Hours'[3] (North gate). Outside the South gate, here called the 'Gate of Beth Shemesh', stood the Monastery of the Orientals. In the moat here were slain about 400 Monophysite monks in the reign of Maurice and later a martyry was erected on this spot.[4] Severus, the Melkite bishop at this time, built for himself a palace beside the river and other buildings, and also a street (or market) called the 'New portico'. It was this Severus whom the general Narseh summoned to his lodgings at the house of Marinus, which was evidently beside the fish-pools. The chronicles relate that after a summary trial the bishop was conducted out by a 'small gate', taken round the West gate, and stoned by the hippodrome while the Edessans, unaware of what had happened, stood near the house of Marinus. The 'small gate' may be the present entrance to the city in the south-west beside the fish-pools, which is today called the Sakabun Kapısı, probably the Bishop's gate.[5] Emperor Heraclius visited Edessa during his campaign against the Persians; he resided at 'the palace near the source of the spring', possibly the house of Marinus.[6]

[1] See pp. 218, 239 below.

[2] This classification of shrines as Monophysite and Melkite is based on the hypothesis that the churches and monasteries listed in Ch. 43 of *Chr. ad 1234*, belonged to the former sect, those in Ch. 44 to the latter sect.

[3] He calls it the 'Soinian' gate attempting to reproduce in Greek the Syriac *ša'e*, 'hours' (referring to a sun-dial?), pp. 244, 250 n. 2. Mas'udi, who visited Harran in the tenth century, has misled later writers (including Bar Hebraeus) by confusing the gate 'called

ša'a' with the Harran gate in his *Kitab al-tanbih*. The name *ša'e* for the North gate was still in use in the thirteenth century.

[4] See p. 98 above.

[5] Syriac *episqopa*, Arabic *usquf*. In this district of Edessa was the garden of the Metropolitan, p. 250 below, perhaps beside the Monastery and Church of the Mother of God (above, this page).

[6] The churches and monasteries outside the city whose names are recorded are probably all Monophysite; see n. 2 this page. They are:

These allusions to the streets and buildings of Edessa are few and uninformative. But we receive the impression that the city was populous and wealthy and sophisticated. It was a tempting prize for its Moslem captors.

the Church of Jacob in the village of Karmush north of Edessa (this Jacob is said by a late chronicle to have suffered martyrdom in the days of Julian, but there is no independent support for this statement); two Monasteries of St. Barbara; the Monastery of Qubbe ('domes', or 'cisterns' if we read Qube), mentioned already by 'Joshua the Stylite', p. 158 above, and lying south of the shrine of Cosmas and in the direction of Harran; the Monastery of John Theologus on a crag on the summit of the hills; the Monastery of the Mother of God and the Monastery of the Orientals at the foot of the hills, the latter well-known in the history of this period, pp. 96, 98 above; the Monastery of the Exedra on the summit of the hills, which had an *exedra* (gallery) of its archimandrites (in which probably their dead bodies dressed in their robes were seated on thrones—as at, for example, the present-day Monastery of Qartamin near Midyat). It was here that 12,000 stonemasons were baptized, it was reported, on a certain Feast of the Epiphany. There are also the 'splendid' Church of Jacob of the *naphshatha* (tomb-towers) among the hills, where there stood till a late period the 'great altar of the pagans',—the monastery already existed in the time of Jacob of Serug (p. 105 above) and still stands today as Deyr Yakup with its ruined towers and inscriptions in Greek and a form of Palmyrene, p. 29 above; a Church of the Mother of God south of the Monastery of Jacob of the *naphshatha*; monasteries of Zakkai, of Qanon, of Samuel, of Hendibana (perhaps the Adiabenian), of Eusebius, and, on the river Gullab, of Julian Saba. In 449 the boundary of the city area of Edessa was at the shrine of Zakkai; here the new Byzantine Governor was met by Monophysite demonstrations against Bishop Hiba. There were, we are told, 90,000 monks in the hills of Edessa at the time.

V

THE LAST FIVE CENTURIES
A.D. 639-1146

FOR MUCH OF THE LAST PHASE OF ITS HISTORY Edessa was ruled by men of alien stock, professing a faith alien to that of most of its inhabitants. The Edessans were, however, already accustomed to rule by strangers. Since the end of the Abgar dynasty the city had been administered by Governors nominated from Constantinople, and these were rarely natives of Osrhoene. Difference in religion between themselves and their rulers was also no novelty to the Edessans. From the end of the fifth century the largest community in the city was Monophysite, whereas most of the Governors were Melkite. Between the two sects animosity had become so bitter and the record of active persecution so violent that the Edessans had welcomed the Moslems to their city as deliverers.

The establishment of Moslem domination over the whole of Mesopotamia brought welcome relief to Edessa. The political frontiers that had artificially divided the region disappeared; no longer was the countryside a battlefield between the major powers of East and West. This new situation, however, diminished the importance of Edessa in the same measure as it decreased its exposure to danger. It was no longer a fortress whose possession was essential for the control of north-west Mesopotamia. Its slow decline was, it is true, delayed briefly by the tumultuous events of the First Crusade when once again Western forces crossed the Euphrates and sought to maintain themselves in this area. But the failure of the Crusaders only hastened the end of Christian ascendancy at Edessa. Nevertheless, although the five centuries whose events are described in this chapter are a period of decay, their story is not without a piquant interest. Some chronicles of the time are written in Greek, Armenian, and Latin, and the most important for the study of local developments are in Syriac; little of detail is recorded in Arabic, the language of the rulers of the country. We are given a rare and sometimes refreshing insight into the life of a minority group in the Moslem empire.

In 637 the Byzantine Governor of Osrhoene, John Cateas, attempted to buy off the advancing Moslems by an offer of tribute, but his action was repudiated by Emperor Heraclius and he was removed from office. His successor Ptolemy could do nothing to retrieve the fortunes of Byzantium in this region. Moslem armies rapidly overran Syria and Babylonia, and their occupation of north Mesopotamia was only a matter of time. The principal cities, Harran, Edessa, Resaina, Mardin, and Amid, capitulated in 639. Tella and Dara were taken by storm. The Byzantine commander had no course but to withdraw across the Euphrates.

There are varying accounts of the surrender of Edessa. The Moslem general 'Iyaḍ ibn Ghanm appears to have laid siege first to Harran. According to one writer, the 'Harranians'—in this context we should understand by the term the pagans of Harran—informed him that they controlled part of the city, and would abide by whatever decision was taken by the people, meaning presumably the pagans, of Edessa. 'Iyaḍ proceeded to invest Edessa. After some deliberation its citizens sent out a force against the Moslems; it was routed and compelled to retire behind the walls. The Edessans then sued for peace. The terms granted by 'Iyaḍ to the Bishop of Edessa secured the lives and property of the Christian inhabitants as *ahl al-dhimma*; in return they were required to pay one dinar and two measures of flour[1] for each male citizen, to maintain the roads and bridges in good repair, to give help to Moslem stragglers and to support in good faith the Moslem cause.[2] This formula became, we are told, the model for treaties between the Moslems and other cities of Mesopotamia. The first Moslem Governor of Edessa is said to have been a certain Abu Badr.

The early years of the Islamic period saw a deliberate attempt to change the structure of the area that had previously been called Osrhoene. Mu'awiya was instructed by Caliph 'Umar I to settle members of the Muḍar group of tribes in the region between the Khabur and the great loop of the Euphrates, in the region later known as Diyar Muḍar. A principal tribe among the group was Qais. The newcomers were given land that had no owners and was far removed from cities and large villages; in the towns Mu'awiya stationed troops to assure the security of the Mudarite settlers. The migration of these tribes continued through the centuries that followed; the nomads in the area continued to be largely Qais. Some sections of Qais, notably Numair, 'Uqail, and Sulaim, took a considerable part, as we shall see, in the history of the region. They did not all remain nomadic. Some followed the historical trend towards settlement; and the antagonism between Beduins on the one hand and cultivators and townsmen on the other was perpetuated, though both sections were members of the same tribal family.

Edessa was used by the Moslems as a military base to contain a Byzantine

---

[1] One source has, one dinar, a measure of flour and some honey, oil, and vinegar.

[2] Another version of the treaty inserts the usual condition that the Christians could retain the shrines they already owned but were forbidden to build new churches; see p. 196 below.

attack on Batnae in 644. But afterwards it was Harran which assumed greatest importance in this area, partly it may be, because Harran was little identified with Christianity. It was a centre of Qais, and when we recall the planet worship of Harran we are not surprised to learn that some members of Qais were reputed to worship the stars. In the conflict between 'Ali and Mu'awiya the people of Harran supported, we are told, the latter. 'Ali came to Harran and slaughtered its inhabitants so that 'the blood flowed out of the city gate'.[1] But when the Umayyads favoured the tribe of Kalb, heredi-tary enemies of Qais, the loyalties of the latter swung violently against them. The great majority of Kalb, it should be noted, professed Christianity, chiefly of the Jacobite persuasion, and we have here an odd extension of the ancient enmity between Monophysite Edessa and pagan Harran. In 686–7 Ibrahim al-Ashtar, a leader of the Alid opponents of Caliph 'Abd al-Malik, granted Edessa, Harran, and Samosata to Hatim ibn al-Nu'man, The Caliph's brother Muḥammad succeeded, however, in occupying Edessa 'without a fight';[1] from it he regained control over all Mesopotamia.

The struggle between Umayyads and Abbasids in the following century again brought the district of Edessa and Harran into prominence. Marwan II had attached himself to the Qais. He took up residence at Harran and transferred to it his treasure. But the role of Harran as imperial capital was short-lived; like Nabonidus, who had settled at the city thirteen centuries earlier, Marwan was the last of his dynasty. He was forced to flee westwards, and was killed in Egypt in 750. In the same year Isḥaq ibn Muslim, a sup-porter of Marwan, seized Edessa. He later transferred to Samosata, leaving his brother Bakkar in charge of Edessa. The city was attacked by Abu Ga'far, later Caliph al-Manṣur, who had several encounters with Bakkar and also invested Samosata. Isḥaq's opposition to the Abbasid regime came to an end when he learned of the death of Marwan.

Forces at Edessa under a certain Manṣur ibn Ga'wana maintained their loyalty to the Umayyads. The Abbasids captured the city; ibn Ga'wana was sent to Raqqa (Callinicos), and executed in 758–9. For nine months the army of Caliph Manṣur camped by the 'river of the Medes',[1] the Gullab, and devastated the countryside. By order of the Caliph the walls of Edessa, like those of other cities of Mesopotamia with the exception of Harran and Maiperqaṭ, were razed to the ground. A Syriac chronicle relates that Manṣur requested the Edessans to give him marble columns from the Great church for the palace he was building at Raqqa.[2] They refused. He then besieged Edessa, and destroyed the church of Sergius outside the east wall. The 'elders and notables of the place' offered to hand over the city if he would guarantee their safety. Manṣur agreed, asking only that they should return to him a 'white horse' that belonged to him. Upon the surrender of the city, the

---

[1] *Chr. ad 1234.*   [2] Or al-Rafiqa, near Raqqa.

Edessans were informed that the Caliph's phrase referred to the city walls; all were demolished 'except for a single tower by which the waters go out to the mills' to the east of Edessa.

During his later years Caliph Harun al-Rashid resided at Raqqa, and he visited Edessa in 797. Edessa was involved in the struggle, between al-Amin and al-Ma'mun, for the succession, which followed the death of this Caliph; its citizens seem to have favoured Amin. Without walls, however, the city was at the mercy of every unscrupulous general. In 811–12 Naṣr ibn Shabath al-'Uqaili, a leader of the Qais and supporter of Amin, was besieging Harran. He was dissuaded from laying waste the church of Edessa only on payment of 5,000 zuze through the mediation of a Moslem chief.[1] A few years later the Edessans regained their security; in about 814 the walls were rebuilt by a certain Abu Shaikh Ganawaya,[2] who collected the expenses of the work from the 'notables and rich men of the city'.

Ma'mun, now Caliph, installed his general al-Ṭahir ibn Ḥusain as Governor to restore order in this region of Mesopotamia. Edessa was garrisoned by Ṭahir's troops. So unruly were they that Ṭahir himself barely escaped with his life, when they mutinied because he had withheld what they considered to be their 'rights'. He let himself down over the wall by night and fled to Raqqa where he was quickly followed by some of the mutineers who feared that Naṣr ibn Shabath might attack Edessa in the absence of the redoubtable Ṭahir. This, indeed, occurred shortly afterwards. Dionysius of Tell-Maḥre, an eyewitness of the scene, describes how the people of Edessa helped their 'Persian' garrison to defend the city with resolution:

[They] went up to the wall, and even the women brought up stones to the wall [and water to quench the thirst][3] of those fighting, and those who could not go up to the wall were bowed in prayer. I[4] was one of these. We asked that the Persian [soldiers of Ma'mun] should prevail so that the rebels should not take possession of the city. The Lord was merciful; 'Amr, one of the rebels, was struck, and they turned back in confusion.[5]

Naṣr continued to terrorize the countryside from Aleppo. It was not until 825 that the central administration effectively asserted its power under 'Abdallah ibn Ṭahir, who had succeeded his father as Governor of Mesopotamia. Naṣr was taken prisoner and sent to Baghdad. In the same year, however, 'Abdallah, a just and considerate ruler, was transferred to the command in Egypt; his place in Mesopotamia was taken by his younger brother, Muhammad, who was less well-disposed towards his Christian subjects. Nevertheless, the active warfare between Byzantium and the

---

[1] One source holds that the money was paid to Yaḥya, the Moslem who acted as mediator, not to Naṣr ibn Shabath.

[2] Basil bar Shumana, in Michael Qindasi

the Syrian, has Gunadiya.

[3] The words are supplied from Bar Hebraeus.

[4] That is, Dionysius.

[5] Dion. T-M., in Mich. Syr.

Moslems which flared up at this time showed the latter in a favourable light. They gave their Christian minorities, no less than the Moslem population, the benefits of firm rule. The Caliphate still maintained a stable government, able to repulse foreign aggression. The situation was to be very different, as we shall see, when Edessa reappeared in history a century later.

During the first centuries of Islam, the Christians of Edessa, who composed the large majority of the inhabitants of the city until the final débâcle in 1146, shared the advantages and the disabilities common to 'People of the Book' throughout the Moslem empire. Their lives were secure on payment of the *gizya*, poll-tax; Christian landowners paid the *kharag*. In general they were permitted to carry out the practices of their religion, provided that they did not seek to win converts from Islam. Their churches and the surrounding land were protected, but they were forbidden to erect new places of worship within a certain distance from a town or large village. Christians were frequently subject to minor restraints, some of them invidious and humiliating, that were modified from time to time by the Caliph on the advice of his jurists. These included regulations concerning dress, housing, and property. Christians were prohibited from displaying the Cross in public and from sounding their church bells[1] at the hours of prayer in the mosques. Caliph 'Abd al-Malik (685–705) introduced a fiscal reform known as the *ta'dil*, which involved some change in the method of taxation, although the effect for the former citizens of the Byzantine empire was little different from the earlier system.[2] A Syriac chronicler declares bitterly, if not quite accurately:

[The Caliph] issued a severe order that everyone should go to his country and his village and his father's house, and everyone should be inscribed by his name and his father's name, his vineyard, his olives, and his possessions, his children and everything that he had. From here began the poll-tax taken according to the heads of persons. From here all the misfortunes of the Christian people took their origin. Until this point the kings took taxes from the land, not from persons. . . . Slaves are ruling over us. That was the first *ta'dil* made by the Moslems.[3]

Under 'Abd al-Malik's successor, al-Walid (705–15), the 'taxes and burdens' on Christians were increased. Syriac writers attribute variously to Walid, 'Umar II (717–20), and Yazid II (720–4) the rulings that the blood price for a Christian was fixed at half that for a Moslem, that the evidence of Christians against a Moslem was to be invalid in court, and that no Christian should hold the office of judge, or raise his voice in prayer, or wear a *qabiya*

---

[1] More precisely, sounding-boards.
[2] See p. 121 above.
[3] '*Chr. Zuqnin*'. Syriac writers of the Moslem period normally apply the expression 'Tayyaye' to the dominant religious group, the Moslems, rather than (as previously) to the Beduins.

or ride upon a saddle. Caliph Manṣur (754–75) ordered that all Christians should be branded on neck, forehead, hands, chest, or shoulders. The tax reforms of 'Umar II brought financial advantage to those Christians who adopted Islam, and led to widespread apostasy.[1] On the other hand, churches and monasteries benefited by the exemption from taxation of dwelling-places, legacies, and land produce set aside for the maintenance of the poor.

These ordinances were of general application throughout the Moslem empire. The interpretation of Islamic law ranged from the rigorous to the lenient according to the caprice of an individual Caliph or Governor; for Christians the effect was more serious than for Moslems, who maintained well-defined rights of appeal. The arbitrariness of the system was displayed at its worst in regions remote from the centre of power. We are told, for example, that Muḥammad ibn Marwan, appointed by his brother, Caliph 'Abd al-Malik, to the governorship of Mesopotamia, showed zeal for his religion by putting to death anyone who refused to accept Islam. During his residence at Edessa he assembled Armenians in a church and set fire to the building. Muḥammad, it is stated, also killed Anastasius son of Andrew, Administrator of the city—for at this time, observes a chronicler, Christians were still appointed to this office—and plundered his house.

A Syriac chronicle of the eighth century relates at considerable length the extortions of the tax collectors. Unscrupulous and greedy, they exploited, he claims, townsfolk and countryfolk alike by demanding more than the legal dues; they imprisoned and tortured their victims. Shopkeepers fled into the villages, and the markets were deserted. Villages were at the mercy not only of representatives of the government but also of their own chiefs, to whom the collection of the capitation tax had been farmed out. Not even the poorest were spared; the notables filled their houses with loot, and villagers who could not meet their demands were reduced to slavery. In about 770 the Governor discovered that the sum at which the capitation tax had been fixed had not been paid. Orders were given for the people to be assembled in the great church in each place,

all free men, and even women whose husbands were far away or absent temporarily because of the persecution. These were dragged from their homes. . . . Women who had never shown themselves in the streets were compelled to come down and were shame-lessly placed in the midst of men. . . . People trampled on the holy [altar] with their unclean feet. Even in the sanctuary they washed off the filth of their limbs, and commit-ted there many other impurities. . . . For three days and nights they remained in the church. Among them arose a bitter wailing . . . . Some persons threw themselves upon the wealth of churches and monasteries, and even remote churches . . . had to suffer this profanation . . . for they were despoiled of their property . . . by the inhabitants. . . . The Church of Edessa suffered more than all others, and lost its property.[2]

[1] See p. 206 below.   [2] 'Chr. Zuqnin'.

Of Edessa in about 773 the same chronicler writes:

the notables suffered afflictions . . . more than at any other city. There was set over them a cruel man called Razin. When he had seized and judged a poor man and knew that he had nothing, he would attach to him two policemen and instruct him, 'Go out to the public square. Find someone, and say to him, "Act as surety for me", and then run away'. He would agree, go out to a public square and take hold of someone. The guards would let him escape and seize the other, though he had not exchanged a word with the [first man], and drag him to the Governor. 'It is you who are that man's surety; bring us what he owes'[, he would order]. When he answered, 'I am not his surety; I do not even know him', they would fling him down, and put shackles on his feet until his legs were broken. They would not let him be until he brought the sum they had fixed for him.

The writer describes in great detail the forms of torture which were employed; racks and thumb-screws and flogging were among the mildest.

But, we are told, the Edessans were not blameless:

What nobles, princes, thieves and robbers who fill their houses with theft and fraud from the poor and orphans and widows were worse than the people of Edessa? . . . Their exactions knew neither beginning nor end, and they were not sated with the plunder that they had obtained.

The Edessans were to receive their deserts. Some forty years later, under the governorship of Ṭahir ibn Ḥusain, the Administrator of Edessa was a certain 'Abd al-'Ala who had little sympathy for Christians:

He loaded the city with taxes. When he wanted one of their villages, he multiplied the burdens on the village to the point at which they were obliged to sell it, and he obtained it at a low price. He had the idea of driving the Edessans from their city and establishing there the Sulaimanites, members of his own tribe. For this reason a numerous crowd [of citizens] gathered and came to find him to complain of what they had to undergo at the hands of those who lodged in their houses, in the city and in the villages. He answered them, 'What have you to complain of, Christians? From the time of the Romans you have devoured this land while our ancestors wandered in the arid desert, in the cold and heat that dries and burns, pasturing their cattle or sheep. Now that we have conquered this land from the Romans with our sword, why do you make trouble instead of leaving it to us and removing yourselves from it. Arise, and leave my presence; endure your situation. Pay the tribute and remain in peace!' The Edessans went out in affliction.[1]

Already under Byzantine rule the Edessans were under an obligation to provide quarters for garrison troops.[2] The continuance of this obligation was implicit in the peace terms dictated to the Christians of Edessa by 'Iyaḍ ibn Ghanm. It was at times exploited unscrupulously. Abu Shaikh Ganawaya, who had rebuilt the walls of the city in 814 at the expense of its notables, sought to introduce his fellow-tribesmen into Edessa to occupy the houses of Christians. We have seen that a similar demand was made somewhat later by 'Abd al-'Ala on behalf of the 'Sulaimanites', the members, possibly, of the tribe of Sulaim of Qais.[3] The tolerant Caliph Ma'mun

[1] Dion. T-M., in Mich. Syr.   [2] See p. 161 above.   [3] See p. 193 above.

revoked the rule, urging ingenuously that none of the Arabs or Persians should harm the Christians. But Ma'mun's dispensation seems not to have survived his death.

The vicissitudes to which the Edessans were exposed are best illustrated by events of the reign of Ma'mun. We have recounted the exactions of 'Abd al-'Ala during the governorship of Ṭahir. When Ṭahir and later also his comrades fled to Raqqa, the Edessans felt 'relieved from heavy burdens'. Ṭahir's son 'Abdallah, on the other hand, was a kindly and scrupulous man. Learning that civilians had been killed by the stones slung by his troops against the walls of a city which they were besieging, he immediately adopted different methods of warfare. 'Abdallah was requested by the Moslems of Harran and Edessa and even of Samosata:

[to] order the destruction of churches that had been built in about the previous ten years and stop the ringing [of bells in the churches]. But the good Governor 'Abdallah replied to them that not even one tenth of the churches that had been destroyed and set on fire had been rebuilt by the poor Christians. He ordered that none of these earlier laws and customs should be withheld from the Christians and that none of their churches should be demolished. And during his days the Christians were in tranquillity and peace.[1]

'Abdallah, however, was sent by the Caliph to Alexandria in 825 and his authority in Mesopotamia was taken over by his young brother Muḥammad. The Administrator of Edessa at that time, Yaqdan, had a Melkite secretary called Walid who 'hated the Christians', in this context presumably the Jacobites. The latter complained to Yaqdan, but received no satisfaction, for the Administrator evidently approved of his secretary's malice. The Jacobite patriarch Dionysius of Tell-Maḥre and his brother Theodosius, Metropolitan of Edessa, then travelled to Egypt to seek the personal intervention of 'Abdallah. Meanwhile, Yaqdan and his secretary solicited the help of a notable of Raqqa, who persuaded Muḥammad to decree the destruction of 'all new buildings' at Edessa—the Church of the Forty Martyrs, the sacristy and treasury of the Great church, a northern inner-room at the northern end of the Baptistry, and basilicas and other constructions of Bishop Theodosius, as well as the nunnery and a church of the Melkites.[2] At the eleventh hour instructions arrived from 'Abdallah to rescind the decision of his deputy.[3]

'Abdallah's policy was in keeping with that of the 'humane and merciful'

---

[1] *Chr. ad 1234.*

[2] At this time, if we may trust the biography of Theodore of Edessa, the Melkites there were in possession of the Cathedral (p. 99) and a Church of the Holy Apostles inside the city, and a Church of St. George and a nunnery outside the city.

[3] Dion. T-M., in Mich. Syr. At Harran in 820–1 the Governor ordered the demolition of 'new' churches—only to countermand the order on the following day. In 834–5 the Moslems of Harran destroyed two Christian churches belonging to the people of Tagrit.

Caliph Ma'mun. The assertion that Ma'mun, on a visit to Harran in about 830, held a disputation on theological questions with its bishop Theodore abu Qurra may be rejected as spurious, but it reflects the attitude of this Caliph towards his Christian subjects.[1] He ordered that no church should be demolished anywhere without his express permission. When he visited Edessa on his way to a campaign against Byzantium,

he entered the Great church and wondered at its beauty. He asked the Metropolitan how much was the revenue of this shrine. The bishop replied, 'Through your bounty, O king, its property is great. But, indeed, even though it is great, it is spent by the exaction of the *gizya* which is set on its revenues.' Then Ma'mun commanded that the *gizya* should not be taken by them on inns, shops, baths and mills—only on gardens and lands. For he affirmed that it is not right that anything that has a roof on it should pay the *gizya*.[2]

But another chronicle adds pointedly, 'This order was decreed for all Mesopotamia, but after a little while the Moslems abolished it.'[3]

When there was full-scale fighting between the Moslems and the Byzantines, it might have been expected that the Moslems would regard their Christians neighbours with distrust. There is little evidence that this feeling was general. In 736–7 there appeared at Harran a certain Bashir who claimed to be Tiberius, son of the Byzantine Emperor Justinian II. He called on the local Jews to summon up his ancestors by enchantment and on the pagans of Harran to examine liver omens for him in order to determine and proclaim his family origin. The Moslem authorities, even Sulaiman son of the Caliph Hisham, credited his claim. He was treated with special honour by the Christians of Edessa—'according to their senselessness, for they are swayed by every wind',[4] adds the chronicler who describes this incident. They allowed him to receive the oblation at the altar, a privilege reserved for reigning emperors.[5] Bashir was conducted to the capital to receive recognition from the Caliph and then returned to Edessa. At Constantinople these developments threw Emperor Leo III into considerable trepidation. His anxiety was not prolonged. Bashir was exposed shortly afterwards as an impostor, and he was crucified at Edessa.

In 796–7 Harun al-Rashid passed by Edessa on his way to conduct a campaign against the Byzantines. The Moslems of Edessa (in one account of this incident a Syriac writer uses the exact transliteration of the Arabic word for Moslem, which in Syriac has the connotation of 'traitor'[6]) laid

---

[1] Theological debates were frequent in this period. We have reference to two in the reign of Harun al-Rashid, in one of which a certain John of Edessa debated with the Jew Phineas, in another a monk of Edessa named Abraham took part in a debate in the presence of the Governor of Jerusalem. Legend greatly multiplied the number of these contests.

[2] *Chr. ad 1234.*
[3] Mich. Syr.
[4] *Chr. ad 1234.*
[5] This privilege had been denied to Emperor Heraclius when he passed through Edessa a century earlier; p. 99 above.
[6] Mich. Syr. But *Chr. ad 1234* has simply 'Ṭayyaye'.

information against their Christian fellow-townsmen. The latter, they maintained, were spies on behalf of Byzantium, and every year the Emperor came to pray in their church at Edessa. The Caliph was requested to destroy the church and to ban the ringing of the church bells. The chronicler continues: 'The king said to Yaḥya [al-Barmaki], his counsellor, "What do you think of this accusation?" He answered wisely, "It should in no way be accepted". And straightway the Moslems were expelled and also flogged.'[1] In 837, however, when Emperor Theophilus invaded Moslem territory the situation was more serious, although the Byzantines massacred Christians and Jews no less than Moslems. Syriac chroniclers record:

the hatred of Moslems against the rest of us who were Christians grew because of the invasion of the Byzantines. The Christians of Edessa especially had to suffer because of an audacious man called Shmona who . . . attached himself to the Byzantines and encouraged them to destroy the Moslems.[1]

It was, however, the lawlessness of Arab military leaders in times of civil unrest that proved the greatest threat to the safety of the Christians of Edessa. There is a significant story that should probably be ascribed to the end of the seventh century. A large sum of money was entrusted by an Arab officer, about to depart on a campaign, to the care of the door-keeper of a monastery outside Edessa. Three years later the warrior returned to find that the door-keeper had died and that the whereabouts of the treasure was not known. The officer threatened to demolish the monastery if he did not receive satisfaction, and the Governor of Edessa insisted that the monastery would be sold and its occupants enslaved. The Bishop of Edessa, Ḥabbib,[2] summoned up the spirit of the dead man, learned from him the place where the money had been deposited, and restored it to its owner.

This simple tale illustrates the insecurity in which the Christians lived. During the fighting between Umayyads and Abbasids a certain 'Ubaidallah ibn Bukhtari terrorized the region of Edessa. He took the nobles, we are informed, and burned them alive 'like fish for the sake of gold'.[3] He enslaved many people, slew the monks of some nine monasteries, sacked villages, and seized their property. It was especially the clergy who were the target of 'Ubaidallah's cruelty. Naṣr ibn Shabath acted with more subtlety. Although he 'was a tyrant', nevertheless, we are assured:

he loved the Christians. He used to oppress without pity [and] with all sorts of taxes Christians who had apostatized to Islam.[4] He would say, 'Provided you pay me the *gizya*, accept each one of you whatever confession he wishes'—and many returned from the mosques to the churches.[5]

We may suspect that Naṣr was motivated not by a liberal attitude towards the Christians—Islamic lawyers regarded the renunciation of Islam as

---

[1] Mich. Syr.
[2] Ḥabbib became Bishop of Edessa when Jacob withdrew from the see in 687.
[3] '*Chr. Zuqnin*'.
[4] Lit., 'paganism'.
[5] Mich. Syr.

impermissible—but by the need to ease the collection of taxes in this pre-
dominantly Christian area. When Naṣr was laying siege to Harran he was
persuaded by the Moslems of Edessa to threaten to destroy the *ciborium*, the
canopied shrine in which was kept the host, in the 'Church of the Christians' at
Edessa. The Christians, it was hinted, would give untold wealth to save their
relics. The citizens were in despair; they could not resist, for the walls of the
city had been broken down by Manṣur. They resorted to fasting and prayer,
and their call was answered. Naṣr was persuaded by a Moslem mediator to
receive a sum of 5,000 *zuze* as ransom and to save himself the trouble of
attacking the city.[1] What would have been the fate of Edessa had it fallen to
him—he was beaten off from Edessa shortly afterwards—we may judge from
his conduct elsewhere in Mesopotamia. His troops devastated the countryside, massacred, pillaged, violated married women, virgins, and children, and
set fire to villages and monasteries. But the people of Mesopotamia suffered
little less from the armies of the Government who opposed Naṣr. The
villagers were compelled to gather in the wheat and barley and other cereals
before they were ripe, to winnow them and to hand all the produce to the
commissariat. As they did this, they were the object of Naṣr's fury; he laid
waste the crops and burned the harvesters alive.

There was, it is true, money to be gained from trade with the military.
At the time of the siege of Erzerum by the Abbasids in 766–7, 'the advance
of the soldiers was of great profit for all the North, for they scattered *zuze*
in it, especially new ones.' This liberality, however, brought no benefit to
ordinary traders, rather the reverse. 'Henceforth whoever wished could
make *zuze* without fear, and new *zuze*—particularly false ones—multiplied.
This caused loss to the public.'[2] Wealth was no longer to be won at Edessa
by caravans and commerce. Its merchants may still have been prosperous
enough, and the fertility of the countryside provided, as we shall see, a
sufficient livelihood. But it was in Government service that fortunes were
amassed; Athanasius, a member of the well-known Edessan family of the
Gumaye who was distinguished for his erudition, was appointed tutor to
'Abd al-'Aziz, younger brother of Caliph 'Abd al-Malik. He accompanied
'Abd al-'Aziz to Egypt where his charge was Governor, and there he remained for twenty-one years. Athanasius acquired immense riches, the details of which are recounted with obvious pride by Syriac chroniclers—four
thousand slaves, villages, mansions, gardens, gold and silver, and jewels
innumerable as pebbles. He was a pious Jacobite, and devoted some of the
revenues he received at Edessa to the building of churches.[3] A Melkite
official at the court of the Umayyads, who was envious of Athanasius, brought
accusations against him to the Caliph. 'Abd al-Malik summoned him,

---

[1] But see above p. 195 n. 1.   [2] '*Chr. Zuqnin*'.   [3] See p. 213 below.

[and] received him quietly. He said to him gently, 'Athanasius, we do not think it right that all this wealth should belong to a Christian. Give us part of it.' Athanasius gave until the Caliph said, 'Enough!'; and there still remained much for him.[1]

A hundred years later, in the reign of Harun al-Rashid, the great fortune of the Roṣpaye comes again to our notice. The fate of the wife of Iwannis Roṣpaya who was deported to Persia by Khusraw and killed there by subtle torture has already been recorded.[2] Before she left Edessa she hid the family treasure in her house, so cunningly that her son Sergius could not find it when he returned from Persia. The Roṣpaya inheritance passed subsequently through the family of the Tell-Maḥraye to the Gumaye. At the end of the eighth century Silvestrus Gumaya at his death bequeathed riches and property 'without end' to his two sons. But the young men quickly dissipated it. They then sought to retrieve their fortunes by digging for the legendary treasure of the Roṣpaye:

They dug in various places and found the treasure. Because they were shameless young men they did not know how to use it sensibly, but squandered it yet more lavishly on horses and hounds [and retainers and maidservants.][3]

Their story came to the notice of Harun al-Rashid in 803-4 when he was residing at Raqqa. The youths were thrown into prison there, and a eunuch was dispatched to impound whatever they had sold at Edessa. He seized their old mother and their wives and sister and ordered them to reveal the whereabouts of the treasure that remained—pots of gold and silver and plate and hoards of Byzantine coins, and gold and silver snakes and scorpions filled with elixir which 'the fools' thought was dust and scattered on the ground. There was an unhappy sequel to this saga of the Roṣpaya treasure. The eunuch imprisoned each of the womenfolk separately.

The sister [of the youths], a virgin, was incarcerated in the house of a Melkite; and he put her in an upper room four storeys high, and set Persian [guards] to watch her. She remained awake and kept vigil lest they might enter and violate her by force. Hearing the sound of footsteps, she cried to God and threw herself down through the window. They found her in the street, and a day later the blessed girl died.[4]

The Caliph himself was overcome by remorse. He ordered the girl's brothers to be released from gaol, to be given one-fifth of the treasure and dismissed.[5]

This was a solitary echo from a more spacious past. Christian Edessans lived more modestly under Moslem domination. There was the usual toll of natural disasters. In spite of Justinian's dam, the waters of the river Daiṣan overflowed into the city once in each century. In November 667,[6] 'there was a great flood of water in the middle of the night. The water

[1] Mich. Syr.   [2] See p. 154 above.
[3] Mich. Syr., with insertions from *Chr. ad 1234.*
[4] Mich. Syr.
[5] We owe the story, with its wealth of detail, to Dion. T-M., a member of the family of Tell-Maḥraye who were related to the Roṣpaye, this page above.
[6] In 666 according to Mich. Syr., in 668 according to Theophanes.

destroyed and broke the wall of Edessa; the city was full of water and thousands of people were drowned.'[1] In March 740[2] occurred another flood, this time without loss of life:

The waters accumulated outside the walls of Edessa and broke them, and the waters entered with a great rush and the city was filled. Houses and courtyards were destroyed, and streets[3] and mills beside the river swept away, and the Old church and its courtyards were filled [with water]. Had people not hurried and opened the eastern [water-]gates, in a trice the whole city would have been submerged by water.[4]

A flood took place in 834–5 at night when the inhabitants were asleep. Again it forced its way through the western wall, and entered the streets and courtyards; some three thousand souls were drowned in their houses before the waters demolished the eastern wall and flowed out into the plain.

In April 679 an earthquake, which completely razed Batnae, killed many people at Edessa. The *ciborium* of the Great church of Edessa collapsed, as well as its two outer sides, and was rebuilt at the order of Mu'awiya. Forty years later, probably in 717–18, occurred another earthquake and there were many victims. The Baptistry and again the Old church were destroyed, as well as many high buildings; where buildings did not fall, cracks appeared and 'those who lived in them would tremble before the Lord whenever they saw these traces of the earthquake'.[5]

Locusts caused terrible hardship in Mesopotamia in 784. They were everywhere, as Dionysius, an eyewitness, describes:

The floors and roofs were covered with them, and also pitchers of water, carpets, tables, and vessels. When they entered a house from the south, they went out by the north, marching straight ahead. When they passed over the roofs and tiles, they went as though over a plain without stopping, eating everything they encountered—grass, trees, woollen material, people's clothing. They spread especially at Edessa [and the neighbourhood. Then] . . . they made, as it were, their route towards the West. . . . As a result of this severe plague, [there was a famine in the land] during the following three years on account of the dearth of bread and wine and oil and all sorts of vegetables.[6]

In March 842 the seeds did not germinate after a rainless winter and hard frosts. With the scarcity of money—aggravated by the cruelty of the Government who, 'greedy for the blood of the poor', insisted on the payment of tribute in full—and the high price of grain, famine and sickness and plague pressed heavily on the poor. They would go out to

collect wood for fire or a little grass for nourishment in place of bread; they perished from cold and from hunger in the midst of their dwellings. The rich, seeing that there was no longer any bread or seeds in the earth, ceased to have pity and to sell grain to give solace to the poor.[6]

---

[1] *Chr. ad 1234.*

[2] The date is slightly different in the '*Chr. Zuqnin*', Theophanes, and Mich. Syr. Fifteen years earlier a flood at Edessa is recorded, but not by Michael.

[3] Or 'markets'.

[4] *Chr. ad 1234.*

[5] '*Chr. Zuqnin*'.

[6] Dion. T-M., in Mich. Syr.

In the following month rain fell and the seeds flourished. But hail and locusts and violent winds destroyed the crops. Pestilence continued for two years.

Nevertheless, in spite of this chronicle of disaster—not a long one for a space of three centuries—the region of Edessa was prosperous from its agriculture. In an account of the year 766–7 we read:

all the countryside . . . was beautiful with vineyards and fields and cattle in profusion. There was not a single wretched pauper in a village who did not possess a plough, donkeys, and goats, and there was not a place cultivable to a greater or lesser degree that was not planted with a vineyard. . . . Wheat and vines grew in abundance.[1]

Prosperity led to luxurious living, to greed and oppression:

The avarice [of the wealthy] became so great that they seized whatever had been given by their ancestors to the churches and to the monasteries. . . . Fights, quarrels and disputes about boundaries were frequent, and sometimes these came even to the point of murder. . . . While the masters were rich in goats and sheep and camels and horses and slaves, and rode on Arab horses accompanied by slaves on mules, their servants carried their children on their shoulders; they were bent and naked and hungry and thirsty, begging from gate to gate for a crust of bread, driven from place to place, the women . . . carrying their infants, naked and pale.[1]

In another passage on the events of some two years later, the chronicler repeats his description of the abundance of produce in the corn fields and vineyards, and the wealth of the landowners:

They were exceedingly rich, they had all good things—and they were proud, presumptuous and jealous, adulterers, fornicators, drunkards, extortioners, false witnesses. . . . [Even] the honourable order of monasticism transgressed the bounds of . . . propriety. . . . They acquired horses and herds of oxen, flocks of goats and sheep; each of them owned plots of land, apart from the land of the [monastic] community. They went outside to acquire vineyards and houses in the villages and to ride horses with saddles like the unbelievers, to walk according to the desire of their heart without subjecting themselves to the Superior who had been given authority over them by God.

When the ignorant villagers, hard pressed by the tax collectors, came to the cities to request loans, they fell into the hands of money-lenders:

They brought the money-lenders presents. The latter, seeing them, would say 'Welcome!' and . . . would add, 'I shall give you all you desire. Have no care . . . I demand no witness or securities or pledge; I ask for no interest or repayment. Take, and when the harvest comes, bring me my [money], or give me wheat or wine at the price current at the time.' . . . The wretched man . . . would stay tranquilly in his house until the tax collectors came. When they took hold of him, he would say, 'Wait a moment; I will fetch it for you'. He would go in haste to [the money-lender] who had led him to hope that he would give it to him. 'Please, sir', he would say, 'give me what I ask.' But the latter would reply, 'Wait a little', and leave him and go off. Or he would mock him with words, saying, 'Go away today; come back in the morning. For the moment I have not

[1] 'Chr. Zuqnin'.

enough for you.' So for many days he would act in this way with him. And when [the poor man] was afflicted to death . . . he would content himself with saying either, 'I shall not give [it] to you because I have not got it to give', or 'I want a written undertaking from you.' . . . Then he would dismiss him, saying 'Go this night and come in the morning.' When they came early in the morning he would say, 'I shall give it only if you provide a pledge.' The pledge would be given and he would then say, 'How much will you give as interest on this money? As for repayment, how much wheat will you give me? I shall not take it at the current price.'

The end was inevitable. The wretched peasant would sell his produce to repay some of his debts and he himself would remain in the power of the usurer with the pledge unredeemed.

There is no mention of pagans at Edessa after the capture of the city by 'Iyaḍ, except for an allusion by Bishop Jacob of Edessa (died 708) to a disciple of Bardaiṣan who discoursed learnedly on Fate and the influence of the planets. At Harran, however, heathens maintained their cults for several centuries longer. Bashir, pretender to the Imperial throne of Byzantium, had demanded their assistance.[1] An idol of these 'Manichaeans'[2] was revealed in an earthquake at Paddana Rabbetha near Harran in 768–9. In the following years many Moslems who had been 'ensnared' by paganism were put to death. Eight members of the Gumaye family, presumably Christian, were implicated; after much torture, three of them died in prison, the rest were released. But in 816–17, the pagans of Harran were permitted to carry out their rites in public by the same Moslem Governor who ordered the demolition of churches in the city on the ground that they had been newly constructed. Such, at any rate, was the story current among the Christians of Edessa; whatever its truth, it indicates the awareness of the Edessans that not far away was Harran, that 'nest of paganism', its inhabitants 'afflicted with the ulcers of idolatry'.[3]

The legal toleration extended to Christianity under Islam, conceded only grudgingly and arbitrarily by some Governors, did not halt the slow erosion of the Christian community at Edessa. A Syriac chronicler writes:

the gates were opened to them to [enter] Islam.[4] The wanton and the dissolute slipped towards the pit and the abyss of perdition, and lost their souls as well as their bodies— all, that is, that we possess. . . . Without blows or tortures[5] they slipped towards apostasy in great precipitancy; they formed groups of ten or twenty or thirty or a hundred or two hundred or three hundred without any sort of compulsion. . . , going down to Harran and becoming Moslems in the presence of [government] officials. A great crowd did so . . . from the districts of Edessa and of Harran and of Tella and of Resaina . . .[6]

[1] See p. 200 above.

[2] The term is used by Moslem writers as a general epithet for pagans.

[3] Letter of David bar Paul, in Rahmani, *Studia Syriaca*, i. 46. See further the present writer's article 'The Planet Cult of Ancient

Harran', in E. Bacon (ed.), *Vanished Civilizations*, 1963, 211 ff.

[4] Lit., 'paganism'.   [5] Lit., 'combings',

[6] British Museum MS. Add. 14665, foll. 2–3, ed. J. B. Chabot (*CSCO*, Scriptores syri 53), 1952, pp. 381, 385.

The anonymous author goes on to describe the wave of deceit and slander that passed through the Christian villages; in this atmosphere of mistrust it was safer to adopt the dominant religion. Once this step was taken there was no return,[1] and we are given accounts of Christians of the neighbourhood of Edessa who had accepted Islam and were afflicted by remorse for their apostasy. But it was not only the timid but also the more ambitious and able among the Christians who were impelled to seek the economic and social advantages that accrued to those who professed Islam. Here, in the gradual alienation of the most talented of its members, may lie the explanation of the strange fact that the community did not close its ranks against its common adversary Islam. Sectarian strife continued unabated at Edessa.

When Edessa fell to the Moslems in 639 the three main sects of Mesopotamian Christianity, Nestorian Dyophysites, Melkites, and Monophysites, were represented in the city. The Nestorians, whose bishop had been installed, largely on political grounds, by Khusraw Abarwez when the Persians overran Mesopotamia, evidently made little headway. Indeed, a Nestorian called Sahdona, who had held the rank of bishop in the East, is said to have been converted to Jacobite views at Edessa and to have been elected as bishop there in the first half of the seventh century; other sources maintain that he was bishop of the Melkite community. After a short time, however, he returned to his earlier beliefs and was expelled from his office; he ended his days as a hermit in the hills outside the city. A letter, written in about 651, from Adiabene to the Nestorians of Edessa mentions a chief-priest, an archdeacon, a lay representative, and other clerics and laymen; there seems not to have been a priest of the standing of bishop. The community still continued at Edessa in the late eighth century and beyond.[2]

The Melkites, like the Nestorians, are scarcely alluded to by our local chroniclers, most of whom were Monophysite, during the first three centuries of Islam. We have, however, a list of the Melkite hierarchy at Edessa in 723.[3] It consisted of a Metropolitan, a chief priest and Steward, a 'second priest', a priest who was in charge (*higoumenos*) of the church in which was kept the 'icon of the Lord', the portrait of Jesus,[4] another who maintained the records (*chartularios*) of the church, an archdeacon, a deacon who was the storekeeper, a chief of the sub-deacons who acted as secretary, the chief of the lectors, the leader of the 'choir[5] of the Greeks' and the leader of the 'choir of the Syrians' and a deacon of the baptistry. In, probably, 836 the office of Melkite bishop of Edessa was occupied by a certain Theodore, if

---

[1] Above p. 201 foot.

[2] See p. 98 above. Job of Edessa was a Nestorian, pp. 212, 216 below.

[3] Thomson, *JTS*, N.S. xiii, 1962, 249.

[4] It is interesting to compare this claim that the portrait of Jesus was in the Melkite cathedral with the counter-claim of the Jacobites that they had acquired the genuine portrait; p. 214 below.

[5] Syriac, *gawda*.

we may credit a biography attributed to his nephew.[1] Born at Edessa, Theodore is stated to have spent over twenty years in retreat near Jerusalem before he returned to assume the bishopric in his native town. He died about thirty years later. Legend improbably ascribes to him the healing of the Caliph at Baghdad and of the Emperor at Constantinople, and a successful campaign against heresy at Edessa itself. One of Theodore's advisers was a stylite named Theodosius, who lived on his pillar at Edessa for forty-nine years. Melkite churches at Edessa, mentioned in this biography of Theodore, are the Cathedral of our Lord and the Church of the Holy Apostles; outside the city were a nunnery and the Church of St. George.

The third denomination, the anti-Chalcedonian Monophysites, consisted already in the middle of the fifth century of two separate groups, the 'Syrians' or Jacobites, and the Armenians. Like the Persians, both the Syrian community and the Armenian community each maintained its own School at Edessa at that time. The Armenians were a recognized section of the population in the reign of Caliph 'Abd al-Malik. In 728 a Council of the Armenian Church at Manzikert was attended by the Metropolitan of Edessa; then the Council of Chalcedon was repudiated, union was established between the Armenians and the Jacobites, and certain ritual practices were instituted, which are still in force.

The largest faction at Edessa was undoubtedly that of the Jacobites. Perhaps they had no stronger a tendency towards dissension than other sects, and those, too, no doubt contained obstreperous and venal priests. It is the misfortune of the Jacobites that most of our contemporary chroniclers belonged to that community and recorded its affairs in intimate detail. One declares, without mincing words, that the Jacobite bishops were 'proud, overbearing, truculent, quarrelsome, and crafty..., and did not set the law of God before their eyes'. It is significant that the Jacobite leader Dionysius protested when Ma'mun decreed that any ten persons belonging to a single group could petition the Caliph for official recognition as a religious confession. The Patriarch explained that this would encourage schism in his Church. To this Ma'mun retorted tartly, 'You trouble us..., you Christians, and most of all you Jacobites—even if we overlook the complaints that you bring against each other'.

If one regards only the second half of the eighth century, the story of discord and depravity among the Jacobite leaders is astonishing. Patriarch Iwannis was traduced before the Caliph himself by one of his principal

---

[1] It has, however, been credibly argued that this Bishop Theodore was not a historical personage, and that his 'biography' is based on that of the well-known Bishop of Harran, Theodore abu Qurra, who died in the early ninth century and was also a native of Edessa; below p. 212. A Melkite bishop of Harran called Theodoricus Pugla, and said to have been deposed in 813-14 for teaching heretical doctrines, is no doubt to be identified with Theodore abu Qurra.

bishops, Athanasius Sandalaya, Bishop of Maiperqaṭ, who apparently accused his Superior of uttering blasphemy against Islam. A reconciliation between the two prelates in 751–2 was short-lived. The successor of Iwannis, Isaac, was believed to have killed a wandering monk whom he had entertained in his monastery of Beth Purkse ('the place of towers') in the hills outside Edessa. The monk had claimed to have an elixir which would transmute lead into gold, and Isaac hoped to find the secret formula on the body of the dead man; he found nothing but his empty scrip. Nevertheless, Isaac hinted in certain circles that he had learned the magic process, and through the personal intervention of Caliph Manṣur he obtained rapid promotion, to the see of Harran and finally to the patriarchal throne. But the falsity of Isaac's claim was exposed to the Caliph, and the Patriarch was strangled in 755–6 and his corpse unceremoniously thrown into the Euphrates. He was succeeded by Athanasius Sandalaya, who was murdered at night by the people of Harran on whom he had sought to foist his own nominee to their vacant diocese. The next Patriarch, George, was calumniated at the court of the Caliph by David, Bishop of Dara, and others, tortured, imprisoned for nine years, and finally deposed. The rule of his successor, John of Callinicos, was not recognized as legitimate by some Jacobites—nor, indeed, had been the reigns of his predecessors Isaac and Athanasius. On the death of John in 762–3 David of Dara was elected to the patriarchate; he went everywhere escorted by a 'Persian' bodyguard and shunned by his colleagues of the Church. In 775 the former Patriarch George was restored to liberty by Caliph al-Mahdi. But the story of the Church continued to be stormy. At the turn of the eighth century Patriarch Cyriacus met with constant opposition from his clergy, and countered with anathemas and ineffective synods.

During these centuries Harran was an important centre of Jacobite activity; patriarchs were elected and several synods were convened at monasteries in its vicinity. Inevitably the attention of the Church was directed also to Edessa. Edessa, in any case, maintained that it had been 'proclaimed the Metropolis of Mesopotamia from the time of Addai'; its bishop Timothy reacted with anger when it was not he but Athanasius Sandalaya, then Bishop of Maiperqaṭ, who was granted the status of Metropolitan.[1] On Timothy's death in 760–61, the Jacobites wished to appoint in his place a recluse named Simeon who had endeared himself not only to them but to Moslems and heretics by his virtues, particularly by his liberality towards strangers and the poor. He was seized and ordained bishop by force. The next two days he spent in fasting; then, 'because he found the air of

---

[1] Timothy's objection was not wholly valid. It is true that the Bishop of Edessa was usually Metropolitan of Osrhoene; but Athanasius was now given the title of Metropolitan of Mesopotamia which was normally the prerogative of the Bishop of Amid.

Edessa oppressive', he retired to the Monastery of the Mother of God in the hills to the south of the city. Protesting that the Edessans were 'difficult people', Simeon enticed an Ethiopian monk from Amid to Edessa, but the latter fled from the city by night when he learned that it was intended to inveigle him into accepting the see. Finally, a certain Zacharias was appointed bishop. He died in 768–9, and a monk from Qartamin, 'a villainous man, who did not consider God at all, became bishop, not because he deserved the bishopric, but because the Edessans deserved him'[1]. But his appointment was not confirmed and the diocese remained without an incumbent.

In 783–4 Zacharias, the Metropolitan of Edessa, was removed by the Patriarch at the instance of the citizens, who declared that he had refused to rebuke his brother for evil conduct. Another bishop of the name of Zacharias was then nominated to the see. He, however, was opposed by 'all the clergy, apart from the populace' in 785–6, and was expelled by Patriarch George. Later Patriarch Joseph, elected to his office largely through the efforts of Zacharias, came to Edessa with the latter, hoping to bring about his return to the diocese. They stayed at the shrine of St. Cosmas in 789–90. But the Edessans refused to accede to the arguments of the Patriarch, and he withdrew in irritation without entering the city. Two years later the pleas on behalf of Zacharias were renewed by another Patriarch, Cyriacus, but with no greater success, Finally, a compromise was arrived at whereby Zacharias was granted authority over four districts of the diocese, but not over the city itself. Cyriacus ordained a certain Basil as bishop of Edessa. When the see again became vacant Cyriacus appointed a priest called Theodosius, but against the wishes of the people; and negotiations at Raqqa between the Patriarch and the Edessans were necessary before they would accept his nominee.

In the first centuries of Islam the Syriac-speaking population of the Moslem empire attained prominence in the fields of science and literature. They had, as we have noted, long been active in the translation of the masterpieces of Greek thought into Syriac, Now they played the role of transmitters of western civilization to the emergent civilization of the Arabs. Their function continued even when Moslems themselves were able to understand Greek and to translate it direct into Arabic; competence in transferring modes of thought and expression from one language to another is derived not so much from the simple control of languages as from that elasticity of mind and mastery of idiom that were a peculiar quality of this minority group. The great contribution of the people of Harran, especially the pagans, to Islamic civilization lies outside the scope of the present work.[2] Those who were

[1] 'Chr. Zuqnin'.

[2] Practically nothing has remained of the writings of the pagans of Harran in Syriac except brief extracts from the works of Baba. The date of these fragments is uncertain, they almost certainly belong to the Moslem era; F. Rosenthal, in *A Locust's Leg*, 1962, 220.

natives of Edessa or resident there contributed less; nevertheless their work was of real significance.

Jacob of Edessa was born near Antioch and was appointed Bishop of Edessa in, probably, 684. In 687, angered by the laxity with which Church rules were interpreted, he resigned after publicly burning a copy of the ecclesiastical regulations, and withdrew to monastic life. He was recalled to the see of Edessa in 708, but died only four months after his return.[1] He was a noted Bible scholar and completed a revision of the Syriac text of the Old Testament in 705. Outstanding as a theologian, his commentaries on the Bible earned him the title of 'Interpreter of the Scriptures'; he was also a historian, but unfortunately little of his work in this field has survived. Jacob made a signal contribution too as translator, as philosopher, as an indefatigable correspondent, and, above all, as grammarian; his invention of symbols to represent Syriac vowels—to be written on the line beside the consonants—was an achievement of unusual ingenuity.

Most significant is Jacob's unfinished *Hexaemeron*, the first attempt in Syriac to describe the world and its phenomena within the framework of the Bible narrative of the Creation. His lively bent towards scientific analysis is illustrated by experiments which remind us of those of St. Ephraim three centuries earlier. Jacob puts water and dust in a glass vessel to show the relationship of air, water and dust in the universe; a narrow-throated glass jug is plunged suddenly into water to show the 'struggle' between air and water seeking to enter a confined space. The *Hexaemeron* reflects the extent to which natural sciences, and especially geography, were studied in Mesopotamia at this time. But Jacob was not satisfied with hearsay. He insisted on himself interrogating the stonemasons who claimed to have seen fossilized human remains in the 'hill country of the Harranians'. He uses rationalist arguments to confute theories on the influence of the planets on human affairs that were held by the pagans of Harran. Jacob writes in effective style, although his choice of vocabulary is stilted:

How great is the variety of the earth in its location and structure! It contains mountains lofty and difficult—that is, inaccessible—that are cut and cleft by impassable crags and by deep chasms, by valleys and gullies and abysses, by pits and heights and depths. It is spread out over plains and wide, impassable deserts. It is damp, sending forth trickling waters and producing springs and pools of water, causing rivers to flow, and bringing forth trees and thickets and making the meadows to sprout. But it is also dry and arid where nothing of value grows. Moreover, it is habitable, used as the dwelling-place of animals—but it is uninhabitable too, without equable temperature that can be endured by men and animals, whether through great cold or through the searing heat of the sun.

[1] He was buried at the monastery of Tell 'Ada, where he had lived, and to which he had gone to bring his library to Edessa. Later, miracles were reported to have been performed at his tomb.

Jacob was associated with Edessa only through his tenure of its see. Theophilus bar Thomas was a native of the city in the eighth century. He was apparently a Maronite and a skilled astrologer: we are told, indeed, that he was 'raised by (the Caliph) al-Mahdi to very high honour because of his superiority in this craft'. He wrote a history which is commended by Bar Hebraeus, although 'in it he reviled and abused orthodox folk'. Most remarkable was the translation into Syriac by Theophilus of the 'two books of the poet Homer on the conquest of the city of Ilion'—that is, presumably, the *Iliad* and the *Odyssey*.

Theodore abu Qurra, born at Edessa in about 750, became Melkite bishop of Harran, after a period in a monastery at Jerusalem. His polemical writings were directed against Moslems, Jews, and heretics, and he wrote in Greek as well as in Arabic. He appears to have died in about 820. A contemporary of Theodore was Job of Edessa, also called Job al-Abrash (the spotted); he was born at Edessa in about 760, and was a Nestorian. Job translated the works of Galen from Greek to Syriac. In about 817 this polymath wrote his *Book of Treasures* which deals with metaphysics, theology, psychology, biology, anatomy, physiology, medicine, chemistry and physics, music, mathematics, and astronomy. The work is largely dependent on Galen, and has many borrowings from Aristotle and Hippocrates, and from Persian and Indian sages who are not mentioned by name.

Another contemporary was Dionysius of Tell-Maḥre, a member of a family that no doubt originated from the village of that name near the river Balikh. A self-effacing monk, he was suddenly raised to the patriarchate in the summer of 818. He travelled widely to visit his co-religionists. He went to Egypt in 825–6 to intervene with 'Abdallah ibn Ṭahir over the order issued by 'Abdallah's brother for the demolition of churches at Edessa, and he travelled to Egypt a second time in the company of Caliph Ma'mun. Several times he visited the court of the Caliphs. Dionysius died in 845, leaving as his memorial a history of affairs from A.D. 582 to 842.[1] Little has survived in independent form, but long excerpts are preserved, some evidently in the original wording, in later chronicles. In particular, an autobiographical narrative by Dionysius gives a lively and lucid account of contemporary events of which the writer was an eyewitness and in some of which he played an important part.[2] Theodosius, Metropolitan of Edessa and brother of Dionysius, who accompanied him on his visit to 'Abdallah ibn Ṭahir in

[1] Scholars have clearly demonstrated that the important history of world affairs from the Creation to A.D. 774–5, which previously had been attributed to Dion. T-M., was in fact the work of an anonymous monk of the monastery of Zuqnin; see in particular R. Abramowski, *Dionysius von Tellmahre*, 1940. Extracts from the fourth part of this chronicle appear on pp. 196–8, 204–6; in it are incorporated writings that might otherwise have been lost—notably the *Chronicle of Edessa*, the chronicle attributed to 'Josh. St.' and much of the *History* of John Ephes.

[2] Extracts have been cited on pp. 195, 198, 204.

Egypt was a well-known scholar. He translated into Syriac some of the writings of Gregory of Nazianzus.

The Moslems who captured Edessa were evidently filled with wonder at the sight of its buildings. Al-Istakhri is followed by other Arab geographers in writing of the 'more than three hundred monasteries and great cells' in the city, and of the monks who lived there. In the ninth century Ibn Khordadhbeh reported that the Byzantines themselves held that no building constructed of stone was ever fairer than the Cathedral of Edessa.[1] A century later it was still called the largest church in the Moslem empire; in the view of al-Muqaddasi, its vaults covered with mosaics made it one of the three wonders of the world, until it was superseded by the mosque of al-Aqsa at Jerusalem. The Moslems themselves built little at Edessa. Sa'id ibn 'Amir, Governor of Mesopotamia after 'Iyaḍ, had a mosque erected 'in the middle of the city [where were] the Churches of St. John and of the Mother of God'.[2] This was built, according to a late tradition, before 644 when Caliph 'Umar I died; it evidently sufficed for the Moslems of the time. It was not until 825–6 that Muḥammad ibn Ṭahir ordered not only the destruction of the church buildings erected by Bishop Theodosius, but also the construction of a new mosque. The site chosen, it should be noted, was not a church but the Tetrapylon (building with four gates) in front of the Old church, rebuilt by the Melkite bishop Amazonius.[3] The place was called the 'synagogue';[4] here, in the ninth century, the 'elders and leaders' used to meet after morning service to discuss problems from ecclesiastical and profane books until dinner time. The Tetrapylon was surmounted by a dome, but this was removed when it was converted into a mosque.

The building of new churches in the city was, we have observed, forbidden. But Athanasius bar Gumaye, favourite of Caliph 'Abd al-Malik and a devout Jacobite, donated the revenue of his shops and other property at Edessa[5] to the construction of two churches in about 700. They were the Church of the Mother of God, standing perhaps on the place of the present Halil Rahman Camii by the fish-pools, and a baptistry. It is likely that Athanasius received permission to carry out this work because these buildings took the place of the churches of St. John and the Mother of God that had been removed when Sa'id ibn 'Amir had built his mosque. It may be, however, that Athanasius's churches were no more than the extension of buildings that already existed.

[1] This is presumably the Melkite cathedral built by Amazonius; p. 189 above. No building in wood, the Arab geographers add, was fairer than the church of Mabbog, and none in marble fairer than the church of Antioch.

[2] See Plan I. This mosque may be the present Ulu Cami (Pl. 33a), but the identification is hazardous.

[3] This mosque may be on the site of the present Hasan Paşa Camii; Pl. 33b.

[4] Syriac, *beth shabbetha*.

[5] One chronicle estimates this at three shops, another at four hundred shops, a third at three hundred shops and nine inns.

However this may be, this Jacobite baptistry became the resting-place of the relic to which, it has been suggested, the Melkites had shown special reverence, the portrait of Jesus.[1] The account merits citation in full:

The Edessans owed part of the taxes which they had to pay and had nothing with which to pay it. A crafty man . . . advised the collector of taxes, 'If you take the portrait they will sell their children and themselves rather than allow it [to be removed]'. When [he] did this, the Edessans were in consternation. . . . They came to the noble Athanasius and asked him to give them the 5,000 dinars of the taxes, and to take the portrait to his place until they repaid him. He gladly took the portrait to his place and gave the gold. Then he brought a clever painter and asked him to paint one like it. When the work was finished and there was a portrait as exactly as possible like [the original] because the painter had dulled the paints of the portrait so that they would appear old, the Edessans after a time returned the gold and asked him for the portrait. He gave them the one that had been made recently and kept the old one in his place. After a while he revealed the affair to the faithful [Jacobites], and built the wonderful shrine of the baptistry. He completed it at expense great beyond reckoning, spent in honour of the portrait, because he knew that the genuine portrait sent through John the *tabellara*[2] had remained in his place. After several years he brought it and put it in the baptistry.

The story is vouched for on the authority of Dionysius of Tell-Maḥre;[3] he was convinced that the genuine portrait was 'in the charge of the Melkites in Edessa . . . from the time of the Greek kings and that Athanasius bar Gumaye took it from them'. We have already cited the *sugitha* which claims that the portrait stood in the Hagia Sophia church built by Amazonius (now called the 'Old church') in the sixth century.[4] Confirmation of the view of Dionysius may be found from the other works carried out by Athanasius. 'He made channels [of water] like those made by Bishop Amazonius in the Old church of Edessa, and he decorated it with gold and silver and marble plating.'[5] Athanasius wished the new setting of the portrait to resemble its former home. The Melkites, however, continued to maintain that they preserved the genuine relic in their 'house of the icon of the Lord'.[6] And in 787, about a century after Athanasius, when the veneration of holy images was debated at the Council of Nicaea, it must have been the Melkite relic of Edessa to which reference was made. Leo, lector of Constantinople declared that he had been in the city, and had seen 'the holy icon made without the aid of [mortal] hands revered and adored by the faithful'.[7]

The portrait of Jesus at Edessa was by now widely celebrated in Christendom, especially at Byzantium. At the capital icons were regarded with

[1] See p. 77 above.

[2] This should be Ḥannan the *tabulara*, the secretary of King Abgar; see above p. 76, and Ch. III.

[3] Mich. Syr., who prefaces this passage with the words, 'Dionysius . . . , the historian of these things, says, "I have taken these things from the account of Daniel . . . , my maternal grandfather"'. The Armenian version of this incident translated by Langlois and reproduced by von Dobschütz, *Christusbilder*, 228, cf. 148, should be regarded with caution.

[4] See p. 189 above.

[5] Mich. Syr.

[6] See p. 207 above.

[7] Mansi, xiii, 192c.

devotion approaching worship. There was, it is true, violent and prolonged opposition to the veneration of images—but it was in vain; popular sentiment was too deeply entrenched. It was towards the end of this struggle, in 836, that the three Melkite Patriarchs of Alexandria, Antioch, and Jerusalem addressed an epistle to the iconoclastic Emperor Theophilus. In it they set out a list of icons 'made without the aid of [mortal] hand' and performing miracles for the pious; at the head of the list stands the portrait of Jesus at Edessa. It is little wonder that the portrait has a central role in the next appearance of Edessa in history.

The misrule and disunity of the Moslem empire had encouraged the Byzantines to launch vigorous offensives across the eastern frontier. Already under Leo VI (886–912) Byzantium had established an administrative enclave east of the upper reaches of the Euphrates. Her objective was no longer isolated raids into the Moslem empire but territorial annexation; the local Arab princes, even the energetic Hamdanids, were on the defensive and without a consistent plan of strategy. In 915, and particularly from 927 under the leadership of John Curcuas, Byzantine incursions met with little resistance. In 942, in a new campaign in Mesopotamia, Dara and Nisibis fell to the Byzantines. They then invested Edessa in the summer of 943. Here their prize was not military conquest but the portrait of Jesus, the *mandylion*.[1]

What followed is obscure. Byzantine historians claim that the Edessans offered the portrait in return for the raising of the siege. More probably the initiative came from the Byzantines, who 'requested the inhabitants [of Edessa] to deliver to them the holy portrait of the *mandylion* kept in the church of Edessa on which our Saviour Jesus Christ had wiped his countenance and on which the features of his face had remained imprinted'. The Byzantine general proposed the exchange of Moslem prisoners for the portrait and this unusual bargain was referred to the Caliph at Baghdad. Moslem jurists ruled that the release of prisoners outweighed other considerations and that the *mandylion* was the joint property of the Christians of Edessa and the Moslem community. Negotiations were protracted. The Edessans were evidently reluctant to part with their treasure, and it was perhaps to exert pressure on them that the Byzantine army returned to the region in November 943, captured Resaina and carried off prisoners. Finally, two hundred Moslem captives were handed to the Caliph's officers. The Byzantines paid the Edessans 12,000 pieces of silver and granted an undertaking of perpetual peace between the Empire and Edessa, Harran, Serug, and Samosata.

The Bishop of Samosata on the edge of Byzantine territory was deputed to take possession of the portrait, accompanied by the Bishop of Edessa.

[1] This Greek term seems to emerge only during the Moslem period, and most scholars therefore regard it as derived from Arabic *mandil*, kerchief. It has been suggested, however, that it is the Greek μαντίλιον that is earlier, and from it have been derived the Aramaic *mantila* and the late Greek μανδύλη.

Still the Edessans sought to avoid parting with the portrait, and complied only after the Moslem commander threatened the use of force. Apparently three copies of the portrait, the property no doubt of each of the three sects, Nestorians, Jacobites and Melkites, were surrendered; two were returned, and we may assume that it was the portrait vouched for by their fellow-Melkites that the Byzantines accepted as genuine. To the end some Edessans resisted. A storm broke out suddenly when the portrait, together with a copy of the 'letter of Jesus', was about to leave the city.[1] The people interpreted this as a sign of divine displeasure and rioted. Their recalcitrance was in vain. The relics were escorted with reverence, and reached the capital on 15 August 944 after, it was related, a journey marked by extraordinary miracles. They were introduced with pomp and jubilation into the Church of St. Sophia and the Imperial palace 'for the glory of the faithful, for the safety of the Emperors, for the preservation of the entire city and of the way of life of the Christian empire'.[2]

The Byzantines carried out their side of the bargain with the Edessans. When they captured Resaina in 943 and pillaged the city, they made no attack on Edessa. In 949–50, however, the Edessans themselves seem to have infringed the terms of the agreement. The powerful Hamdanid ruler of the area, Saif al-Dawla, forced them to take part in a raid on the Byzantine fortress of Mopsuestia, in which great numbers of them perished. During the next twenty years the countryside suffered from repeated Byzantine invasions, in 952, 959–60, and 963. A terrible famine, according to Matthew of Edessa, began in Mesopotamia in 952–3, and in Edessa especially:

the inhabitants were a prey to all sorts of torments and calamities. The dearth lasted seven years and destroyed an incalculable number of persons. . . . Locusts spread . . . in clouds . . . and ravaged all the fields, increasing the rigour of the dearth. A crowd of people, exasperated by the anguish of hunger, threw themselves upon each other with the cruelty of wild beasts and devoured each other. Great and rich were reduced to finding nourishment in vegetables and fruit because animals had been destroyed by disease.

The ravages of war continued. In 966 Byzantine forces seized Dara and Nisibis; in 968 or 969 under Nicephorus Phocas they 'plundered, took captive, burned and laid waste' regions nearer to Edessa.[3] When, however,

---

[1] Local chroniclers, all of them Monophysite, are remarkably uncommunicative about the transaction.

[2] The later adventures of the portrait are outlined in von Dobschütz, *Christusbilder*, 156 ff.; see also S. Runciman, *Cambridge Historical Journal* iii, 1931, 250 ff., V. Grumel, *Anal. Boll.* lxiii, 1950, 135, and K. Weitzmann, *Cah. arch.* xi, 1960, 163.

[3] But possibly in the winter of 971 or 972. The chroniclers that report that Edessa was razed to the ground in October–November, 968 have, however, confused it with Emesa. In 966 Nicephorus Phocas removed from Mabbog (Hierapolis) to Constantinople the sacred tile on which, as on the *mandylion* of Edessa, were engraved the features of Jesus, see p. 78 above.

John Tzimisces campaigned in the area in 974–5, he is said by Matthew of Edessa to have 'spared Edessa out of consideration for the monks who dwelt in the nearby hills and the environs to the number of about ten thousand'. Some twenty years later a threat appeared from another direction. Fatimid forces from Egypt had invaded Syria and laid siege to Aleppo in, probably, 993–4. They crossed the Euphrates and devastated the lands of Edessa and did 'immense harm to the city'.

The fighting between the rival empires was vexatious enough; but, as in earlier centuries, a greater danger to the security of Edessa were the petty Moslem warlords who, with their bands, terrorized the countryside, and imposed heavy exactions on the townspeople. At the beginning of the eleventh century—from this point in our history of Edessa the documentation by sources in Arabic, Syriac, Armenian, and later in Latin, becomes excellent—Edessa was in the hands of 'Uṭair, cousin of Waththab, chief of the Banu Numair and ruler of Harran. As his deputy in the city, 'Uṭair installed a certain Aḥmad ibn Muḥammad; later, jealous of Aḥmad's popularity, he caused him to be assassinated. In despair the people of Edessa turned to the powerful Marwanid prince of Amid, Naṣr al-Dawla. 'Uṭair was permitted by Naṣr al-Dawla to return to Edessa; shortly afterwards he was murdered by a rival chieftain. Naṣr al-Dawla then divided control of the city. The Citadel he gave to the son of 'Uṭair, and a smaller fort, probably in the east wall, he gave to the son of Shibl al-Dawla, another Numairid sheikh.

The events that followed are confused, but their effect was far-reaching. The two chiefs plotted and wrangled against each other. In the winter of 1031–2[1] Salman, Naṣr al-Dawla's Turkish deputy who was hard pressed by 'Uṭair's widow or by Shibl al-Dawla[2] (another source holds that it was not Salman but the son of 'Uṭair), entered into negotiations with the Byzantine general George Maniaces, who held the Byzantine title of *protospatharios*. George was *strategos* of the *thema*, or Byzantine administrative area, of Telukh, and then resided at Samosata as *strategos* of the 'cities of the Euphrates'. His victory over Arab forces in about 1030 had won him local fame and he had been appointed *catepano*, Governor, also of the Byzantine *thema* of Lower Media (ceded to Byzantium by its king in 1021). The Citadel of Edessa was handed over to Maniaces, in return for an annual pension and a patent of nobility from the Emperor.[3] We have a vivid account in a Syriac chronicle.

It was arranged that Maniaces should come secretly to meet Salman. They fixed a certain night on which he would come from the western gate of the Citadel on the hill.

---

[1] A Byzantine source has 1034.

[2] According to Matthew of Edessa, 'Uṭair's followers assassinated Shibl in 1032 at 'a place called the Convent of Arjej where a stone column rises opposite the fortress'. Salman was, he holds, Shibl's lieutenant.

[3] Another version sets the price at 20,000 dinars and a number of villages in Byzantine territory.

When this had been decided between them, Maniaces came with a small number of soldiers and hid them in tens and twenties in the hills. He himself with his two attendants came near the gate according to the arrangement. He knocked at the gate. Salman was standing behind the gate, waiting; he opened the gate and the two met in the gate, Maniaces standing outside and Salman inside, speaking to each other by night and in a low voice, with no outsider aware of the secret. Maniaces had appointed a sign for his soldiers. When they perceived the sign they were to approach the gate, and he had ordered those who accompanied him to take some little stone pebbles from the wadi. But when Salman and Maniaces conversed, the affair was not resolved in any way. Salman said to Maniaces . . . , 'Go in peace, and let the secret and our friendship be preserved between us'. When he came as though to close the gate, the attendants of Maniaces threw the stones at the gate of the Citadel and roused the soldiers who were in hiding and they came forward. Salman wanted to close the gate of the Citadel but it could not be closed. Maniaces and those with him leapt up and seized the Citadel, slew the guards and brought out Salman and his family and wealth and possessions without out in any way harming him.[1]

The Byzantine forces were strong enough to hold the Citadel, but too weak to occupy the city. They seem, however, to have slain Moslems in the city and to have sacked a mosque. The Christian inhabitants, perhaps principally Melkites who were known to favour the Byzantine cause,[2] feared reprisals and fled to the Hagia Sophia Church. After three days the Moslem commander broke down the doors, slew the menfolk and carried off women and children as prisoners. The rest of the city was deserted. But even Naṣr al-Dawla's army could not dislodge Maniaces from the Citadel. With the approach of winter they withdrew, after setting fire to houses and shrines.[3] Among the latter were the Jacobite Church of the Mother of God, restored by Athanasius bar Gumaye, and the Church of St. Theodore; they were rebuilt, however, by the next Metropolitan Athanasius (Joshua), who brought wood for this purpose from Armenia, encouraged by the Governor of Edessa, Abu-K'ab.

The Byzantine garrison in the Citadel of Edessa was reinforced by the Emperor.[4] It took possession also of the city, and the walls were repaired. Edessa was, we are assured, a prosperous place, 'full of many people, Christians and Moslems, and resounding with innumerable crowds and artisans of all sorts'. Unfortunately, our sources tell us nothing about the government of Edessa at this time and we have no information about the fiscal and judicial

[1] *Chr. ad 1234.* According to another account Maniaces took possession of three towers in the wall.

[2] Though Matthew of Edessa refers to them as the 'Syrians', that is, Jacobites.

[3] According to Basil bar Shumana (in Mich. Syr.), the Turks fled when Maniaces occupied the Citadel. With them went the 'Christians'— presumably the Jacobites—who were well acquainted with Arabs both in speech and

writing and who hated the Melkite Byzantines. When the city had been evacuated, a Moslem set fire to the houses and churches and abandoned the deserted city to the Byzantines.

[4] At the same time, however, Emperor Romanus Argyrus in a letter to Naṣr al-Dawla ingenuously asserted that the Byzantine forces had occupied Edessa without first obtaining the approval of Constantinople.

administration of the city. It probably became the seat of a *thema* under the rule of a *catepano* or *strategos*. But it is likely that Maniaces maintained a degree of semi-independence, since he paid annual tribute to Constantinople. He is said to have discovered at Edessa another copy of the 'letter of Jesus' to king Abgar and to have sent it to Constantinople.

Maniaces is unlikely to have remained long at Edessa. On his transfer to the command of the province of Upper Media, he was replaced by Leo Lependrenus in 1035; under Leo, however, Byzantine control of the area was in jeopardy and, in 1037, Edessa was saved by troops sent from Antioch by Constantine, brother of Emperor Michael IV. Leo's successor at Edessa was the Armenian patrician Abu-K'ab, who had previously been an officer of David the Great, King of Iberia and ally of Byzantium. This Abu-K'ab may be identified as that Barasbatzes,[1] *strategos* of Edessa, in whose time there were abortive attempts by Arabs to recover the city. We have an account of the smuggling of armed soldiers into the gates of Edessa, probably in 1038, in boxes laden on camels. They were detected by a poor Armenian who understood Arabic; he heard one of the soldiers inside a box ask where they were. The Armenian alerted the commander of the city, and the soldiers were put to death; their leaders already inside the city were killed, except one who was mutilated and sent to report to his friends the outcome of their venture. Abu-K'ab settled new inhabitants in Edessa.

The Byzantine hold on Edessa was tenuous. The region of which it was the centre was small. It extended no more than eighty kilometres to the north-east to include Severak; strong Moslem kingdoms lay to the east, Harran was less than forty kilometres to the south and Serug the same distance to the west. The direct route from Edessa to the great Byzantine base at Antioch was frequently cut by Moslem forces from Aleppo. Samosata, on the Euphrates, north-east of Edessa, provided the only safe link with Christian territory, but even the road to Samosata was threatened by Moslem bands. It was, indeed, only dissension between the petty Arab chieftains on the borders of the Moslem empires of Baghdad and Cairo that permitted the Christian enclave at Edessa to survive. Yet disunity and the fragmentation of areas of rule was not confined to the Moslem side. This period, as we shall see, witnessed the mushroom growth of Christian principalities, set up by Armenian warriors driven from their homelands in the East, and extending from the valleys of the Upper Euphrates across the Anatolian plateau. Armenians commanded Byzantine garrisons and were favoured for their courage. But they had no sense of allegiance towards the central administration of the Empire.

From Edessa the Byzantines carried out raids over the neighbouring territory of Kisas, Harran, and Serug. Their suzerainty seems to have been acknowledged by Shabib ibn Waththab, ruler of Harran, and the Byzantines

---

[1] See J. Laurent, *Byzantion* i, 1924, 393 f.

of Edessa and Shabib made a joint expedition against Naṣr al-Dawla, in 1034–5. Shabib, however, was an unreliable ally. In 1036 he seized Severak from the Byzantines and laid siege to Edessa itself, with forces also sent by Naṣr. The commander of Edessa succeeded in escaping, but as he was returning to Edessa at the head of 5,000 reinforcements, he fell into an ambush; and Shabib demanded the city as the price of his release. For the citizens, hard pressed by famine, there was no course but capitulation. The Moslems defeated a mixed force of Arabs and Byzantines under a Beduin leader that sought to come to the help of Edessa; they were unable, however, to dislodge the Byzantine garrison from the Citadel, and are said to have lost two hundred men in the attempt. Instead, they plundered the city, seized, chroniclers tell us, three thousand young men and women and sent one hundred and sixty camel-loads of heads to Amid. But without possession of the Citadel they could not hold Edessa. When the Byzantines made a diversionary feint against Harran, Shabib withdrew altogether. In 1037 a formidable threat had appeared on his eastern flank in the emergent power of the Saljuqs. Shabib prudently ceded the city of Edessa to the Byzantine garrison, which was reinforced by troops sent, as we have already observed, from Antioch by Constantine, brother of the Emperor.

The following years are a wearisome chronicle of violence. In about 1045 the Saljuqs are reported to have captured the city of Edessa (as well as Melitene and Samosata) but to have retired shortly afterwards. The *catepano* of Edessa in 1059 was John Ducetzes. Under the *dux* Tavadanos, the city militia of Edessa participated in a successful Byzantine raid on Amid. But the Saljuqs were growing in strength, and their threat to Edessa came ever closer. They invaded the district several times in 1065–6 and the following year, and defeated Byzantine armies—once through the ill will or treachery of the Governor of Edessa and his lieutenant—and carried off many prisoners. In 1067 the Byzantine commander of a nearby fortress offered battle to the Saljuqs; he was defeated, and the *strategos* of Edessa bought his freedom for 20,000 dinars—a precedent that was frequently to be followed in the next century.

Four years later, in the spring of 1071, Alp Arslan marched westwards 'like a river overflowing its banks'. Severak paid him ransom, another nearby fort capitulated. The citizens of Edessa, recovering from their initial dismay at the onset of this 'drinker of blood', defended the walls bravely, under the *dux* of Mesopotamia, the Bulgar prince Basil, who was in command in the absence of the *catepano* Paul. The Saljuqs attacked the city from the east, cutting down trees and gardens and filling in the moat on that side of the walls. After fifty (one source has thirty) days spent in battering the walls with siege towers and in tunnelling and counter-tunnelling, they failed to break through the defences. Only the shrine of St. Sergius outside the city seems to have fallen once again victim to a frustrated enemy; we need not credit the Armenian Matthew of Edessa, who writes that the Turks miraculously found themselves unable to dislodge even a fragment of the altar. Alp Arslan agreed to withdraw on payment of 50,000 dinars. When, however, he had destroyed his siege engines, the Edessans refused to honour their side of the bargain and the Sultan continued his march westwards in great indignation. Such, at any rate, is the version of local chroniclers. The true facts may have been different, for it is more probable that Edessa accepted the nominal suzerainty of the Saljuqs. Shortly afterwards Alp Arslan passed by Edessa on his return to the East; he received from its commander gifts of horses and mules and supplies, and he spared the city from attack.

In the same year Emperor Romanus Diogenes advanced in person against the Saljuqs. Alp Arslan turned to meet him, and defeated him decisively at Manzikert in August. The Emperor was released after undertaking to hand over the principal cities of Mesopotamia, in addition to large sums of money. He was, however, in no position to exercise authority, for in the meantime he had been deposed. Edessa remained in Christian hands, but its *catepano* Paul had fled to Constantinople. With the defeat of Manzikert the whole defensive organization of Byzantium in Mesopotamia collapsed; and internal discord at the capital weakened its power to recover the lost ground. Until 1078 the Court at Constantinople, it is true, maintained the fiction of rule over Edessa, but there was no reality in the claim. Local Christians felt no loyalty towards Byzantium. The Jacobites were unfriendly, or at best neutral; the Armenians were hostile to the Melkites of Byzantium, and the petty Armenian chieftains hastened to come to terms with the Turkish armies that ranged over the countryside and destroyed its crops. Constant warfare led to the depopulation of the region, and the fields were neglected. Only at Edessa was there security and plenty. Elsewhere, writes a chronicler of the year 1079–80, 'illustrious persons, nobles, chiefs and women of high condition wandered, begging their bread . . . Corpses lay without burial . . . Priests and venerable monks died . . . , dragging their wandering steps on foreign land.'

The most powerful Christian chief in the region was Philaretos Brachamios who had been a commander under Romanus Diogenes and, after Manzikert, remained in control of a broad area to the west of the Euphrates. He held the Byzantine rank of *curopalates*, and Romanus had granted him the title of Grand Domesticus (Commander-in-chief). Armenian by birth but Melkite by religion, Philaretos, 'the first born of Satan' as Matthew of Edessa calls him, was liked by neither Armenian nor Byzantine. While other Armenian principalities disappeared under the onslaught of Turkish arms, he extended his domains until they reached from Mar'ash to Melitene, including Samosata. He came to agreements with both the rival Saljuqs, Malikshah in the east and Soliman ibn Qutlumush in the west. It was as agent of Philaretos that Vasil, son of that Abu-K'ab who had himself been Governor of the city forty years earlier, invested Edessa in 1077–8. The ruler of the city at that time was Leo, brother of Tavadanos who had been *dux* of Edessa until his death at the hands of the Turks in 1062. Leo refused to surrender to Vasil. But the citizens turned against him. He fled to the Citadel, his lieutenant was murdered as he clung to the side of the altar in the Church of the Mother of God. Vasil was then admitted to the city. The son of a Georgian mother, holding the Byzantine offices of patrician and *magister*, he had had a distinguished military career and had himself been resident at Edessa. But he could maintain himself at Edessa only by holding a precarious balance between Malikshah (who succeeded Alp Arslan in 1072) and his brother Tutush and their respective protégés at Mosul and Aleppo. The territory of Edessa continued to be ravaged by war. It was invaded by an army from the East, in 1081–2, which inflicted widespread slaughter and devastation. Troops from Harran came to the rescue of Edessa; and in return for his help the ruler of Harran received from Edessa the right to mint coins.

In 1083 Vasil died, leaving behind a name as 'a good man, pious and merciful towards widows, peaceful and a benefactor of the people'. He was buried in the Church of St. George of the Baldric.[1] The citizens then assembled in the Church of Hagia Sophia; they elected as successor the Armenian Sembat. Perhaps they wished in this way to assert their independence of Philaretos, Vasil's protector—but without success. Six months later, in September 1083, the new ruler was overthrown in the name of Philaretos, 'who had many adherents among the families and persons of upper class of Edessa'. Philaretos now entered the city in person. Sembat was blinded, even the men of Philaretos who had organized the coup were tortured and imprisoned.

The position of Philaretos himself, however rapidly became untenable. Inside Edessa his cruelty soon made him obnoxious; outside he lost Samosata in 1085 to the ruler of Harran. He had acknowledged the suzerainty of Constantinople in 1078—he held, after all, dignities conferred upon him by Byzantium—but this was of little assistance, for Edessa was exposed to the cross-fire of warring Moslem generals. In 1086–7, eager to enlist support from a closer quarter, Philaretos took gifts of gold and silver, horses, mules, and costly garments to Malikshah, leaving Edessa in the hands of his son. The Sultan, however, treated Philaretos with contempt (although the latter

---

[1] So Matthew of Edessa; the phrase is explained by Dulaurier with a reference to the Armenian practice of representing St. George in paintings wearing a belt.

in an effort to ingratiate himself, is said to have apostatized to Islam), and sent his general Buzan to take possession of Edessa. Meanwhile, in the absence of Philaretos, his deputy at Edessa had been assassinated by a certain Barṣauma, 'with the knowledge and help of the chief men of Edessa',[1] as he prayed at the shrine of St. Theodore in the Citadel. Buzan laid siege to the city. The citizens, tormented by hunger and without hope of relief, now turned upon Barṣauma; he threw himself from the ramparts, broke his spine and died in Buzan's camp. In March 1087 the 'leaders and administrators' of Edessa capitulated to Buzan.

Buzan's appointment meant direct control of the city by the tolerant Sultan and the prospect of peace was received with relief by the Christians of Edessa. Buzan delegated the command of the Citadel to a Saljuq general. He also maintained the ancient practice of appointing an Administrator of the city. In the first century of Moslem rule, we have noted, Christians had been nominated to the post; later the position was held by Moslems. Buzan reverted to the earlier practice. He installed as his representative vis-à-vis the populace the Armenian, Thoros son of Hethum, who had, according to one source, acted as representative of Philaretos at Melitene and had the Byzantine rank of *curopalates*. Buzan discovered and executed the persons who had brought about the death of twelve Armenian notables of the city.[2] He also had a minaret constructed on the mosque built at the beginning of the Moslem occupation over four centuries earlier.

With the death of Malikshah in 1092 his vast empire, in which Moslems and Christians had lived in amity, fell apart. Dissension arose between the claimants to the Sultanate and fighting again broke out. In 1094 Buzan was captured in a battle against Tutush. Tutush immediately sent to Edessa demanding the surrender of the city. But Buzan had evidently made a good impression on Edessa; fifty years later we read of the 'garden of Buzan' that lay outside the eastern wall, named probably after the general.[3] At any rate, both the citizens and the garrison in the Citadel refused to yield without some sign from Buzan himself, and the messenger of Tutush was dismissed empty-handed. Thoros, the Administrator, fearing that the Saljuqs in the Citadel might admit foreign troops and gain control also of the city, quickly constructed an inner wall with twenty-five towers alongside the river to the north of the Citadel, from the river gate in the west and as far as the Church of St. Theodore. It was complete before a grisly reply arrived from Tutush, the head of Buzan conveyed by a general, Alp Yaruq.[4] The latter carried instructions to take possession of the Citadel; the city was to be given as plunder to the troops because it had disobeyed Tutush's orders. Alp Yaruq

---

[1] Matthew of Edessa.

[2] Matthew of Edessa gives the impression that it was the twelve notables of the city who were slain by Buzan; but see p. 228 below.

[3] See p. 245 below.

[4] Bar Hebraeus gives the name as Al-Fariq.

installed himself in the Citadel and his soldiers camped in the west of the city around the church of St. John the Baptist. There is a Biblical flavour about the sequel, as related by a local chronicler:

One day [Alp Yaruq] gave a banquet in the Citadel for his officers, and he brought singers from the city, among them one called Madame Gali, a Christian. When he was merry with wine . . . he swore to [his officers] that he would give order for the sack of the city. They spoke in Persian and the woman understood their words. Immediately she devised a bold scheme. She began to complain of a pain which, she said, had taken hold of her stomach. They asked her, 'What do you want us to bring you?' She replied that this pain was usual with her, and when it came upon her nothing would avail except a bath. [Alp Yaruq] gave order that she should go down to the baths.

[Gali] went down from the Citadel and went straight to Thoros son of Hethum, and informed him of the whole affair. 'Woman', he said to her, 'it seems the whole city is in your hands. See how you can save [it]!' He gave her a ring that he had, which would immediately kill if it came into contact with food or drink. She took the ring and went up to the fortress as if her pain had been eased. The guests rejoiced over her, and when they were gay she arose to dance. She took a cup of wine and danced lasciviously, and dipped the ring into the cup. After the dance [Gali] approached and held out the cup to Alp Yaruq. As soon as he had drunk it he gave a cry on account of his stomach. She said, 'My Lord, hasten to the baths. My own pain was dispersed by [my] bath.' When he went down to the baths, she took off his clothes and went in with him. He entered the inner room and immediately his life departed.

[Gali] went out and said to the eunuchs and servants at the door, 'The Commander is asleep; see that you do not disturb him'. Now all the Edessans armed themselves and went out in a great force to meet the Turks who were unprepared. When the Turks saw them they were in despair, since they were very few compared with the force of the Edessans. The Turks ran to the baths to inform the general and found him dead.[1]

The Saljuq soldiers in the city were permitted by the Edessans to leave by the West gate. Those who were in the Citadel were no less vulnerable, because they were cut off from the city by the inner wall which Thoros had built. Tutush, to whom they appealed for help, died at this very moment (February 1095). Thoros, however, agreed to buy the Citadel and to allow its garrison to depart without hindrance. Edessa, both Citadel and city, was again in the hands of Christians. We may suppose that Thoros acknowledged the authority of Byzantium; he held, as we have seen, the Byzantine title of *curopalates*.[2]

---

[1] *Chr. ad 1234.*

[2] It was perhaps in commemoration of this success of the Edessans in occupying both the city and the Citadel that the Greek inscription still to be seen on the Harran gate of Urfa was erected. In 1925 it was examined by Max von Oppenheim who reported that it contained the name of Emperor Alexius Comnenus and recorded the rescue of the city from τῆς τῶν

Τούρκων ἐπικρατείας. Today scarcely one-sixth of the text remains, and it does not include these allusions. It was studied by Dr. M. Ballance in 1956 who suggests the reading:
ε]σωθη τη Ρωμαικη εξουσια
]μα κιρωτατ[
]ναλ [. .]ν[. . .] συ [.] αιτου
αυτο]κρατορας βασιλεας
]ινου εν ετει [- - - -

Shortly afterwards, in 1095–6, the Artuqid Suqman of Serug and the ruler of Samosata, Balduq, laid siege to Edessa. They made breaches in the wall, but before they could take advantage of their success, news of the approach of rival Saljuq forces under Tutush's son, Riḍwan, ruler of Aleppo, and Alusian of Antioch caused them to flee. The newcomers invested Edessa in their turn; the city withstood their assaults or they quarrelled and abandoned the siege.[1] But the people of Edessa, harassed from all sides, were now weary of the perils to which they were constantly exposed. Their communications were cut by Turkish garrisons at Samosata, at Amid, at Harran, and at Serug; their fields were constantly ravaged, the sons of their notables were held as hostages by the Turks. They looked elsewhere for succour, and so opened the strange interlude which was to seal irrevocably the fate of Christian Edessa.

News of the arrival of the Crusader forces on the Euphrates under Count Baldwin de Bouillon had reached Edessa; Matthew of Edessa claims, indeed, that Baldwin announced his departure from Nicaea to Thoros. Warriors from the West were no novelty in this region. European mercenaries had already won a reputation as seasoned fighters, both among Byzantines and among Moslems. European units were incorporated in the Byzantine army in Mesopotamia. A force of 8,000 Franks under Raimbaud served in 1073 in the army of Philaretos. In 1063–4 a high command was held by a Norman captain, Francopoulos, in the attack on Amid by the Governor of Edessa. He had already distinguished himself under Maniaces in Sicily, and although our chronicler accuses him of treachery at Amid, he cannot conceal the great feats of valour that he performed. Two years later a company of two hundred Frankish cavalry garrisoned Severak near Edessa. At the same time there were Franks serving under their own commander in the army of Edessa, and one of them was famous for his prodigies of courage. Crusaders, in their turn, availed themselves readily of the help of their eastern co-religionists. Armenians, notably Prince Bagrat, accompanied Baldwin's army on its advance to the Euphrates. Cities with Christian populations expelled their Turkish garrisons and opened their gates to the Franks. Baldwin was in

The reference to multiple Emperors in the words . . κρατορας βασιλεας may well allude to Alexius and his son John; the latter was born in 1088, but was associated with his father on the throne in 1092. Pl. 2a.

[1] These events are related in different order by Matthew of Edessa and Arab writers. It was, according to them, Tutush who appointed Thoros as Administrator of Edessa. After the death of Tutush in February 1095 Riḍwan, his son, and his guardians, the rulers of Antioch and Aleppo, approached Edessa and caused Suqman and Balduq to abandon the siege. Riḍwan's guardians quarrelled between themselves and returned to Aleppo. An officer in the Citadel of Edessa, Mekhitar, betrayed the Turks and handed the fortress to Thoros. Meanwhile, Thoros had called for the help of Alpilek (Alp Yaruq) against the Turks; Alpilek wished to seize Edessa, but Thoros killed him by poison and expelled his troops from the city after thirty-five days. At the same time Gabriel, father-in-law of Thoros, obtained Melitene after an operation against the Turks.

touch with Bagrat's brother, Gogh Vasil, the powerful lord of fortresses in Commagene. The Edessans could not have failed to mark the nervousness aroused among the Turks by the progress of Crusader forces.

Whether the initiative then taken by the Edessans was at the prompting of Thoros son of Hethum is uncertain. One account, which may well be a later invention, maintains that he realized that the Edessans would send for the Crusaders, whatever his own view might be, and that he therefore co-operated against his will. However this may be, a deputation of notables of the city under the leadership of the bishop (probably the Bishop of the Armenian community) waited upon Baldwin at Tell Bashir and invited him to Edessa. Their proposal was accepted with alacrity. Edessa 'at that time was a very prosperous city, filled with voices of many peoples; it was renowned for its clergy, and worshippers and large population. Its territory was prosperous with villages, estates and hamlets'.[1] It was a happy omen, the Crusaders felt, that 'just as Edessa believed in Christ before Jerusalem, so [Edessa] had been given [to them] by Christ the Saviour before Jerusalem'.[2] Tactical considerations reinforced their religious zeal. Possession of the great fortress would protect the left flank of the Crusader advance. Towards the end of February 1098 with eighty knights and their retainers[3] Baldwin accomplished the journey to Edessa across hostile country, for a large force of Turkish cavalry from Samosata sought to intercept him and he was forced to lie low for two days behind the walls of an Armenian fortress. Western chroniclers record with interest the ceremony by which, on arrival at Edessa, he was adopted as heir and co-ruler of the childless Armenian. He was introduced with naked breast under Thoros's tunic and embraced by the prince; the ritual was repeated with Thoros's wife.

Edessa had summoned the Crusaders as hired mercenaries to rescue their eastern co-religionists from the Moslem yoke; it was quickly to discover that it had exchanged one master for another. The city, it is true, assumed its former prominence as a bastion of Christendom. But its new rulers were foreigners out of sympathy with the traditions and the way of life of the region. Edessa was set upon a dangerous course.

Baldwin insisted on a share in the actual government of the city, which Thoros ruled through a Council of twelve. What followed is obscure. Not more than fifteen days after Baldwin's arrival a plot was hatched against Thoros son of Hethum and disorder broke out in the city probably on Sunday 7 March. According to Western sources Thoros was fearful of the populace whom he had oppressed and who had acclaimed the Crusaders. He offered to buy off his enemies with his treasure; his offer was spurned. He then sought to flee by lowering himself from the window of a tower, and

[1] *Chr. ad 1234.*   [2] Mich. Syr.
[3] According to another account, sixty; a third account has two hundred.

was slain by his enemies, to the 'great distress' of the Crusaders.[1] The view of the Armenian historian, Matthew of Edessa, is significantly different; and it is the more plausible when we consider that Baldwin had everything to gain from Thoros's downfall, and when we consider, too, the Frankish Count's subsequent conduct. Baldwin, with a small detachment of Crusaders and a large force of the city militia had attacked Samosata a few days after his arrival at Edessa. He had been beaten off and withdrew after leaving a garrison at a nearby fort. He was, Matthew maintains, eager to divert the blame for his failure. He was privy to the conspiracy against Thoros; a leading part in it was taken by Constantine, the Armenian prince of Gargar. It is suggested that Thoros had been hostile to some nobles of Edessa, others assert that he was hated for his avarice and his extortions. The mob were incited to fall upon the houses of the leading adherents of Thoros and to seize the outer wall of the fortress in which he lived. On the following day Thoros, reduced to extremities, offered to hand over the city in return for a safe conduct for his wife and himself, permitting them to withdraw to Melitene. Baldwin swore solemn oaths on the sacred relics of Varag and Mak'enis[2] in the Church of the Holy Apostles that no harm would befall them, and then with the city notables took possession of the Citadel. But on the Tuesday the populace, armed with swords and sticks, threw themselves upon Thoros in the lower fortress over the East gate, which he himself had fortified and where he had fled for refuge. They cast him, clad only in a loin-cloth, from the walls; they slew him with fearful torments, dragged his body through the streets and set his head upon a pole outside the Church of the Saviour. This version is confirmed by a Syriac chronicle, not usually well-disposed towards the Armenian community. The Edessans, it declares, 'raved like wild beasts, incited and egged one another on, gathered in a great crowd and raised a tumult . . . , not from love of the Franks but from the malice of those who hated Thoros.'[3]

Thoros had been the representative of the wealthy and aristocratic order, who at this period were evidently most of them Armenian. Behind them stood the Council of twelve members, the descendant of the council of the Aryu dynasty and the city Council of Byzantine times. They had maintained their prestige and standing under Moslem rule. Caliph Manṣur issued instructions for the destruction of the city walls to the 'elders and leaders of the place'; and the walls were rebuilt by money collected from the same source. Bishop Zacharias was expelled in 785–6 at the instance of the 'chiefs in alliance with the clergy'. Antagonism between the citizen body and the aristocracy had grown in the decades preceding the arrival of Baldwin. At this time of constant warfare, great power lay in the hands of the citizen body from whom the militia of Edessa was drawn, and who went armed in helmet and cuirass

---

[1] Fulcher of Chartres.   [2] See p. 239 below.   [3] *Chr. ad 1234.*

when occasion arose. It was they who elected their leader; this pattern of organization was the same at other cities in this area with which the Crusaders came into contact. The entry into Edessa of Vasil, son of Abu-K'ab, 'benefactor of the people', was evidently brought about by the populace, who overthrew with violence the government of the city. It was they who elected Vasil's successor Sembat in 1083. Shortly afterwards it was the turn of the 'persons of the upper class' to replace Sembat by Philaretos. Barṣauma also had the support of the 'chief men of Edessa' in his conspiracy against Philaretos. When, in consequence, Edessa was besieged by Buzan it was the populace who forced their rulers to surrender the city, and killed the twelve Councillors; the ringleaders were later executed by Buzan.

In their campaign to reduce the power of the Council, the people of Edessa found a ready ally in Baldwin. First Baldwin assured his lines of supply by the purchase of Samosata for 10,000 pieces of gold, for he had come into possession of the treasure amassed by Thoros. At Samosata he found prisoners from Edessa, and his stock in the city rose when the released captives returned home. The former ruler of Samosata, Balduq, and his troops were invited to take service in the employ of the Count. Baldwin then captured Serug which was largely Moslem, slew its fickle Artuqid master and left there a Frankish garrison. With the occupation of Birtha on the Euphrates, the road to Tell Bashir and Antioch was now open. Baldwin withstood a siege of Edessa by the Turks; after three, or according to another version, six, weeks the enemy turned to mount an attack on the Franks at Antioch itself. By this time the notables of Edessa had come to regret their invitation to Baldwin to come to the city. True, he had married the daughter of an Armenian prince who brought him a dowry of 60,000 bezants. But the local burghers found that the Franks grew in number and 'prospered', acquiring estates in the region. The Franks supplanted the members of the city Council in their influence on the conduct of affairs and interfered in the administration.

The aristocrats of Edessa conspired to kill or expel Baldwin. But he learned of the plot. On Christmas Day Baldwin went to church as though nothing was afoot but surrounded on every side by armed soldiers. On the next day he summoned the leading citizens and upbraided them for their treachery. They confessed; the leaders were arrested. They tried to purchase their freedom, but now Baldwin's appetite had been whetted by rumours of hidden treasure. He consented to receive some gifts, then he ordered the donors to be blinded or mutilated in other ways and driven out of the city. Other Edessans, less directly implicated in the plot, were thrown into prison.[1] Baldwin had now acquired great wealth in money, vessels and ornaments of gold and silver, horses and mules, 'From that day', comments a chronicler

[1] Guibert, Abbot of Nogent.

ingenuously, 'he was feared at Edessa and his name was known to the ends of the earth.'[1] Even his Armenian father-in-law, we are told, fled in panic from Edessa to the mountains, taking with him the bulk of his daughter's dowry. Providence, it is true, reminded the simple townsfolk of their misdeeds. In 1099 there were drought and famine at Edessa, and this was looked upon as divine retribution for their slaughter of Thoros despite their solemn pledge of loyalty. But abundance returned in the next year. Baldwin's position at Edessa was unchallenged.

On Christmas Day 1100, Baldwin succeeded his brother Godfrey as king of Jerusalem. Matthew of Edessa, who had no love for Baldwin de Bouillon, declares darkly that he had bought the crown of Jerusalem with the 'enormous sums' which he had extorted from the inhabitants of Edessa. The County of Edessa now became a fief of the kingdom of Jerusalem; its ruler in common with the ruler of Antioch shared the right of the king of Jerusalem to strike coins. The prince of Antioch, it is true, also regarded the ruler of Edessa as his vassal; and the Comneni emperors still continued, hopefully, to insist on treating both Antioch and Edessa as subject to Constantinople, by virtue of the oath of allegiance which the Franks had sworn to them at the outset of the Crusade.[2] But it was the King of Jerusalem who, after a brief visit to Edessa, bestowed the County on his kinsman and namesake, Baldwin du Bourg. The second Crusader ruler of Edessa married the daughter of Gabriel, prince of Melitene, an Armenian of Melkite persuasion. Baldwin appeared to follow a pro-Armenian policy even more pronounced than that of his predecessor, and Gabriel supported him with his great wealth. Of Baldwin du Bourg his contemporary Matthew of Edessa writes:

[he was] one of the most illustrious Franks in rank, a valorous warrior, of exemplary purity of habits, enemy of sin and full of gentleness and modesty. But these qualities were tarnished by [the] ingenious cunning [which he employed] to seize the riches of others and to accumulate them, through an insatiable love of gold and lack of generosity. For the rest he was very orthodox in his faith and very firm in his conduct and character.

Between the Edessans and the warrior Crusaders there was now little sympathy. The former complained, according to Matthew, that the Frankish princes 'had nothing in their mind but ill will and fraud; they loved all evil works, with no thought of doing good or performing a noble action'. This is, no doubt, an exaggerated judgement. But the code of chivalry of the Crusader nobles certainly had more in common with that of the Moslem generals than with the way of life of their native fellow-Christians. There is some justification for Matthew's comment that Baldwin du Bourg 'had more hatred for Christians than for the Turks'.

---

[1] Albert of Aix.
[2] In 1108 Bohemund of Antioch formally acknowledged Emperor Alexius Comnenus as his liege lord, and was confirmed by the Emperor in his title to (among other lands) the territory of Edessa.

The first care of the new ruler of Edessa, as it had been of Baldwin de Bouillon, was to secure Serug and safeguard his supply-route. This city was 'prosperous and rich, with many Moslems and Christians and all sorts of famous merchants; the valley also was rich, prosperous, and resounding with hamlets.'[1] Shortly afterwards the town of Serug was recaptured by the Turk Suqman, with the complicity of its Numairid population. The citadel remained, however, in the hands of its Christian garrison under the command of Benedict, the Latin Archbishop of Edessa, who happened to be there at the time. Baldwin brought troops from Antioch, and the Moslems were expelled from the city in January–February 1101. So great was the carnage that 'the prosperous city was destroyed; the Christians who remained gathered around the citadel and lived there in misery'.[1]

Two years later Edessa had a serious flood:

> The air, violently agitated, was condensed in the atmosphere; noises were heard, accompanied by the crashing of thunder, and the whole surface of the sky was over-thrown with a terrible tumult. Some thought it was the end of the city. . . . From dawn there fell torrents of rain mingled with hail. At sunrise the waters opened an exit on the western side and spread through the whole area from one end to the other. They were precipitated against the ramparts, and half-opening [a path], they invaded the whole city. Part of it was destroyed; a great many houses collapsed and many animals perished. But no-one lost his life in this disaster, although it was so sudden and unexpected, because it occurred by day and everyone was able to escape.[2]

Fighting continued. In 1101 or 1102, Baldwin entrusted his lands west of the Euphrates into the charge of his kinsman Joscelyn de Courtenay, with his base at Tell Bashir. Joscelyn attacked Turkish communications between Aleppo and the Euphrates, while Baldwin made successful raids in the direction of Mardin and Raqqa and even as far as Mar'ash. The Turkish leaders were at loggerheads with each other, and the time seemed propitious for a Crusader drive to remove the threat to Edessa from Harran and to extend the territory under Frankish control. Forces sent from Antioch by Bohemund and Tancred congregated ostentatiously at Edessa, local chroniclers relate, in 1104 to co-ordinate the campaign with the forces of Baldwin and Joscelyn. But the jealousy and fractiousness among the Crusaders were no less un-bridled than among the Turks; days were lost in wrangling over the division of spoils that had not yet been won—the wealthy cities and lands to the North and East and even beyond the Tigris.

Eventually the Crusaders, 3,000 knights and 7,000 foot, laid siege to Har-ran. The river Gullab, some twenty kilometres from Harran and eleven from Edessa, had been 'from ancient times' the boundary between the territory of Edessa and that of Harran; its channels irrigated the plains on both sides. While, however, the fields of Edessa were fertile and provided

---

[1] *Chr. ad 1234.*   [2] Matthew of Edessa.

food in plenty, those of the Harranians had been devastated by Crusader raids, and their city had no other source of supplies.[1] Reduced to extremities of hunger, the Moslems of Harran brought out the keys of the city in token of unconditional surrender. Baldwin, however, who would have become lord of Harran because of its proximity to Edessa, feared the effect on the discipline of his troops if so rich a prize were to fall into their hands at the opening of the campaign. He therefore refused to occupy the city, to the anger of the formidable Tancred of Antioch. Meanwhile, the Turkish armies had rallied. At the river Balikh they gave battle on 7 May. A hail of arrows from their bowmen, followed by a charge by the swordsmen, decimated the van of the Crusader army from Edessa, and threw the remainder into retreat. (According to another version, the Edessan forces pursued the Turks across the river, only to fall into an ambush.) Baldwin and Joscelyn de Courtenay were taken prisoner; Benedict, the Latin Archbishop of Edessa, was captured but later made good his escape. The fugitives were massacred by the Harranians. The Crusader contingents from Antioch had been more successful against the Turks, and were able to extricate themselves. Now Harran returned to Turkish control. Fortunately for Edessa, discord between the Turkish commanders, Suqman and Jekermish, gave it a brief respite. But soon it was invested by Jekermish, with, we are told, troops occupying thousands of tents. Tancred, who had retired to the city after the defeat on the Balikh, encouraged the few troops who had remained there and, with the help of the loyal citizens, beat off the Turkish attack by a sudden night sortie. Jekermish withdrew a fortnight later, Edessa was saved; but it had been near to falling into the hands of the enemy, so tenuous was the hold of the Crusaders on the town.

The County of Edessa was entrusted to Tancred until Baldwin should be released. Tancred, however, was recalled to Antioch whose prince, Bohemund, was on a visit to Europe, and rule at Edessa was delegated to Richard, a kinsman of Bohemund. This man is described by a contemporary chronicler as

a bad, tyrannical, unjust and greedy man. The worthless people of Edessa found for themselves an opportunity that suited their wickedness; they began to traduce each other. . . . [Richard] began to inflict on the Edessans cruel tortures, imprisonment, and disgrace. He collected much money, especially as he knew that he was a sojourner and a passer-by, not the true lord and heir.[2]

Cultivation of vineyards and orchards was neglected, churches deserted. Significantly, the temporary rulers of Edessa made no effort to obtain the release of Baldwin, though the seizure of a Moslem princess at this time presented the occasion for an admirable exchange. The occupation of the

[1] William of Tyre.   [2] *Chr. ad 1234.*

city—its revenue in taxes and tolls amounted to 40,000 bezants a year—was too profitable.

It was perhaps during Richard's tenure at Edessa, in 1105 or 1106, that the city was again besieged by Jekermish. It is related that Edessan troops sallied out of the East gate into the plain. The Turks, feigning to retreat, drew the Christians forward; then they turned and drove them towards the walls. But meanwhile the citizens had closed the gate. The Franks 'could not reach the bridge over the moat to cross between the walls'. Some 450 soldiers were killed, and 'in a moment the moat was filled with the dead, blood ran like a river flowing down the moat'. Satisfied with this victory, the Turks withdrew. For the rest, the four years which followed Baldwin's capture were largely uneventful. In 1105-6, the western side of the Church of Hagia Sophia collapsed and a great part of the building was ruined. Raids of Turkish soldiers, who killed the labourers in the fields, led to a scarcity of food in the city, until Tancred broke the blockade with supplies from the West.

Both Baldwin and Joscelyn obtained their freedom in 1108. But Tancred was reluctant to hand over the County of Edessa, unless Baldwin swore allegiance to him. Baldwin returned in dudgeon to Tell Bashir and was joined there by Joscelyn. Smarting with anger against Tancred, Baldwin engaged him in battle, with indecisive results. He then sought the help of his former Turkish captor against Tancred. The latter also found allies among the Turks, and there ensued the unedifying spectacle of Crusader fighting Crusader for the control of the County, each with the aid of Moslems. Baldwin had reoccupied the city (through the good offices of the Patriarch of Antioch, Bernard), only to leave it shortly afterwards to meet Tancred's forces near Tell Bashir. The accounts of the battle are confused. Baldwin's Turkish allies seem to have been more attracted by the fine thorough-breds in his camp than by the justice of his cause, and although they were on the point of victory, they mounted the horses and disappeared. The outcome was a victory for Tancred.

News of Baldwin's defeat came to the people of Edessa:

They held an assembly in the Church of St. John, where was the Frankish Archbishop of the city, to decide on the action they should take; for they feared that the city might again fall into the hands of Tancred who would probably hand it back to Richard. At this assembly the inhabitants violently blamed the Archbishop. 'Let your men', they added, 'and ours guard the Citadel until we know who is the master who will govern us.' But on the next day Baldwin and Joscelyn arrived and made their entry into Edessa. They inquired into the speech which had been made at the meeting. They considered [it] very dangerous, and interpreted it in a wholly criminal way. They had the houses of a great number of inhabitants looted, and put out the eyes of people who were in no way guilty. They inflicted . . . cruel tortures on the Christians, for the Franks readily lent an ear to the most calumnious denunciations and took pleasure in shedding innocent blood.

They pushed cruelty to such an excess that they wanted to tear out the eyes of Stephen, the Armenian Archbishop. The inhabitants, knowing that there was nothing for which he could be reproached, ransomed him.[1]

It can have been little comfort to the Edessans to learn shortly afterwards that Baldwin and Tancred were reconciled through the intervention of Baldwin of Jerusalem and that there was 'great and perfect amity between them'.[2] Baldwin remained at Edessa; Richard had already carried off to his own city of Mar'ash the booty he had extorted during his brief rule in the County.

In 1110 a new and more serious threat appeared; a great army under a united group of Turkish commanders, including the able Mawdud, Governor of Mosul, who came, insinuates Matthew of Edessa, at the invitation of Baldwin; other sources allege that Tancred had summoned him. The Turks encamped near the fort of Kisas to the east of Edessa. They did not lay siege to the city, but contented themselves with the destruction of the crops and monasteries. After much delay, a relief army arrived under Baldwin of Jerusalem and Tancred. The Frankish force on this occasion is said to have numbered well over 25,000 and to have been the largest ever assembled. Mawdud withdrew southwards to the Gullab. The Crusaders, however, began to suffer from scarcity of food, for not only had the crops been destroyed by the Turks, but the population of Edessa had been swollen by an influx of refugees from the villages. Their generals, 'having no patience, as is the bad habit of the Franks',[2] decided to return westwards, Tancred towards Samosata, King Baldwin to meet an Egyptian threat to Jerusalem. The garrison at Edessa was to be reinforced, the rural population to be evacuated. But a treacherous Frank divulged the plan to the enemy. The retreating army reached the Euphrates, 'faint from hunger and weakened by the fatigues of the journey'.[2] When the fighting men had crossed the river, the Turks fell upon the foot soldiers and baggage attendants, most of them Edessans, who remained on the eastern bank. They were cut down or drowned or carried into captivity. Mawdud returned to his own country with the booty.

In the spring of 1112, Mawdud besieged Edessa. Again he devastated the countryside; the harvest was ruined, and the city was in great distress. 'Some traitors', according to Matthew of Edessa (a Syriac chronicle calls them more precisely 'some twenty Armenians'[2]) conspired to hand over a tower in the east of Edessa to the enemy. A number of picked Turkish soldiers came on foot through the orchards on a Sunday dawn to an agreed point near the wall inside the lower bridge over the moat. Here was a wide corner with room for movement and a great tower dominating the city,

---

[1] Matthew of Edessa.   [2] *Chr. ad 1234.*

perhaps the tower from which Thoros son of Hethum met his death; it was guarded by a well-known notable named Cyrus. The traitors let down ropes and pulled up silken ladders which they then attached to the wall. Turkish troops climbed the tower and killed the guards, Cyrus being silent from fear, while others created a diversion by shouting, beating drums, and blowing trumpets to the west of the city. At daybreak some sixty Turks had established themselves on the tower; the Franks and the chief citizens were panic-stricken. But by good fortune Joscelyn de Courtenay happened to be at Edessa. He ran to the tower through a shower of arrows and stones, entered, thrust his sword through a window and cut the ladder by which the enemy were ascending, and they fell to their death. He mounted to the roof of the tower. His shield was broken into fragments by arrows and stones; seizing a sack filled with straw to protect his helmet, he charged upon the Turks. Thirty he cut down with his sword, the rest leapt from the tower, breaking their limbs in their fall. Joscelyn's courage had foiled the plot; Mawdud retired. But at Edessa the treachery was followed by swift retribution. Citizens, innocent as well as guilty, were arrested by the Franks, some put to death, others mutilated. 'This unjust severity', declares Matthew of Edessa, 'was odious in the eyes of the Lord.'

Mutual suspicion continued to poison the relations between the people of Edessa and their ruler. The Crusaders had crushed the aristocratic families; now it was the turn of the populace. In 1113, Mawdud was at Harran. Baldwin, at Tell Bashir, was informed by 'pernicious Franks'[1] that some Edessans intended to surrender their city to the Turks. Orders were given by the Count to expel all the inhabitants[2] and settle them at Samosata, and to burn in their houses those who presumed to remain at Edessa in defiance of the command. All departed but twenty-four,[3] who had taken refuge in the Church of St. Theodore and were transferred to the Citadel under military guard. The city was deserted, 'like a widow who before had been the mother of all. . . . In return for the benefits which Edessa had showered upon them, [the Franks] heaped most shameful treatment upon her'.[4] Only when Mawdud left Harran did Baldwin revoke his decree, and 'at the end of three days each [of the Edessans] saw his hearth again'.[5] But it was not only the Edessans who suffered from Baldwin's evil temper. In this year there was famine at Edessa. Baldwin, in residence there at the time, heard that Joscelyn at Tell Bashir had food in plenty, and summoned him to Edessa. He found Baldwin in the Citadel[6] in his inner bedchamber; the Count flung him into a dungeon, deprived him of food, and finally stripped him of his lands and wealth and

---

[1] Matthew of Edessa.

[2] Perhaps here we should understand (with Grousset, *Histoire des Croisades* i, 490) the Armenian inhabitants.

[3] Another account has eighty.

[4] Matthew of Edessa. [5] Ibid.

[6] The text has, 'the quarter called Rangulath'; this is a rendering of the Arabic *al-qal'a*, the Citadel, or *'ain al-qal'a*, the Citadel fountain.

banished him from the territory of Edessa. Joscelyn went to Palestine, and there the king of Jerusalem gave him a command in Galilee.

Shortly afterwards, in October 1113, Mawdud was assassinated. Edessa, however, was again besieged in 1114, by al-Barsuqi, and for one month, or possibly two months, gardens and crops outside the city were systematically destroyed. The Franks defended the place with courage. Moslems who had been captured in ambush were impaled on the ramparts; the Turks apparently retaliated by slaying fifty Christian officers. Lack of provisions forced the Turks to withdraw. In the next year the Edessan countryside was laid waste once more, but this time the Franks engaged the enemy and won a decisive victory. Edessa had its domestic troubles also. In November 1114 a violent earthquake caused much damage in the neighbouring cities; at Edessa thirteen towers of the wall collapsed. A flood demolished the dam, which by now was attributed to the Apostle Addai, in the following year. There must nevertheless have been a shortage of water in the city, for at this period a certain Bar Ḥalabi caused a spring of water to be conveyed to Edessa.[1]

Baldwin du Bourg went to spend Easter at Jerusalem in 1118. During the previous three years he had reduced to submission the petty Armenian lords of the surrounding districts, often with the approval of the Jacobite populace. The latter, whose monks had been supplanted in their monasteries by Armenians, saw in this an occasion for satisfaction. Baldwin now felt so secure that he did not appoint a successor to himself at Edessa; he left as his deputy there Waleran, lord of Birtha, 'an excellent young man'. Baldwin, however, was not to return to the County. While he was in the West his namesake, King Baldwin of Jerusalem, died, and in April 1118 he was consecrated in his place.

In the absence of Baldwin, Waleran was emboldened to attack Turkoman camps east of Edessa in March 1119; he killed many soldiers, took prisoners and carried off to Edessa large numbers of horses and cattle. Seizing upon the pretext offered by this act of aggression, Ilghazi, the Artuqid ruler of Mardin, came with his army at harvest time, 'near to Edessa but at some distance from the fields and crops of the city'.[2] Waleran's courage was not equal to this challenge; he quickly proposed terms of peace, the Turkish prisoners were released, and after only three or four days, Ilghazi pursued his march westwards. To the relief of the Edessans, Waleran did not continue in command of the city for Baldwin appointed Joscelyn de Courtenay as his successor in the County. With the passing of time Joscelyn's temper had mellowed; he returned, writes Matthew, with 'feelings of kindness and humanity towards the inhabitants of Edessa, and abjured the feelings of cruelty which he had shown previously'. His fame throughout North Mesopotamia was at its

---

[1] That is, the Aleppine; the name should perhaps be Barṣauma bar Shalabi; p. 240 below.
[2] *Chr. ad 1234.*

height. Although Ilghazi ravaged the region of Edessa in May 1120, again he did not dare to attack the city itself. The fortifications of the city were strengthened.[1]

In September 1122, however, Joscelyn and Waleran with a small retinue fell into the hands of Balak, nephew of Ilghazi. The news of Joscelyn's capture reached Edessa on the eve of the Feast of the Cross; that year, we are told, there was no procession, instead, everyone lamented. Seven months later King Baldwin, after reinforcing the garrison at Edessa and leaving Geoffrey, lord of Mar'ash, in command, was himself captured by Balak. But, in August 1123, twenty (another text has fifty) Armenians from Edessa,[2] disguised as poor villagers, broke into Kharput where Joscelyn was confined, snatched some swords hanging by the gates, slew the guards and released the Count from confinement. Joscelyn managed, after remarkable adventures, to reach Tell Bashir, but his brave rescuers were caught and slain. Thereafter he spent little time at Edessa. Towards the end of 1131, Joscelyn, now an old man, was wounded in an attempt to destroy a castle near Mabbog that was in the hands of freebooters. He died of wounds received in an earlier campaign, in the same year as his patron, King Baldwin. We are told that the Turkish commander, hearing of Joscelyn's death:

showed magnanimity. He halted the fighting, sent his condolences and wrote to the Franks, 'I shall not engage you in combat today lest anyone say that I have triumphed over your army through the death of your king. Arrange your affairs, then, in tranquillity, choose a leader according to your customs, and govern your land in peace, for you have nothing to fear on my part or that of my troops.[3]

Joscelyn's son and namesake succeeded to the County of Edessa; thick-set, with dark hair and complexion, prominent nose and bright eyes, he was Armenian on his mother's side. 'A youth void of understanding', he is called by Matthew of Edessa, and events were to prove the shrewdness of the historian's judgement. The desultory fighting was continued with varying outcome, but now, significantly, it was invariably in the close neighbourhood

---

[1] Evidence is to be found in an Armenian inscription on a tower at the Bey kapısı in the east wall of Urfa. It reads; 'In the 571st year of the Greater Armenian era (beginning 19 February 1122) in the days of the pious, excellent, and valorous soldier of Christ, the great Count Joscelyn, and in the administration (epistasia) of the God-loving prince Vasil who held the locum-tenancy of the duchy of this great city of Edessa, this fortified stronghold was completed with great industry and at great expense (lit., with greatly industrious expenditure), wherefore may God likewise keep its builders victorious and unshaken, and at His [second] coming may He crown them with glory. Amen.' I owe this translation to the kind-

ness of Professor C. J. Dowsett. See his article, 'A twelfth-century Armenian inscription at Edessa', in In Memoriam Vladimir Minorsky, 1970, and the photograph of the round tower at the Bey Gate shown at Pl. 5b. The three stones on which the inscription is engraved are larger than the neighbouring stones of the tower and there has also been some recent reconstruction of this building; nevertheless, it is not unreasonable to assume that the fort restored by the Administrator Vasil in 1122-3 is the tower in which his inscription still stands.

[2] Another version has it that they were from Hanzit, and were disguised as merchants.

[3] Mich. Syr.

of Edessa itself. The Artuqid Timurtash made frequent raids into Edessan territory, pillaging villages and farms. On one occasion, it is reported, 600 Franks killed 1,000 Turks, and burned their commander at the gate of Edessa. In 1135 a Turkish army was apparently beaten off outside the city. Three years later Edessa was again besieged. A great company of Franks, 300 horse and 4,000 foot, set out from Samosata to raise the blockade; they escorted supplies of corn, wine, and other necessities, as well as reinforcements in men and pack-animals. When they had advanced a few miles they were suddenly attacked by the army of Timurtash. Most of the Franks were killed. The rest, with great booty of horses and mules, were paraded in rows, bound with ropes, below the walls of Edessa. 'Fools', proclaimed the Turkish commander, 'why are you confident? Deliver the town to me, and I shall free these prisoners . . .'[1] But the Edessans trusted in the strength of their walls; the Turks had no siege engines, and after capturing the important fort of Kisas east of Edessa they withdrew. The Turks, as we shall see, were soon to profit by this lesson in tactics.

While the Crusaders were masters of Edessa there were four principal groups of Christians in the city. A Latin Archbishop of Edessa, for whom the Syriac chronicles use the title 'Papias', was consecrated by Dagobert at Jerusalem at the end of 1099, a year before the installation of a Latin Patriarch at Antioch, with authority over the eastern archbishoprics. The first occupant of the Latin see of Edessa was Benedict (Benoît, Syriac Berikha). He was a warlike priest; he briefly took command of the garrison at Serug, as we have seen, and narrowly escaped capture at the hands of the Turks at the battle of the Balikh in 1104. A later Archbishop of Edessa was Hugo; he already held the office in 1122, and was killed in 1144. Whether he had a successor is not known. The cathedral church of the Latin community was the Church of St. John the Baptist. Here the remains of Addai (Thaddaeus) and Abgar, both transferred by, probably, the end of the fifth century,[2] rested in a silver coffin, as we learn from an interesting description of the church in 1145.[3] Beside it stood a monastery. The Latins worshipped also in the Church of St. Stephen in the middle of the city and in the Church of St. Thomas, probably also in a Church of the Virgin Mary.

With Edessa under the rule of the Franks, the head of the Latin confession in the city had, for political reasons, influence out of all proportion to the

[1] *Chr. ad 1234.*

[2] See p. 174 above. According to Mich. Syr., Archbishop Benedict had a vision about the relics of Addai and Abgar. They were then discovered in the Church of St. John in a *sqm'*. The Syriac word *sqm'*, in both the Syriac and Arabic versions, is no doubt a copyist's error, possibly for *smq'*, red (the

Church of St. John the Baptist was celebrated for its red pillars), or for *glwsqm' smq'*, red tomb (like that which was later erected for Archbishop Hugo, p. 249 below). The story of the vision may have been a pretext for the appropriation of this church by the Latins as their cathedral.

[3] See p. 249 below.

size of his flock. He was warrior and spokesman of the citizens as well as churchman, and among the religious groups in the city he naturally assumed leadership. With matters of dogma he appears to have had little concern. But when negotiations with an enemy were to be opened it was the Latin Archbishop who took the initiative. When Baldwin was defeated by Tancred in 1108, it was evidently the Latin Archbishop who convened the citizens, and in 1144 the Jacobite Metropolitan Basil submitted his truce proposals to Zangi through his Latin colleague.

The Melkites were in a difficult position in those areas under Crusader control where the political influence of Constantinople had suffered complete eclipse. The Franks insisted that the Greeks were subject to the authority of the Latin Church; and at Antioch, for example, the ascendancy of the Latin Patriarch was scarcely challenged by the Melkites. Nor did the Melkites fare better with the two Monophysite groups, the Armenians and the Jacobites, who were nominally independent of the Latins; for they had not abandoned their traditional distrust and hatred of the Greek Church. There was no Melkite bishop at Edessa. But the community, though small in numbers, continued in existence. Their cathedral church was the famous Church of Hagia Sophia; among their members was ʿAbd al-Masiḥ, a philosopher well known in his time. A Melkite inscription has survived in the neighbourhood of Edessa; dated probably 1118–19, it is written in the Serṭa script employed in the regions under Byzantine rule.[1]

Among the Armenian community were counted some of the wealthiest citizens of Edessa. Their prestige had been especially high because several rulers of Edessa and of other cities in the region were Armenians, though some of them, it is true, were Armenian by race only but by religion adherents of the Greek, not the Armenian, Church.[2] With the fall of Thoros son of Hethum in 1098 and the gradual elimination by Baldwin du Bourg of the Armenian princes of the neighbouring principalities, the prominence of the community, whether as a confessional or an ethnic unit, declined. The Armenians of Edessa acted as individuals rather than as a group, and they were sharply divided in their loyalties. Some had, it was alleged, conspired to admit the Turks into the city in 1112; on the other hand, it was, according to one account, Armenians from Edessa who rescued Count Joscelyn from prison in 1123, and the Count's son, Joscelyn the Younger, was Armenian on his mother's side. The Armenian Catholicus, on a visit to Edessa in 1103, was received by Baldwin du Bourg with extravagant honour and lavish gifts. On the whole, indeed, the Latin princes showed partiality for rich Armenian

[1] The inscription may be reconstructed to read; 'This is the grave of the body of Constantine [in the yea]r 1400 and thirty; let who [ever] reads [this, ask p]ardon [for] his sou[l].'

[2] Philaretos, Thoros son of Hethum, Vasak at Antioch, Gabriel at Melitene, Bagrat of Tell Bashir and his powerful brother Gogh Vasil, Constantine of Gargar—to mention only the most notable.

chieftains. But this did not save the latter when political expediency was involved; ultimately the goodwill of the Franks brought upon the Armenian leaders, as Matthew of Edessa oddly puts it, 'terrible chastisement . . . on the part of the Turks and their brothers, the Byzantines'.

Edessa was the seat of an Armenian Archbishop. His cathedral is called by one writer the Church of St. Euphemia—this may well be in error for St. Ephraim. An Armenian church stood near the tomb of St. Ephraim outside the walls of Urfa until recent times.[1] Another Armenian church was the Church of the Holy Apostles. The Armenian Patriarch Basil spent a year at Edessa, after receiving his diploma from Malikshah in 1090-1. In the following year the 'sacred cross of Varag and the image of the Holy Mother of God'[2] were brought to Edessa by Paul, who had been created Metropolitan of Mar'ash through the influence of Philaretos. It was at the Church of the Holy Apostles that they were kept; their transfer to Edessa may have been prompted by a sense of rivalry with the other sect of Monophysites, the Jacobites, who now, it will be recalled, claimed to be in possession of the portrait of Jesus.[3] Paul survived only one year at Edessa, and he was interred with great pomp beside the tomb of the 'Doctor', Jacob K'arap'netzi of Sanahin, 'at the gate of the holy Church [of the twelve Apostles] to the north of the city, a bowshot from the ramparts'. It was on the cross of Varag that Baldwin de Bouillon took an oath to spare the life of Thoros son of Hethum, and, perhaps significantly, only a few years passed before the cross was 'purloined by sacrilegious hands'.

It is, however, of the other Monophysite community, the Jacobites, that we hear most at this period; contemporary chroniclers, belonging to that sect, describe their affairs in great detail. A Jacobite, Michael bar Shumana, held the responsible position of Administrator of the city under Count Joscelyn the Elder. But it was the humbler citizens who belonged to this sect, and sheer numbers made it by far the most important denomination in the city and its neighbourhood.

The Jacobites were probably in possession of several churches under Crusader rule, principally the Church of St. Theodore, used as their cathedral church, and the Church of the Mother of God. Local historians complain of a decline in devoutness in the Jacobite community. Towards the end of the eleventh century Edessa was visited by the Jacobite Patriarch. But his followers there did not come to pay their respects; they did not even contribute to the cost of his maintenance at Edessa with his large retinue. Unlike

---

[1] There was a 'lower monastry' of St. Ephraim in the late twelfth century.

[2] Legend relates that the cross of Varag, ten kilometres south-east of Van, appeared to a hermit in the middle of the seventh century. Mak'enis, where the celebrated monastery of the Holy Mother of God of Gegham was situated, is near Lake Sevan.

[3] See p. 214 above. It has been suggested, p. 216 above, that it was the portrait of the Melkites that was transferred to Constantinople in 944.

their fathers, laments a chronicler, who had 'lavished reverence and the desire to show honour and submission to their pastors', the Edessans of this time were, 'on the contrary, devoid of these [feelings] altogether. The Patriarch left Edessa grieved, and with resentment towards them in his mind.'[1]

The Jacobite Metropolitan of Edessa, Athanasius, better known by his baptismal name of Barṣauma, was now an old man and wearied by the 'worthless' Edessans. He built a small monastery dedicated to Sergius and Bacchus outside the North gate and beside the garden which he owned in that district,[2] and there he lived. At that time there were many priests and deacons from places outside Edessa, particularly from Melitene. All the officiants in the 'great' Church of the Mother of God, built or rebuilt by Athanasius bar Gumaye, were foreign. They included the chief priest, the Secretary, the Steward of the church, the Archdeacon, and a physician who was also deacon and who administered the church and was in charge of the treasury. Another foreigner who was a Jacobite deacon was a city notable and is styled 'builder of churches', while yet another is called the City Elder; a certain Barṣauma bar Shalabi restored the springs of water which flowed near this church at his own expense. The congregation of the other principal Jacobite church, the Church of St. Theodore, where the Jacobite bishops were buried, seem to have been poorer, since they are described as workmen and gardeners and men 'from the plains', who had settled at Edessa.

Athanasius died in 1099–1100 to the grief of Edessans, because he had been an ornament to the Church. The Jacobite Patriarch, another Athanasius and a man distinguished for his learning and much respected both within and outside his own Church, then hoped to leave the see vacant, and reside at Edessa himself. In his opinion Edessa was the most convenient centre of his community, for Amid at that time had a Moslem ruler who was intolerant to Christians, while Melitene was too close to the troublesome monks of the Monastery of Barṣauma. The Jacobites of Edessa insisted, however, on exercising their prerogative of electing a Metropolitan of their own choosing. They selected a monk distinguished for his eloquence and erudition, Abu Ghalib bar Ṣabuni of Melitene, whose brother had been Metropolitan of that city and had been killed by its ruler shortly after taking up residence in the diocese. The choice of Abu Ghalib greatly vexed the Patriarch; not only had he hoped to make no appointment to the see of Edessa, but also he regarded Abu Ghalib himself with distrust. Nevertheless, he had no alternative but to accept the nomination. First, however, he imposed a condition. Volumes of the Gospel bound in silver and gold and belonging to the treasury of the Patriarch had, we are told, been used as a pledge by a Jacobite leader of Edessa to obtain money with which to bribe the rulers of the city; these

---

[1] *Chr. ad 1234.*   [2] Not far from the present Soliman pınar, p. 244 below.

volumes, the Patriarch insisted, were to be returned to the patriarchate. Abu Ghalib assented to the condition in writing. He was consecrated in 1100-1 under the name of Basil, the Patriarch contenting himself with the words of a popular proverb, 'Take him and may you have no pleasure from him'.[1]

Basil, under the influence of obstinate trouble-makers among his congregation, then refused to return the Gospels. There ensued a period of discord which was exploited by persons of ill will: on both sides the quarrel was exacerbated by unprincipled advisers. The Patriarch excommunicated Basil. Basil continued to ordain priests, the Patriarch would not recognize them unless he himself ordained them a second time. Several times priests and leading laymen begged him to release Basil from excommunication; he refused. The intrigues and dissension in the Jacobite church came to the notice of Count Baldwin of Edessa, of Joscelyn, and even of the king of Jerusalem. Bernard, the Latin Patriarch of Antioch, intervened personally in the dispute. The details of the incidents that followed illustrate the relations between the Jacobites and the Frankish authorities.

Bernard summoned the Jacobite Patriarch to Antioch and asked him to absolve Basil. Told by the interpreter that Basil owed the Patriarch money, Bernard exclaimed that 'Christians should not deprive a bishop of his office for a debt of silver'. Changing his tone, he went on to suggest that the Patriarch should regard the transaction as though he had given a loan to the Latin Church. Then he had a document brought declaring that Basil had been absolved and, in the presence of the Metropolitan of Edessa, invited Athanasius to sign. 'See, Abu Ghalib, to what a pass you have brought me', shouted the Patriarch. 'If I am [to be called familiarly] Abu Ghalib', retorted the other, 'you, [the Jacobite Patriarch, should be called equally] Abu l-Farag'. In a rage Athanasius swore that he would rather risk his neck than release the Metropolitan from his ban. Bernard would have had Athanasius beaten on the spot, had not a bishop protested at the unseemliness of these proceedings in a church. Athanasius fled to another church, and on the instructions of Bernard no one was permitted to communicate with him. The Jacobites were in great distress. But the Melkite philosopher, 'Abd al-Masiḥ of Edessa, advised Athanasius to appeal to Roger, prince of Antioch, and to reinforce his petition with a gift. The effect was immediate. Roger remonstrated with Bernard, reminding him that he had no authority over the 'Syrians'; Athanasius found himself free to leave Antioch for the Monastery of Barṣauma.

The breach widened. The Patriarch deposed the Metropolitan, but Count Baldwin, who, like other Edessans, supported Basil, forbade him to depart from the city. Then the Patriarch used his last weapon—the churches

[1] This Abu Ghalib is not to be confused with his contemporary and namesake, who was Bishop of Giḥon until his death in 1178-9, and was a prolific writer on ecclesiastical questions.

of Edessa were to remain closed, no bells were to be rung, and the services were suspended until Pentecost. For the Jacobites of Edessa the situation was critical. Some began to frequent 'heterodox' services and they acquired the habit of baptizing their children in Latin churches. The leading priests interceded with the Patriarch, and undertook not to associate with the Metropolitan; the churches were then reopened. Basil was now isolated. He no longer carried his pastoral staff, and he attended services without mitre or stole. He retired to an estate which he had planted with trees to the north-west of the city in the wadi Sulaiman.[1] At the same time, an opponent of the Metropolitan Basil (who had been replaced by a certain Ignatius), established, in the same area and with the help of rich men from Amid, a nunnery built by monks from the hills outside Edessa.

The Patriarch, now at Amid, succeeded, with some difficulty, in leaving the town only through the intervention of the Jacobite Michael bar Shumana, Administrator of Edessa and Count Joscelyn's deputy in that city. He visited Joscelyn at Tell Bashir on his way to the Monastery of Barṣauma. There his powers left him suddenly while he was conducting a service, and six days later he died. Now the Franks felt free to interfere in the ecclesiastical affairs of their Jacobite subjects. Joscelyn seized the patriarchal insignia, declaring that the election to the office of Patriarch should take place in his territory. This was done; the ceremony was held in February 1130 in the great church of the Latins, in the presence not only of the Maphrian of the East but also of Joscelyn and his officers. The new Patriarch, John, is des-cribed as dissolute, feeble in theological matters, but vigorous in anger and strife. His first act, no doubt on the advice of his Frankish masters, was to release Basil of Edessa from excommunication; but it was too late, for the letter of absolution reached the Metropolitan as he lay on his death-bed.

Power among the Jacobite community now passed into the hands of persons whom our sources term 'evil men'—'Abdun, the chief priest and Steward, and a certain Ṣaliba, a rich priest, who was proud of his scholarly ability. When the see of Edessa fell vacant, they arranged for the election of the Archdeacon and Steward of the church to the position of Metropolitan; he was 'Abdun's uncle by marriage. He received the formal name of Atha-nasius. His appointment was well received by the citizens, because he was a good and modest man. For five or six years he endured the intrigue and insolence of his patrons.

On the death of Athanasius in 1143 or 1144, Basil Abu l-Farag bar Shu-mana, brother of Michael bar Shumana, who had previously been Bishop of Kaishum, was translated to the diocese of Edessa. It may have been the influence of his brother, the Administrator of Edessa, that procured for Basil the appointment to the Metropolitan see. Indeed, he was obliged to

---

[1] Near, we may assume, the present Soliman pınar; see p. 240 n. 2, and the site on Plan II.

defend himself publicly against the charge of having received the preferment at the instance of the Count of Edessa, and he brought witnesses to prove that he had consented only when the Patriarch himself had ordered him to do so. As an Edessan, Basil had the support of his fellow citizens, and it was through him that the Jacobite Patriarch recovered control over the affairs of his co-religionists in the city. An agile man of the world, as well as theologian, poet, and historian, Basil succeeded in winning the confidence of the rulers of Edessa, Moslem and Christian alike, during the violent changes of fortune through which the city passed at this period.

There was not only internal discord among the Jacobites; they were also at loggerheads with the members of other Christian sects. In 1102 a dispute arose over that vexed problem, the date of Easter. The Latins of Edessa showed no interest in the matter. The Jacobites had previously acted in concert with the Armenians, their fellow anti-Chalcedonians. But now, out of fear, according to the Armenian Matthew of Edessa, they joined the camp of the Melkites and 'renounced the alliance which they had formed with the Armenians'. A curious incident occurred in 1133–4 that portrays more clearly this background of sectarian strife. Swarms of locusts had appeared in the countryside of Edessa. The Jacobites brought from Melitene the coffin of Barṣauma, in which was preserved the saint's right hand; as soon as the holy relic was displayed the locusts disappeared without causing damage to the crops. But the Melkites, 'in accordance', remarks our Jacobite narrator, 'with their detestable habit, burned with jealousy',[1] and incited the Latin Archbishop to insist on opening the coffin. The Jacobites were unwilling to permit it, warning that such irreverence would bring disaster in its train; the Melkites mocked them, and alleged that the coffin was empty. Accordingly, the relic was exposed in the church of the Latins. Straightway there was a terrifying peal of thunder, the sky was covered with clouds, and a heavy downpour of hail burst upon the streets. The people cried for mercy, the Franks, both priests and laymen, prostrated themselves, and the Melkites fled and hid themselves. When the hail ceased, all the city assembled and proclaimed the next three days a time of solemn intercession. The Moslems of Harran begged that the relic might be sent to their town to preserve it from the locusts; the Jacobites declined, and returned it to Melitene where it was welcomed with processions and prayer. The locusts did no more damage to the crops, but fed upon straw and withdrew to the desert and the semi-cultivated lands.

The Crusaders had not extended their domain east of Edessa, but they had, in spite of their private jealousies, managed to maintain their hold on the immediate neighbourhood of the city. In no small degree this was due to

[1] *Chr. ad 1234.*

the ineptitude of the Turkish commanders, with the exception of Mawdud in 1110–13. Now, however, the Franks met in the Atabeg of Mosul, 'Imad al-din Zangi, an opponent of skill, resourcefulness, and determination at the time when the ruler of Edessa was the ineffective Joscelyn the Younger. Edessa was a thorn in the side of the Moslems, and Zangi exerted every effort to neutralize it. Already in 1129 Zangi, passing by Edessa, had conveyed a message of friendship, declaring that he desired peace with the Franks. In return the Edessans sent him presents and food and drink. But now the situation had changed. Joscelyn had drawn upon himself the Atabeg's enmity by making a pact with his Artuqid rival Qara arslan. The latter handed over a fortress to the Count, and Joscelyn sought to make good his side of the bargain by extending military aid. It was at this moment, in 1143, that the two Christian princes who might have contained the expansionist schemes of Zangi died; in April the Byzantine Emperor, John II Comnenus, who nursed the hope of establishing his claim to the suzerainty of both Edessa and Antioch, and in November Fulk, king of Jerusalem.

Zangi bided his time, and kept a watch on developments at Edessa through the Moslem rulers of Harran. At the end of 1144, Joscelyn left the city accompanied by a large force; according to one writer he was preparing to raid the area of Raqqa in order to cut Zangi's lines of communication, according to another he intended to go to Antioch, according to yet a third he wished to return to the debaucheries of Tell Bashir.[1] Immediately Zangi sent an army to surprise Edessa. They marched through the day and the following night. Had they arrived then, they would have found the inhabitants wholly unprepared. But rain fell and they lost the way. They approached the city along the Harran road at dawn on Tuesday, 28 latter Teshrin (November 1144). Passing through the country south of the walls, they quickly perceived that the city was lightly defended; a message was sent to Zangi by pigeon post, and two days later he came to surround the city on all sides.

The events that followed are described graphically in eyewitness accounts. The Turks pitched their tents within the outer works. Zangi stationed himself opposite the Gate of Hours in the north, on the hill above the Church of the Confessors. To his east was the Sultan's son, the vizier was further north on Watchmen's Hill. Another detachment encamped to the north-west, at the head of wadi Sulaiman at the 'fence of Barṣauma' (evidently called after the orchard of the Metropolitan Athanasius[2]) and another to the west of the city, at the Gate of the spring [of water], on a hill in the cemetery where the tomb of St. Ephraim was. There was a detachment east of the East gate, where the road led to the fort of Kisas, now

---

[1] Wholly improbable is the story that Joscelyn was at Edessa at the time of its capture by Zangi and fled from the city disguised as a beggar.   [2] See p. 240 above.

in Turkish hands, others were to the north, north-east, and south of this point, by the garden of Buzan (perhaps that Buzan who was the Governor of Edessa under Malikshah sixty years earlier). Other soldiers were outside the Harran gate to the south, and yet others to their west opposite the Citadel.

The city had few troops, and these mercenaries had received no pay for a year or more. Present were the Archbishops of three denominations: the Archbishop of the Armenians, John; the Metropolitan of the Jacobites, Basil bar Shumana (who was the author of a history of these events[1]); and finally the Latin Hugo who was in overall command of the defence. The citizens, declares one chronicler, were 'only cobblers, weavers, mercers, tailors, priests, and deacons'.[2] William of Tyre is more scathing. Edessa, he writes, 'had Syrians[3] and some unwarlike Armenians, and servants wholly ignorant of the use of arms, familiar only with the arts of trade', apart from a few Latins. It had sufficient supply of arms and provisions, it had a solid wall and the upper and lower Citadels with high towers. But, William adds pointedly, 'all these were of avail against an enemy only if there were people willing to fight for freedom and to oppose the enemy with courage'.

William's strictures reflect the contempt of the Franks for the local Christians. They were little deserved; the latter showed, if we may trust Basil bar Shumana, their customary doggedness—and contrariness—in the face of overwhelming odds. 'They resisted stoutly and withstood [the attack] bravely as long as they were able'.[2] This time the Turks left nothing to chance. They prepared mounds and set up siege engines, they battered the walls, they poured a rain of arrows into the city, they dug trenches under the bridge outside the North gate. Zangi 'wished the city to surrender so that its inhabitants should not perish and [the city] be destroyed'.[2] He begged the Edessans to capitulate. But 'there was no one in the city whose word was decisive . . . ; they answered Zangi with insults and abuse'.[2] Yet the defence of the place was hopeless. Hugo, we are told, refused to secure the co-operation of the soldiers by distributing the money he had amassed. The people were exhausted by hunger, for Zangi's blockade was effective. 'Women, girls, and boys were wearied beyond words, carrying stones, water and [other] necessities' to the fighting men. They were under constant attack from the catapults; the wall was broken, its foundations had been mined, and beams and scrap and layers of wood, the interstices stuffed with materials steeped in naphtha, grease, and sulphur, stood ready to be ignited. Basil persuaded the Latin Archbishop to write to Zangi asking for a truce in the hope that the Crusaders might answer their appeal and send a relief force from Antioch or from Jerusalem, and Zangi, we are assured, would

[1] p. 242 above.   [2] *Chr. ad 1234.*   [3] Latin, *Chaldaei.*

have granted this respite. But the letter was seized by an 'ignorant fellow, a mercer' and torn to pieces in public; 'there was great commotion and this useful plan came to naught'.[1]

The Turks, according to one account, invited the Edessans to inspect the siege works in order to convince them that they had no course but surrender. Indeed, the mines had been prepared by Aleppans who were acquainted with the topography of Edessa. Some four weeks after the siege had begun, on 23 former Kanun (December), or on Christmas Eve, Zangi's troops set fire to the beams beside the North gate. The flames consumed the grease and sulphur, a north wind carried the smoke towards the defenders, and the great wall and two towers swayed and fell. The temporary structure which the Edessans had built inside the wall proved to be too short. From dawn men and women, and even the monks from the hills of Edessa, fought in the two breaches; at the third hour the Turks forced their way into the city across the bodies of the dead. Zangi had given the city to his soldiers to sack for three days. On the first day about six thousand helpless Edessans were slain. Seeing the enemy break into the streets, women, children, and youths ran towards the upper Citadel in the south of the city, 'pressing upon each other, row upon row, from fear of death and slavery, pushing upwards, treading upon one another'.[1] But the gate of the Citadel had been closed by order of Archbishop Hugo. The people 'were suffocated, and trampled down into a solid mass',[1] and some five thousand perished miserably. About ten thousand boys and girls were carried into captivity. Hugo, on the point of entering the Citadel, was himself cut down by an axe; many priests, deacons, and monks were killed. Zangi entered the city, and, wondering at its beauty, showed magnanimity and stayed the slaughter. He saw an old man, his head tonsured, stripped of his clothing, dragged along by a rope. He learned that this was the Jacobite Metropolitan Basil. Finding that he spoke Arabic and was a man of spirit, Zangi took him to his tent, and treated him with kindness. At the Citadel gate, the general offered to spare the lives of those within, and two days after the entry of the Turks it was surrendered by a certain Barṣauma. Resistance was at an end.

On the next day guards were set on the city by the Turks so that the citizens would not be at the mercy of the soldiery, and the troops were forbidden to enter. Zangi inspected the prisoners. Some, it seems, were led away; others were sent back to their homes with corn and other necessities. Some two thousand women and children who were found in the upper Citadel were carried into slavery, about ten thousand soldiers were released, and those who had hidden in the two citadels or underground escaped. The Jacobites and Armenians and Melkites were spared. The Franks were plundered of their gold and silver, their church vessels and cups and bowls and crosses

---

[1] *Chr. ad 1234.*

and jewels—according to some accounts, all the Franks who were discovered were killed. Priests and notables of Edessa were stripped and sent to Aleppo, craftsmen were set apart and put to work at their trades as prisoners, about a hundred men were tortured and slain. The citizens who remained were allowed to keep some possessions and were provided with oxen and fodder. Basil was made to swear on the Cross that he would observe loyalty to the new masters of the city. He was assured:

We are ready to treat you well and to set free those of you who are captives. You know well that when the Moslems conquered this city . . . , it remained under them for two hundred years; it was prosperous like a capital city. Today fifty years have passed since the Franks occupied it—and they have ruined and razed its territory.[1]

Four days after his entry into Edessa, Zangi went to Harran and Raqqa. At Edessa he left a Governor, Zain al-din 'Ali Küçük, 'a good man who did much kindness',[1] and seven lieutenants. In January 1145 Serug fell to Zangi. Thence his army marched on Birtha on the Euphrates. After a siege of forty days it was saved only by the withdrawal of Zangi, in March, to deal with an insurrection in his own country.

The capture of Edessa was not a particularly brilliant victory, and it is with evident exaggeration that Ibn al-Athir describes it as 'a feat of arms as glorious as that of Badr'. But he was right in describing Edessa as 'in effect the eye of Mesopotamia and the strongest fortress in the Moslem lands'. Zangi was hailed by the Caliph with extravagant titles—*zain al-Islam, al-malik al-mansur, alp ghazi, nasir amir al-mu'minin*; he was presented with horses with golden harness, a golden sword, a banner, a mantlet, and a black turban.

For the Crusaders, however, the consequences of the fall of Edessa were serious. It had brought to an end their pretensions to dominion east of the Euphrates. The news was carried throughout Christendom that the city of Abgar had fallen to the Moslems. Christian Antioch and even Jerusalem itself seemed threatened, for just as the cession of Edessa to Baldwin in 1098 was regarded as a portent of the conquest of Jerusalem, so its loss was an ill omen for the Latin kingdom.[2] The alarm was sounded by Pope Eugenius III in a summons to Louis VII of France. On Christmas Day 1145 Louis announced his intention of taking the Cross, and confirmed it at Easter in the following year. The ardour and oratory of St. Bernard of Clairvaux roused the princes of Germany, led by King Conrad and followed by a great concourse. King Roger of Sicily and Emperor Manuel Comnenus offered help.

---

[1] *Chr. ad 1234.*

[2] It was at this juncture that rumours reached the papal court of a great potentate to the east of Persia who was both a Nestorian priest and emperor, and who was waging war against the infidel. These stories continued to circulate for centuries in the West—but, though they no doubt have a substratum of fact, the tales of Prester John belong to the realm of legend rather than history.

But the wave of enthusiasm that had prompted the Second Crusade sub-sided. Already in 1147 discord appeared between the Christian princes, and soon they met with military disaster. The siege of Damascus was abandoned in 1148, through jealousy between the Syrian Franks and the western Crusaders; the kings returned to Europe. It was left to St. Bernard to write the epilogue, declaring that the Crusade was 'an abyss so deep that I must call him blessed who is not scandalized thereby'.[1]

To the Christians of Edessa the emotion of their co-religionists in the West brought little consolation. The disaster of 1144 was commemorated by laments in Syriac.[2] The Catholicus Narsai IV Shnorhali wrote an elegy in Armenian on the ruined city.

> Its foundations set deep in the earth, . . . crowned with battlements, wonderful dwellings and a temple enclosed in [its] beautiful circuit; its houses and roads devoted to commerce aligned on a symmetrical plan.

He recounts in exaggerated language the destruction of the city and the massacre of its inhabitants. The Edessans, as best as they could, ransomed the captives out of their own straitened resources.

But the remarkable resilience of the Edessans asserted itself. A Syriac chronicler complains:

> they did not return from their evil ways. . . . Metropolitan Basil urged them to turn from their deeds and their evil ways, especially the leaders and the rich and particularly the members of the Church. They hated one another and spoke malice of each other, and were covetous of each other and wronged each other, and oppressed and took by force. . . . Indeed, they caused even the harassed pastor to suffer many things and like wolves they tore his flesh in secret and spoke malice of him behind his back . . . Edessan women even associated with Turks and became their wives according to their desire; this especially pained the spirit of God, for before the Turks had been a complete year in the city more than a hundred women had married unbelievers.[3]

The strong rule of the Turks had restored security to the city. We have our last glimpse of the Christian community of Edessa at peace and still prosperous in the year 1145.

In that year Zangi visited Edessa at harvest time. He left his troops by the river Gullab, and with his nobles and generals and district commanders and other councillors came to the city in the middle of Pentecost. Zain al-din had now been succeeded as Governor by 'Ain al-Dawla; he was aided by the ruler of Harran 'who was the cause of the capture of the city [of Edessa]' as Administrator. Freed from the stresses of Crusader rule, Edessa had

---

[1] Yet as late as 1150 the Emperor proposed to Beatrice, Countess of Edessa, that she should yield to him her title to the County in return for an annual pension!   [2] See p. 254 below.
[3] *Chr. ad 1234.*

already taken a fresh lease of life. The account of Zangi's visit provides an interesting description of the appearance of the city at this time:

The Metropolitan [Basil], priests, deacons, and all the Christians went out to meet [Zangi] on the one side, and the Moslems who had assembled from all quarters on the other. [Zangi] greeted the Christians with joy and took the Gospel and kissed it, saluted the Metropolitan and asked after his health. He said, 'For your sake have I come to supply your wants'. He passed the East gate of the city and went to enter by the North gate where the city had been captured.

They had rebuilt the breaches in the wall and the seven towers which the siege mounds had destroyed with an even stronger building from the foundations, and had written upon them in Arabic characters the account of the capture and the name of the ruler [Zangi]. They had razed the shrine of the Confessors outside the city and built the wall with its stones. They had begun, moreover, to build a castle for the ruler beside the splendid shrine of St. John in which the ruler lodged.[1] Over this shrine they had set guards so that nothing in it should be destroyed. The Franks had restored it splendidly, altering the roof and renewing the tiles. In it were nearly a hundred great windows; for all of them they had made lead lattices so that the light should enter but not the birds. Many bishops and fathers of early times were buried there. In the middle of the shrine behind the bishops' throne were buried the bishops of the Franks. The bishop[2] who was killed at the capture [of Edessa] was also buried there. Over [his] tomb a block of red marble was carved in the likeness of the bishop; the whole covering of the tomb was a single stone. The bodies of the holy Addai the Apostle and king Abgar were deposited in the shrine in a coffin of silver, plated with gold.[3] At the capture [of Edessa] the coffin was carried away and the bones scattered; but the believers collected them with many [other] fragments of saints and brought and set them in an urn in the northern treasury of the Church of the Syrians known as St. Theodore.[4]

[1] The original West gate of Edessa, the 'Gate of Arches (or Vaults)', was, we have observed (p. 186 above), no longer in use. Travellers from the West entered Edessa either by the North gate or from the south-west by the 'Gate of the spring of water' (p. 244)—probably the present Sakabun Kapısı, south of the sluices and west of Birket Ibrahim and immediately below the Citadel mount. This may have been an enlargement of the little gate through which the Melkite Bishop Severus was led to his death by the soldiers of Narseh in about 604. But the arch of the original Byzantine West gate still remains; it was discovered by the present writer in 1961 and examined by him again, together with Dr. G. Fehérvári, in 1966. The structure beside it was no doubt a guard-room of the later Islamic period, and may well have formed part of the 'castle' built for Zangi in 1145. It stands near and due west of the electricity plant which was itself once a church—probably on the site of the ancient Church of St. John. See Plans I and II and the photographs at Pl. 6a, b.

[2] Syriac, *Papias*.

[3] According to an anonymous semi-poetic western text written before 1109, the relics of Abgar and Addai were placed in a 'silver mausoleum' in the church by the Latin Archbishop Benedict, p. 237. A Latin MS., edited by Röhricht, and giving a description of Edessa after 1144, refers to the 'great monastery dedicated to Thaddaeus the Apostle, John the Baptist and the martyr George'. It 'towered over the city and had four carved and well-designed gates'. But the Latin cathedral was, maintains the writer, the Church of St. Mary, Thaddaeus the Apostle, and the martyr George. This may be in error for the Church of St. John which stood beside a Monastery of St. John.

[4] This was situated north of, and below, the Citadel (and is not to be confused with a church inside the Citadel that later became a mosque). Beside it was, appropriately, the Monastery of Abgar (p. 252 below). The latter is probably alluded to in the Röhricht MS. as the Church of St. Abraham which was the cathedral of the Jacobites. In the same MS. the cathedral of the Armenians is the Church of 'St. Euphemia'; this is possibly an error for St. Ephraim, p. 239.

So too the Moslems took the shrine of St. Stephen and Thomas the Apostle, because, it was said, the Franks prayed in these shrines. That of St. Thomas they made a stable, and that of St. Stephen they made a storehouse for corn and the other crops of the ruler. The shrine of the Confessors outside the city which had been built more or less a hundred years earlier they razed, as we have said. The shrine, too, of St. Theodore and the Angel Michael on the south side of the city they pulled down and from their stones they built the places that had been destroyed in the wall on that side and in the upper Citadel and wherever else [building] was needed.[1] So also the Moslems renewed and restored afresh the mosque and the Moslem chapel which had been made the residence of the bishop of the Franks.

Zangi then entered, as we have said, by this North gate called [the Gate] of Hours[2] and went up in the direction of the shrine of St. John and went down to the sources of the springs of water and examined [them] carefully. He came to the shrine of the Apostle Thomas and ate bread there. Then he mounted again and went up to the round spring called Abgarus, for there in early times was a palace of King Abgar, long since destroyed, and in that place was planted the garden called the Metropolitan's [garden][3] to this day. Late at night he went up to the shrine of St. John, because he was lodging there and around the shrine were pitched the tents of his nobles.[4]

In the morning Zangi enquired of Basil bar Shumana about the well near the monastery of Cosmas, the martyr-physician (now claimed by the Edessans as a resident of their city), outside the Harran gate. The Metropolitan related a popular story of that time about an 'Easterner' who stole the *mandylion*,[5] the portrait of Jesus, from the church in which it was kept. The man spent the night in the monastery of Cosmas. But the *mandylion* burned in his pocket and in fear he threw it into the well. Immediately a pillar of fire arose from the well and in the waters appeared a disc bright as the sun. The *mandylion* was retrieved.[6] Thereafter the sick, especially non-Christians, bathed in the waters of the well and were healed of elephantiasis, leprosy and 'Abgar's disease', gout.[7] Then,

[1] According to the Röhricht MS., Zangi destroyed twelve monasteries at Edessa.

[2] The Röhricht MS. states that there were four gates, and one through which the Apostle Thaddaeus entered which was kept closed. The four are: the Gate of 'soys' (Hours, cf. p. 190); a gate of a 'hanging rock' (perhaps Sakabun Kapısı in the south-west below the great rock of the Citadel); the Gate of 'na'm' beside the 'turris naimam' which is strong and high and well built and commands the whole city (probably referring to the Citadel that is called the 'great fortress of Maniaces' by Matthew of Edessa; the gate may be the Harran Gate to the south of the city, not far from the Citadel—or it may be a gate inside the Citadel); the fourth gate is where the river, after flowing around the walls of the city, 'enters the city through some small caves, runs under the foundations of a large monastery and becomes a stream over which hang [the remains of] the two Apostles Thomas and Barnabas in a golden vessel excellently set with jewels' (presumably the East gate). These identifications are, however, far from certain. The MS. adds that Edessa's walls had 145 towers and bastions (*munitiones*) and an outer wall with a barbican.

[3] See p. 190 and n. 5 there above.

[4] *Chr. ad 1234.*

[5] On this term, see p. 215.

[6] The story is told already in the *Epistola Abgari* of about A.D. 900.

[7] See pp. 72 f. above. But the western text written before 1109, referred to on p. 249 n. 3 above, declares that it was of leprosy that Thaddaeus cleansed Abgar in a sacred fountain.

Zangi . . . said, 'I believe that the blessing of Christ can perform wonders like these'. [He] had gout in his legs and he suffered greatly from it. He arose and mounted and came to the well; he drew water from it and bathed his legs. This monastery had been destroyed for a while and nothing remained of it save only the altar in its east part. The ruler Zangi ordered that a great hospice should be built there for the use and repose of the sick and suffering who congregated [there]. He ordered that all the fields around it should be for the use of the hospice. But God did not wish this to be fulfilled; it was annulled by the death of the ruler [shortly afterwards].

Zangi came to our Jacobite churches and examined their beauty. He ordered that they should be given two great bells which were to be placed on them as was the practice at the time of the Franks. Then he made ready to depart. He ordered the Metropolitan and the people to be vigilant in guarding the city and not to plot against his rule. He departed from them on the Friday after Pentecost and went to Harran and thence to Raqqa. . . . He brought about three hundred Jewish families with their wives and children and settled them at Edessa.[1]

Unhappily the story of Edessa does not close with this pleasing incident. In September 1146, as he was laying siege to the castle of Qal'at Ga'bar, Zangi was assassinated, to the joy of his enemies who had never acknowledged his tolerance and generosity.[2] One western poetaster punned on his name:

> Quem bonus eventus! fit sanguine sanguinolentus
> Vir homicida, reus, nomine Sanguineus.

Joscelyn had been tormented by the loss of his County. Already shortly after the fall of Edessa in 1144, Armenians in the city had plotted to seize it for him. The conspiracy had been discovered and the guilty men executed. With the death of Zangi, Joscelyn's hope re-awakened. Scarcely forty days had passed before he set out with Baldwin of Mar'ash and a small troop of soldiers to surprise the city by night; the prince of Antioch refused to take part in the enterprise. But the element of surprise had been lost. The Moslems of Aleppo heard of Joscelyn's plan and warned the Turkish garrison at Edessa. They took about fifty Christian master-builders, smiths, and artisans as hostages and prepared to defend the citadels.

Joscelyn's advance party reached Edessa on Sunday 27 former Teshrin (October). When darkness fell they scaled the walls, apparently with the aid of some Armenians inside the city, slew the guards, and opened the gate 'beside the source [of water]', that is, in the south-west of the walls. The main body of Frank cavalry and infantry entered the city. But the 'brainless fools', as a chronicler calls them,[3] did not engage the Turks in the citadels;

---

[1] *Chr. ad 1234.*

[2] So Gregory the Priest, who continued the history of Matthew of Edessa, writes of Zangi as 'pouring forth torrents of blood'. But he is also compelled to admit grudgingly that at the capture of Edessa 'the tyrant felt compassion in his heart' and 'the arrogant victor wished to pacify the city and had an order proclaimed that no more hurt should be done to the Christians'.

[3] *Chr. ad 1234.*

on that very night they turned to plunder the shops and houses of the citizens, Moslem and Christian, good and bad, alike. The Moslems imme-diately retired with their families and property to the citadels, and were received quietly—not, our narrator comments, 'like the evil behaviour of the Franks at the first capture of Edessa when they closed the gates and caused the calamity in which [people were] bitterly suffocated'.[1] Some Moslems escaped to Harran during the night. The Franks instructed Basil, the Jacobite Metropolitan, to prepare engines to attack the lower Citadel; the upper Citadel, they realized, was impregnable. But the lower Citadel also proved too strong. The Crusaders spent six days in futile activity, in the meantime the Turks were massing around the city. Joscelyn and his com-panions were now in despair, and the wretched Christians of Edessa passed each night in fear near the camp beside the Monastery of Abgar, the church of the Jacobites.[2]

On the sixth day, a spy informed Joscelyn that about ten thousand Turkish soldiers were in the hills and the plain ready to join forces on the morrow with their compatriots inside the city. He determined to leave the same night. The North gate, the Gate of Hours, was opened and the Frank army began to withdraw. But, asks the chronicler bitterly:

how was it possible that many thousands of men and horses and beasts of burden should go out by one gate without its being known? . . . The Edessans . . . saw that the Franks were departing, abandoning them to the hands of the pagan oppressors. . . . The city arose in great terror, and screams were raised in bitter anguish by women and children. . . . The night was dark, there was no light; all ran headlong through the street which led to the Gate of Hours—soldiers, men in armour, horses, and pack-animals were mingled with boys, women, and children, crushing and trampling on one another without pity. . . . No one grieved or stretched out a hand. Such was their bitter exodus; they left houses full of goods and all necessities, the doors open, lamps lighted and beds spread.[3]

The Frank forces and the people with them halted around a tower, the pillar of the anchorites in front of the shrine of the Confessors. Turks ringed them around, 'pouring arrows on them like rain. . . . They mingled with the crowd and began to slay like butchers, and a noise was heard like axes hewing in the forest.'[3] When dawn broke, order was restored. Baldwin of Mar'ash passed to the front of the crowd, Joscelyn brought up the rear, infantry marched to the right and left.

The soldiers resisted valiantly and did not let the Turks approach near the crowd. . . . And so they went [on the road to Samosata] in weariness and great danger. . . . The pursuers slaughtered them like sheep. Children and babes ran unshod among the thorns, their tender feet bleeding, the skin torn away by sharp spikes, their tongues hanging out with thirst, their mouths bitter as aloes, their teeth black as soot . . . , crushed in the

---

[1] See p. 246.
[2] Cf. p. 249 n. 4 above.
[3] *Chr. ad 1234*. According, however, to the account of Mich. Syr., Joscelyn's men set fire to the houses and goods of the Christians of Edessa before leaving the city.

mob, trampled under the horses' hoofs. . . . In the plain through which they journeyed were brushwood and great thickets. The enemy set fire to this and it blazed in front and around them; they found no path to turn aside, but continued towards the fire in great peril, their feet scorched by the burning.[1]

Many of the Turkish soldiers, wearied by the fighting, returned to Edessa; some feared lest the Franks should make a stand in one of the forts and turn upon them, others wished to secure their share of the plunder of the city. Joscelyn's cavalry then sounded the trumpets and attacked the enemy. Their disorderly charge was allowed to pass, only to be assaulted by the Turks from the rear. The Franks fled in panic, 'casting away their spears and shields, smashing their coats of mail and all their armour—even the drawn swords in their hands they cast away out of the terror that had taken hold of them.'[1] Joscelyn escaped with a few followers,[2] Baldwin was slain with many more soldiers. Thirty thousand souls were killed. Women, youths, and children to the number of sixteen thousand were carried into slavery, stripped of their clothes, barefoot, their hands bound, forced to run beside their captors on horses. Those who could not endure were pierced by lances or arrows, or abandoned to wild animals and birds of prey. Priests were killed out of hand or captured, few escaped. The Archbishop of the Armenians was sold at Aleppo, Basil bar Shumana narrowly made his escape to Samosata.

['Abdun,][3] that disturber of the Church, was caught . . . outside the city gate. He fell into the moat and, thinking that Christians would come down and pull him out, cried, 'Who will earn a hundred dinars by pulling me out?' A Turk went down, killed him, took his purse of gold and the wealth he had on him.[4]

The whole city was given over to looting.

The Turks and various tribes entered and became masters of this famous city which had not been sacked since its foundation by Seleucus, 1,460 years [before]. At the first destruction when it was captured, the pillage lasted two days only, and the city was hurriedly saved and destruction . . . was restrained at the command of Zangi; all went back to their homes and inheritances. In this, complete ruin—not for two days only, but for a whole year they went about the town digging, searching secret places, foundations and roofs. They found many treasures hidden from the earliest times of the fathers and elders, and many [treasures] of which the citizens knew nothing. . . . They brought out of [the Jacobite cathedral] great wealth and church valuables. [There were] crosses, Gospels, goblets, bowls, censers, and the great splendid pot of the chrism and the spice vessel and the tops of the pastoral staffs, and other objects all of silver plated with gold,

---

[1] *Chr. ad 1234.*

[2] Another, less probable, account relates that Joscelyn fled from the Moslems with twenty of his chief knights to the 'Water tower'. Surrounded by Turks who had made a breach in the tower and threatened to bring it down, Joscelyn deserted his companions. They were all killed—and so too were all the Christians of Edessa. Mich. Syr. states that Joscelyn entered Edessa by the 'Water gate' and then took refuge in 'a great, derelict fort called the "Star [tower]"'.

[3] See p. 242 above.

[4] *Chr. ad 1234.*

and many splendid, expensive, regal carpets, with the coverings of the altars and of the vessels for Mass which had been collected for a long time and put aside by the early kings and leaders. [There were also] other regal objects and carpets that had been made at this later time, and those that were sent each year from the capital by an Edessan believer . . . and by [another] . . . who lived in the capital and had constant care for the churches of Edessa and each year used to send much gold for the churches and for the monasteries and for the poor and sick . . .[1]

From this disaster the Christian community of Edessa never recovered. By the West, they felt they had been abandoned. 'In the Christians who lived in those [western] regions', wrote a Syriac chronicler, 'was no mercy, but only cruelty, callousness, hardness of heart, and wickedness of thought—especially among the priests, monks, and bishops.'[1] Christians east of the Euphrates used their meagre substance to ransom the Edessans who had been carried into captivity; John, Bishop of Mardin, an Edessan by origin, is singled out for special praise. The tragedy of Edessa was commemorated in sermons and elegies by Dionysius bar Ṣalibi, Basil bar Shumana, and others. 'It was not the Lord who decreed that Turks should rule at Edessa', boldly declared the humane Bishop of Mardin; 'had a Frank army been in the city, Zangi would not have taken it.' His fellow theologians rebuked him. 'It is not for us to say why Edessa was struck nor why the sword devastated it without pity'. After the passage of a few years, the story of the city of Abgar, whose traditions were woven into the fabric of Christian history, had become no more than a subject for academic argument on the workings of Providence.

[1] *Chr. ad 1234.*

EPILOGUE

OUNT JOSCELYN'S ATTEMPT TO RECOVER HIS DOMAINS east of the Euphrates had failed miserably.[1] But even if he had been a man of integrity, of ability and resourcefulness, he could not have arrested the course of history. Edessa could no longer survive as a Christian city alone and isolated in a cohesive Moslem empire. On the death of Zangi's son it passed to his lieutenants; later it became the property of Saladin and his Ayyubid successors. True, a flash of the old spirit of independence flared up in 1234 when the citizens defied the troops of Mosul, but this was the mechanical—and unavailing—reflex of a moment. The soldiers breached the walls, sacked the town and deported its inhabitants to the West. Thereafter it shared passively the fate of its neighbours. It experienced the visitation of the Tatars in 1244, it surrendered to Hulagu in 1260, by the beginning of the fifteenth century it had been repopulated when Timur and his court 'drank with great devotion the waters' of its famous springs. In 1637 the city was incorporated in the Ottoman empire by the campaign of Murad IV in the East. It was again, and finally, under the rule of Asia Minor; history had come full circle.

There is symbolic significance in the gradual change in the nomenclature of the city. The name of Orhay was little altered as the Arabic al-Ruha; in the Turkish Urfa it became scarcely recognizable.[2] By the same token its Christian population, now a pitiful minority, virtually disappear from view. Less than thirty years after the catastrophe of 1146 they staged a half-hearted demonstration, 'like the old practices of the days of the Franks'. The church bells pealed, the populace were sworn on the Cross and the Gospels, meetings were summoned, deputations dispatched. By a deft and contemptuous use of bribes, the Governor thwarted the movement and banished its authors. 'The only result', comments our chronicler sadly, 'was that the Christians became unpopular . . . and won a bad name.'

The moral decline of the Christian community was swift. Metropolitan Basil bar Shumana had been a man of culture, at ease with princes and

[1] In 1148 Joscelyn earned the maledictions of Jacobite writers when he rifled the celebrated Monastery of Barṣauma. Two years later, in an ill-conceived assault on Antioch, he was captured by the Moslems, taken to Aleppo and blinded; after nine years of confinement he died there, receiving at the end the consolations of the Syrian bishop.

[2] Urfa is presumably from an earlier form Rufa. For the mutation of *h* to *f* see J. Deny, *Principes de grammaire turque* ('*Türk*' de Turquie), 1955, 109, and J. Németh, *Die Türken von Vidin, Sprache, Folklore, Religion*, 1965, 74. (I owe these references to my colleague Dr. V. L. Ménage.) It is difficult to assess the point of time at which the name Urfa became standard.

prelates.[1] But his successor owed his position to the prestige of his wealth, and the following bishop was inducted only after the payment of 500 dinars to the Governor from Church funds. So venal had become the leaders of the community that the clergy of the two Jacobite churches quarrelled over the distribution of the fees that they received on festival days, and the scandal was resolved by the intervention of the Moslem ruler.[2]

Christian shrines which had long been a memorial of Roman and Byzantine Edessa were now empty and deserted. In Zangi's lifetime the famous churches of St. Thomas and St. Stephen were put to menial use as stable and granary;[3] as other churches fell into disrepair they were dismantled to provide stone for the Citadel and the walls. Even the church of Hagia Sophia, once accounted one of the wonders of the world, had so far deteriorated that it was demolished and its fabric transferred to the Citadel and to the mosque of Harran. The beautiful church of St. John the Baptist had been employed as a storehouse for wool, and the pigeons that formerly had been excluded by lead lattices now nested in its lofts. In 1183 a lighted lamp set fire to the inflammable material, and the whole building perished in a molten blaze.

Meanwhile the Moslem population of Urfa grew, and so too did the number of its mosques, side by side with the public baths, khans, and markets.[4] Yet a sense of the continuity of history was not lost. On his visit to the city some ten years after its incorporation into Turkey, Evliya Çelebi enumerates mosques and shrines that still bear the same names today, and were themselves erected on more ancient places of worship. Evliya, like a succession of other travellers over the centuries,[5] records also legends of the city that have been recounted in the present volume.

The same spirit is abroad in modern Urfa, not only in official circles but now among the people too. The neglect of time—among the casualties were mosaics (notably the 'Tripod' mosaic) which the present writer had happily been able to record in 1952, 1956, and 1959—is being arrested. A few years

[1] After his escape to Samosata in 1146, Basil was thrown into prison by Joscelyn on a charge of favouring the Turks. There he wrote treatises on the fall of Edessa. On his release three years later, he travelled widely in both Crusader and Turkish territory, collecting money for the ransom of Edessan captives; he was received with great honour on both sides of the frontier. Basil subsequently retired to Severak near Edessa, over which he was granted ecclesiastical authority by the Jacobite patriarch. He died in 1169.

[2] The Jews of Edessa were no less mercenary at this time, if we may believe Judah al-Ḥarizi. The poet pillories them (with a few honourable exceptions) for their meanness—in spite of their protestations to the contrary. An inscription indicating the presence of Edessan Jews at Ruṣafa in Syria in 1102 is edited by A. Caquot, *Syria* xxxii, 1955, 70.

[3] See p. 250 above.

[4] To the late twelfth century belong the octagonal minaret of the Ulu Cami and the square minaret of the Halil Camii. On the latter is an Arabic inscription dated 1211-12, near the former is an inscription of Saladin, dated 1191. Inside the Harran gate is an Arabic inscription of the late thirteenth century, while the Hasan Paşa Camii has three inscriptions of the sixteenth century.

[5] Notably Rauwolff (1575), Tavernier (1644), Otter (1734), Pococke (1738), Niebuhr (1766), Olivier (1794), Buckingham (1823), Badger (1843), Sachau (1879), and Guyer (1910).

ago a fine mosque was built outside the eastern wall near the place where once stood the historic shrine of St. Sergius. Amid popular approbation two Christian Syriac inscriptions that were formerly in that shrine were reverently inserted in the walls of the mosque.[1]

[1] Named Circis Peyamber. Of the inscriptions one commemorates the rebuilding of the Church of St. George in Sel. 2156 (A.D. 1844–5). The other records a 'wonderful event' which took place when the Patriarch officiated at the Church of St. George on the great feast of Saints Peter and Paul on 29th Haziran, Sel. 1869 (A.D. 1557). Both inscriptions are shortly to be published in *B.S.O.A.S.*

MAP AND PLANS

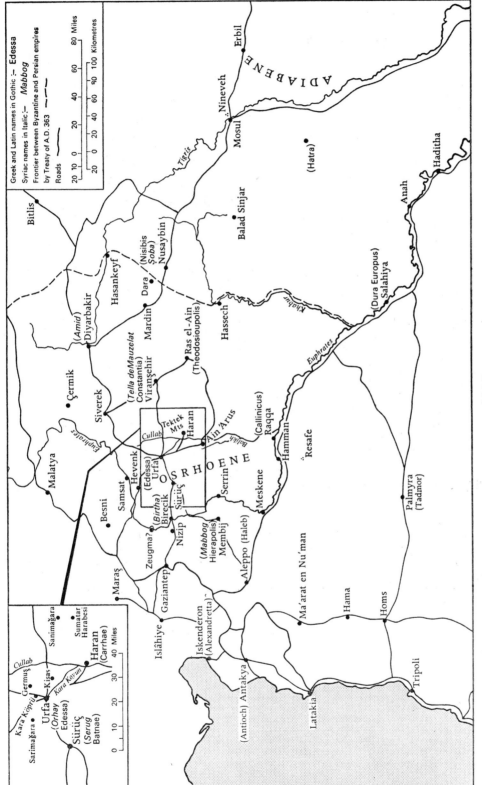

MAP

Greek and Latin names in Gothic :- **Edessa**
Syriac names in Italic:- *Mabbog*
Frontier between Byzantine and Persian empires by Treaty of A.D. 363
Roads

80 Miles
60
40
20
0

100 Kilometres
90
60
40
20 10
20
0

ADIABENE

Erbil
Nineveh
Mosul
(Hatra)
Haditha
Anah
Balad Sinjar
Bitlis
(Nisibis)
Şoba
Nusaybin
Dara
Hasankeyf
Diyarbakir
(*Amid*)
Çermik
Siverek
Tigris
(Tella deMauzelat)
Constantia
Viranşehir
Mardin
Ras el-Ain
(Theodosioupolis)
Hassech
Khabur
Salahiya
(Dura Europus)
Euphrates
Malatya
Euphrates
Besni
Samsat
Hevenk
(*Birtha*)
Zeugma?
Birecik
Cullab
Tektek
Mts
Haran
(Edessa)
Urfa
Ain 'Arus
Balikh
Raqqa
(Callinicus)
OSRHOENE
Serrin
Meskene
Hamman
Resafe
Nizip
(*Mabbog*)
Hierapolis)
Membij
Aleppo (Haleb)
Palmyra
(Tadmor)
Maraş
Gaziantep
Islâhiye
Iskenderon
(Alexandretta)
(Antioch) Antakya
Latakia
Ma'arat en Nu'man
Hama
Homs
Tripoli

Sanimağara
Sumatar
Harabesi
Cullab
Germuş
Kısas
Kara Koyun
Haran
(Carrhae)
Sarimağara
Kara Köprü
Urfa
(*Orhay*)
Edessa
Süruç
(Serug)
Batnae)

40 Miles
30
20
10
0

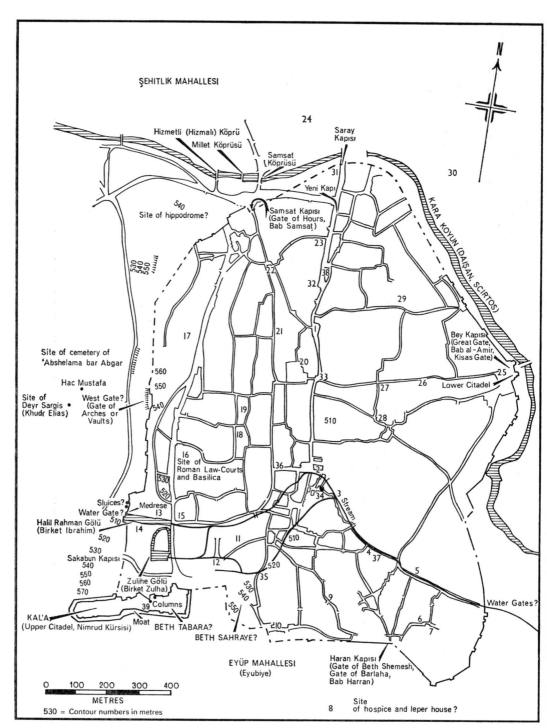

ŞEHITLIK MAHALLESI

24

Hizmetli (Hizmalı) Köprü
Millet Köprüsü
Samsat Köprüsü

Saray Kapısı

31

30

Yeni Kapı

540
Site of hippodrome?

Samsat Kapısı
(Gate of Hours,
Bab Samsat)

23

KARA KOYUN (DAISAN, SCIRTOS)

22

38
32

29

530
540
550

17

21

20

Bey Kapısı
(Great Gate,
Bab al-Amir,
Kisas Gate)

Site of cemetery of
'Abshelama bar Abgar

33

27

26

25
Lower Citadel

Hac Mustafa

560
550

Site of
Deyr Sargis
(Khudr Elias)

West Gate?
(Gate of
Arches or
Vaults)

540

19

510

28

18

16
Site of
Roman Law-Courts
and Basilica

36

530
520

3
34

Sluices?
Water Gate?
Medrese
13

15

510

11

510

Stream

Halil Rahman Gölü
(Birket Ibrahim)
520

14

4 37

12

520
35

5

530
540
Sakabun Kapısı
550
560
570

Zulihe Gölü
(Birket Zulha)
39 Columns

530
540
550

9

6
7

Water Gates?

KAL'A
(Upper Citadel, Nimrud Kürsisi)

Moat
BETH TABARA?

510

BETH SAHRAYE?

EYÜP MAHALLESI
(Eyubiye)

Haran Kapısı
(Gate of Beth Shemesh,
Gate of Barlaha,
Bab Harran)

0   100   200   300   400
METRES

530 = Contour numbers in metres

8

Site
of hospice and leper house?

PLAN I

PLAN I. URFA (EDESSA). The City

Key

1. HÜSEYIN PAŞA CAMII (KARA MEYDAN CAMII; site of the Melkite Church of the Mother of God?)
2. PAZAR CAMII (HAŞIMIYE CAMII; site of the Byzantine Town Hall?)
3. DEBAĞHANE CAMII
4. HIZANOĞLU CAMII
5. ÇAKARI CAMII (site of the Byzantine Theatre?)
6. HAYRULLAH CAMII (site of the Church of St. Barlaha?)
7. HAVRA
8. EYUBIYE CAMII
9. ARABI CAMII (site of the Church of St. Michael?)
10. YENI CAMI
11. HASAN PAŞA CAMII (site of the Tetrapylon, formerly a synagogue?)
12. DERSA CAMI (MAKAM IBRAHIM, MEVLUD HALIL; site of the Cathedral Church of the Saviour, built beside the Old Church, and later of the Melkite Cathedral or Hagia Sophia?)
13. RIDWANIYE CAMII (AHMET PAŞA CAMII, ZULUMIYE CAMII; site of the Church of St. Thomas?)
14. HALIL RAHMAN CAMII (YEŞIL KILISE; site of the Monophysite Church of the Mother of God and baptistry, formerly the School of the Persians?)
15. SITE OF THE WINTER BATHS
16. ELECTRICITY POWER STATION (site of the Church of St. John the Baptist and St. Addai?)
17. FIRFILI CAMI (site of the Armenian Church of the Twelve Apostles?)
18. IMAM SEKKÂKI MESCIDI (site of the Melkite Church of the Mother of God?)
19. ŞEYHNEBI TEKKESI (site of the Melkite Church of the Cross?)
20. ULU CAMI (KIZIL KILISE; site of the Church of St. Stephen, formerly a synagogue?)
21. KUTBEDDIN CAMII
22. KADIOĞLU CAMII (site of the Church of the Confessors?)
23. YUSUF PAŞA CAMII (site of the Church of St. Cyriacus?)
24. SÜLEYMANIYE CAMII
25. KARA MUSA CAMII (BEY KAPISI CAMII)
26. TÜZEKEN CAMI
27. HACIYADIGÂR MESCIDI (site of the Church of the Twelve Apostles?)
28. AK CAMI (site of the Church of St. Sergius?)
29. HEKIM DEDE CAMII
30. CIRCIS PEYAMBER (site of the Church of St. Sergius and St. Simeon?)
31. PUBLIC BUILDING
32. POST OFFICE
33. YILDIZ HAMAMI
34. VELI BEY HAMAMI
35. SULTAN HAMAMI
36. MÜHACIR ÇARŞISI HAMAMI
37. CINCIKLA HAMAMI
38. VEZIR HAMAMI
39. RUINS OF CHURCH (site of the Church of St. Theodore?)

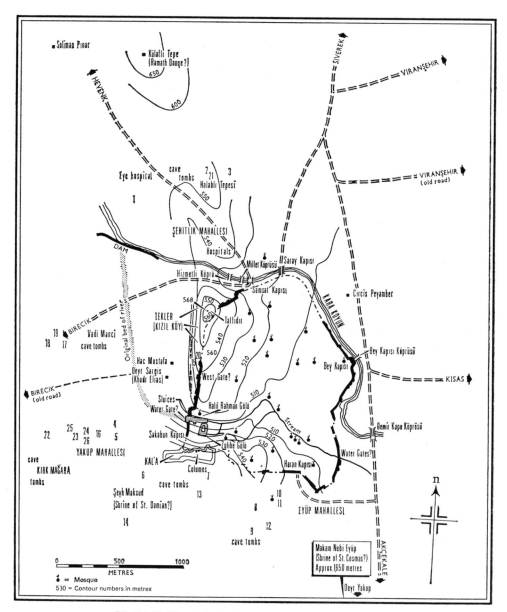

PLAN II. URFA (EDESSA). The City and its environs

Key

1. Cave-tomb with busts in relief
2. 'Tripod' mosaic
3. 'Animal' mosaic
4. Cave-tomb with Jewish inscriptions in Hebrew and Greek
5. Cave-tomb with Funerary couch in relief
6. Cave-tomb with Winged Victory in relief
7. 'Family Portrait' mosaic
8. 'Phoenix' mosaic
9. Double cave-tomb with Winged Victory in relief
10. 'Orpheus' mosaic
11. 'Funerary couch' mosaic
12. Cave-tomb with Funerary couch in relief
13. Cave-tomb with entrance through vertical shaft
14. Syriac inscription of Shalman
15. Double cave-tomb with serpents in relief

16. Double cave-tomb with ornamental arched entrance
17. Cave-tomb with relief
18. Cave-tomb with Funerary couch in relief (unfinished)
19. Cave-tomb with Christian inscription in Syriac and cross
20. Cave-tomb with Funerary couch in relief
21. Cave-tomb with Christian inscription in Greek
22. Cave-tomb with Syriac inscription of G'W
23. Cave-tomb with candelabra carved on entrance wall
24. Cave-tomb with Jewish inscription in Hebrew at entrance
25. Double cave-tomb with ornamental interior
26. Double cave-tomb with Syriac inscription and cross at entrance

SELECT BIBLIOGRAPHY

A. TEXTS

(Texts whose author has not been identified appear under their subject or the title by which they are commonly known.)

Aaron of Serug: F. Nau, *Les légendes syriaques d'Aaron de Saroug* .., (*PO* v), 1910, 697.

Abraham Qidunaya, Acts of: T. J. Lamy, 'Acta Beati Abrahae Kidunaiae Monachi . . .', *Anal. Boll.* x, 1891, 5.

Abu Shama, Shihab al-din abu l-Qasim 'Abd al-raḥman b. Isma'il, *Kitab al-rawḍatayni, Recueil, hist. or.* iv. 1.

Abu l-Fida, Isma'il b. 'Ali 'Imad al-din: J. T. Reinaud and S. Guyard, *Géographie . . .*, 1848–83.

Acts of Abraham Qidunaya, *see Abraham Qidunaya, Acts of.*

—— Addai, *see Addai, Doctrine of.*

—— Mari, *see Mari, Acts of St.*

—— the Apostles, *see Apostles, Acts of the.*

—— the Martyrs, *see Bedjan, Acta . . .*

—— the Martyrs of Beth Slokh, *see Beth Slokh, Acts of the Martyrs of.*

—— the Martyrs of Edessa, *see Edessa, Acts of the Martyrs of.*

Addai, Doctrine of: W. Cureton, *Ancient Syriac Documents . . .*

—— G. Phillips, *The Doctrine of Addai . . .*, 1876.

Aelian, Claudius, *On the Nature of Animals*, ed. R. Hercher, 1864–6.

Aetheria, *see Egeria.*

Agapius (Maḥbub) of Mabbog: A. A. Vasiliev, *Kitab al-'Unvan. Histoire universelle écrite par Agapius (Maḥboub) de Menbidj (PO* v, vii, viii, xi), 1909–15.

Agathias, *History*, ed. B. G. Niebuhr (*CSHB* i), 1828.

Albert of Aix, *Historia Hierosolymitana, Recueil, hist. occ.* iv. 265.

Alexius, Story of St.: A. Amiaud, *La Légende syriaque de Saint Alexis, l'homme de Dieu,* 1889.

Ammian Marcellinus, *Res gestae*, ed. V. Gardthausen, 1874–5.

'Ananisho': E. A. W. Budge, *The Book of Paradise . . . by Palladius . . . according to the recension of 'Anan-Îsho' . . .*, 1904.

Aphraates, Homilies of: J. Parisot, *Aphraatis Sapientis Persae Demonstrationes* (*Pat. Syr.* i), 1894–7.

Apostles, Acts of the: R. A. Lipsius and M. Bonnet, *Acta Apostolorum Apocrypha*, 1951.

Appian, *Roman History*, ed. P. Viereck and A. G. Roos, 1905–39.

Arrian, *Works*, ed. A. G. Roos, 1907–28.

Attaleiates, Michael, *History*, ed. I. Bekker (*CSHB* xxxiv), 1853.

Augustan History, *see Scriptores Historiae Augustae.*

Augustine, St., *Epistolae*, Migne *Patrologia Latina* xxxiii.

Baba of Harran: F. Rosenthal, 'The Prophecies of Bâbâ the Ḥarrânian', in W. B. Henning and E. Yarshater (ed.), *A Locust's Leg. Studies in honour of S. H. Taqizadeh,* 1962, 220.

al-Baladhuri, Aḥmad b. Yahya, *Kitab futuḥ al-buldan*, ed. M. J. de Goeje, 1863–6.

Baldric of Dol, *Historia Jerosolimitana, Recueil, hist. occ.* iv, 1.

Bar Hebraeus, Gregory abu l-Farag: J. B. Abbeloos and T. J. Lamy, *Gregorii Barhe-braei Chronicon Ecclesiasticum* . . . , 1872–7.

—— —— P. Bedjan, *Gregorii Barhebraei Chronicon Syriacum*, 1890.

—— —— P. J. Bruns and C. G. Kirsch, *Gregorii Abulpharagii sive Bar-Hebraei Chronicon Syriacum* . . . , 1789.

—— —— E. A. W. Budge, *The Chronography of Gregory Abu'l Faraj*, 1932.

—— —— W. E. W. Carr, *Commentary on the Gospels from Horreum Mysteriorum*, 1925.

—— —— E. Pocock, *Historia compendiosa Dynastiarum*, 1663.

—— —— M. Sprengling and W. C. Graham, *Barhebraeus' Scholia on the Old Testament*, 1931.

Bardaiṣan, School of: F. Nau, *Bardesanes. Liber Legum Regionum* (*Pat. Syr.* i), 1907.

Barḥadbeshabba 'Arbaya: F. Nau, . . . *Histoire de l'Église nestorienne* (*PO* ix, xxiii), 1913, 1932.

—— A. Scher, *Cause de la Fondation des Écoles* (*PO* iv), 1908.

Basil of Caesarea, St., *Letters*, Migne *PG* xxxii.

Bedjan, P., *Acta Martyrum et Sanctorum*, 1890–7.

Beth Slokh, Acts of the Martyrs of, *see* Bedjan, *Acta* . . .

Burkitt, F. C., *Euphemia and the Goth, with the Acts of Martyrdom of the Confessors of Edessa*, 1913.

Canons, Church: J. Mounayer, 'Les Canons relatifs aux moines, attribués à Rabboula', *Orientalia christiana periodica* xx, 1954, 406.

—— —— *see* Overbeck, *S. Ephraemi Syri . . . Opera*; Vööbus, *Syriac and Arabic Documents* . . .

Cassiodorus: R. A. B. Mynors, *Cassiodori Senatoris Institutiones*, 1937.

Cedrenus, George: I. Bekker, *Compendium Historiarum* (*CSHB* xxiv), 1838.

Chabot, J. B., *Anonymi auctoris Chronicon ad annum Christi 1234 pertinens* (*CSCO* 81–2, *Scr. syri* 36–7), 1953.

—— *Documenta ad origines Monophysitarum illustrandas* (*CSCO* 17, *Scr. syri* 17), 1955.

—— *Incerti auctoris Chronicon Pseudo-Dionysianum vulgo dictum* (*CSCO* 91, 104, *Scr. syri* 43, 53), 1952–3.

Chronicle, Nestorian, *see* I. Guidi, etc., *Chronica Minora*.

—— Sasanian, *see* I. Guidi, etc., *Chronica Minora*.

—— to the year 664, Maronite, *see* I. Guidi, etc., *Chronica Minora*.

—— —— 724, Maronite, *see* I. Guidi, etc., *Chronica Minora*.

—— —— 813, Maronite, *see* I. Guidi, etc., *Chronica Minora*.

—— —— 846, Maronite, *see* I. Guidi, etc., *Chronica Minora*.

—— —— —— E. W. Brooks, 'A Syriac Fragment', *ZDMG* liv, 1900, 195.

—— —— 1234, *see* Chabot, . . . *Chronicon ad . . . 1234*.

Chronicle of Edessa, *see* Guidi, etc., *Chronica Minora*.

'Chronicle of Zuqnin', *see* Chabot, . . . *Chronicon Pseudo-Dionysianum* . . . .

Chronicon Paschale, ed. G. Dindorf (*CSHB* ix), 1832.

Codes, *see* Law Codes.

Constantine Porphyrogenitus, Emperor, *On the Portrait of Edessa*, *see below*, E. von Dobschütz, *Christusbilder*.

Councils, Church: J. B. Chabot, *Synodicon orientale, ou Recueil de synodes nestoriens*, 1902.

—— —— J. Flemming, *Akten der Ephesenischen Synode vom Jahre 449* (Abhandl. d. königl. Gesellsch. d. Wissensch. zu Göttingen, Phil.-hist. Kl., N.F. xv), 1917.

—— —— G. D. Mansi, *Sanctorum Conciliorum nova et amplissima collectio*, 1759.

—— —— F. Schulthess, *Die syrischen Kanones der Synoden von Nicaea bis Chalcedon . . .* (Abhandl. d. königl. Gesellsch. d. Wissensch. zu Göttingen, Phil.-hist. Kl., x), 1908.

—— —— E. Schwartz, *Acta Conciliorum Oecumenicorum* i. 5–8, 1927–30.

Cureton, W., *Ancient Syriac Documents relative to the Earliest Establishment of Christianity in Edessa . . .* , 1864.

—— *Spicilegium Syriacum . . .* , 1855.

Cyriacus, Bishop of Amid: M. A. Kugener, 'Récit de Mar Cyriaque racontant comment le corps de Jacques Baradée fut enlevé . . .', *ROC* vii, 1902, 196.

Denḥa, *History of Marutha*: F. Nau, *Histoires d'Ahoudemmeh et de Marouta . . .* (*PO* iii), 1905.

Dio Cassius, *Roman History*, ed. L. Dindorf and I. Melber, 1863–1928.

Dionysius of Tell-Maḥre, Pseudo-, *see* Chabot, . . . *Chronicon Pseudo-Dionysianum . . .*

Edessa, Acts of the Martyrs of: Burkitt, *Euphemia . . .*

—— —— E. von Dobschütz, *Die Akten der Edessenichen Bekenner Gurjas, Samonas und Abibos . . .* , 1911.

—— *Sugitha* on the Cathedral of: H. Goussen, 'Über ein 'Sugītha' auf die Kathedrale von Edessa', *Muséon* xxxviii, 1925, 117.

—— Topography of: R. Röhricht, 'Studien zur mittelalterlichen Geographie und Topographie Syriens, no. XVI, 'De civitatibus Persarum in terra promissionis imprimis de Edissa vel Roas et de ejus expugnatione et de bello quod christiani parant' ', *ZDPV* x, 1887, 295.

Egeria: O. Prinz, *Itinerarium Egeriae (Peregrinatio Aetheriae)*, 1960.

Elias b. Shinaya: F. W. A. Baethgen, *Fragmente syrischer und arabischer Historiker*, 1884.

—— E. W. Brookes and J. B. Chabot, *Eliae Metropolitae Nisibeni Opus Chronologicum* (*CSCO* 62* 62**, Scr. syri 21–2), 1954.

Ephraim of Edessa, St.: E. Beck, *Des Heiligen Ephraem des Syrers Carmina Nisibena* (*CSCO* 218, 240, Scr. syri 92, 102), 1961–3.

—— —— E. Beck, *Des heiligen Ephraem des Syrers Hymnen Contra Haereses* (*CSCO* 169, Scr. syri 76), 1957.

—— —— E. Beck, *Des Heiligen Ephraem des Syrers Hymnen De Fide* (*CSCO* 154, 212, Scr. syri 58, 73), 1955–61.

—— —— E. Beck, *Des Heiligen Ephraem des Syrers Hymnen De Paradiso und Contra Julianum* (*CSCO* 174, Scr. syri 78), 1957.

—— —— E. Beck, *Des Heiligen Ephraem des Syrers Hymnen De Virginitate* (*CSCO* 223, Scr. syri 94), 1962.

—— —— T. J. Lamy, *S. Ephraemi Syri Hymni et Sermones*, 1882–1902.

—— —— S. J. Mercati, *S. Ephraem Syri Opera* i, 1915.

—— —— C. W. Mitchell, etc., *S. Ephraim's Prose Refutations of Mani, Marcion and Bardaisan*, 1912–21.

—— —— R. M. Tonneau, *Sancti Ephraem Syri in Genesim et in Exodum commentarii* (*CSCO* 152, Scr. syri 71), 1955.

—— —— *Life* of, *see* Bedjan, *Acta . . .* iii.

—— —— *Testament* of: R. Duval, 'Le Testament de saint Ephrem', *JA* 9 Ser. xviii, 1901, 234.

Epiphanius, *Works*, ed. K. Holl, 1915–33.

Euphemia of Edessa, *see* Burkitt, *Euphemia . . .*

Eusebius of Caesarea: *Works*, ed. G. Dindorf, 1867.

—— W. Wright and N. McLean, *The Ecclesiastical History of Eusebius in Syriac*, 1898.

Eutropius, *Breviarium ab urbe condita*, ed. F. Ruehl, 1887.

Evagrius Scholasticus: J. Bidez and L. Parmentier, *The Ecclesiastical History of Evagrius* . . . , 1898.

Evliya Çelebi (Mahomet Zilli b. Dervish), *Seyahatname*.

Florus, Publius Annius, *Epitome*, ed. O. Rossbach, 1896.

Fulcher of Chartres, *Historia Iherosolymitana. Gesta Francorum Iherusalem peregrinantium, Recueil, hist. occ.* iii. 311.

Furlani, F., 'Un Recueil d'énigmes philosophiques en langue syriaque', *ROC* 3 Ser. i (xxi), 1918–9, 113.

George Monachus, *Lives*, ed. I. Bekker (*CSHB* xxii), 1838.

George Syncellus, *Chronography*, ed. G. Dindorf (*CSHB* vii), 1829.

Gesta Francorum expugnantium Iherusalem, Recueil, hist. occ. iii, 487.

Goussen, H., *Martyrius-Sahdona's Leben und Werke* . . . , 1897.

Gregory of Nyssa, St., *Works*, Migne *PG* xliv–xlvi.

Gregory of Tours, *De gloria martyrum*, Migne *Patrologia Latina* lxxi.

Gregory the Priest, *see* Matthew of Edessa.

Guidi, I., etc., *Chronica Minora* (fragments of the Chronicle of Jacob of Edessa and various anonymous chronicles, including the Chronicle of Edessa) (*CSCO* 1, 3, 5, Scr. syri 1, 3, 5), 1955.

Guibert of Nogent, *Gesta Dei per Francos* . . . , *Recueil, hist. occ.* iv. 113.

al-Hamadhani, Abu Bakr Aḥmad b. Muḥammad, *Kitab al-buldan*, ed. M. J. de Goeje, *BGA* v, 1885.

al-Harawi, 'Ali b. Abu Bakr: J. Sourdel-Thoumin, *Guide des lieux de pèlerinage*, 1957.

'Hierotheos': F. S. Marsh, *The Book Which is Called the Book of the Holy Hierotheos* . . . , 1927.

Himyarites: A. Moberg, *The Book of the Himyarites*, 1924.

'Hymn of the Soul', *see* Thomas, Acts of Judas.

Ibn al-Athir, 'Izz al-din abu l-Ḥasan 'Ali Muhammad, *Al-Kamil fi l-ta'rikh*, ed. C. J. Tornberg, 1867–76.

—— —— *Ta'rikh al-dawla al-atabakiya muluk al-Mawṣil, Recueil, hist. or.* ii/2, 1.

Ibn Gubair, Muḥammad b. Aḥmad; W. Wright and M. J. de Goeje, *The Travels of Ibn Jubayr*, 1907.

Ibn Ḥawqal, Muḥammad abu l-Qasim, *Kitab al-masalik wal-mamalik*, ed. M. J. de Goeje, *BGA* ii, 1873.

—— —— *Kitab ṣurat al-arḍ*, ed. J. H. Kramers, 1938–9.

Ibn Khordadhbeh, Abu l-Qasim 'Ubaidallah b. 'Abdallah, *Kitab al-masalik wal-mamalik*, ed. M. J. de Goeje, *BGA* vi, 1889.

Ibn al-Nadim, Abu l-Farag Muḥammad b. (abu Ya'qub) Isḥaq al-Warraq, *Kitab al-Fihrist*, ed. G. L. Flügel, etc., 1871–2.

Ibn al-Qalanisi, Ḥamza b. Asad: H. A. R. Gibb, *The Damascus Chronicle of the Crusades*, 1932.

Ibn Rosta, 'Ali Aḥmad b. 'Umar, *Kitab al-a'laq al-nafisa*, ed. M. J. de Goeje, *BGA* vii, 1892.

Ibn Shaddad, 'Izz al-din b. 'Abdallah Muḥammad, *Al-A'laq al-ḥaṭira fi dhikr umara' al-Sham wal-Gazira*, Bodl. ms. Marsh 333 (unpublished.)

Isaac of Antioch: P. Bedjan, *Homiliae S. Isaaci Syri Antiocheni* i. 1903.

—— G. Bickell, *S. Isaaci Antiocheni . . . opera omnia* i–ii, 1873–7.

Isho'denaḥ: J. B. Chabot, *Le Livre de Chasteté* . . . (École Française de Rome. Mélanges d'Archéologie et d'histoire xvi/3–4, 1891.

Isidore of Charax: W. H. Schoff, *Parthian Stations*, 1914.

Isidore of Seville, St., *Works*, Migne *Patrologia Latina* lxxxi–lxxxiv.

al-Istakhri, Ibrahim b. Muḥammad abu Isḥaq al-Farisi, *Kitab al-masalik wal-mamalik*, ed. M. J. de Goeje, *BGA* i, 1870.

Jacob, Bishop of Edessa: *Chronicle, see* Guidi, etc., *Chronica Minora.*

—— —— *Hexaemeron*: J. B. Chabot, *Jacobi Edesseni Hexaemeron . . . (CSCO* 92, Scr. syri 44), 1953.

—— —— F. Nau, 'Lettre de Jacques d'Édesse à Jean le Stylite . . . ', *ROC* v, 1900, 581.

Jacob, Bishop of Serug: J. P. Martin, 'Discours de Jacques de Saroug sur la chute des idoles', *ZDMG* xxix, 1876, 107.

—— —— C. Moss, 'Jacob of Serugh's Homilies on the Spectacles of the Theatre', *Muséon* xlviii, 1935, 87.

—— —— P. Mouterde, 'Deux homélies inédites de Jacques de Saroug', *Mél. S-J* xxvi, 1944–6, 1.

—— —— O. G. Olinder, *Jacobi Sarugensis Epistulae quotquot supersunt (CSCO* 110, Scr. syri 57), 1952.

—— —— R. Schröter, 'Gedicht des Jakob von Sarug über den Palast', *ZDMG* xxv, 1871, 321.

—— —— *See also* Cureton, *Ancient Syriac Documents.*

Jerome, St., *Works*, Migne *Patrologia Latina* xx–xxx.

Job of Edessa: A. Mingana, *Encyclopaedia of Philosophical and Natural Sciences . . . or Book of Treasures*, 1935.

John, Bishop of Ephesus: E. W. Brooks, *Lives of the Eastern Saints (PO* xvii, xviii, xix), 1923–5.

—— *Johannis Ephesini Historiae Ecclesiasticae pars tertia (CSCO* 105, Scr. syri 54), 1952.

John, Bishop of Tella, *see* A. Vööbus, *Syriac and Arabic Documents . . . .*

John Chrysostom, St., *Works*, Migne *PG* xlvii–lxiv.

John Malalas, *Chronography*, ed. G. Dindorf (*CSHB* viii), 1831.

John Rufus, Bishop of Mayuma, *Plerophories*, ed. F. Nau (*PO* viii), 1912.

Josephus, *Works*, ed. S. A. Naber, 1888–96.

'Joshua the Stylite': W. Wright, *The Chronicle of Joshua the Stylite . . .*, 1882.

Julian, Emperor: J. Bidez and G. Rochefort, *L'Empereur Julien. Œuvres complètes*, 1924–63.

Julian, Romance of: J. G. E. Hoffman, *Julianus der Abtruennige . . .*, 1880.

Julius Africanus: H. Gelzer, *Sextus Julius Africanus und die byzantinische Chronographie*, 1880–98.

—— J. R. Vieillefond, *Fragments des Cestes . . .*, 1932.

Kethaba deMasseqatha (Liber Graduum), ed. M. Kmosko (*Pat. Syr.* i), 1926.

Khalil b. Shahin al-Ẓahiri, *Zubdat kashf al-mamalik*, ed. P. Ravaisse, 1894.

Law Codes: K. G. Bruns and C. E. Sachau, *Syrisch-Römisches Rechtsbuch aus dem fünften Jahrhundert . . .*, 1880.

—— —— C. E. Sachau, *Syrische Rechtsbücher . . .*, 1907–14.

Leo the Deacon, *History*, ed. C. B. Hase (*CSHB* ii), 1828.

Leo the Grammarian, *Chronography*, ed. I. Bekker (*CSHB* xxx), 1842.

Libanius, *Works*, ed. R. Foerster, 1903–23.

Liber Graduum, see Kethaba deMasseqatha.

Lives of Monophysites: E. W. Brooks, *Vitae virorum apud Monophysitas celeberrimorum (CSCO* 7, Scr. syri 7), 1955.

Lucian of Samosata, *De dea syria*, ed. A. M. Harmon, 1925.

Macrobius, *Saturnalia*, ed. J. Willis, 1963.

al-Makin, Girgis b. al-'Amid: P. Erpenius, *Historia saracenica*, 1625.
al-Maqrizi, Aḥmad b. 'Ali: H. F. Wüstenfeld, *Macrizis Geschichte der Copten*, 1845.
Mara b. Serapion, *see* Cureton, *Spicilegium Syriacum* . . .
Marcellinus, Count, *Chronicon*, Migne *Patrologia Latina* li.
Mari, Acts of St.: J. B. Abbeloos, 'Acta Sancti Maris, Assyriae, Babyloniae ac Persidis . . . Apostoli', *Anal. Boll.* iv, 1885, 43.
Marutha, Bishop of Maiperqat: C. G. A. von Harnack, *Der Ketzer-Katalog des Bischofs Maruta*, 1899.
al-Mas'udi, 'Ali b. Ḥusain, *Murug al-dhahab*, ed. C. Barbier de Meynard, etc., 1861–77.
—— —— *Kitab al-tanbih wal-ishraf*, ed. M. J. de Goeje, *BGA* viii, 1894.
Matthew of Edessa: J. P. L. F. E. Dulaurier, *Chronique de Matthieu d'Édesse (962–1136) avec la continuation de Grégoire le Prêtre jusqu'en 1162*, 1858.
Me'arrath Gazze: C. Bezold, *Die Schatzhöhle*, 1883.
Melito of Sardis, Pseudo-, *see* Cureton, *Spicilegium Syriacum* . . .
Menander Protector, *History*, ed. I. Bekker and B. G. Niebuhr (*CSHB* vi), 1829.
Menologies: F. Nau, *Un Martyrologe et douze Ménologes syriaques* (*PO* x), 1915.
Meshiḥazekha: A. Mingana, *Histoire de l'Église d'Adiabène sous les Parthes et Sassanides* (*Sources syriaques* i), 1908.
Michael Qindasi 'the Syrian', Patriarch: J. B. Chabot, *Chronique de Michel le Syrien . . .*, 1899–1924.
Moses of Khoren: P. E. Le Vaillant de Florival, *Histoire d'Arménie*, 1841.
—— —— M. Lauer, *Des Moses von Chorene Geschichte Gross-Armeniens*, 1869.
—— —— N. Tommaséo, *Storia di Mosè Corenese*, 1841.
Mueller, K., *Geographi Graeci Minores*, 1855–61.
—— and T. Mueller, *Fragmenta Historicorum Graecorum*, 1841–84.
al-Muqaddasi, Shams al-din abu 'Abdallah Muḥammad b. Aḥmad, *Kitab aḥsan al-taqasim*, ed. M. J. de Goeje, *BGA* iii, 1906.
al-Mustawfi, Aḥmad b. Abu Bakr b. Naṣr Ḥamdallah: G. le Strange, *The Geographical Part of the* Nuzhat al-Qulub, 1915.
Narratives of Holy Women, Select, ed. A. S. Lewis, 1900.
Narsai (Narseh): A. Mingana, *Narsai Doctoris Syri Homiliae et Carmina*, 1905.
Nau, F., 'Hagiographie syriaque', *ROC* 2 Ser. v (xv), 1910, 53, 173.
—— *La Didascalie de Jacob* (*PO* viii), 1912.
—— 'Littérature canonique syriaque inédite . . .', *ROC* 2 Ser. iv (xiv), 1909, 1, 113.
Nestorian History: A. Scher, *Histoire Nestorienne inédite* (*Chronique de Séert*), *PO* iv–xiii, 1908–19.
Nicetas (Choniates) Acominatus: *History*, ed. I. Bekker (*CSHB* xiv), 1835.
Nisibis, Statutes of the Academy of: I. Guidi, 'Gli Statuti della Scuola di Nisibi', *Giornale della Società Asiatica italiana* iv, 1890, 165.
Nöldeke, T., *Geschichte der Perser und Araber zur Zeit der Sasaniden. Aus der arabischen Chronik des Tabari . . .*, 1879.
Overbeck, J. J., *S. Ephraemi Syri, Rabbulae . . . Balaei aliorumque Opera selecta*, 1865.
Philostratus, *Life of Apollonius of Tyana*, ed. C. L. Kayser, 1870–1.
Philoxenus, Bishop of Mabbug: E. A. W. Budge, *The Discourses of Philoxenus . . .*, 1894.
—— —— R. Lavenant, *La Lettre à Patricius de Philoxène de Mabboug* (*PO* xxx), 1963.
—— —— A. Vaschalde, *Philoxeni Mabbugensis Tractatus tres . . .* (*CSCO* 9, *Scr. syri* 9), 1955.
Pliny, *Natural History*, ed. L. John and C. Mayhoff, 1870–97.
Plutarch, *Lives*, ed. C. Lindskog and K. Ziegler, 1914–39.

Porphyry, *On Abstinence*, ed. A. Nauck, 1886.

Procopius, *Works*, ed. G. Dindorf (*CSHB* x), 1833.

al-Qalqashandi, Aḥmad b. 'Abdallah: M. Gaudefroy-Demombynes, *La Syrie à l'époque des Mamelouks . . .*, 1923.

Rabbula, Life of, see Overbeck, *S. Ephraemi Syri . . .*

Rabbula, *Rules* of, see Vööbus, *Syriac and Arabic Documents . . .*

Raimond de Aguilers, *Historia Francorum qui ceperunt Iherusalem, Recueil, hist. occ.* iii, 231.

Raoul of Caens, *Gesta Tancredi in Expeditione Hierosolymitana, Recueil, hist. occ.* iii, 587.

Rufinus of Aquileia, *Ecclesiastical History*, Migne *Patrologia Latina* xxi.

Samuel of Ani, *Chronography, Recueil des historiens des Croisades. Documents arméniens* i, 447.

Scriptores Historiae Augustae, ed. E. Hohl, etc., 1965.

Secunda pars Historiae Iherosolimitanae, Recueil, hist. occ. iii, 545.

Seert, Chronicle of, *see* Nestorian History.

Sempad, Le Connétable, *Chronicle of the Kingdom of Lesser Armenia, Recueil des historiens des Croisades. Documents arméniens* i. 605.

Sharaf al-din Yazdi, 'Ali: P. de la Croix, *Histoire de Timur-Bec . . .*, 1722.

Simocatta, Theophylact, *History*, ed. I. Bekker (*CSHB* xi), 1834.

Socrates Scholasticus, *Ecclesiastical History*, Migne *PG* lxvii.

Solomon of Basra: E. A. W. Budge, *Book of the Bee . . .*, 1886.

Sozomen: J. Bidez and G. C. Hansen, *Sozomenus Kirchengeschichte*, 1960.

Stephen of Taron: J. P. L. F. E. Dulaurier, *Histoire universelle par Étienne Acogh'ig de Daron*, i. 1883.

———— F. Macler, *Histoire universelle par Étienne Asolik de Tarôn . . .* ii, 1917.

Stephen b. Ṣudaile, *see* 'Hierotheos'

de Stoop, E., *Vie d'Alexandre l'Acémète* (*PO* vi), 1911.

Strabo, *Geography*, ed. A. Meinecke, 1852.

Symeon Magister, *Annals*, ed. I. Bekker (*CSHB* xxii), 1838.

Symeon Metaphrastes, *Lives of the Martyrs Gurias, Samonas and Abibus*, Migne *PG* cxvi.

Synods, *see* Councils, Church.

al-Ṭabari, Muḥammad b. Garir: H. Zotenberg, *Chronique d'Abou Djafar . . . Tabari*, 1867–74.

———— *See also* Nöldeke, *Geschichte der Perser*.

Tacitus, *Annals*, ed. E. Koestermann, 1965.

Theodore b. Koni: A. Scher, *Liber Scholiorum* (*CSCO* 55, 69, *Scr. syri* 19, 26), 1954.

Theodoret, Bishop of Cyrus, *Ecclesiastical History*, ed. L. Parmentier, 1954.

———— *Religious History*, Migne *PG* lxxxii.

Theophanes, *Chronography*, ed. F. Combefis (*CSHB* xxvi), 1839–41.

Theophanes continuatus, *Chronography*, ed. I. Bekker (*CSHB* xxii), 1838.

Thomas, Acts of Judas: P. Bedjan, *Acta . . .* iii.

———— M. Bonnet, *Supplementum Codicis Apocryphi. Acta Thomae*, 1883.

———— W. Wright, *Apocryphal Acts of the Apostles* i, 1871.

———— *See* A. A. Bevan, *Hymn of the Soul*, 1897; *Narratives of Holy Women*, Select.

Thomas, Bishop of Marga: E. A. W. Budge, *The Book of Governors: the Historia Monastica of Thomas, Bishop of Marga A.D. 840*, 1893.

Vööbus, A, *Syriac and Arabic Documents regarding Legislation relative to Syrian Asceticism*, 1960.

William of Tyre, *Historia rerum in partibus transmarinis gestarum, Recueil, hist. occ.* i. 1.
Xenophon, *Anabasis*, ed. G. Gemoll, 1909.
Yahballaha III, Catholicus: P. Bedjan, *Histoire de Mar Jabalaha*, 1895.
Yaḥya b. Saʿid al-Anṭaki: I. Kratchkovsky and A. A. Vasiliev, *Histoire de Yaḥya-ibn-Saʿid d'Antioche* (*PO* xviii), 1924.
al-Yaʿqubi, Aḥmad b. abu Yaʿqub b. Waḍiḥ, *Kitab al-buldan*, ed. M. J. de Goeje, *BGA* vii, 1892.
Yaqut b. ʿAbdallah, *Muʿgam al-buldan*: H. F. Wüstenfeld, *Jacuts Geographisches Wörterbuch*, 1866–73.
Zacharias Rhetor Pseudo-: E. W. Brooks, *Historia Ecclesiastica Zachariae Rhetori vulgo adscripta* (*CSCO* 83–4, *Scr. syri* 38–9), 1953.
Zonaras, John, *Annals*, ed. M. Pinder (*CSHB* xxix), 1841–97.
Zosimus, *New History*, ed. I. Bekker (*CSHB* xx), 1837.

B. OTHER WORKS (INCLUDING INSCRIPTIONS)

Abbott, F. F., and A. C. Johnson, *Municipal Administration in the Roman Empire*, 1926.
ʿAbd al-Masiḥ, Y., 'An unedited Boḥairic letter of Abgar', *Bulletin de l'Institut français d'archéologie orientale du Caire* xlv, 1947, 65.
Abel, A., 'Étude sur l'inscription d'Abercius', *Byzantion* iii, 1926, 321.
Abramowski, R., *Dionysius von Tellmahre, jakobitischer Patriarch von 818–845 . . .*, 1940.
Adam, A., *Die Psalmen des Thomas und das Perlenlied als Zeugnisse vorchristlicher Gnosis*, 1959.
Adler, E. N., *Jewish Travellers*, 1930.
Adnès, A., and P. Canivet, 'Guérisons miraculeuses et exorcismes dans l' "Histoire Philothée" de Théodoret de Cyr', *RHR* clxxi, 1967, 53, 149.
Adontz, N., 'Notes arméno-byzantines', *Byzantion* ix, 1934, 367.
Ainsworth, W. F., *A Personal Narrative of the Euphrates Expedition*, 1888.
—— *Researches in Assyria, Babylonia and Chaldaea*, 1838.
—— *Travels and Researches in Asia Minor, Mesopotamia, Chaldea, and Armenia*, 1842.
Albrecht, K., *Die in Taḥkemoni vorkommenden Angaben über Ḥarizis Leben, Studien und Reisen*, 1890.
d'Alès, A., 'La Lettre d'Ibas à Marès le Persan', *Recherches de science religieuse* xxii, 1932, 5.
Alföldi, A., 'Die Hauptereignisse der Jahre 253–61 n. Chr. im Orient im Spiegel der Münzprägung', *Berytus* iv, 1937, 41.
Allemand-Lavigerie, C. M., *Essai historique sur l'école chrétienne d'Édesse*, 1850.
Altheim, F. and R. Stiehl, *Die Araber in der alten Welt*, 1964– .
Amedroz, H. F., 'The Marwānid Dynasty at Mayyafariqin in the Tenth and Eleventh Centuries A.D.', *JRAS*, 1903, 123.
—— and D. S. Margoliouth, *The Eclipse of the Abbasid Caliphate*, 1920–1.
Arewean, A., *History of Edessa* (in Armenian), 1881.
Assemanus, J. S., *Bibliotheca Orientalis Clementino-Vaticana*, 1719–28.
Babelon, E. C. F., *Les Rois de Syrie, d'Arménie et de Commagène*, 1890.
—— *Mélanges numismatiques*, 1892–1912.
Babelon, J., *Catalogue de la Collection de Luynes* iv, 1936.
Badger, G. P., *The Nestorians and their Rituals . . .*, 1852.
Baldwin, M. W., *The First Hundred Years* (K. M. Setton, *A History of the Crusades* i), 1955.

Bardenhewer, O., *Geschichte der altkirchlichen Literatur*, 1913–32.

Baumstark, A., 'Bruchstücke eines Taufsymbols der Euphratesia oder Osrhoëne', *OC* iii, 1903, 208.

—— 'Das Alter der Peregrinatio Aetheriae', *OC* N.s. i, 1911, 32.

—— 'Das Todesjahr der edessenischen Märtyrer Guria und Shamona', *Atti del IIo Congresso internazionale di Archeologia cristiana tenuto in . . . 1900*, 1902, 23.

—— *Die Petrus- und Paulusacten in der literarischen Ueberlieferung der syrischen Literatur*, 1902.

—— 'Eine syrische 'traditio legis' und ihre Parallelen', *OC* iii, 1903, 173.

—— *Festbrevier und Kirchenjahr der syrischen Jacobiten*, 1910.

—— *Geschichte der syrischen Literatur*, 1922.

—— 'Îwannîs von Dara über Bardaiṣan', *OC* 3 Ser. viii, 1933, 62.

—— 'Vorjustinianische kirchliche Bauten in Edessa', *OC* iv, 1904, 164.

Baur, P. V. C., etc., *The Excavations at Dura-Europos*, 1929– .

Bayer, T. S., *Historia Osrhoene et Edessena, ex numis illustrata*, 1734.

Baynes, N. H., *Byzantine Studies and other Essays*, 1955.

—— 'The Supernatural Defenders of Constantinople', *Anal. Boll.* lxvii, 1949, 165.

Beck, E., 'Ascétisme et monachisme chez saint Ephrem', *Orient syrien* iii, 1958, 273.

—— 'Das Bild vom Spiegel bei Ephräm', *Orientalia christiana periodica* xix, 1953, 1.

—— *Ephraems Reden über den Glauben . . .* (Studia Anselmiana 33), 1953.

—— art. 'Ephraem Syrus' in T. Klauser (ed.), *Reallexikon für Antike und Christentum*.

Beck, H. G., *Kirche und theologische Literatur im byzantinischen Reich*, 1959.

Beckingham, C. F., *The Achievements of Prester John. An Inaugural Lecture*, 1966.

Bell, G. M. L., *Amurath to Amurath . . .* , 1924.

Bellinger, A. R., 'Hyspaosines of Charax', *YCS* viii, 1942, 53.

—— 'The Coins . . .', in M. I. Rostovtzeff, etc., *The Excavations at Dura-Europos . . . 1933–1934 and 1934–1935*, 1939, 391.

—— and C. B. Welles, 'A Third-Century Contract of Sale from Edessa in Osrhoene', *YCS* v, 1935, 93.

Benz, E., *Indische Einflüsse auf die frühchristliche Theologie*, 1951.

van Berchem, M., and J. Strzygowski, *Amida . . .* , 1910.

Bidez, J., *La Vie de l'empereur Julien*, 1930.

—— and F. V. M. Cumont, *Les Mages hellénisés . . .* , 1938.

Bivar, A. D. H., and S. Shaked, 'The Inscriptions at Shīmbār', *BSOAS* xxvii, 1964, 265.

Bludau, A., *Die Pilgerreise der Aetheria*, 1927.

Bossert, H. T., *Altanatolien*, 1942.

Bowen, H., *The Life and Times of 'Ali ibn 'Isa ,'the Good Vizier'*, 1928.

Braun, O., *Ausgewählte Akten Persischer Märtyrer*, 1915.

—— *Das Buch der Synhados . . .* , 1900.

Breasted, J. H., 'Peintures d'époque romaine dans le désert de Syrie', *Syria* iii, 1922, 177.

Bréhier, L., 'Byzance et empire byzantin', *BZ* xxx, 1929–30, 360.

—— 'Icones non faites de main d'homme', *Rev. arch.* 5 Ser. xxxv, 1932, 68.

—— *La Civilisation byzantine*, 1950.

—— *Les Institutions de l'Empire byzantin*, 1948.

—— *Vie et mort de Byzance*, 1947.

Brière, M., 'Quelques fragments syriaques de Diodore, évêque de Tarse', *ROC* 3 Ser. x (xxx), 1935–6, 231.

Brock, S., 'The Armenian and Syriac Versions of the Ps.-Nonnus Mythological Scholia', *Muséon* lxxix, 1966, 401.

Brockelmann, C., *Syrische Grammatik mit . . . Literatur . . .* , 1962.

Brooks, E. W., 'Byzantines and Arabs in the time of the early Abbasids', *English Historical Review* xv, 1900, 728; xvi, 1901, 84.

—— 'The Chronological Canon of James of Edessa' *ZDMG* liii, 1899, 261.

—— 'The Sources of Theophanes and the Syriac Chroniclers', *BZ* xv, 1906, 578.

Brown, L. W., *The Indian Christians of St. Thomas*, 1956.

Buckingham, J. S., *Travels in Mesopotamia . . .* , 1827.

Buckler, G., 'Women in Byzantine Law about 1100 A.D.', *Byzantion* xi, 1936, 391.

Burckhardt, A., *Hieroclis Synecdemus*, 1893.

Burkitt, F. C., *Church and Gnosis . . .* , 1932.

—— *Early Eastern Christianity*, 1904.

—— *The Religion of the Manichees*, 1925.

——'The Throne of Nimrod', *Proceedings of the Society of Biblical Archaeology* xxviii, 1906, 149.

Bury, J. B., *History of the Later Roman Empire from the death of Theodosius I to the death of Justinian, A.D. 395 to A.D. 565*, 1923.

Butler, H. C., *Ancient Architecture in Syria*, 1907–21.

Cahen, C., 'La Djazira au milieu du treizième siècle d'après 'Izz ad-din ibn Chaddad', *REI* viii, 1934, 109.

—— 'La Première pénétration turque en Asie-Mineure (seconde moitié du XIe S.)', *Byzantion* xviii, 1948, 5.

—— *La Syrie du Nord à l'époque des croisades*, 1940.

—— 'Le Diyarbakr au temps des premiers Urtukides', *JA* ccxxvii, 1935, 219.

Canard, M., *Histoire de la Dynastie des H'amdanides de Jazîra et de Syrie*, 1953.

—— 'Quelques 'à-côté' de l'histoire des relations entre Byzance et les Arabes', *Studi Orientalistici in onore di Giorgio Levi della Vida*, 1956, i, 98.

—— *Recueil de textes relatifs à l'émir Sayf al-Daula le Ḥamdanide . . .* , 1934.

Cantineau, J., *Grammaire du palmyrénien épigraphique*, 1935.

—— *Le Nabatéen*, 1930.

—— and J. Starcky, *Inventaire des inscriptions de Palmyre*, 1930–.

Caquot, A., 'Inscriptions judéo-arabes de Ruṣāfa (Sergiopolis)', *Syria* xxxii, 1955, 70.

—— 'Note sur le *Semeion* et les inscriptions araméennes de Hatra', *Syria* xxxii, 1955, 59.

—— 'Nouvelles inscriptions araméennes de Hatra', *Syria* xxix, 1952, 89; xxx, 1953, 234; xxxii, 1955, 49, 261; xl, 1963, 1; xli, 1964, 251.

Carrière, A., *La Légende d'Abgar dans l'histoire d'Arménie de Moïse de Khoren* (Centenaire de l'École des langues vivantes), 1895.

Casson, L., and E. L. Hettich, *Excavations at Nessana* ii, 1950.

Cerfaux, L., art. 'Bardesanes' in T. Klauser (ed.), *Reallexikon für Antike und Christentum*.

Cerulli, E., *Storia della letteratura etiopica*, 1956.

Chabot, J. B. 'Édesse pendant la première croisade', *CRAI*, 1918, 431.

—— 'L'École de Nisibe, son histoire, ses statuts', *JA* 9 Ser. viii, 1896, 43.

—— 'Les Évêques jacobites du VIIIe au XIIIe siècle d'après la chronique de Michel le Syrien', *ROC* iv, 1899, 444, 495; v, 1900, 605; vi, 1901, 189.

—— 'Notes sur quelques monuments épigraphiques araméens', *JA* 10 Ser. vii, 1906, 281.

—— 'Un Épisode inédit de l'histoire des croisades', *CRAI*, 1917, 77.

Chalandon, F., *Les Comnène*, 1900–12.

Chalandon, H., *Histoire de la première croisade, jusqu'à l'élection de Godefroi de Bouillon*, 1925.

Chapot, V., 'Antiquités de la Syrie du Nord', *Bull. corr. hell.* xxvi, 1902, 161.

—— *La Frontière de l'Euphrate de Pompée à la conquête arabe*, 1907.

Charanis, P., *Church and State in the Later Roman Empire. The Religious Policy of Anastasius the First 491–518*, 1939.

Charles, H., *Le Christianisme des arabes nomades sur le Limes . . .* , 1936.

Charlesworth, M. P., *Trade-Routes and Commerce of the Roman Empire*, 1926.

Chaumont, M. L., 'Les Sassanides et la christianisation de l'empire iranien au IIIᵉ siècle de notre ère', *RHR* clxv, 1964, 165.

Chesney, F. R., *The Expedition for the Survey of the Rivers Euphrates and Tigris . . .* , 1850.

Christensen, A. E., *L'Iran sous les Sassanides*, 1936.

Chwolson, D. A., *Die Ssabier und der Ssabismus*, 1856.

Clemen, C., *Lukians Schrift über die syrische Göttin*, 1938.

—— 'Tempel und Kult in Hierapolis', in *Pisciculi. Studien zur Religion und Kultur des Altertums Franz Joseph Dölger . . . dargeboten*, 1939, 66.

Clermont-Ganneau, C., *Recueil d'archéologie orientale*, 1888–1924.

Connolly, R. H., *Didascalia Apostolorum*, 1929.

Conybeare, F. C., 'The Date of Moses of Khoren', *BZ* x, 1901, 489.

Cook, A. B., *Zeus. A Study in Ancient Religion*, 1914–40.

Cumont, F. V. M., *Die Mysterien des Mithra*, 1911.

—— *Études syriennes*, 1917.

—— *Fouilles de Doura-Europos, 1922–1923*, 1926.

—— 'Gaionas le δειπνοκρίτης', *CRAI*, 1917, 275.

—— 'Le Culte de Mithra à Édesse', *Rev. arch.* 3 Ser. xii, 1888, 95.

—— *Les Religions orientales dans le paganisme romain*, 1929.

—— 'Peintures d'époque romaine dans le désert de Syrie', *Syria* iii, 1922, 177.

—— *Recherches sur le symbolisme funéraire des Romains*, 1942.

Debevoise, N. C., *A Political History of Parthia*, 1938.

Deconinck, J., review in *RB* N.S. vii, 1910, 432.

Delaporte, L. J., *La Chronographie d'Élie Bar-Šinaya . . .* , 1910.

Delcor, M., 'Une Inscription funéraire araméenne trouvée à Daskyleion en Turquie', *Muséon* lxxx, 1967, 301.

Delehaye, H., *Les Origines du culte des martyrs*, 1933.

—— *Les Saints stylites*, 1923.

Deonna, W., 'Questions d'archéologie religieuse et symbolique. V', *RHR* lxx, 1914, 43.

Der Nersessian, S., 'The Illustrations of the Metaphrastian Menologium', in *Late Classical and Mediaeval Studies in Honor of A. M. Friend*, 1955, 222.

Devos, P., 'Actes de Thomas et Actes de Paul', *Anal. Boll.* lxix, 1951, 119.

—— 'Égérie à Édesse. S. Thomas l'Apôtre; le roi Abgar', *Anal. Boll.* lxxxv, 1967, 381.

—— 'La Date du voyage d'Égérie', *Anal. Boll.* lxxxv, 1967, 165.

—— 'Le Miracle posthume de S. Thomas l'Apôtre', *Anal. Boll.* lxvi, 1948, 231.

Devreese, R., *Le Patriarcat d'Antioche depuis la paix de l'église jusqu'à la conquête arabe*, 1945.

Dhorme, E., 'Les Religions arabes préislamiques d'après une publication récente', *RHR* cxxxiii, 1948, 34.

Diehl, C., *Dans l'Orient byzantin*, 1917.

—— *Justinien et la civilisation byzantine au VIᵉ siècle*, 1901.

Diekamp, F., 'Der Mönch und Presbyter Georgios, ein unbekannter Schriftsteller des 7. Jahrhunderts', *BZ* ix, 1900, 14.

Dillemann, L., *Haute Mésopotamie orientale et pays adjacents*, 1962.

Dj'afar al-Ḥassani and J. Starcky, 'Autels palmyréniens découverts près de la source Efca', *Annales archéologiques de Syrie* vii, 1957, 95.

Dobiáš, J., 'Les Premiers rapports des Romains avec les Parthas et l'occupation de la Syrie', *Arch. or*, iii. 1931, 215.

von Dobschütz, E., *Christusbilder. Untersuchungen zur christlichen Legende*, 1899.

—— 'Der Briefwechsel zwischen Abgar und Jesus', *ZWT* xliii, 1900, 422.

—— 'Die Chronik Michael des Syrers', *ZWT* xli, 1898, 456.

—— 'Die confessionellen Verhältnisse in Edessa unter der Araberherrschaft . . .', *ZWT* xli, 1898, 364.

Dölger, F., *Regesten der Kaiserurkunden des oströmischen Reiches von 565–1453*, 1924–65.

Dölger, F. X. J., *Ἰχθύς. Das Fischsymbol in frühchristlicher Zeit*, 1910–57.

Donner, H., and W. Roellig, *Kanaanäische und aramäische Inschriften*, 1962–4.

Doresse, J., *The Secret Books of the Egyptian Gnostics*, 1960.

Downey, R. E. G., *A History of Antioch in Syria from Seleucus to the Arab Conquest*, 1961.

Dowsett, C. J. 'A Twelfth-century Armenian Inscription at Edessa', in *In Memoriam Vladimir Minorsky*, 1970.

Drijvers, H. J. W., *Bardaiṣan of Edessa*, 1966.

—— 'Quq and the Quqites. An Unknown sect in Edessa in the Second Century A.D.', *Numen* xiv, 1967, 104.

Drioton, E., 'Un Apocryphe anti-arien: la version copte de la correspondence d'Abgar roi d'Édesse avec Notre-Seigneur', *ROC* 2 Ser. x, 1915–7, 306, 337.

Duchesne, L., *L'Église au VIe siècle*, 1925.

—— 'L'Iconographie byzantine dans un document grec du IX siècle', *Roma e l'Oriente* anno III, v, Nov. 1912–Apr. 1913, 222, 273, 349.

Duchesne-Guillemin, J., 'Die drei Weisen aus dem Morgenlande und die Anbetung der Zeit', *Antaios* vii, 1965, 234.

Dulaurier, J. P. L. F. E., 'Die Chronik Michael des Syrers', *ZWT* N.F. vi (xli), 1898, 456.

Du Mesnil du Buisson, R., *Les Peintures de la synagogue de Doura-Europos, 245–256 après J. C.*, 1939.

Dupont-Sommer, A., 'Une Hymne syriaque sur la Cathédrale d'Édesse', *Cah. arch.* ii, 1947, 29.

Dussaud, R., *La Pénétration des arabes en Syrie avant l'Islam*, 1955.

—— *Topographie historique de la Syrie antique et médiévale*, 1927.

Duval, R., *Histoire politique, religieuse et littéraire d'Édesse jusqu'à la première croisade*, 1892.

—— 'Notes sur la Peschitto', *REJ* xiv, 1887, 49.

Ebersholt, J., *Sanctuaires de Byzance*, 1921.

Eissfeldt, O. H. W. L., *Tempel und Kulte syrischer Städte in hellenistisch-römischer Zeit*, 1941.

Eméreau, C., *Saint Éphrem le Syrien: son œuvre littéraire grecque*, 1919.

Emerton, J. A., 'Some Problems of Text and Language in the Odes of Solomon', *JTS* N.S. xviii, 1967, 372.

Ensslin, W., *Zu den Kriegen des Sassaniden Schapur I*, 1949.

van Esbroeck, M., 'Chronique arménienne', *Anal. Boll.* lxxx, 1962, 423.

Euting, J., 'Notulae epigraphicae 1. Mosaïque syrienne d'Ourfah', in *Florilegium ou Recueil de travaux d'érudition dédiés à . . . de Vogüé*, 1909, 231.

Faris, N. A., and H. Glidden, 'The Development of the Meaning of the Koranic *Ḥanif*', *Journal of the Palestine Oriental Society* xix, 1939–40, 1.

de Faye, E., 'Introduction à l'étude du gnosticisme au IIe et au IIIe siècle', *RHR* xlv, 1902, 299; xlvi, 1902, 31, 145, 363; xlvii, 1903, 336.

Férotin, M., 'Le Véritable auteur de la *Peregrinatio Silviae*; la vierge espagnole Éthéria', *RQH* N.S. xxx, 1903, 367.

Festugière, A. M. J., *Antioche païenne et chrétienne*, 1959.

Février, J. G. *La Religion des Palmyréniens*, 1931.

—— 'Simia–Némésis, *JA* ccxxiv, 1934, 308.

Fiey, J. M. 'Auteur et date de la Chronique d'Arbèles', *Orient syrien* xii, 1967, 265.

—— 'Diptyques nestoriens du XIVe siècle', *Anal. Boll.* lxxxi, 1963, 371.

—— 'Vers la réhabilitation de l'*Histoire de Karka d^eBeṯ Slōḥ*', *Anal. Boll.* lxxxii, 1964, 189.

Fliche, A., and V. Martin (ed.), *Histoire de l'église*: iii. J. R. Palanque, etc., *De la paix constantinienne à la mort de Théodose*, 1947; iv, P. de Labriolle, etc., *De la mort de Théodose a l'élection de Grégoire le Grand*, 1945.

Forrer, E. O. G., *Die Provinzeinteilung des assyrischen Reiches*, 1920.

Frank, T. (ed.), *An Economic Survey of Ancient Rome*, 1933–40.

Frey, J. B., *Corpus inscriptionum judaicarum*, 1936– .

Frézouls, E., 'Recherches sur les théâtres de l'Orient syrien', *Syria* xxxvi, 1959, 202.

Frolow, A., *La Relique de la Vraie Croix. Recherches sur le développement d'un culte,* 1961.

—— *Les Reliquaires de la Vraie Croix*, 1965.

Frothingham, A. L., *Stephen bar Sudaili, the Syrian Mystic, and the Book of Hierotheos*, 1886.

Frye, R. N., 'Notes on the Early Sassanian State and Church', *in Studi orientalistici in onore di Giorgio Levi della Vida*, 1956, i, 314.

—— etc., 'Inscriptions from Dura-Europos', *YCS* xiv, 1955, 127.

Gabriel, A., *Voyages archéologiques dans la Turquie orientale*, 1940.

Gadd, C. J., 'The Harran Inscriptions of Nabonidus', *AS* viii, 1958, 35.

von Gaertringen, F. Hiller, review in *Byzantinisch-Neugriechische Jahrbücher* v, 1926–7, 213.

Gagé, J., 'Comment Sapor a-t-il 'triomphé' de Valérien?', *Syria* xlii, 1965, 343.

—— *La Montée des Sassanides et l'heure de Palmyre*, 1964.

de Gaiffier, B., 'Les Sources de la Passion de S. Eutrope de Saintes dans le 'Liber Sancti Jacobi' ', *Anal. Boll.* lxix, 1951, 57.

Galust, Ter-Grigorian Iskenderian, *Die Kreuzfahrer und ihre Beziehungen zu den armenischen Nachbarfürsten bis zum Untergang der Grafschaft Edessa*, 1915.

Garcia, Z., 'Egeria ou Aetheria?', *Anal. Boll.* xxx, 1911, 444.

—— 'La Lettre de Valérius aux moines de Vierzo sur la bienheureuse Aetheria', *Anal. Boll.* xxix, 1910, 377.

Gavin, F., 'Aphraates and the Jews', *Journal of the Society of Oriental Research* vii, 1923, 95.

Geary, G., *Through Asiatic Turkey. Narrative of a Journey from Bombay to the Bosphorus*, 1878.

Geffcken, J., *Der Ausgang des griechisch-römischen Heidentums*, 1929.

Gelzer, H., *Georgii Cyprii Descriptio Orbis Romani*, 1890.

—— 'Josua Stylites und die damaligen kirchlichen Parteien des Ostens', *BZ* i, 1892, 34.

—— 'Ungedruckte und wenig bekannte Bistümerverzeichnisse der orientalischen Kirche', *BZ* i, 1892, 245; ii, 1893, 22.

Gelzer, H., and A. Burckhardt, *Des Stephanos von Taron Armenische Geschichte*, 1907.

Gershevitch, I. 'A Parthian Title in the Hymn of the Soul', *JRAS*, 1954, 124.

Gerson, D., 'Die Commentarien des Ephraem Syrus im Verhältniss zur jüdischen Exegese . . .', *Monatschrift für Geschichte und Wissenschaft des Judenthums* xvii, 1868, 15, 64, 98, 141.

Gibson, J. C. L., 'From Qumran to Edessa: or the Aramaic Speaking Church before and after 70 A.D.', *Annual of the Leeds University Oriental Society* v, 1963–5, 24.

Giron, N., 'Notes épigraphiques (Damas, Alep, Orfa)', *Mél. S-J* v. 1911, 71.

Gollancz, H., *Julian the Apostate*, 1928.

Goodenough, E. R., *Jewish Symbols in the Greco-Roman Period*, 1953–6.

Goossens, G., *Hiérapolis de Syrie. Essai de monographie historique*, 1943.

Gordon, C. H., 'Abraham and the Merchants of Ura', *JNES* xvii, 1958, 28.

—— *Before the Bible*, 1962.

Gottheil, R. J. H., 'A Tract on the Syriac conjunctions', *Hebraica* iv, 1887–8, 167.

Goubert, P., *Byzance avant l'Islam*, 1951–5.

Gouillard, J., 'Supercheries et méprises littéraires: L'œuvre de Saint Théodore d'Édesse', *Revue des études byzantines* v, 1947, 137.

Grabar, A. N., *L'Iconoclasme byzantin. Dossier archéologique*, 1957.

—— *La Sainte Face de Laon, le Mandylion dans l'Art orthodoxe* (Seminarium Kondakovianum), 1931.

—— 'Le Témoignage d'une hymne syriaque sur l'architecture de la cathédrale d'Édesse au VIe siècle et sur la symbolique de l'édifice chrétien', *Cah. arch.* ii, 1947, 41.

—— *Martyrium. Recherches sur le culte des reliques et l'art chrétien antique*, 1946.

Graf, G., 'Die Ṣâbier', *OC* xii–xiv, 1925, 214.

—— *Geschichte der christlichen arabischen Literatur*, 1944–53.

—— 'Zur Gebetsostung', *Jahrbuch für Liturgiewissenschaft* vii, 1927, 153.

Grébaut, S., 'Les Relations entre Abgar et Jésus, texte éthiopien', *ROC* 3 Ser. i (xxi), 1918–9, 73, 190, 253.

Grégoire, H., 'Bardesane et S. Abercius', *Byzantion* xxv–xxvii, 1955–7, 363.

—— 'Le Tombeau et la date de Digénis Akritas', *Byzantion* vi, 1931, 481.

—— *Les Persécutions dans l'Empire romain*, 1964.

—— 'Sainte Euphémie et l'Empereur Maurice', *Muséon* lix, 1946, 295.

—— and M. Canard, *La Dynastie d'Amorium (820–867)*, 1935.

Grintz, J. M. 'On the Original Home of the Semites', *JNES* xxi, 1962, 186.

Grohmann, A., *Griechische, koptische und arabische Texte zur Religion und religiösen Literatur in Ägyptens Spätzeit*, 1934.

Grousset, R., *Histoire de l'Arménie des origines à 1071*, 1947.

—— *Histoire des Croisades et du royaume franc de Jérusalem*, 1934–6.

Grumel, V., 'Léon de Chalcédoine et le canon de la fête du saint Mandilion', *Anal. Boll.* lxviii, 1950, 135.

Grünbaum, M., *Neue Beiträge zur semitischen Sagenkunde*, 1893.

von Grunebaum, G. E., 'Eine poetische Polemik zwischen Byzanz und Bagdad im X. Jahrhundert', *Studia Arabica I*, 1937, 41.

Güterbock, C., *Byzanz und Persien in ihren diplomatisch-völkerrechtlichen Beziehungen im Zeitalter Justinians . . .*, 1906.

von Gutschmid, A., *Untersuchungen über die Geschichte des Königreichs Osroene*, 1887.

Guyer, S., *My Journey down the Tigris*, 1925.

—— 'Reisen in Mesopotamien', *Dr. A. Petermanns Mitteilungen aus Justus Perthes' Geographischer Anstalt* lxii, 1916, 168.

Haase, F., *Altchristliche Kirchengeschichte nach orientalischen Quellen*, 1925.
—— 'Die Abfassungszeit der Edessenischen Chronik', *OC* N.S. vii–viii, 1918, 88.
—— 'Neue Bardesanesstudien', *OC* N.S. xii–xiv, 1925, 129.
—— 'Untersuchungen zur Chronik des Pseudo-Dionysios von Tell-Maḥre', *OC* N.S. vi, 1916, 65, 240.
—— *Zur bardesanischen Gnosis*, 1910.
Hage, W., *Die syrisch-jakobitische Kirche in frühislamischer Zeit*, 1966.
Hallier, L., *Untersuchungen über die edessenische Chronik . . .*, 1892.
Hallo, W. W., 'The Road to Emar', *Journal of Cuneiform Studies* xviii, 1964, 57.
Hammerschmidt, E., etc., *Symbolik des orthodoxen und orientalischen Christentums*, 1962.
von Harnack, C. G. A., *The Mission and Expansion of Christianity in the First Three Centuries . . .*, 1908.
—— 'Der Brief des britischen Königs Lucius an den Papst Eleutherus', *Sitzungsberichte der königlich preussischen Akademie der Wissenschaften*, 1904, 909.
Harris, J. R., *Boanerges*, 1913.
—— *The Cult of the Heavenly Twins*, 1906.
—— *The Dioscuri in the Christian Legends*, 1903.
Hartmann, M., *Bohtan* (Mitteilungen der vorderasiatischen Gesellschaft), 1896.
Hasluck, F. W., *Christianity and Islam under the Sultans*, 1929.
Hayes, E. R., *L'école d'Édesse*, 1930.
Head, B. V., *Historia nummorum*, 1911.
von Hefele, C. J., *Histoire des Conciles d'après les documents originaux*, 1907.
Henderson, M. I., review in *JRS* xxxix, 1949, 121.
Henning, W. B., 'A New Parthian Inscription', *JRAS* 1953, 132.
—— 'The Monuments and Inscriptions of Tang-i Sarvak', *Asia Major* N.S. ii, 1951–2, 151.
Herrmann, A., *Die alten Seidenstrassen zwischen China und Syrien*, 1910.
Herrmann, L., 'Qui est Saint Alexis?', *L'Antiquité classique* xi, 1942, 235.
Herrmann, T., 'Die Schule von Nisibis vom 5. bis 7. Jahrhundert', *ZNW* xxv, 1926, 89.
Herzfeld, E., 'Hatra', *ZDMG* lxviii, 1914, 655.
Hilgenfeld, A., *Bardesanes, der letzte Gnostiker*, 1864.
Hill, G. F., *Catalogue of the Greek Coins of Arabia, Mesopotamia, and Persia . . .*, 1922.
Hjelt, A., *Die altsyrische Evangelienübersetzung und Tatians Diatessaron*, 1903.
Hoffmann, J. G. E., *Akten der Ephesinischen Synode vom Jahre 449*, 1917.
—— *Auszüge aus syrischen Akten persischer Märtyrer*, 1880.
Hogarth, D. G., 'Hierapolis Syriae', *The Annual of the British School of Athens* xiv, 1907–8, 183.
Hölscher, G., *Syrische Verskunst*, 1932.
Homes, D., 'A propos d'une statue 'parthe',' *Syria* xxxvii, 1960, 321.
Honigmann, E., 'A Trial for Sorcery on August 22, A.D. 449', *Isis* xxv, 1944, 281.
—— *Die Ostgrenze des byzantinischen Reiches von 363 bis 1071 . . .*, 1935.
—— *Évêques et évêchés monophysites d'Asie antérieure au VIᵉ siècle*, 1951.
—— *Le Couvent de Barsauma et le patriarcat jacobite d'Antioche et de Syrie*, 1954.
—— *Patristic Studies*, 1953.
—— 'Studien zur Notitia Antiochene', *BZ* xxv, 1925, 60.
—— 'The Original Lists of the Members of the Council of Nicaea, the Robber-Synod and the Council of Chalcedon', *Byzantion* xvi, 1942–3, 20.
—— 'Urfa keilschriftlich nachweisbar?', *ZA* N.F. v (xxxix), 1930, 301.
—— art. 'Orfa' in *EI*.

Honigmann, E., and A. Maricq, *Recherches sur les Res gestae divi Saporis*, 1953.

Hopfner, T., 'Apollonis von Tyana und Philostratos', *Seminarium Kondakovianum* iv, 1931, 135.

Hopkins, C., 'Aspects of Parthian Art in the Light of Discoveries from Dura-Europos', *Berytus* iii, 1936, 1.

Huart, C., *La Perse antique et la civilisation iranienne*, 1925.

Humann, K., and O. Puchstein, *Reisen in Kleinasien und Nordsyrien*, 1890.

Ingholt, H., 'Inscriptions and Sculptures from Palmyra, I–II', *Berytus* iii, 1936, 83; v, 1938, 93.

—— *Parthian Sculptures from Hatra* . . . . 1954.

—— etc., *Recueil des Tessères de Palmyre*, 1955.

Işiltan, F., *Urfa bölgesi tarihi* . . . (in Turkish), 1960.

Jannare, A. N., 'Κατεπάνω—Capitano—Captain', *BZ* x, 1901, 204.

Jansma, T., 'Die Christologie Jakobs von Serugh und ihre Abhängigkeit von der alexandrinischen Theologie und der Frömmigkeit Ephraems des Syrers', *Muséon* lxxviii, 1965, 5.

—— 'L'Hexaméron de Jacques de Sarug', *Orient syrien* iv, 1959, 3, 129, 363.

Jargy, S., 'Les 'fils et filles du Pacte' dans la littérature monastique syriaque', *Orientalia christiana periodica* xvii, 1951, 304.

Jenni, E., 'Die altsyrischen Inschriften 1–3 Jahrhundert n. Chr.', *Theologische Zeitschrift* xxi, 1965, 371.

Jensen, P., 'Nik(k)al . . . in Harran', *ZA* xi, 1896, 293.

Johns, C. H. W., *An Assyrian Doomsday Book . . . of the District round Harran*, 1901.

Jones, A. H. M., *The Cities of the Eastern Roman Provinces*, 1937.

—— *The Greek City from Alexander to Justinian*, 1940.

—— *The Later Roman Empire, 284–602*, 1964.

Juster, J., *Les Juifs dans l'Empire romain. Leur condition juridique, économique et sociale*, 1914.

Kahle, P. E. *The Cairo Genizah*, 1959.

Kaufmann, C. M., *Handbuch der christlichen Archäologie*, 1922.

Kawar, I., 'The Arabs in the Peace Treaty of A.D. 561', *Arabica* iii, 1956, 181.

Kawerau, P., *Die jakobitische Kirche im Zeitalter der syrischen Renaissance, Idee und Wirklichkeit*, 1960.

Kazan, S., 'Isaac of Antioch's Homily against the Jews', *OC* 4 Ser. ix (xlv), 1961, 30; x (xlvi), 1962, 87; xi (xlvii), 1963, 89; xiii (xlix), 1965, 57.

Keseling, P., 'Die Chronik des Eusebius in der syrischen Überlieferung', *OC* 3 Ser. i (xxiii), 1926–7, 23, 223; ii (xxiv), 1927, 33.

Lord Kinross, *Within the Taurus*, 1954.

Kirsten, E., art. 'Edessa', in T. Klauser (ed.), *Reallexikon für Antike und Christentum*.

Klijn, A. F. J., *Edessa; de Stad van de Apostel Thomas* . . . , 1962.

—— *The Acts of Thomas*, 1962.

Kraemer, C. J., *Excavations at Nessana* iii. Non-literary papyri, 1958.

Krauss, S., *Griechische und lateinische Lehnwörter im Talmud, Midrasch und Targum*, 1898–9.

Kromayer, J., and G. Veith, *Heerwesen und Kriegführung der Griechen und Römer*, 1928.

Krueger, P., *Codex Justinianus*, 1954.

Krüger, P., *Das syrisch-monophysitische Mönchtum im Tur-'Abdin* . . . , 1938.

Krumbacher, C., *Der heilige Georg in der griechischen Überlieferung*, 1911.

—— *Geschichte der byzantinischen Literatur von Justinian bis zum Ende des oströmischen Reiches, 527–1453*, 1897.

Kugener, M. A., 'La Compilation historique de pseudo-Zacharie le Rhéteur', *ROC* v, 1900, 201, 461.

—— 'Observations sur la vie de l'ascète Isaïe et sur les vies de Pierre l'Ibérien et de Théodore d'Antinoé par Zacharie le Scolastique', *BZ* ix, 1900, 464.

—— 'Une Inscription syriaque de Biredjik', *RSO* i, 1907, 587.

Kupper, J. R., *Les Nomades en Mésopotamie au temps des rois de Mari*, 1957.

—— 'Uršu', *RA* xliii, 1949, 79.

Kuypers, A. B., *The Prayer Book of Aedeluald the Bishop, commonly called the Book of Cerne*, 1902.

Labourt, J., *Le Christianisme dans l'Empire perse sous la dynastie Sassanide (224–632)*, 1904.

de Labriolle, P., *La Réaction païenne*, 1934.

Lammens, H., *Études sur le siècle des Omayyades*, 1930.

—— *L'Arabie occidentale avant l'hégire*, 1928.

—— 'La Mecque à la veille de l'hégire', *Mél. S-J* ix, 1923–4, 97.

—— 'Le Culte des bétyles et les processions religieuses chez les Arabes préislamites', *Bulletin de l'Institut français d'archéologie orientale du Caire* xvii, 1919, 39.

La Monte, J. L., *Feudal Monarchy in the Latin Kingdom of Jerusalem, 1100 to 1291*, 1932.

Landersdorfer, S., *Die Götterliste des Mar Jakob von Sarug in seiner Homilie über den Fall der Götzenbilder . . .* , 1914.

Langlois, V., *Voyage dans la Cilicie et dans les montagnes du Taurus, exécuté pendant les années 1852–1853 . . .* , 1861.

Laroche, E., 'Divinités lunaires d'Anatolie', *RHR* cxlviii, 1955, 1.

Lassus, J., *Sanctuaires chrétiens de Syrie . . . du III siècle à la conquête musulmane*, 1947.

Laurent, J., *Byzance et les Turcs seldjoucides dans l'Asie occidentale jusqu'en 1081*, 1913.

—— 'Des Grecs aux Croisés: étude sur l'histoire d'Édesse entre 1071 et 1098', *Byzantion* i, 1924, 367.

Leclercq, H., art. 'Édesse' in F. Cabrol and H. Leclercq (ed.) *DACL*.

Leloir, L., *Doctrines et Méthodes de S. Éphrem . . .* , 1961.

—— 'Le Diatessaron de Tatien', *Orient syrien* i, 1956, 208, 313.

—— *Le Témoignage d'Éphrem sur le Diatessaron*, 1962.

—— *Saint Éphrem. Commentaire de l'Évangile concordant . . .* , 1963.

Lemoine, E., 'Physionomie d'un moine syrien: Philoxène de Mabboug', *Orient syrien* iii, 1958, 91.

Lepper, F. A., *Trajan's Parthian War*, 1948.

Le Rider, G. G., 'Monnaies de Characène', *Syria* xxxvi, 1959, 229.

Leroy, J., 'Mosaïques funéraires d'Édesse', *Syria* xxxiv, 1957, 306.

—— 'Nouvelles découvertes archéologiques relatives à Édesse', *Syria* xxxviii, 1961, 159.

Le Strange, G., *The Lands of the Eastern Caliphate*, 1930.

Levi, D., *Antioch Mosaic Pavements*, 1947.

Levy, R., *The Social Structure of Islam*, 1957.

Lewy, H., 'Points of Comparison between Zoroastrianism and the moon-cult of Harran', in W. B. Henning and E. Yarshater (ed.), *A Locust's Leg. Studies in honour of S. H. Taqizadeh*, 1962, 139.

Lewy, J., 'Studies in the Historic Geography of the Ancient Near East. I–II', *Orientalia* xxi, 1952, 265, 393.

Lewy, J., 'The Late Assyro-Babylonian Cult of the Moon and its Culmination at the Time of Nabonidus', *HUCA* xix, 1945–6, 405.

Lidzbarski, M., *Ephemeris für semitische Epigraphik*, 1900–15.

—— *Handbuch der nordsemitischen Epigraphik nebst ausgewählten Inschriften*, 1898.

Lietzman, H., *A History of the Early Church*, 1949–51.

—— *Das Leben des heiligen Symeon Stylites*, 1908.

Lipsius, R. A., *Die Edessenische Abgar-Sage* . . . , 1880.

Littmann, E., 'Eine altsyrische Inschrift', *ZA* xxvii, 1912, 379.

—— *Semitic Inscriptions* (Part IV of the *Publications of an American Archaeological Expedition to Syria in 1899–1900*), 1904.

—— *Semitic Inscriptions* (*Publications of the Princeton University Archaeological Expeditions to Syria in 1904–05 and 1909. Division IV*), 1914–49.

Liu, G. K–C., 'The Silkworm and Chinese Culture', *Osiris* x, 1952, 129.

Lloyd, S., and W. Brice, etc., 'Harran', *AS* i, 1951, 77.

Longden, R. P., 'Notes on the Parthian Campaigns of Trajan', *JRS* xxi, 1931, 1.

de Lorey, E., 'Les Mosaïques de la mosquée des Omayyades à Damas', *Syria* xii, 1931, 326.

Lucius, E., *Die Anfänge des Heiligenkults in der christlichen Kirche*, 1904.

Luckenbill, D. D., *Ancient Records of Assyria and Babylonia*, 1926–7.

Lüders, A., *Die Kreuzzüge im Urteil syrischer und armenischer Quellen*, 1964.

Lüdtke, W., and T. Nissen, *Die Grabschrift des Aberkios. Ihre Überlieferung und ihr Text*, 1910.

Macdonald, G., *Catalogue of Greek Coins in the Hunterian Collection. University of Glasgow* iii, 1905.

McDowell, R. H., *Stamped and Inscribed Objects from Seleucia on the Tigris*, 1935.

MacLean, A. J., and W. H. Browne, *The Catholicos of the East* . . . , 1892.

Maricq, A., *Classica et Orientalia* (revised by J. Pirenne, etc.), 1965.

—— 'Hatra de Sanatrouq', *Syria* xxxii, 1955, 273.

Marmardji, M. S., 'Les Dieux du paganisme d'après Ibn Al-Kalbi', *RB* xxxv, 1926, 397.

Marquart, J., *Eranšahr nach der Geographie des Ps. Moses Xorenac'i*, 1901.

—— *Osteuropäische und ostasiatische Streifzüge*, 1903.

Martin, J. P., 'Le Brigandage d'Éphèse d'après ses Actes récemment découverts', *RSE* 3 Ser. ix (xxix), 1874, 505; x (xxx), 1874, 22, 209, 305, 385, 518.

—— *Le Pseudo-Synode connu dans l'histoire sous le nom de Brigandage d'Éphèse* . . . , 1875.

Maspéro, J., 'Φοιδερᾶτοι et Στρατιῶται dans l'armée byzantine au VIᵉ siècle', *BZ* xxi, 1912, 97.

Matthes, K. C. A., *Die edessenische Abgarsage* . . . , 1882.

Maude, M. M., 'Who were the B'nai Q'yama?', *JTS* xxxvi, 1935, 13.

Maundrell, H., *A Journey from Aleppo to Jerusalem at Easter, A.D. 1697, The Third Edition. To which is now added an Account of the Author's Journey to the Banks of the Euphrates at Beer, and the Country of Mesopotamia*, 1749.

Mayer, L. A., *Mamluk Costume; A Survey*, 1952.

Meister, C., 'De itinerario Aetheriae abbatissae perperam nomini S. Silviae addicto', *Rheinisches Museum für Philologie* lxiv, 1909, 337.

Mendel, G., *Catalogue des sculptures grecques, romaines, et byzantines*, 1912–4.

Messina, G., 'La Celebrazione della festa . . . in Adiabene', *Orientalia* N.S. vi, 1934, 234.

—— 'La Cronaca di Arbela', *Civiltà Cattolica* lxxxiii, 1932, 362.

Meyer, E., art 'Edessa' in Pauly–Wissowa *Real-Encyclopädie der classischen Altertumswissenschaft*.

Mez, A., *Geschichte der Stadt Harran in Mesopotamia bis zum Einfall der Araber*, 1892.

Moberg, B., 'Die syrische grammatik des Johannes Esṭōnājā', *Monde Oriental* iii, 1909, 24.

von Moltke, H. C. B., *Briefe über Zustände und Begebenheiten in der Türkei aus den Jahren 1835 bis 1839 . . .*, 1891.

Mommsen, T., and P. M. Meyer, *Theodosiani libri XVI cum constitutionibus Sirmondianis . . .*, 1905.

Monneret de Villard, U., 'La Fierà di Batnae e la traslazione di S. Tomaso a Edessa', *Rendic. Lincei*, Classe di Scienze morali, storiche e filologiche, 8 Ser. vi, 1951, 77.

—— *Le Chiese della Mesopotamia*, 1940.

Moore, G. F., 'The Theological School at Nisibis', in D. G. Lyon (ed.), *Studies in the History of Religions presented to C. H. Toy . . .*, 1912, 255.

Moritz, B., 'Syrische Inschriften', in M. von Oppenheim, *Inschriften aus Syrien, Mesopotamien und Kleinasien . . .*, 1913, 157.

—— 'Syrische Inschriften aus Syrien und Mesopotamien', *Westasiatische Studien. Mittheilungen des Seminars für Orientalische Sprachen zu Berlin* i/2, 1898, 124.

Moss, C., *Catalogue of Syriac Printed Books and Related Literature in the British Museum*, 1962.

Mouterde, R., 'Dea Syria en Syrie', *Mél. S-J* xxv, 1942–3, 135.

—— and A. Poidebard, 'La Voie antique des caravanes entre Palmyre et Hît, au IIᵉ siècle après Jésus-Christ, d'après une inscription retrouvée au Sud-Est de Palmyre (1930)', *Syria* xii, 1931, 101.

—— —— *Le Limes de Chalcis. Organisation de la steppe en Haute Syrie romaine*, 1945.

Müller, N., art, 'Koimeterien, die altchristlichen Begräbnisstätten', in Herzog, *Realencyklopädie für protestantische Theologie und Kirche*.

Müller, V. P. P., *En Syrie avec les bédouins*, 1931.

Myslivec, J., 'Die Abgaros-Legende auf einer Ikone des XVII Jhdts.', *Seminarium Kondakovianum* v, 1932, 190.

Naster, P., 'Les Monnaies d'Édesse révèlent-elles un Dieu 'Elul?', *Revue belge de Numismatique* cxiv, 1968, 5.

Nau, F., 'Analyse de la seconde parte inédite de l'histoire ecclésiastique de Jean d'Asie . . .', *ROC* ii, 1897, 455.

—— 'Étude sur les parties inédites de la chronique ecclésiastique attribuée à Denys de Tellmahré . . .', *ROC* ii, 1897, 41.

—— *Les Arabes chrétiens de Mésopotamie et de Syrie du VIIᵉ au VIIIᵉ siècle*, 1933.

—— 'Notice des manuscrits syriaques . . ., entrés à la bibliothèque nationale de Paris . . .', *ROC* 2 Ser. vi (xvi), 1911, 271.

—— 'Une inscription grecque d'Édesse: la lettre de N.-S. J.-C. à Abgar', *ROC* 3 Ser. i (xxi), 1918–9, 217.

Nestle, E., Die Statuten der Schule von Nisibis aus den Jahren 496 und 590', *Zeitschrift für Kirchengeschichte* xviii, 1898, 211.

Neusner, J., *A History of the Jews in Babylonia* i. The Parthian Period, 1965.

Niebuhr, C., *Reisebeschreibung nach Arabien und andern umliegenden Ländern*, 1774–8.

Nissen, T., 'Die Petrusakten und ein bardesanitischer Dialog in der Aberkiosvita', *ZNW* ix, 1908, 190, 315.

—— *S. Abercii Vita*, 1912.

Nodelman, S. A., 'A Preliminary History of Characene', *Berytus* xiii, 1960, 83.

Nöldeke, T., 'ΑΣΣΥΡΙΟΣ ΣΥΡΙΟΣ ΣΥΡΟΣ', *Hermes* v, 1871, 443.

Nöldeke, T., 'Die von Guidi herausgegebene syrische Chronik', *Sitzungsberichte d. Kaiserl. Akademie d. Wissenschaften in Wien*, Phil.-hist. Classe, cxxviii–cxxix, 1893.

—— 'Ein zweiter syrischer Julianusroman', *ZDMG* xxviii, 1874, 660.

—— *Neue Beiträge zur semitischen Sprachwissenschaft*, 1910.

—— 'Syrische Inschriften', *ZA* xxi, 1908, 151.

—— 'Ueber den syrischen Roman von Kaiser Julian', *ZDMG* xxviii, 1873, 263.

—— 'Über einige Edessenische Märtyrerakten', *Strassburger Festschrift zur XLVI. Versammlung deutscher Philologen und Schulmänner*, 1901, 13.

—— 'Zur Alexiuslegende', *ZDMG* liii, 1899, 256.

Olivier, G. A., *Voyage dans l'Empire Othoman, l'Égypte et la Perse*, 1801–7.

von Oppenheim, M., *Inschriften aus Syrien, Mesopotamien und Kleinasien gesammelt im Jahre 1899*, 1913.

—— *Vom Mittelmeer zum Persischen Golf . . .*, 1899–1900.

—— and F. Hiller von Gaertringen, 'Höhleninschrift von Edessa mit dem Briefe Jesu an Abgar', *Sitzungsberichte der königlich preussischen Akademie der Wissenschaften*, 1914, 817.

—— and H. Lucas, 'Griechische und lateinische Inschriften aus Syrien, Mesopotamien und Kleinasien', *BZ* xiv, 1905, 1.

Ortiz de Urbina, I., *Patrologia syriaca*, 1958.

Ostrogorski, G., *History of the Byzantine State*, 1956.

Otter, J., *Voyage en Turquie et en Perse*, 1748.

Parrot, A., etc., *Archives royales de Mari*, 1950– .

Parry, O. H., *Six Months in a Syrian Monastery*, 1895.

Parthey, G., and M. Pinder, *Itinerarium Antonini Augusti et Hierosolymitanum*, 1848.

Peeters, P., 'Glanures martyrologiques. II. La Basilique des Confesseurs à Édesse', *Anal. Boll.* lviii, 1940, 110.

—— 'Jacques de Saroug appartient-il à la secte monophysite?', *Anal. Boll.* lxvi, 1948, 134.

—— 'La Légende de saint Jacques de Nisibe', *Anal. Boll.* xxxviii, 1920, 285.

—— 'La Passion de S. Michel le Sabaïte', *Anal. Boll.* xlviii, 1930, 65.

—— 'Le "Passionaire d'Adiabène"', *Anal. Boll.* xliii, 1925, 261.

—— *Orient et Byzance. Le tréfonds oriental de l'hagiographie byzantine*, 1950.

—— *Recherches d'histoire et de philologie orientales*, 1951.

—— 'S. Dometios le martyr et S. Dometios le médecin', *Anal. Boll.* lvii, 1939, 72.

—— 'S. Syméon Stylite et ses premiers biographes', *Anal. Boll.* lxi, 1943, 29.

—— 'Traductions et traducteurs dans l'hagiographie orientale à l'époque byzantine', *Anal. Boll.* xl, 1922, 241.

Perdrizet, R., 'D'une gravure relative à la légende de S. Jude Thaddée', *Seminarium Kondakovianum* vi, 1933, 67.

—— 'De la Véronique et de Sainte Véronique', *Seminarium Kondakovianum* v, 1932, 1.

Pereira, F. M. E., 'Légende grecque de l'Homme de Dieu saint Alexis', *Anal. Boll.* xix, 1900, 241.

—— 'Note sur la date de la légende grecque de saint Alexis', *Anal. Boll.* xix, 1900, 254.

Perry, S. G. F., *The Second Synod of Ephesus*, 1881.

Petermann, J. H., *Reisen im Orient*, 1860–1.

Peters, C., *Das Diatessaron Tatians. Seine Überlieferung und sein Nachwerken im Morgen- und Abendland . . .*, 1939.

Peterson, E., *Frühkirche, Judentum und Gnosis*, 1959.

Pétré, H., *Journal de Voyage*, 1948.

Philipsborn, A., 'Der Fortschritt in der Entwicklung des byzantinischen Kranken-hauswesens', *BZ* liv, 1961, 338.

Picard, C., 'Un Texte nouveau de la correspondance entre Abgar d'Osrhoène et Jésus-Christ', *Bull. corr. hell.* xliv, 1920, 41.

Piganiol, A., *L'Empire chrétien (325–95)*, 1947.

Pigulevskaya, N. V., *Les Villes de l'état iranien aux époques parthe et sassanide*, 1963.

Pinkerton, J., 'The Origin and the Early History of the Syriac Pentateuch', *JTS* xv, 1914, 14.

Pirenne, J., 'Aux origines de la graphie syriaque', *Syria* xl, 1963, 101.

Platnauer, M., *The Life and Reign of the Emperor Lucius Septimius Severus*, 1918.

Pococke, R., *A Description of the East and some other Countries*, 1743–5.

Pognon, H., *Inscriptions mandaïtes des coupes de Khouabir*, 1898–9.

—— *Inscriptions sémitiques de la Syrie, de la Mésopotamie et de la région de Mossoul*, 1907.

Pomjalovskij, J., *Das Leben unseres verewigten Vaters Theodor, Erzbischofs von Edessa*, 1892.

Poujoulat, B., *Voyage à Constantinople, dans l'Asie mineure, en Mésopotamie, à Palmyre, en Syrie, en Palestine et en Égypte*, 1840–1.

Poullet, *Nouvelles Relations du Levant*, 1668.

Preusser, C., *Nordmesopotamische Baudenkmäler altchristlicher und islamischer Zeit*, 1911.

Puech, H. C., *Le Manichéisme*, 1949.

Ramusio, G. B., *Delle Navigationi et Viaggi*, 1583–1613.

Rauwolfen L., *Aigentliche beschreibung der Raisz, so er . . . gegen Auffgang inn die Morgen-länder . . . vollbracht*, 1582–3.

—— *Itinerary into the Eastern countries . . .* (tr. N. Staphorst), 1693.

Renan, J. E., 'Deux monuments épigraphiques d'Édesse,' *JA* 8 Ser. i. 1883, 246.

—— *Mission de Phénicie*, 1864.

Rey, E. G., *Les Colonies francques de Syrie au XIIme et XIIIme siècles*, 1883.

—— *Les Grandes Écoles Syriennes du IVᵉ au XIIᵉ siècle*, 1898.

Rice, D. S., 'Medieval Harran . . .', *AS* ii, 1952, 36.

Richter, G., 'Über die älteste Auseinandersetzung der syrischen Christen mit den Juden', *ZNW* xxxv, 1936, 101.

Richter, G. M. A., 'Silk in Greece', *American Journal of Archaeology* xxxiii, 1929, 27.

Ritter, H., and M. Plessner, *'Picatrix'. Das Ziel des Weisen von Pseudo-Maǧrīṭī*, 1962.

Röhricht, R., *Geschichte des ersten Kreuzzuges*, 1901.

—— *Geschichte des Königreichs Jerusalem 1100–1291*, 1898.

Ronzevalle, S., 'Les Monnaies de la dynastie de 'Abd-Hadad et les cultes de Hiérapolis-Bambycé', *Mél. S-J* xxiii, 1940, 1.

—— 'Notes et études d'archéologie orientale' 2 Ser. Venus lugens et Adonis byblius, *Mél. S-J* xv, 1930–1, 139.

—— 'Notes et études d'archéologie orientale' 3 Ser. II: Jupiter héliopolitain, nova et vetera, *Mél. S-J* xxi, 1937–8, 1.

Rosenthal, F., *Die aramäistische Forschung seit Th. Nöldeke's Veröffentlichungen*, 1939.

—— 'The Prophecies of Bâbâ the Ḥarrânian', in W. B. Henning and E. Yarshater (ed.), *A Locust's Leg. Studies in Honour of S. H. Taqizadeh*, 1962, 220.

Rosmarin, T. W., 'Aribi und Arabien in den Babylonisch-Assyrischen Quellen', *Journal of the Society of Oriental Research* xvi, 1932, 1.

Rostovtzeff, M. I., 'Dura and the Problem of Parthian Art', *YCS* v, 1935, 155.

—— *The Social and Economic History of the Hellenistic World*, 1941.

—— *The Social and Economic History of the Roman Empire*, 1957.

Rubin, B. *Das Zeitalter Justinians* i, 1960.

Rucker, I., 'Florilegium Edessenum anonymum (syriace ante 562)', *Sitzungsberichte der bayerischen Akademie d. Wissensch.*, Phil.-hist. Abteilung, 1933.

Rücker, A., 'Aus der Geschichte der jakobitischen Kirche von Edessa in der Zeit der Kreuzfahrer', *OC* 3 Ser. x (xxxii), 1935, 124.

Runciman, J. C. S., *A History of the Crusades*, 1965.

—— 'Some Remarks on the Image of Edessa', *Cambridge Historical Journal* iii, 1929–31, 238.

—— *The Emperor Romanus Lecapenus and his Reign*, 1963.

Ryckmans, G., *Les Religions arabes préislamiques*, 1951.

Sachau, C. E., *Die Chronik von Arbela*, 1915.

—— 'Edessenische Inschriften', *ZDMG* xxxvi, 1882, 142.

—— *Reise in Syrien und Mesopotamien*, 1883.

Saggs, H. W. F., *The Greatness that was Babylon*, 1962.

—— 'Ur of the Chaldees', *Iraq* xxii, 1960, 200.

Saxl, F., 'Beiträge zu einer Geschichte der Planetendarstellungen im Orient und im Okzident', *Der Islam* iii, 1912, 151.

Schaeder, H. H., 'Bardesanes von Edessa in der Überlieferung der griechischen und der syrischen Kirche', *Zeitschrift fur Kirchengeschichte* li, 1932, 21.

—— review in *Gnomon* ix, 1933, 337.

Schall, A., *Studien über griechische Fremdwörter im Syrischen*, 1960.

Schiwietz, S., *Das morgenländische Mönchtum*, 1904–38.

Schlumberger, D., 'Descendants non-méditerranéens de l'art grec', *Syria* xxxvii, 1960, 131, 253.

—— 'Études sur Palmyre', *Berytus* ii, 1935, 149.

—— 'Les Formes anciennes du chapiteau corinthien en Syrie, en Palestine et en Arabie', *Syria* xiv, 1933, 283.

—— 'Palmyre et la Mesène', *Syria* xxxviii, 1961, 256.

—— etc., *La Palmyrène du nord-ouest*, 1951.

Schneider, A. M., 'Die Kathedrale von Edessa', *OC* 3 Ser. xiv (xxxvi), 1941, 161.

Schoeps, H. J., *Urgemeinde. Judenchristentum. Gnosis*, 1956.

Seeck, O., *Geschichte des Untergangs der antiken Welt*, 1895–1921.

Segal, J. B., 'A Syriac Seal inscription', *Iraq* xxix, 1967, 6.

—— *Edessa and Harran. An Inaugural Lecture*, 1963.

—— 'Mesopotamian Communities from Julian to the Rise of Islam', *Proceedings of the British Academy* xli, 1955, 109.

—— 'New Syriac Inscriptions from Edessa', *BSOAS* xxii, 1959, 23.

—— 'Pagan Syriac Monuments in the Vilayet of Urfa', *AS* iii, 1953, 97.

—— 'Some Syriac Inscriptions of the 2nd–3rd century A.D.', *BSOAS* xvi, 1954, 13.

—— 'The Jews of North Mesopotamia', in J. M. Grintz and J. Liver (ed.), *Sepher Segal*, 1964, 32*.

—— 'The Sabian Mysteries. The Planet Cult of Ancient Harran', in E. Bacon (ed.), *Vanished Civilizations*, 1963, 201.

—— 'Two Syriac Inscriptions from Harran', *BSOAS* xx, 1957, 513.

Seligman, C. G., 'The Roman Orient and the Far East', *Antiquity* xi, 1937, 5.

Seybold, C. F., review in *ZDMG* lxvi, 1912, 742.

Seyrig, H., 'Antiquités syriennes': nos. 13, 14, 20, 27, 32, 39–41, 57, 78, *Syria* xiv, 1933, 238, 253; xviii, 1937, 4; xx, 1939, 183; xxi, 1940, 277; xxiv, 1944–5, 62; xxvi, 1949, 17, 29; xxxi, 1954, 80; xxxvii, 1960, 233.

—— 'Le Repas de Morts et le 'Banquet funèbre' à Palmyre', *Annales archéologiques de Syrie* i, 1951, 32.

Sharf, A., 'Byzantine Jewry in the Seventh Century', *BZ* xlviii, 1955, 103.

Sidersky, D., *Les Origines des légendes musulmanes dans le Coran et dans las vies des Prophètes*, 1933.

Simon, M., *Verus Israel. Étude sur les relations entre Chrétiens et Juifs dans l'empire romain (135–425)*, 1948.

Smith, S., 'Events in Arabia in the 6th century A.D.', *BSOAS* xvi, 1954, 425.

Smith, W. R., *Lectures on the Religion of the Semites*, 1927.

Soane, E. B., *To Mesopotamia and Kurdistan in Disguise*, 1912.

Spinka, M., *Chronicle of John Malalas . . .* , 1940.

Spuler, B., etc., *Handbuch der Orientalistik*, 1952– .

Starcky, J., *Palmyre: Guide archéologique*, 1941.

Starr, J., 'Byzantine Jewry on the Eve of the Arab Conquest (565–638)', *Journal of the Palestine Oriental Society* xv, 1935, 280.

—— *The Jews in the Byzantine Empire, 641–1204*, 1939.

Stein, E., *Histoire du Bas-Empire*, 1949–59.

Stern, H. 'La Mosaïque d'Orphée de Blanzy-lès-Fismes', *Gallia* xiii, 1955, 41.

—— 'The Orpheus in the Synagogue of Dura-Europos', *Journal of the Warburg and Courtauld Institutes* xxi, 1958, 1.

Stern, S. M. ''Abd al-Jabbar's Account of How Christ's Religion was Falsified by the Adoption of Roman Customs', *JTS* N.S. xix, 1968, 128.

Stocks, H., 'Studien zur Lukian's "De syria dea"', *Berytus* iv, 1937, 1.

Straubinger, J., *Die Kreuzauffindungslegende*, 1912.

Strong, H. A., and J. Garstang, *The Syrian Goddess*, 1913.

Strugnell, J., 'The Nabataean Goddess 'Al-Kutba' and Her Sanctuaries', *Bulletin of the American Schools of Oriental Research*, no. 156, 1959, 29.

Strzygowski, J., *Asiens bildende Kunst in Stichproben, ihr Wesen und ihre Entwicklung*, 1930.

Sykes, M., *The Caliph's Last Heritage*, 1915.

Tarn, W. W., *Hellenistic Military and Naval Developments*, 1930.

—— and G. T. Griffith, *Hellenistic Civilisation*, 1952.

Tavernier, J. B., *Collection of Travels through Turkey into Persia and the East-Indies*, 1684.

Teixidor, J., 'Deux inscriptions palmyréniennes du musée de Bagdad', *Syria* xl, 1963, 33.

—— 'Notes hatréennes', *Syria* xli, 1964, 273.

—— 'The Kingdom of Adiabene and Hatra', *Berytus* xvii, 1967–8, 1.

Texier, C. F. M., 'La Ville et les monuments d'Édesse', *Revue américaine et orientale* i, 1858–9, 326.

de Thévenot, J., *Relation d'un voyage fait au Levant . . .* , 1664–84.

Thomson, R. W., 'An Eighth-century Melkite Colophon from Edessa', *JTS* N.S. xiii, 1962, 249.

Tisserant, E., *Eastern Christianity in India . . .* , 1957.

—— art. '(L'église) nestorienne' in A. Vacant (ed.), *Dictionnaire de Théologie catholique*.

Tixeront, L. J., *Les Origines de l'église d'Édesse et la légende d'Abgar*, 1888.

Tobler, T., and A. Molinier, *Itinera Hierosolymitana et descriptiones Terrae Sanctae bellis sacris anteriora . . .* , 1877–80.

Torrey, C. C., 'A Syriac Parchment from Edessa of the Year 243 A.D.', *ZS* x, 1935, 33.

Toumanoff, C., 'Introduction to Christian Caucasian History: The Formative Centuries (IVth–VIIIth)', *Traditio* xv, 1959, 1.

Tournebize, F., 'Étude sur la conversion de l'Arménie au christianisme . . .', *ROC* 2 Ser. ii (xii), 1907, 22, 152, 280, 356; iii (xiii), 1908, 72, 142.

—— *Histoire politique et religieuse de l'Arménie*, 1910.

Toutain, J., 'La Légende chrétienne de saint Siméon stylite et ses origines païennes' *RHR* lxv, 1912, 171.

Tritton, A. S., and H. A. R. Gibb, 'The First and Second Crusades from an Anonymous Syriac Chronicle', *JRAS*, 1933, 69, 273.

Tscherikower, V., *Die hellenistischen Städtegründungen von Alexander dem Grossen bis auf die Römerzeit*, 1927.

van den Ven, P, 'A propos de la vie de S. Syméon Stylite le jeune', *Anal. Boll.* lxvii, 1949, 425.

—— 'S. Jérome et la vie du moine Malchus le Captif', *Muséon* N.S. i, 1900, 413; ii, 1901, 208.

Vandenhoff, B., 'Die Götterliste des Mar Jakob von Sarug in seiner Homilie über den Fall der Götzenbilder', *OC* N.S. v, 1915, 234.

Vasiliev, A. A., *History of the Byzantine Empire*, 1952.

—— *Justin the First. An Introduction to the Epoch of Justinian the Great*, 1950.

—— 'Notes on Some Episodes Concerning the Relations between the Arabs and the Byzantine Empire from the Fourth to the Sixth Century', *Dumbarton Oaks Papers* ix–x, 1956, 306.

—— 'The Life of St. Theodore of Edessa', *Byzantion* xvi, 1942–3, 165.

Väth, A., *Der hl. Thomas, der Apostel Indiens*, 1925.

Vincent, L. H., 'Les Épigraphes judéo-araméennes postexiliques', *RB* lvi, 1949, 274.

Vogt, J., *Kaiser Julian und das Judentum*, 1939.

de Vogüé, C. J. M., *Syrie Centrale. Inscriptions sémitiques*, 1868–77.

Vööbus, A., *A letter of Ephrem to the Mountaineers*, 1947.

—— 'Beiträge zur kritischen Sichtung der asketischen Schriften, die unter dem Namen Ephraem des Syrers überliefert sind', *OC* 4 Ser. iii (xxxix), 1955, 48.

—— 'Das Alter der Peschitta', *OC* 4 Ser. ii (xxxviii), 1954, 1.

—— *Early Versions of the New Testament*, 1954.

—— *History of Asceticism in the Syrian Orient*, 1958– .

—— *Investigations into the Text of the New Testament used by Rabbula of Edessa*, 1947.

—— *La Vie d'Alexandre en grec—un témoin d'une biographie inconnue de Rabbula écrite en syriaque*, 1948.

—— *Studies in the History of the Gospel Text in Syriac*, 1951.

—— *Untersuchungen über die Authentizität einiger asketischer Texte, überliefert unter dem Namen Ephraem Syrus*, 1947.

Vosté, J. M. 'Athanasios Abougaleb', *ROC* 3 Ser. vi (xxvi), 1927–8, 432.

Walker, J., 'The Coins of Hatra', *Numismatic Chronicle* 6 Ser. xviii, 1958, 167.

Warmington, E. H., *The Commerce between the Roman Empire and India*, 1928.

Weigand, E., 'Zur Datierung der Peregrinatio Aetheriae', *BZ* xx, 1911, 1.

—— review in *BZ* xxviii, 1928, 401.

Weitzmann, K., 'The Mandylion and Constantine Porphyrogennetos', *Cah. arch.* xi, 1960, 163.

Welles, C. B., *Royal Correspondence in the Hellenistic Period*, 1934.

—— etc., *The Excavations at Dura-Europos. Final Report V/1. The Parchments and Papyri*, 1959.

Wellhausen, J., *Skizzen und Vorarbeiten*, 1884–99.

Wensinck, A. J. 'Qejāmā und Benai Qejāmā in der älteren Syrischen Literatur', *ZDMG* lxiv, 1910, 561.

Widengren, G., *Iranisch-semitische Kulturbegegnung in parthischer Zeit*, 1960.

—— *Mani and Manichaeism*, 1965.

Wiegand, T., *Palmyra. Ergebnisse der Ausgrabungen und Untersuchungen seit dem Jahre 1899*, 1932.

Wigand, K., 'Thymiateria', *Bonner Jahrbücher* cxxii, 1912, l.

Wigram, W. A., *The Separation of the Monophysites*, 1923.

Will, E., 'L'Art sassanide et ses prédécesseurs', *Syria* xxxix, 1962, 45.

—— 'La Tour funéraire de la Syrie et les monuments apparentés', *Syria* xxvi, 1949, 258.

—— 'La Tour funéraire de Palmyre', *Syria* xxvi, 1949, 87.

—— 'Marchands et chefs de caravanes à Palmyre', *Syria* xxxiv, 1957, 262.

Wilmart, A., 'Le Souvenir d'Eusèbe d'Émèse. Un discours en l'honneur des saintes d'Antioche Bernice, Prosdoce et Domnine', *Anal. Boll.* xxxviii, 1920, 241.

Winckworth, C., and F. C. Burkitt, 'On Heathen Deities in the Doctrine of Addai', *JTS* xxv, 1924, 402.

Wischnitzer, R., *The Messianic Theme in the Paintings of the Dura Synagogue*, 1948.

Wiseman, D. J., 'A Fragmentary Inscription of Tiglath-Pileser III from Nimrud', *Iraq* xviii, 1956, 117.

Wittek, P., 'Deux chapitres de l'histoire des Turcs de Rûm', *Byzantion* xi, 1936, 285.

—— *The Rise of the Ottoman Empire*, 1938.

Wright, W., *A Short History of Syriac Literature*, 1894.

—— *Catalogue of the Syriac manuscripts in the British Museum*, 1870–2.

Youtie, H. C., 'A Gothenburg Papyrus and the Letter to Abgar', *HTR* xxiii, 1930, 299.

—— 'Gothenburg Papyrus 21 and the Coptic Version of the Letter to Abgar', *HTR* xxiv, 1931, 61.

de Zwaan, J., 'The Edessene Origin of the Odes of Solomon', in R. P. Casey, etc. (ed.), *Quantulacumque. Studies presented to Kirsopp Lake . . .* , 1937, 285.

PLATES

PLATE 1

THE FAMILY PORTRAIT MOSAIC, with names in Syriac; probably second or early third century A.D.

THE FUNERARY COUCH MOSAIC, with Syriac inscriptions; dated A.D. 278.

PLATE 3

THE TRIPOD MOSAIC, with Syriac inscriptions including an epitaph (p. 34); probably second or third century A.D.

PLATE 4

a. THE CITADEL WALL AND MOAT. In the distance is the plain of Harran

b. BRIDGE OVER THE KARA KOYUN

PLATE 5

a. OUTSIDE THE HARRAN GATE (Haran Kapısı). In the section of Byzantine wall at right is a fragmentary Greek inscription (p. 224 n. 2)

b. ROUND TOWER AT THE BEY GATE (Bey Kapısı); at top an Armenian inscription (p. 236 n. 1). The bridge over the moat leads to Kisas

PLATE 6

a. SITE OF THE WEST GATE. At right is a section of the Byzantine wall, at left may have stood a guard-room of the twelfth century

b. VIEW WESTWARDS FROM THE WEST GATE. The buildings at left centre mark the site of the tomb of St. Ephraim and Deyr Sargis

PLATE 7

DAM first constructed in the reign of Justinian I

PLATE 8

a. SLUICES in the original bed of the river Daişan

b. WESTERN WATER-GATE beside the Pool of Abraham

PLATE 9

a. THE CITADEL MOUNT AND COLUMNS from the Pool of Zulha (Zulihe Gölü)

b. DETAIL OF COLUMN on the Citadel mount
(with acknowledgements to G. Fehérvári)

PLATE 10

a. SOURCE OF THE SPRING in Makam Ibrahim

b. 'SACRED' FISH in the Pool of Zulha (Zulihe Gölü)

PLATE 11

STREAM from the springs of water flowing through a public courtyard

PLATE 12

b. STATUE OF AN EDESSAN LADY, with the figure of her daughter in miniature at bottom left. Their names are recorded in Syriac (p. 33). In the Diyarbakir Museum

a. BUST OF AN EDESSAN LADY, with the figure of her daughter in miniature at right. Their names are recorded in Syriac (p. 33). In the Urfa Museum

PLATE 13

b. STATUE FOUND AT HARRAN

a. STATUE AT SUMATAR HARABESI

PLATE 14

a. RELIEF OF MALE PERSONAGE from Urfa, with Syriac inscription (p. 40 n. 4). At Istanbul

b. RELIEF found near Urfa, with Greek inscription (p. 30 n. 5). In the Urfa Museum

PLATE 15

b. COUPLE EMBRACING: relief. In the Urfa Museum (with

a. TRITON; relief. In the Urfa Museum (with acknowledgements to G. Fehérvári)

PLATE 16

a. MENORAH (candelabrum), outside Jewish tomb at Kırk Mağara

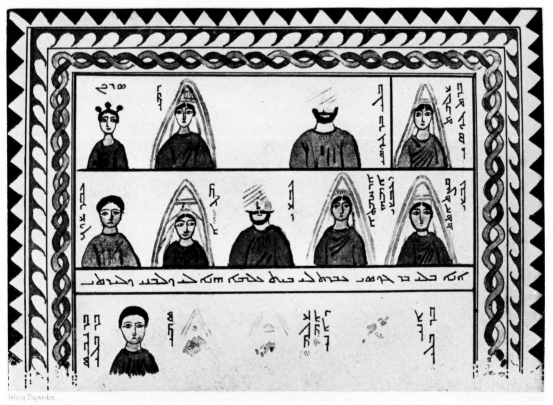

b. MOSAIC with Syriac inscriptions at Urfa, drawn by J. Euting (*Florilegium . . . de Vogüé,* 1909). Now destroyed

PLATE 17

a. MOSAIC from Urfa, with Syriac inscriptions. At Istanbul

b. GENERAL VIEW OF THE ANIMAL MOSAIC at Urfa; at centre a wing, and a forearm with a staff

PLATE 18

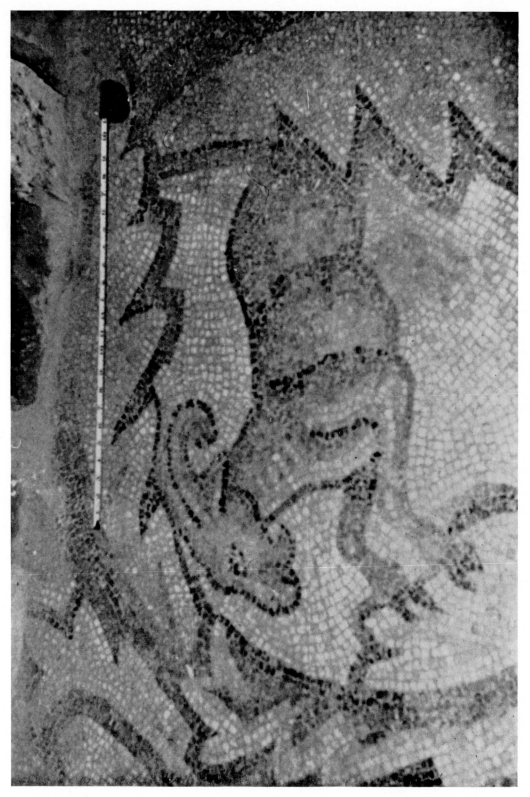

DETAIL from border of the Animal mosaic

PLATE 19

DETAIL from border of the Animal mosaic

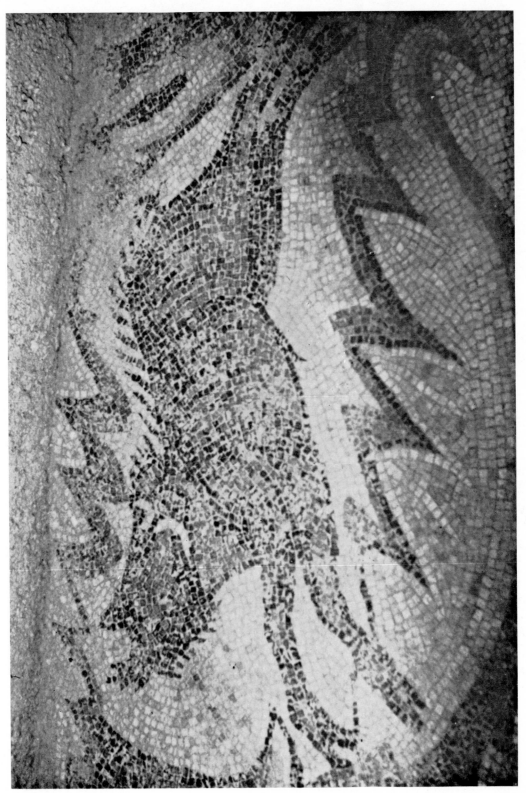

PLATE 20

DETAIL from border of the Animal mosaic

PLATE 21

a. ENTRANCE TO CAVE-TOMB in Eyüp Mahallesi

b. VERTICAL SHAFT ENTRANCE TO
TOMB in Eyüp Mahallesi, with loculi inside

PLATE 22

a. ENTRANCE TO DOUBLE CAVE-TOMB, in hills south-west of Urfa

b. DETAIL of arch

PLATE 23

a. INTERIOR OF CAVE-TOMB at Kırk Mağara, with arched entrance to an inner chamber

b. 'FLYING BUST' IN CAVE-TOMB at Şehitlik Mahallesi

PLATE 24

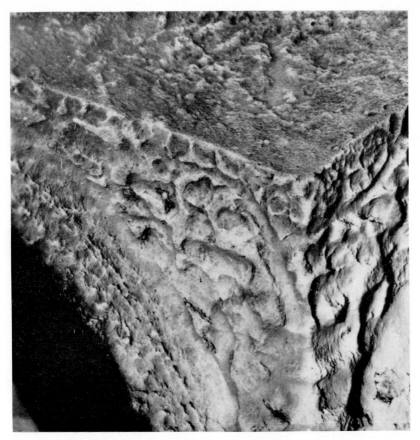

a. VINE MOTIF ON WALLS OF CAVE-TOMB

b. CARVING OF SERPENT INSIDE CAVE-TOMB, at Kızıl Köy; at left is a bull's head with a disc between the horns (with acknowledgements to G. Fehérvári)

PLATE 25

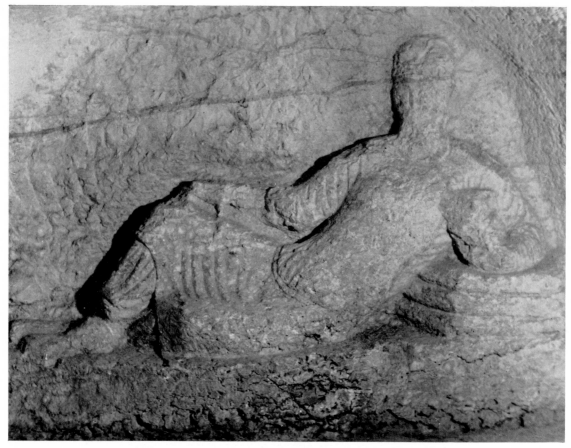

a. FIGURE ON COUCH; relief in arcosolium of cave-tomb

FUNERARY BANQUET; relief inside cave-tomb at Kırk Mağara

PLATE 26

INTERIOR OF CAVE-TOMB

PLATE 27

PLATE 28

(i)

(ii)

(iii)

(iv)

a. COINS: SACRAL STOOL AND PILLAR IN SHRINE

  (i) Reverse; reign of Wa'el bar Sahru. The Syriac legend is probably
    to be read, The go d Naḥai

 (ii) Reverse; reign of Wa'el bar Sahru. The Syriac legend is probably
    to be read, The go d Naḥai.

(iii) Reverse; reign of Elegabalus (or Caracalla). Two busts of City-
    goddess

(iv) Obverse; busts of Elegabalus and Alexander Severus

(i)

(ii)

b. COINS: KINGS OF EDESSA

  (i) Obverse; Abgar the Great
 (ii) Obverse; Wa'el bar Sahru

PLATE 29

a. SYRIAC INSCRIPTION TO QUEEN SHALMATH, on a column on the Citadel mount (p. 19)

b. SYRIAC TOMB-INSCRIPTION in memory of G'W, at Kırk Mağara (p. 59)

PLATE 30

a. SYRIAC EPITAPH on a rock-face south-west of Urfa (pp. 34 f.)

b. BILINGUAL INSCRIPTION ON TOMB-TOWER at Deyr Yakup, in 'Palmyrene' and Greek (p. 29)

PLATE 31

a. JEWISH INSCRIPTION IN GREEK, outside cave-tomb at Kırk Mağara

b. LETTER OF JESUS TO ABGAR in Greek, found at Kırk Mağara (H. von Oppenheim and F. Hiller von Gaertring
Sitzungsber. D. Königl. Preuss. Akad. D. Wissensch. zu Berlin, phil.-hist. Kl., 1914, 824)

PLATE 32

a. PANORAMA NORTHWARDS FROM THE CITADEL MOUNT. In the foreground is the Pool of Abraham, at left the original bed of the river Daişan and Vadi Manci; the rectangular building at right centre is the Electricity Power station

b. IN THE COURTYARD OF MAKAM IBRAHIM

PLATE 33

b. HASAN PAŞA CAMII, with the Citadel in the background.
Storks are nesting in the minaret

a. ULU CAMI

PLATE 34

STREET SCENE, in front of Kara Meydan Camii

PLATE 35

COURTYARD OF THE GÜMRÜKHANE

PLATE 36

PANORAMIC VIEW FROM KIRK MAĞARA, with the Citadel at right and the Pool of Abraham at centre

PLATE 37

PANORAMIC VIEW LOOKING EASTWARDS, from hill in north-west of Urfa (Talfidir)

PLATE 38

'WELL OF JOB' at Makam Nebi Eyüp

PLATE 39

a. RUINS AT DEYR YAKUP

b. RECUMBENT STATUE AT DEYR YAKUP

PLATE 40

a. BUILDING AT SUMATAR HARABESI (circular on square base)

b. THE 'SACRED MOUNT' AT SUMATAR HARABESI. Right of centre are a bust and a statue in relief

PLATE 41

BUST AT SIDE OF THE 'SACRED MOUNT' at Sumatar Harabesi, with three Syriac inscriptions (pp. 56 f.)

PLATE 42

ALTAR AT SANIMAĞARA. The stone stands in the direction of Sumatar Harabesi

PLATE 43

THE PHOENIX MOSAIC, with Syriac inscriptions; dated A.D. 235–6

PLATE 44

THE ORPHEUS MOSAIC, with Syriac inscriptions; dated A.D. 228

GENERAL INDEX

U

GENERAL INDEX

295

Babai, legendary martyr, 82 f., 86.
Babylon, Babylonians, 1, 4 f., 35 n. 5, 46, 58, 60
68.
Bagrat, of Tell Bashir, 225, 238 n. 2.
Bakru, 'patrician' of Edessa, 43, 69.
Balak, Artuqid general, 236.
Balawat, Gates of, 4, 18 n. 7.
Balduq, lord of Samosata, 225, 228.
Baldwin, lord of Mar'ash, 251-3.
Baldwin de Bouillon, King of Jerusalem, 225–
30, 233, 235, 239, 241, 247.
Baldwin du Bourg, King of Jerusalem, 229–36,
238, 241.
Balikh, river, 4, 5, n. 3, 6, 18 n. 7, 49, 54 f., 112,
126 n. 2, 156, 231, 237.
Balthi, deity, 48 n. 1, 104, 168; see Beltis.
Bambyce, see Mabbog.
Barasbatzes, Governor of Edessa, 219.
Bardaiṣan of Edessa, 31 f., 34–7, 44 f., 49 f.,
55 f., 69–71, 81, 86, 90–2, 100, 105, 108, 168,
206.
Barhadad, Bishop of Tella, 127 f.
Barḥadbeshabba 'Arbaya, History of, 149 n. 2.
Bar Ḥalabi, benefactor of Edessa, 235.
Bar Hebraeus, 2 n. 2, 101 n. 1, 106, 190 n. 3,
195 n. 3, 223 n. 4.
Bar Nemre, deity, 2 n. 2, 171.
Barsai, Bishop of Edessa, 88, 91, 104, 175, 182
Barsamya, disciple of Addai, 79, 82 f., 86.
Barṣauma, Jacobite Bishop of Edessa, see
Athanasius.
Barṣauma, noble of Edessa, 223, 228.
Barṣauma b. Shalabi, 235 n. 1, 240.
Barṣauma, Monastery of, 240–3, 255 n. 1.
Barshelama ('Abshelama), disciple of Addai,
79; see 'Abshelama.
Bashir, pretender to the throne of Byzantium,
200, 206.
Basil, Armenian Patriarch, 239.
Basil, dux of Mesopotamia, 220.
Basil, Jacobite Bishop of Edessa, 210.
Basil abu Ghalib b. Ṣabuni, Jacobite Bishop of
Edessa, 240–2.
Basil abu l-Farag b. Shumana, Jacobite Bishop
of Edessa, 3, 195 n. 2, 218 n. 3, 238, 242 f.,
245–50, 252–5, 256 n. 1.
Basilicas, 83, 122, 148, 182, 184, 199.
Bassus of Edessa, Count, 170.
Bath Nikal, deity, 51.
Baths, Municipal, 32, 83, 99, 122, 124 f., 129,
133, 148, 156, 164, 184, 186, 200, 256.
Batnae, 1 n. 2, 10, 13, 15, 24, 50, 111, 117, 123,
131, 134, 137, 170, 174 n. 7, 176 n. 3, 179,
194, 204; see also Serug.
Beatrice, Countess of Edessa, 248 n. 1.
Beduins (Saracens), 22 f., 42, 104, 112, 115,
117 f., 134 n. 1, 137, 143–5, 156, 158 f., 166,
168, 179, 193; see also Ṭayyaye.
Be'elshamin, deity, 45, 59 f., 171.

Beirut, 31, 94, 104, 130, 151.
Bel, deity, 2 n. 2, 45, 47 f., 50 f., 53, 59, 68, 79 f.,
83, 171.
Beltis, deity, 45.
Belaṭ, 51.
Belisarius, Byzantine general, 142, 146.
Benedict, Latin Archbishop of Edessa, 230–2,
237, 249 n. 3.
Benoît, Archbishop, see Benedict.
Berikha, Archbishop, see Benedict.
Bernard, Latin Patriarch of Antioch, 232,
241.
Bernard of Clairvaux, St., 247 f.
Beth Alah Qiqla, see Edessa, Districts of.
Beth Ḥur, 168.
Beth Lapaṭ, 71.
Beth Saḥraye, see Edessa, Districts of.
Beth Shemesh, see Gates: South gate.
Beth Tabara, see Edessa, Districts of.
Bible, 35, 37, 42 f., 79 f., 93, 95, 135, 149, 151,
165, 170, 180, 211; see also Diatessaron,
Separate Gospels.
Bir Eyüp, see Wells.
Birecik, see Birtha.
Birket Ibrahim, see Fish-pools.
Birket Zulha, see Fish-pools.
Birtha (Birecik), 5, 23, 38, 117, 129, 134, 228,
235, 247.
Bishops, 27, 87 f., 91, 94, 123–5, 127–35, 142 f.,
152, 182, 185 n. 8, 209 f., 237 ff., 249, 251,
256.
Bohemund I, Prince of Antioch, 229 n. 2,
230 f.
Book of the Holy Hierotheos, 107 n. 1.
Book of the Laws of Countries, 31, 36, 44, 45
n. 1, 50, 56, 100.
Borborians, Sect of, 92.
Boule of Edessa, see Town Council.
Bread-making, 140, 161 f.
Budar, 23 n. 4, 57–9.
Bughdariyyun, 58 f.
Buzan, Saljuq general, 223, 228, 245.
Byzantium, Byzantines, 71, 75, 77, 80, 87, 95,
98–104, 108, 111–18, 120, 122 f., 125, 127,
129 n. 2, 136, 138–46, 148, 151 f., 154–9,
161–4, 167 f., 174 n. 6, 183 n. 4, 184, 198,
200 f., 213–25, 227, 229, 238; see also
Constantinople.

Caeciliana, 10, 46.
Callinicos, 10, 101, 112, 117, 134, 136, 194;
see also Raqqa.
Callirhoe, see Edessa, Names of.
Camuliana, Portrait of Jesus at, 77.
Caracalla, Emperor, 14 f., 21, 36, 58 n. 3.
Carus, Emperor, 110.
Cassiodoros, 151.
Castration, Ritual, 47, 56, 69 f.
Cateas, John, Governor of Osrhoene, 192.

PRINTED IN GREAT BRITAIN
AT THE UNIVERSITY PRESS, OXFORD
BY VIVIAN RIDLER
PRINTER TO THE UNIVERSITY